DISCARDED

ALSO BY STEVEN BRILL

The Teamsters

*After: How America
Confronted the September 12 Era*

*Class Warfare: Inside the Fight to
Fix America's Schools*

AMERICA'S BITTER PILL

AMERICA'S BITTER PILL

MONEY, POLITICS, BACKROOM DEALS,

AND THE FIGHT TO FIX OUR BROKEN

HEALTHCARE SYSTEM

STEVEN BRILL

RANDOM HOUSE

NEW YORK

Copyright © 2015 by Brill Journalism Enterprises, LLC

Published in the United States by Random House,
an imprint and division of Random House LLC,
a Penguin Random House Company, New York.

RANDOM HOUSE and the HOUSE colophon
are registered trademarks of Random House LLC.

ISBN 978-0-8129-9695-1
eBook ISBN 978-0-8129-9696-8

Printed in the United States of America on acid-free paper

www.atrandom.com

2 4 6 8 9 7 5 3 1

FIRST EDITION

Book design by Barbara M. Bachman

To Cynthia

CONTENTS

PART ONE

LOOKING UP FROM
THE GURNEY

I USUALLY KEEP MYSELF OUT OF THE STORIES I WRITE, BUT THE ONLY way to tell this one is to start with the dream I had on the night of April 3, 2014.

Actually, I should start with the three hours before the dream, when I tried to fall asleep but couldn't because of what I thought was my exploding heart.

THUMP. THUMP. THUMP. If I lay on my stomach it seemed to be pushing down through the mattress. If I turned over, it seemed to want to burst out of my chest.

When I pushed the button for the nurse, she told me there was nothing wrong. She even showed me how to read the screen of the machine monitoring my heart so I could see for myself that all was normal. But she said she understood. A lot of patients in my situation imagined something was going haywire with their hearts when it wasn't. Everything was fine, she promised, and then gave me a sedative.

All might have looked normal on that monitor, but there was nothing fine about my heart. It had a time bomb appended to it. It could explode at any moment—tonight or three years from tonight—and kill me almost instantly. No heart attack. No stroke. I'd just be gone, having bled to death.

That's what had brought me to the fourth-floor cardiac surgery unit at New York–Presbyterian Hospital. The next morning I was having open-heart surgery to fix something called an aortic aneurysm.

It's a condition I had never heard of until a week before, when a routine checkup by my extraordinarily careful doctor had found it.

And that's when everything changed.

Until then, my family and I had enjoyed great health. I hadn't missed a day of work for illness in years. Instead, my view of the world of healthcare was pretty much centered on a special issue I had written for *Time* magazine a year before about the astronomical cost of care in the United States and the dysfunctions and abuses in our system that generated and protected those high prices.

For me, an MRI had been a symbol of profligate American healthcare—a high-tech profit machine that had become a bonanza for manufacturers such as General Electric and Siemens and for the hospitals and doctors who billed billions to patients for MRIs they might not have needed.

But now the MRI was the miraculous lifesaver that had found and taken a crystal clear picture of the bomb hiding in my chest. Now a surgeon was going to use that MRI blueprint to save my life.

Because of the reporting I had done for the *Time* article, until a week before, I had been like Dustin Hoffman's savant character in *Rain Man*—able and eager to recite all varieties of stats on how screwed up and avaricious the American healthcare system was.

We spend $17 billion a year on artificial knees and hips, which is 55 percent more than Hollywood takes in at the box office.

America's total healthcare bill for 2014 is $3 trillion. That's more than the next ten biggest spenders combined: Japan, Germany, France, China, the United Kingdom, Italy, Canada, Brazil, Spain, and Australia. All that extra money produces no better, and in many cases worse, results.

There are 31.5 MRI machines per million people in the United States but just 5.9 per million in England.

Another favorite: We spend $85.9 billion trying to treat back pain, which is as much as we spend on all of the country's state, city, county, and town police forces. And experts say that as much as half of that is unnecessary.

We've created a system with 1.5 million people working in the health insurance industry but with barely half as many doctors providing the actual care. And most do not ride the healthcare gravy train the way hospital administrators, drug company bosses, and imaging equipment salesmen do.

I liked to point out that Medtronic, which makes all varieties of medical devices—from surgical tools to pacemakers—is so able to charge sky-high prices that it enjoys nearly double the gross profit margin of Apple, considered to be the jewel of American high-tech companies.

And all of those high-tech advances—pacemakers, MRIs, 3-D mammograms—have produced an irony that epitomized how upside-down the healthcare marketplace is: This is the only industry where technology advances have increased costs instead of lowering them. When it comes to medical care, cutting-edge products are irresistible; they are used—and priced—accordingly.

And because we don't control the prices of prescription drugs the way every other developed country does, we typically spend 50 percent more on them than what people or governments everywhere else spend. Meanwhile, nine of the ten largest pharmaceutical companies in the world have signed settlement agreements with federal prosecutors, paying millions or even billions in criminal and civil penalties for violating laws involving kickbacks and illegal marketing of their products. Nine out of ten.

To prove how healthcare had become an alternative-universe economy amid a country struggling with frozen incomes and crushing deficits (much of it from healthcare spending), I could recite from memory how the incomes of drug and medical device industry executives had continued to skyrocket even during the recession and how much more the president of the Yale New Haven Health System made than the president of Yale University.

I even knew the outsized salary of the guy who ran the supposedly nonprofit hospital where I was struggling to fall asleep: $3.58 million.

Which brings me to the dream I had when I finally got to sleep.

As I am being wheeled toward the operating room, a man in a finely tailored suit stands in front of the gurney, puts his hand up, and orders the nurses to stop. It's the hospital's CEO, the $3.58-million-a-year Steven Corwin. He, too, had read the much-publicized *Time* piece, only he hadn't liked it nearly as much as Jon Stewart, who had had me on his *Daily Show* to talk about it.

"We know who you are," he says. "And we are worried about whether this is some kind of undercover stunt. Why don't you go to another hospital?" I don't try to argue with him about gluttonous profits or salaries, or the back pain money, or the possibility that he was overusing his MRI or CT scan equipment. Instead, I swear to him that my surgery is for real and that I would never say anything bad about his hospital.

Remembering a bait and switch billing trick common at some hospitals that I had written about (though not this one, as far as the nondreaming me knew), I even blurt out, "I don't care if the anesthesiologist isn't in [my insurance] network. Just please let me go in."

A week before, I could have given hospital bosses like him the sweats, making them answer questions about the dysfunctional health-care system they prospered from. Their salaries. The operating profits enjoyed by their nonprofit, non-tax-paying institutions. And most of all, the outrageous charges—$77 for a box of gauze pads or hundreds of dollars for a routine blood test—that could be found on what they called their "chargemaster," which was the menu of list prices they used to soak patients who did not have Medicare or private insurance. How could they explain those prices, I loved to ask, let alone explain charging them only to the poor and others without insurance, who could least afford to pay?

But now I am the one sweating. I beg Corwin to let me into his operating room so I can get one of his chargemasters. If one of the nurses peering over me as he stopped me at the door had suggested it, I'd have bought a year's supply of those $77 gauze pads.

I didn't care about the cost of the anesthesiologist, who the afternoon before had told me that her job was to keep my brain supplied with blood and oxygen during the three or four hours that they were going to stop my heart. Stop my heart? No one had told me about that.

In the next part of the dream, the gurney and I are about to go through the doors to the operating room when off to the left side I see two cheerful women at a card table under a sign that proclaims "Obamacare Enrollment Center. Sign Up Now Before It's Too Late. Preexisting Conditions Not a Problem."

Actually, on April 4, 2014, the morning of my surgery, it was already four days too late to sign up for insurance under the Affordable Care Act, or Obamacare. Besides, I already had decent insurance. But at least that dream was more on point with what was happening in my real life. The day I found out about the time bomb in my chest, I was finishing reporting for a book about Obamacare and the fight over how to fix America's healthcare system.

In fact, on March 31, 2014, the day I was told about my aneurysm, I was awaiting the results of the final push by the Obama administration to get people to enroll in the insurance exchanges established under Obamacare.

WHAT FOLLOWS IS THE roller-coaster story of how Obamacare happened, what it means, what it will fix, what it won't fix, and what it means to people like me on that gurney consuming the most personal, most fear-inducing products—the ones meant to keep us alive.

From its historical roots, to the mind-numbing complexity of the furiously lobbied final text of the legislation, to its stumbling implementation, to the bitter fights over it that persist to this day—the story of Obamacare embodies the dilemma of America's longest running economic sinkhole and political struggle.

It's about money: Healthcare is America's largest industry by far, employing a sixth of the country's workforce. And it is the average American family's largest single expense, whether paid out of their pockets or through taxes and insurance premiums.

It's about politics and ideology: In a country that treasures the marketplace, how much of those market forces do we want to tame when trying to cure the sick? And in the cradle of democracy, or swampland, known as Washington, how much taming can we do when the health-care industry spends four times as much on lobbying as the number two Beltway spender, the much-feared military-industrial complex?

It's about the people who determine what comes out of Washington—from drug industry lobbyists to union activists; from senators tweaking a few paragraphs to save billions for a home state industry to Tea Party organizers fighting to upend the Washington status quo; from turf-obsessed procurement bureaucrats who fumbled the government's most ambitious Internet project ever to the selfless high-tech whiz kids who rescued it; and from White House staffers fighting over which faction among them would shape and then implement the law while their president floated above the fray to a governor's staff in Kentucky determined to launch the signature program of a president reviled in their state.

But late in working on this book, on the night of that dream and in the scary days that followed, I learned that when it comes to health-care, all of that political intrigue and special interest jockeying plays out on a stage enveloped in something else: emotion, particularly fear.

Fear of illness. Or pain. Or death. And wanting to do something, anything, to avoid that for yourself or a loved one.

When thrown into the mix, fear became the element that brought a chronically dysfunctional Washington to its knees. Politicians know that they mess with people's healthcare at their peril.

It's the fear I felt on that gurney, not only in my dream, but for real the morning after the dream, when I really was on the gurney on the way into the operating room.

It's the fear that continued to consume me the next day, when I was recovering from a successful defusing of the bomb. The recovery was routine. Routinely horrible.

After all, my chest had just been split open with what, according to the website of Stryker, the Michigan-based company that makes it, was a "Large Bone Battery Power / Heavy Duty" sternum saw, which "has increased cutting speed for a more aggressive cut." And then my heart had been stopped and machines turned on to keep my lungs and brain going.

It's about the fear of a simple cough. The worst, though routine, thing that can happen in the days following surgery like mine, I found out, was to cough. Coughing was torture because of how it assaulted my chest wounds.

I developed a cough that was so painful that I blacked out. Not for a long time; there was a two-two count on Derek Jeter just before one of the episodes, and when I came to Jeter was about to take ball four. However, because I could feel it coming but could do nothing about it, it was terrifying to me and to my wife and kids, who watched me seize up and pass out more than once.

In that moment of terror, I was anything but the well-informed, tough customer with lots of options that a robust free market counts on. I was a puddle.

There were occasions during those days in the hospital when the non-drug-addled part of my brain wondered, when nurses came in for a blood test twice a day, whether once might have been enough. Sometimes, I imagined what those chargemaster charges might look like, or wondered whether the cheerful guy with the wheel-around scale who came to weigh me once a day—and who told me he owned a second home as an investment—was part of the healthcare gravy train.

But most of the time the other part of my brain took over, the part that remembered my terror during those blackouts and the overriding fear, reprised in dreams that persisted for weeks, that lingered in someone whose chest had been sawed open and whose heart had been stopped. And as far as I was concerned they could have tested my blood ten times a day and weighed me every hour if they thought that was best. They could have paid as much as they wanted to that nurse's aide with the scale or to the woman who flawlessly, without even a sting, took my blood. And the doctor who had given me an angiogram the afternoon before the surgery and then came in the following week to check me out became just a nice guy who cared, not someone who might be trying to add on an extra consult bill.

In the days that I was on my back, to have asked that nurse how much this or that test was going to cost, let alone to have grilled my surgeon—a guy I had researched and found was the master of aortic aneurysms—what he was going to charge seemed beside the point. It was like asking Mrs. Lincoln what she had thought of the play.

When you're staring up at someone from the gurney, you have no inclination to be a savvy consumer. You have no power. Only hope. And relief and appreciation when things turn out right. And you certainly don't want politicians messing around with some cost-cutting schemes that might interfere with that result.

New York–Presbyterian's marketing slogan is "Amazing Things Are Happening Here." I'll drink to that (although part of me did wonder why they need a marketing budget and how much it is). To me, it was, indeed, amazing that eight weeks after my bad dream I was back working out aerobically and with weights, just as I had before they had discovered the time bomb. That was more important to me than the hospital's amazing salaries or chargemaster.

That is what makes healthcare and dealing with healthcare costs so different, so hard. It's what makes the Obamacare story so full of twists and turns—so dramatic—because the politics are so treacherous. People care about their health a lot more than they care about healthcare policies or economics. That's what I learned the night I was terrified by my own heartbeat and in the days after when I would have paid anything for a cough suppressant to avoid those blackouts.

It's not that this makes prices and policies allowing—indeed, encouraging—runaway costs unimportant. Hardly. My time on the gurney notwithstanding, I believe everything I have written and will write about the toxicity of our profiteer-dominated healthcare system.

But now I also understand, firsthand, the meaning of what the caregivers who work in that system do every day. They do achieve amazing things, and when it's your life or your child's life or your mother's life on the receiving end of those amazing things, there is no such thing as a runaway cost. You'll pay anything, and if you don't have the money, you'll borrow at any mortgage rate or from any payday lender to come up with the cash. Which is why 60 percent of the nearly one million personal bankruptcies filed in the United States last year resulted from medical bills.

Even when it's not an emergency, even those who would otherwise be the toughest customers lose their leverage.

"When I went in for knee surgery, I couldn't have cared less about healthcare policy or cost containment," Marna Bargstrom, the CEO of the giant Yale New Haven Health System told me. "I was just scared."

That is the perspective that anyone's encounter with a scalpel provides—the "How can I think about the cost at a time like this?" element.

Most of the politicians, lobbyists, congressional staffers, and others who collectively wrote the story of Obamacare had some kind of experience like that, either themselves or vicariously with a friend or loved one. Who hasn't?

Montana's Max Baucus, the chairman of the all-important Senate Finance Committee, had a picture on his desk of a constituent he had befriended who had died after a long fight against a disease stemming from an industrial pollution disaster, the court settlement of which, Baucus believed, had not sufficiently provided for his medical care.

Billy Tauzin, the top lobbyist for the drug industry had, he said, "a cancer where they told me I had a one percent chance of living, until a drug saved my life."

The staffer who was more personally responsible than anyone for the drafting of what became Obamacare had a mother who, in the year before the staffer wrote that draft, had to take an $8.50 an hour job as a nightshift gate agent at the Las Vegas airport. She worked every night not because she needed the $8.50—her semiretired husband was himself a doctor—but because a preexisting condition precluded her from buying health insurance on the individual market. That meant she needed a job, any job, with a large employer. Her daughter's draft of the new law prohibited insurers from stopping people with preexisting conditions from buying insurance on the individual market.

And then there was Senator Edward Kennedy, for fifty years the champion of extending healthcare to all Americans. Beyond his brothers' tragic visits to two hospital emergency rooms, Ted Kennedy's firsthand experience with healthcare began with a sister's severe mental disabilities, extended to a three-month stay in a western Massachusetts hospital following a near-fatal 1964 plane crash, and continued through his son's long battle with cancer.

Although their solutions varied, these four—as well as most of the dozens of other Obamacare players, who to some degree had these kinds of personal stories—saw and understood healthcare as an issue not only more urgent and more emotionally charged than any other, but also bedeviled by one core question: How do you pay for giving millions of new customers the means to participate in a marketplace with inflated prices—and with a damn-the-torpedoes attitude about those prices when they're looking up from the gurney? Is that possible? Or must the marketplace be tamed or tossed aside? Or must costs be pushed aside, to deal with another day?

As we'll see, even the seemingly coldest fish among politicians—the cerebral, "no-drama" Barack Obama—drew on his encounters with people who desperately needed healthcare to frame, and ultimately fuel, his push for a plan.

"Everywhere I went on that first campaign, I heard directly from Americans about what a broken health care system meant to them—the bankruptcies, putting off care until it was too late, not being able to get coverage because of a pre-existing condition," Obama would later tell me.[1]

But as Obama's campaign began, he had not yet met many of those Americans victimized by the broken healthcare system. And it showed.

---

1. President Obama agreed to answer questions put to him in writing. Written answers risk being filtered by the president's communications apparatus, and many of the president's answers deserved the kind of follow-up that only a conversation can facilitate. I was assured by his press office that the president had read all of my questions and personally signed off on the answers. A full text of the questions and the president's answers, as well as those questions that he declined to answer, is included as an Appendix at the back of the book.

CHAPTER 2

CENTER STAGE

"OBAMA WAS DEFINITELY NOT READY FOR PRIME TIME," RECALLED Andy Stern, then president of the two-million-plus-member Service Employees International Union (SEIU). "He thought he knew the issue incredibly well—and he didn't."

Stern was referring to Barack Obama's performance in a Democratic presidential candidates' forum on Saturday night, March 24, 2007, in Las Vegas, Nevada. (Obama declined to answer a question I put to him about his performance that night.)

Coming less than six weeks after he had plunged into the race, it was the long shot candidate's first appearance with those thought to be the leading contenders, Hillary Clinton and John Edwards. Also on the stage were candidates Joe Biden, Bill Richardson, Chris Dodd, Dennis Kucinich, and Mike Gravel.

The Illinois senator's Las Vegas flameout didn't even come at a real debate. It was a one-at-a-time speaking forum sponsored by Stern's union and the Center for American Progress, the center-left Washington think tank that housed refugees from the administration of President Bill Clinton who were considered, at least by each other, as a staff-in-waiting for the next Democratic president. There was to be no give-and-take among the candidates. Each would make an opening statement of three to five minutes to a crowd in the Cox Pavilion auditorium at the University of Nevada, Las Vegas, filled with members of Stern's union and local and national political junkies. The White House hopefuls would then answer fifteen minutes of questions put to them by *Time* magazine's Karen Tumulty and by the audience. Then he or she would exit the stage and the next contestant would be up.

Moreover, it wasn't to be a general debate about the various issues facing the country as the 2008 election season approached. It was about one topic only: healthcare.

Before the candidates were introduced, John Podesta, the former Clinton chief of staff who ran the Center for American Progress, explained the unusual focus this way: "We hope that what happens in Las Vegas today will . . . set the tone for the entire presidential campaign. It's simply time to make affordable, quality coverage for every American a reality."

Podesta offered statistics, the ones that by 2007 had become a mantra for the cause that would roil the country for the next seven years.

> Today 45 million Americans are uninsured, including 9 million children. Since 2000, health care premiums for workers have increased four times faster than wages. . . .
>
> What kind of value do we get for all that money we spend on health care in the United States? Not much. The U.S. currently ranks 31st in the world in terms of life expectancy, and 28th on infant mortality. . . . Our health care system today violates America's deep commitment to human dignity for all and fairness for all, and it hampers our nation's economic competitiveness.

Co-host Stern put it this way to the candidates, still waiting behind the curtain:

> Polling in the four early primary states shows the cost of health care is the number one pocketbook concern for voters of both parties. . . .

So what . . . are we missing? Leadership. Leadership in Washington, D.C.

And for the next president here's the final point of our poll: Voters are saying they're not hearing from you enough about health care. And in a minute we're going to start solving that problem. . . . It's up to us voters . . . to . . . demand detailed answers about what they're going to do.

Barack Obama did not answer the call. He had come to Las Vegas knowing that this would be his first appearance with his opponents on the presidential stage. He knew that his only job would be to talk about healthcare, nothing else. Yet he winged it. He spent the first two of his three minutes sucking up to Stern's union (recalling how he had worked with the SEIU as a community organizer in Chicago) and complaining generally about the plight of the middle class. Then he talked vaguely about the need to tackle costs while providing coverage for all.

But he concluded forcefully: "I want to be held accountable for getting it done," he declared. "I will judge my first term as president based . . . on whether we have delivered the kind of health care that every American deserves and that our system can afford."

Tumulty and the rest of the audience didn't seem to buy it. That this junior senator would make sweeping healthcare reform a priority and deliver on it just didn't jibe with his going-through-the-motions presentation. "You gave a speech in January," Tumulty began, "where you said that the time for half steps and the time for half measures in health care is over. . . . But thus far we haven't seen a plan from you."

She turned the microphone over to a young man in the audience, who complained that "when it came to addressing the health care issue" the only content on Obama's website "was things like HIV, which is very important, and issues like lead poisoning."

"Right," Obama answered, relaxing on a stool. "Well, keep in mind that our campaign now is, I think, a little over eight weeks old. And so we will be putting a very detailed plan on our website."

The other candidates were crisp, knowledgeable, and specific, especially John Edwards, who freely acknowledged that he would end the Bush-era tax cuts for both the middle and upper classes in order to pay for expanded healthcare.

And then there was Hillary Clinton. The New York senator stole the show. Her standing, strolling presentation was a tour de force of personal stories, sophisticated detail, easily understandable data, and great one-liners: "The insurance companies make money by spending a lot of money and employing a lot of people to try to avoid insuring you, and then, if you're insured, to try to avoid paying for the health care you received."

A SWAMP OF CORRUPTION

Most of the candidates aimed similar, if less pungent, attacks on the insurers—an industry whose profit margins are dwarfed by those of the drugmakers, device makers, and even nonprofit hospitals. And except for vague promises to promote efficiency through electronic medical records, Clinton, Edwards, Obama, and the others said little about how they were going to deal with the elephant in the room: costs.

Yet all promised in one way or another to attack every politician's favorite targets—"fraud and abuse." Here, too, they were not specific. However, they would have had plenty to work with had they tried. By 2007, a healthcare system that sucked up as much money as the gross domestic product of France—but whose consumers had little knowledge of what they were consuming and often weren't the ones paying for it, anyway—had metastasized into a swamp of corruption.

As Clinton, Obama, and the others took their turns on the stage, federal prosecutors were deep into fraud investigations against bad actors trolling that swamp, ranging from a high-profile retailer of wheelchairs and motorized scooters to a giant international drug company.

The Scooter Store, based in New Braunfels, Texas, was allegedly using millions of dollars in television ads to get people over sixty-five—which meant that the federal Medicare program paid their bills—to ask their doctors for prescriptions for its scooters and wheelchairs. At the same time, it was deploying salesmen across the country to push doctors to write those prescriptions, even for people who could get around without the scooters or chairs. Investigators were about six weeks away from settling a fraud suit that would require the retailer to pay $4 million in cash and give up more than $43 million in bills that were pending at Medicare.

Meantime, another team of federal prosecutors was pursuing a far bigger target—the Aventis unit of Sanofi, a Paris-based pharmaceutical giant suspected of systematically overbilling Medicare.

"Aventis Pharmaceuticals Inc. has paid . . . over $190 million to resolve allegations that the company caused false claims to be filed with Medicare . . . as a result of the company's alleged fraudulent pricing and marketing of . . . Anzemet, an antiemetic drug used primarily in conjunction with oncology and radiation treatment to prevent nausea and vomiting," the Justice Department would announce in August 2007.

Like the Scooter Store, Sanofi signed a Corporate Integrity Agreement calling for five years of strict government monitoring. There were, in fact, so many of these agreements that in the Washington healthcare bureaucracy "CIA" had become a favorite acronym having to do with renegade drug companies or other suppliers, not spies.

THE DEMOCRATS MOVE RIGHT

Barack Obama, the former *Harvard Law Review* president and boy wonder senator, was not used to not being the smartest guy in the room.

"It wasn't that Obama didn't care," said a former senator who had been close to Obama and recalls the Las Vegas forum well. "It's just that he had been able to wing it most of his life because he's so smart, and he thought he could here. . . . He tends not to buckle down and do the work until he sees that he absolutely has to.

"But I know he knew he blew it. He told me after that debate that he knew he had made a jackass of himself, and it was not going to happen again."

Beyond Obama's poor performance—which was not that noticeable at the time because, after all, he was supposed to be the inexperienced, quixotic underdog—there was something else striking about the Democrats' forum.

Aside from Kucinich, the Ohio congressman who was unabashedly the most left-leaning contender, the other candidates seemed to agree on an approach to healthcare reform more reminiscent of Richard Nixon than of Harry Truman, who had proposed government-sponsored health insurance for all in 1949. The 2008 Democratic contenders outlined reforms that followed the lead set by a Republican governor of Massachusetts, which would give all Americans insurance coverage within the current system.

At its core, theirs was a plan any Republican or chamber of commerce lobbyist would likely love: The government would create tens of millions of new customers for all those profiting from the current system—insurers, drug companies, hospitals, and makers of all varieties of high-margin medical equipment, from CT scans to defibrillators.

Kucinich, the liberal, was having none of that. He stuck to what had been Democratic Party orthodoxy before most of those on the stage had been born. "Today at this forum the sub-message is that you can't break the hold that the insurance companies have," he began. "Not a single candidate up here has challenged the underlying problem with our health care system, and that is insurance companies are holding our health care system hostage and forcing millions of Americans into poverty with unconscionable premiums, co-pays, deductibles.

"So I ask you," he continued, "is it constant with America's greatness that candidates step away from the one solution that could change it all?"

For Kucinich, as with most Democrats in years past, that "one solution" was the way most other developed countries had dealt with healthcare, beginning with Kaiser Wilhelm in late nineteenth-century Germany: "A not-for-profit health care system is not only possible," Kucinich declared, "but . . . a bill that I introduced . . . actually establishes Medicare for all, a single-payer system, and it's a not-for-profit system. It's time we ended this thought that health care is a privilege. It is a basic right. . . . Think for a moment," Kucinich concluded, "if

Lincoln had decided, well, you know, there's just too much resistance to this idea of emancipation."

That, in fact, was exactly what the major Democratic candidates had decided—that there was, indeed, too much resistance to upending a status quo that was consuming a sixth of the entire American economy. There was no way that they could, as Obama would later put it in speeches about healthcare, "put the toothpaste back in the tube," by scrapping the uniquely American system under which private, profit-making insurance companies sold protection to those Americans who could afford it, whereupon the insurers and their customers chipped in to pay unregulated prices in a private marketplace for drugs, hospitals, doctors, diagnostic tests, and other healthcare.

There were multiple analogies that people used for the entrenched, sorry state of the American healthcare system. One man's toothpaste tube was another man's tangle of legacy programs and delivery systems that, piece by piece, had been patched together into an unworkable mess that provided substandard care at exorbitant prices. Trying to tack new programs and systems onto that was a recipe for frustration. It was, to use yet another metaphor, like deciding to fix up a hopelessly dilapidated house, instead of saving time and money by building a new one, because so many people had so much invested in preserving the irredeemably defective plumbing, wiring, and floors in the old house.

AMERICA TAKES A DIFFERENT PATH

The toothpaste had started coming out of the tube slowly, beginning in 1929. That year, a group of Dallas, Texas, schoolteachers signed up to buy health insurance from the local Baylor University Hospital. For six dollars a month they would get all of their care covered for up to twenty-one days in the hospital. The plan was called Blue Cross.

At the time, healthcare costs were not much of a concern—because there was not much healthcare. Hospitals were convalescent homes or places where people went to die, not the high-intensity, high-tech centers of complicated medical cures that they would become. For example, in the early twentieth century—before, for example, the invention of penicillin—the forerunner to New York–Presbyterian, where I had my open-heart surgery, was in a quaint building in lower Manhattan with about fifty beds, and services that featured bloodletting, some surgery, and "lying-in" facilities for the mentally disabled and for women who had given birth. By the time I checked in, it was a 1,483-bed colossus, with more than $3.6 billion in annual revenue, spread across six campuses, some with towering facilities that dominated the skylines of upper Manhattan.

When the Dallas teachers signed up for Blue Cross in 1929, Americans spent about 1 percent of the country's gross domestic product on anything related to healthcare. By 1966, it was 6 percent, and by the time Obama and his opponents took the stage in Las Vegas, it was 16 percent, heading toward 20 percent. A negligible cost in 1929, probably less than the pocket change people spent on candy or snacks, had become the country's and every family's number one financial burden.

THE HISTORY OF THE century-long political debate over healthcare that culminated in this singly focused 2007 Las Vegas candidates' forum mirrors that process of medical care pricing itself into the pubic consciousness.

Theodore Roosevelt had proposed national health insurance during his unsuccessful 1912 campaign to reclaim the presidency on a third-party ticket. However, that plan was aimed mostly at providing compensation to workers who lost wages because of injury or illness, not what was then the relatively inconsequential (for all but the poorest Americans) cost of care.

Those on the left who tried to pick up and expand on TR's cause over the next two decades were successfully attacked from two sides. At a time when Germany had become a prime American enemy, some argued that government-supplied healthcare seemed too much like the kaiser's program. Others, playing off the Red Scare then coursing through American politics, said it smacked of socialism or communism. The attacks worked, in no small part because people were still not reaching into their pockets too deeply when they got sick.

By 1935, insurance programs like the one that had begun in Dallas were slowly popping up around the country. Meanwhile, costs were beginning to rise as medical care progressed beyond bloodletting. This put Franklin D. Roosevelt under pressure from aides and constituents on the left to add health insurance to his proposal for Social Security pension protection. But FDR (despite his own health issues) never had the enthusiasm for health insurance that he demonstrated for Social Security. He held off on including it in his historic 1935 initiative.

By the time FDR came back to the idea during the later years of his presidency, he faced new opposition: labor union leaders, who were the core of his political base.

The reason the unions were against government-supplied healthcare had to do with a quiet decision made during World War II by Franklin Roosevelt's National War Labor Board, a panel he had appointed to enforce wartime wage and price controls. In 1943, the board ruled that fringe benefits—including health insurance—were not subject to wage controls, which prohibited an employer seeking to encourage workers to join or stay at his company from enticing them with higher pay. Under the board's ruling, an employer could lure workers by offering to pay for health insurance, to be supplied by what would soon become a flood of insurance companies flocking into the new market. The decision released much of the political pressure for reform by allowing a large swathe of the population to start getting protected from healthcare bills, while motivating the unions to oppose government intervention.

According to an article published in 2008 by the American Enterprise Institute scholar Robert Helms, "There is no indication that the Board debated this policy or made any prediction of its future consequences."

The Internal Revenue Service then magnified the effect of the National War Labor Board edict by ruling that if health insurance benefits were not wages, they should not be taxed as such. In other words, if a worker in the 20 percent income tax bracket got health insurance worth $1,000 a year, that was $1,000 free of what, at a 20 percent rate, would be a $200 tax. For an executive in the 50 percent bracket, the ruling was worth $500. Years later, when the insurance benefit might be worth $10,000 or even $20,000 because medical costs and insurance premiums had gotten so high, the tax break would be even more addictive.

It was this largely unheralded bureaucratic decision (followed in 1954 by a formal IRS regulation during the Eisenhower administration) that launched America's most gaping tax loophole, one that would forever change the course of healthcare in the United States.

As a result of the labor board's ruling, unions began pushing for and winning health insurance in their contracts with employees. For the government to usurp that with its own insurance (which came to be called a single-payer system), or with a completely government-operated health system—which were generally the models followed in Europe and ultimately in most developed countries—would undercut the important new benefit the unions could offer workers who joined their ranks. With that kind of pressure coming from his base, Roosevelt tabled the idea of healthcare as his last New Deal breakthrough. Had the labor board decided instead that offering health insurance violated the wartime wage-control regime, which it arguably did, the need—and political pressure—in the United States to provide health insurance for all, the way every other country had, would almost certainly have forced a different outcome during the Roosevelt presidency or soon thereafter.

Harry Truman—influenced, historians say, by the number of recruits he had met during the war who showed up for duty too sick to fight—took up the banner after he succeeded Roosevelt in 1945. But by then rulings by the National Labor Relations Board had solidified healthcare coverage as a key ingredient of collectively bargained contracts. As a result, the unions were even more opposed to the idea, and their members were largely indifferent to it.

Meanwhile, the more predictable opponents—the incumbent insurers and hospitals and drug companies worried about having to bargain with one single payer—were arrayed against Truman's push, which he presented to Congress in 1949.

Opposition to Truman's bill from Republicans and the growing healthcare industry was fierce. The most vehement opponent was the American Medical Association, the then-powerful professional association of the nation's doctors. The AMA spent what in 1949 was an astounding $1.5 million to campaign against the plan, labeling it socialized medicine that would be "the key to the arch of a socialist state," which would destroy doctors' independent relationships with their patients and lead to doctors becoming government employees.

The rejection of public insurance for all at the same time that private insurance flourished, courtesy of the National War Labor Board and the IRS, added up to a lot of toothpaste gushing out of the tube. In 1940, fewer than ten million Americans had private health insurance. By 1950, 76.6 million enjoyed that protection, with enrollment growing rapidly.

Yet there were still tens of millions of Americans who were left out because they did not have jobs working for businesses that offered insurance. The largest and fastest-growing group among them were the elderly who had retired.

But then came LBJ. In 1965, President Lyndon B. Johnson and his Great Society took the elderly out of the equation.

Fresh off a landslide presidential election victory and propelled by huge Democratic majorities in Congress, Johnson signed legislation establishing Medicare, the government health insurance program for everyone over sixty-five. Medicare also included a program for the disabled of any age. And the companion Medicaid program that Johnson pushed through at the same time offered limited protection for those living below the poverty line.

By the time the candidates appeared that night in Las Vegas in 2007, 162 million nonelderly Americans had employer-paid health insurance, either in their own name or as family members of workers who had been given coverage. That was more than 80 percent of the people who were not protected by Medicare, by Medicaid, or by a Clinton-era program aimed at insuring poor and lower-middle-class children.

THE STARS ALIGN IN 2007

With all of those people covered either through private insurance or through Medicare or Medicaid, why was healthcare such a crisis that it deserved its own stage that night?

"By 2007, the stars were aligned to do something about healthcare, because we had to," recalled Tom Daschle, the South Dakota Democrat who had been the Senate majority and minority leader and a leading policy thinker on healthcare until losing a reelection bid in 2004.

Here's how those stars were now aligned:

First, there was the galloping cost of advances in the science of medicine. While all that progress was good news—I'm glad they invented that MRI to pinpoint what was going on in my chest—it ballooned healthcare costs across the board.

As a result, insurers now had to pay more for their policyholders' claims, so insurance premiums went up. As John Podesta had pointed out in his introduction to the forum, "Today the average family insurance policy costs $11,841. That's a thousand dollars more than a full-time minimum-wage worker makes in a year."

The cost spikes for the government programs that protected the elderly and the poor were even worse. Better medical care kept people alive longer, and that meant Medicare had to pay for more complicated and more expensive treatment during those prolonged lives. In 1965, Medicare had been projected by a House of Representatives committee to cost $12 billion by 1990. Its actual cost by then was $110 billion. And by 2011—the third year of the prospective first term of the presidential candidates vying on the 2007 Las Vegas stage—government healthcare spending was projected to exceed all private spending and account for nearly a third of the overall federal budget.

And, of course, there was the crushing burden for those forty-five million Americans (a number rising every year) who didn't have insurance at all.

Those who were out of work or in jobs that didn't offer insurance had to face buying insurance on their own in the so-called individual market. The rates they faced were so exorbitant—typically approaching or exceeding $10,000 a year in 2007—that most couldn't even contemplate buying it. And those that tried often couldn't get covered at any price because insurers were allowed to screen them for what were called "preexisting conditions." In other words, the people who needed insurance the most—because they suffered from preexisting conditions—were locked out of the market.

The second star in alignment had to do with the growing plight of people—particularly in low-wage jobs—who did have what they thought was health insurance but were not really covered when they faced a serious—or even not-so-serious but highly billable—medical issue. Their insurance was like a parachute that didn't open.

These were people who might have been indifferent to earlier reform pushes, but were now buttonholing the candidates on the campaign trail with their sad stories about rising medical costs and insurance that was a lot less protective than it used to be. Podesta had pointed out in introducing the forum that healthcare premiums for workers—the amount they had to contribute to their employers' insurance—had increased four times faster than their wages. What he could have added was that the amount they paid that was not covered by insurance—in so-called co-pays, co-insurance, or deductibles—was increasing just as quickly.

Worse, employers were increasingly trying to stem their skyrocketing insurance costs by allowing insurers to set limits on coverage so that the insurers could incur less risk and, therefore, offer lower premiums. This allowed employers to avoid the short-term budget trauma of escalating insurance premiums, but made insurance much less protective. Workers might now be on their own after they hit $50,000 in costs in a year, or maybe $200,000 or $300,000 over their lifetimes. Hitting these limits seemed unlikely until someone got grievously ill and realized that exceeding them was the norm.

Or workers, especially those in low-wage jobs, might be offered insurance that capped daily charges—$1,000 per day in the hospital, for example—that were far below what they were likely to face in the real world of the twenty-first-century American healthcare marketplace.

The bills for my aortic aneurysm topped $197,000 for eight days in the hospital.

As early as 1973, Ted Kennedy had seen how elusive real insurance could be for people who thought they had it. That year, Kennedy spent endless hours with his son, who was being treated for cancer with a variety of trailblazing drugs. According to his widow, Vicki, the Massachusetts senator sat with parents who faced the ultimate good news/bad news roller coaster: being offered the miracles of great new treatments that were unimaginably expensive and either not covered by insurance at all or covered for only a limited period that did not extend through their child's treatment.

"Teddy would tell me," Vicki Kennedy recalled, "that when he was in the hospital ward with his son he would talk to mothers who could only afford five or ten of the twenty-three chemo treatments, and they'd ask him what to do."

By 2007, the problem Kennedy had observed nearly thirty-five years earlier had extended to even mundane, seemingly routine health needs.

THE BUS DRIVER AND THE CHARGEMASTER

Not long after the Las Vegas forum, Emilia Gilbert—a school bus driver earning about $1,800 a month, whom I wrote about in the *Time* article—fell victim to these coverage gaps.

For six years, Gilbert, who was sixty-one at the time, would be forced by a judge to make weekly payments on the bill she got after she slipped and fell on her face in the small yard behind her house in Fairfield, Connecticut. Her nose bleeding heavily, she was taken to the emergency room at Bridgeport Hospital. She went home a few hours later with a half dozen stitches.

"I was there for maybe six hours, until midnight," Gilbert told me, "and most of it was spent waiting." Gilbert got three CT scans—of her head, her chest, and her face. The last one showed a hairline fracture of her nose.

Along with Greenwich Hospital and the Hospital of St. Raphael in New Haven, Bridgeport Hospital is owned by the Yale New Haven Health System, of which Yale–New Haven Hospital is the flagship. Although Yale University and Yale New Haven are separate entities, Yale–New Haven Hospital is the teaching hospital for the Yale School of Medicine. University representatives, including Yale's president, sit on the Yale New Haven Health System board.

Yale New Haven's Bridgeport unit applied its list prices to Gilbert's bill, the way most hospitals do before Medicare or insurance company discounts kick in. In the hospital business, these list prices are derived from what is called the hospital's chargemaster. Decades ago, a chargemaster was a document the size of a phone book; now it's a massive computer file, thousands of items long.

In Gilbert's case, insurance-related discounts off the chargemaster prices didn't kick in, because of what she soon learned were the severe limits on her insurance coverage.

The CT scan bills alone were $6,538. Medicare, which pays hospitals based on their costs, plus overhead and a small profit margin, for providing each service, would have paid about $825 for all three tests.

Also on Emilia Gilbert's bill were items that neither Medicare nor any insurance company would pay anything at all for: basic instruments, bandages, and even the tubing for an IV setup. Under Medicare regulations and the terms of most insurance contracts, these are supposed to be part of the hospital's facility charge, which in this case was $908 for the emergency room.

William Gedge, a senior vice president for payer relations at Yale New Haven Health System, insisted to me that "the chargemaster is fair," but said, after making inquiries, that he had "no way" of explaining how the CT scan bills or anything else, including seemingly inflated bills for blood tests and equipment, were calculated.

Gilbert's total bill was $9,418.

"When I got the bill, I almost had to go back to the hospital," Gilbert told me. "I was hyperventilating." Contributing to her shock was the fact that although her employer supplied insurance from Cigna, one of the country's leading health insurers, Gilbert's policy was from a Cigna subsidiary that insured mostly low-wage earners. The policy covered just $2,500 of Gilbert's bill, leaving her on the hook for about $7,000.

That made Gilbert one of the millions of Americans that Stern and Podesta were asking the candidates that night to focus on. They were routinely categorized as having health insurance but didn't have anything approaching meaningful coverage.

After the hospital sued Gilbert for the full $7,000, a judge ruled that Gilbert, who represented herself in court because she could not afford a lawyer, had to pay all but about $500 of the original charges. The judge put her on a payment schedule of $20 a week.

In describing the forces that impelled the push for healthcare reform, *Harvard Business Review* would later cite a 2007 study reporting that medical bills "had become a factor in 62 per cent of personal bankruptcies, an increase from just 8 per cent in 1981."

If Gilbert had been forced to pay her bill from Yale New Haven Health System in one lump sum, she would likely have been one of those, all for a fall in her backyard and a few hours in the emergency room.

As the candidates took to the Las Vegas stage that night in 2007, Yale New Haven, which has a tax exemption as a nonprofit institution, was on its way to recording operating income of more than $125 million. Its chief executive would earn a salary of more than $2.5 million, roughly 70 percent more than that of the president of Yale University.

HILLARY'S SCARS

During Hillary Clinton's presentation to the crowd in Las Vegas she remarked with a chuckle, "I know probably better than anybody how hard this will be. Yeah, I know. I've got the scars to show for it and I've been through it."

Everyone understood what she was talking about. Soon after he took office in 1993, President Bill Clinton had appointed his wife to come up with a plan for a massive overhaul of the country's healthcare system.

That unusual role for a First Lady, albeit one who was a respected lawyer and policy wonk, produced the scars that Hillary Clinton now kidded about. Following an orgy of expert panels and subpanels, mostly operating in secret, she came up with a plan that was so complex that few could understand it. "Hillarycare" ostensibly proposed to operate within the incumbent private market system but would have overhauled it by organizing a network of insurance-buying cooperatives regulated by the federal government.

To the extent anyone could figure it out, the First Lady's plan seemed likely to force most Americans to give up the insurance they had in favor of these new government-supervised co-ops.

The key industries—insurers, drug companies, hospitals, doctors— had ended up opposing it. The drug companies famously sponsored a series of ads featuring a middle-class couple, "Harry and Louise," whose plain talk about keeping the government out of "our health-care" galvanized the public, most of whom had private insurance and feared radical change.

When the Democrats lost control of the House of Representatives a year later, Hillarycare was tagged as a major cause.

THE DEMOCRATS' NEW REPUBLICAN ALTERNATIVE

So why did Clinton and the other 2008 contenders think they could avoid new scars, even if the problems of costs and poor coverage had only gotten markedly worse?

The answer was Mitt Romney and a young economics professor named Jonathan Gruber. They put the third star—in addition to high costs, and weakening insurance that was pushing those costs onto everyone—into alignment: a new reform model that seemed politically achievable.

When he was a freshly minted Harvard PhD in economics, Gruber had worked in the Clinton administration under Larry Summers, the celebrated Harvard economics professor who had become deputy Treasury secretary. Summers had been Gruber's adviser on his thesis— which was about employer-sponsored health insurance.

As Gruber were preparing to leave government in early 1998, Summers gave Gruber what Gruber says was "the best advice of my life."

Summers told Gruber—an outgoing guy who had the intellectual chops of an Ivy League academic without the withdrawn personality— that he could carve out a great career creating economic models that provided practical advice to politicians and policy makers seeking to understand the implications and likely results of the policies they were debating.

"Academics usually didn't do that," Gruber later explained. "They didn't connect what they knew or what they were doing to specific policy debates in real time so they could chime in with real, practical answers. I loved the thought of that."

In 1998, Gruber, by then thirty-three, became an assistant professor of economics at MIT's Sloan School of Management. He began picking up grants to create algorithms that could produce models of the economic consequences of various healthcare plans and reforms.

Using thousands of lines of code that plotted behavioral patterns, Gruber would program hundreds of variables into a black box and out would pop the likely outcomes of this tweak or that big change in healthcare systems or rules. The young professor would then turn the black box's pronouncements into widely followed articles in scholarly journals and even some publications with broader reach. He earned tenure at MIT, and his reputation grew.

By 2005, aides to Mitt Romney came calling.

Romney, a first-term Republican governor of Massachusetts, was a Harvard MBA, who had been a successful management consultant and private equity investor. In large part because Massachusetts faced losing hundreds of millions of dollars in Medicaid support from Washington unless it came up with a new plan to insure more of its citizens, Romney wanted to create a market-based healthcare reform program. Would Gruber help?

Gruber was taken with Romney from their first meeting. "Here was a guy who seemed to me to be the perfect public servant," he later told me. "He was courteous. Warm, even solicitous. And really smart. He knew this stuff cold. He was deep into the details but also eager to talk about the broader ideas. I really liked him."

Romney and his staff were focused on an idea first floated in 1989 by economist Stuart Butler, then the director of Domestic Policy Studies at the Heritage Foundation, the conservative Washington think tank. The way to fix healthcare, Butler reasoned, was rooted in a classic conservative principle: individual responsibility. An ideal plan would require everyone to buy health insurance, although those who could not afford the full cost would get the government's help. That way, people would not show up in emergency rooms uninsured or with poor insurance.

Butler summarized his argument for compulsory insurance this way: "If a man is struck down by a heart attack in the street, Americans will care for him whether or not he has insurance. If we find that he has spent his money on other things rather than insurance, we may be angry but we will not deny him services—even if that means more prudent citizens end up paying the tab.

"A mandate on individuals recognized this implicit contract. Society does feel a moral obligation to insure that its citizens do not suffer from the unavailability of health care. But on the other hand, each household has the obligation, to the extent it is able, to avoid placing demands on society by protecting itself."

The plan would be financed by eliminating the tax break the government provides by not taxing employees for the value of employer-sponsored health insurance, Butler wrote. The billions the government would save would be applied to subsidize premiums for everyone to buy their own insurance.

Although he was a Democrat, Gruber had been thinking about the Heritage individual responsibility idea for a while. He thought it made sense as a way to make insurance markets work better by getting more people, even healthy people, into the pool of people paying premiums. That way, insurance companies could cover the unlucky ones who got sick while using revenues from the enlarged base of healthy policyholders to charge lower premiums.

However, Gruber judged it politically impractical to try to scrap the federal tax break on employer-paid insurance. The unions would fight it, as would insurance companies and even employers, who liked the idea of being able to offer a tax-free benefit to workers (even if they were being forced to cut back on its scope because of rising costs) and whose executives benefited from the tax break disproportionately because they were in higher tax brackets. Besides, Massachusetts alone couldn't overturn federal tax law.

Gruber began working with Romney and his staff and people from Heritage. Importantly, aides to Senator Ted Kennedy—whose help would be crucial in getting a federal aid package to support the state's reforms—were also involved from the beginning. Together, they came up with a plan that would spread health insurance coverage to almost everyone in the Bay State. Employer-sponsored insurance would not be tampered with. In fact, Gruber and the Romney staff came up with the opposite idea: To keep their plan from threatening the private insurance market status quo, Massachusetts law would be changed to require all but the smallest businesses to offer basic health insurance to their workers.

Requiring big business to ante up this way might have seemed like an un-Republican, even radical, idea. Yet its origins dated back to a proposal Richard Nixon had pushed, beginning in 1973. In part to counter more liberal reforms then being promoted by Kennedy, Nixon announced a plan that would force employers to buy insurance for all of their workers. On top of that, Nixon offered an even more unlikely Republican idea: The government would give subsidies to people of limited means who were not covered at work so that they could buy insurance in the individual market. The insurance would be sold in markets—called exchanges—that would be regulated by the government to ensure that the offerings were consumer friendly and competitive.

Because he had won the support of Wilbur Mills, the Democratic chairman of the all-important House Ways and Means Committee, Nixon seemed on his way to getting Nixoncare through. But then Mills was suddenly dethroned by a scandal involving a female companion who was arrested one night for jumping into the Washington pond known as the Tidal Basin. And soon after that, Nixon was derailed by the Watergate scandal.

The Gruber/Romney team's mandate that employers buy insurance for their workers was not new. But in order to get everyone covered, their plan featured other, more radical, changes to fix the market in which individuals bought insurance for themselves.

THE THREE-LEGGED STOOL

The plan had three major, interrelated features, which everyone began to call "the three legs of the stool."

The first leg was a reform in how insurance was sold that Gruber and other economists had come to believe was a key to eliminating a major flaw in the market for individual insurance. Insurance companies in the individual market would not be allowed to screen people with preexisting conditions in order to exclude them or to charge them more than healthy people. In other words, sick people, who need insurance the most, would be able to buy affordable insurance.

But what would prevent people from waiting to buy insurance until they got sick? The whole idea of insurance is shared risk: We all pay equally into the pot, and those of us who get sick can withdraw funds to pay for care.

That's where the second leg came in: the Heritage Foundation mandate. Gruber and the Romney team paired the requirement that preexisting conditions could no longer be used to deny anyone insurance with a mandate that anyone not in a job where insurance was provided by an employer (or not covered by Medicare or Medicaid) would have to buy insurance or pay a penalty for not doing so. There would be no one filling out insurance applications on their way to the hospital.

The mandate was the linchpin. In fact, in pushing for this plan beginning in 2005, Romney, citing the original Heritage Foundation article, would deride the "free riders" who refuse to buy insurance and call the mandate "the ultimate conservative idea" because it was rooted in the principle of individual responsibility.

To make the mandate more palatable, insurers would compete to sell individual policies on the kind of exchange Nixon had envisioned, so that prices and coverage could be compared. The resulting competition would presumably drive prices down.

But what about people who could not afford insurance, no matter how much competition on the exchanges held the line on prices?

The third leg of the stool addressed that. As with the old Nixon plan, there would be government subsidies for people below certain income levels so that they could buy policies. And, again, to make sure that employers would not stop paying for their workers' insurance and throw them onto these exchanges where they would get government subsidies, the plan, as with the old Nixon proposal, included penalties for companies (other than small businesses) that did not pay for workers' health insurance—a provision that further ensured that the employer-insurance status quo would not be disrupted.

By now Kennedy was enthusiastic about this more conservative approach. "Teddy always told me 'You take what you can get,'" recalled David Blumenthal, a physician and longtime healthcare policy expert who had worked on Kennedy's Senate staff. So Kennedy eagerly partnered with Romney in an effort to corral Democrats and Republicans in the Massachusetts legislature by negotiating all kinds of tweaks and compromises.

A BIPARTISAN CELEBRATION

As a result of that unlikely partnership, less than a year before the Las Vegas forum, on April 12, 2006, there had been an event in Boston's historic Faneuil Hall that made it seem as if healthcare—because it had become such a pressing, personal issue for so many Americans—could be the dilemma that brought the country together.

The vast hall, filled with state legislators from both sides of the aisle, was festooned with banners celebrating "Making History in Healthcare." Romney aides handed out buttons saying the same thing. It all had the air of a revival meeting.

Romney mounted a raised podium in front of statues of John Adams, John Quincy Adams, and Daniel Webster and under the hall's looming iconic painting of Webster debating the fate of the Union on the Senate floor. Not trying to contain his enthusiasm, Romney joked that this was a "Cecil B. DeMille moment," referring to the over-the-top movie director whose extravaganzas had included *The Ten Commandments* and *The Greatest Show on Earth*.

On the stage with Romney, celebrating the governor's signing of what would come to be called Romneycare, were Ted Kennedy and Heritage Foundation senior fellow Robert Moffit. Romney called it "an extraordinary sight, not just because how many people are here but because *who* is here."

After thanking Gruber, Romney noted that for him to be returning to Faneuil Hall, the site of a debate Romney had famously lost to

Kennedy when Romney had run against him for the Senate in 1994, "feels like the *Titanic* returning to visit the iceberg." Unable to resist another acknowledgment of how surreal the moment seemed, he added that his son had said that "having Senator Kennedy and me in a room for this will help slow global warming because hell has frozen over."

Romney introduced Kennedy, applauding heartily as the Senate warhorse, whose brother had come to the same hall on the night of November 8, 1960, to thank Americans for electing him president, took the podium. "Yet again, the pioneering spirit of the people of Massachusetts has prevailed," Kennedy thundered. "And you may well have fired the shot heard round the world on health care in America."

Heritage's Moffit, an icon of conservative orthodoxy, was just as enthusiastic. "We have retained what is best in American healthcare while correcting its deficiencies," he declared when it was his turn to address the crowd, before adding "Too often excessive partisanship corrodes civility. . . . The opposite has happened here."

In the days that followed, some critics on the right, most notably the *Wall Street Journal* editorial page, attacked the plan as an assault on liberty, because of the mandate that everyone had to buy insurance. Some on the left, including progressive activists and union leaders who had been Kennedy's comrades in arms since the 1970s, complained that any reform that didn't scrap private insurance and feature the government as the single payer was a cop-out.

But the optimism prevailing that day in Boston had not waned in the eleven months leading up to the Las Vegas candidates' night. There had been a nerve-rattlingly slow rate of sign-ups in the early days after the Massachusetts exchange had opened in January 2007. But by March, activity was already beginning to pick up. And the bipartisan spirit of the enterprise had stayed so strong that supporting Romneycare had become a matter of civic boosterism, not politics. Even the Boston Red Sox promoted Romneycare.

Meantime, across the country, governors, most notably California's Arnold Schwarzenegger, were taking note and pushing their own versions of Romneycare.

"Romneycare," said Daschle, "was the game changer. We could now see a plan that would extend coverage for all, not upset the private market, and attract broad bipartisan support."

OBAMA TREADS CAUTIOUSLY

It was not surprising, then, that Edwards and Clinton, while not crediting the Republican governor by name, touted the three-legged Romneycare stool as the crux of their solution: prohibit insurance companies from discriminating based on preexisting conditions; keep premiums relatively low by requiring everyone without employer-based insurance to buy insurance on exchanges (while requiring employers to keep offering insurance); and provide subsidies for those who needed it to pay those premiums.

Healthcare had not been much of an issue during the 2004 campaign. To the extent it had been talked about, the Democratic candidates' positions ran the gamut from single-payer to more modest proposals for government programs to take care of a greater share of the still uninsured. Now, everyone except Kucinich, who was never seen as a serious candidate, seemed to be on the same page.

But Barack Obama didn't go as far as the others. In the 2003 run-up to his 2004 U.S. Senate campaign, Obama had promised a union rally that he would fight for the single-payer system that Kucinich now championed. Not anymore. In Las Vegas, Obama not only discarded that position; he also didn't talk about an individual mandate, though he did vaguely back the notion of getting the uninsured into "large pools" where risk could be spread.

Obama's hesitancy was not because he wasn't already schooled in at least that detail. Stern, the service workers union leader who had organized the Las Vegas forum, later told me that months before, over dinner in Washington on the eve of announcing his candidacy, Obama had said he feared a mandate would be so politically unpopular as to be unrealistic. "He wasn't where Hillary or Edwards were," said Stern.

Despite what Stern had said from the Las Vegas podium about the polls showing great voter concern about healthcare, Obama's team was less enthusiastic about the idea that the issue would fire up the troops. His pollsters were finding that, while Americans were worried about it as a pocketbook issue, they were also leery, as they had been in the days of Hillarycare, about the government interfering with the insurance that most of them already had.

There was something else that constrained Obama's view beyond the yellow light his campaign staff was flashing. Obama had not yet put in the time that Clinton and Edwards had on the campaign trail—where so many people had stopped them on rope lines to tell a tale of woe about medical bills their families had faced.

That would change. Obama would soon have his own list of ordinary citizens who had bent his ear about medical bills.

In fact, when he left the stage on March 24, 2007, Obama could have gotten a primer from a gate agent working at the airport that night.

THE GATE AGENT'S DAUGHTER

Checking suitcases and boarding passes for US Airways passengers moving through McCarran International Airport in Las Vegas on a shift that ended at 3:30 A.M. was not how Mary Fowler, then sixty-two, had planned to spend her retirement when her husband ended his Minneapolis medical practice and they moved to Henderson, Nevada, at the beginning of 2006.

At the time of the move, Dr. Robert Fowler was sixty-five and enrolled in Medicare, so health insurance was not an issue for him. For Mary, it was.

Years earlier she had contracted hepatitis C through a contaminated blood transfusion given to her during the birth of their son. The Fowlers were so worried that she was nearing death that they were considering a liver transplant. Then she was put into a clinical trial testing what was thought might be a miracle drug. It worked. By the time Mary Fowler, who had worked as an accountant, got to Nevada, she had been symptom free for seven years.

But WellPoint, which was the only insurer she could initially find selling insurance on the individual market in Nevada, didn't care. Because of her preexisting condition, she was rejected. She then found a plan from another insurer. But because of her prior condition, it was so costly and had such a high deductible that after a few months of paying premiums she leaped at the chance when a neighbor told her about an $8.50 per hour job at the airport that provided full insurance.

It was her only workable alternative.

Insurance plans offered by large employers, called group plans, do not screen individuals for their health history or even their age. That's because the "pool" of people to be insured is large enough that the risks among them average out—which is what insurance is supposed to be about: large groups of people paying premiums in order to share the risk that some of them will need help.

But unlike with Romneycare in Massachusetts, when insurers sold policies to individuals in Nevada and the rest of the country they were allowed to discriminate. Indeed, discrimination was their business model. The individual market was premised on the insurer gauging the risk—which is called underwriting—of each person applying for insurance.

In that sense it was not really insurance at all, because it was not about a large group covering for the losses of one of its members. Rather, it was about the insurance company making a bet on Mary Fowler's risk of getting sick. Only it was making a bet using data about Mary Fowler's age, her health history (which she had to supply to them in pages of excruciating detail and which she had to tell the truth about or the insurance would not apply), and her lifestyle and circumstances. (Did she smoke? Was she likely to get pregnant? How old was she?)

All that data—all that underwriting expertise—gave the insurers a far better sense of the odds than Mary Fowler could ever have. Think of it in terms of another Las Vegas bet. Underwriting was like card counting in blackjack, where the player who can keep track of all the cards that have been played has an advantage in deciding whether to draw another one. Casinos kick out card counters because they believe a good counter's skill puts the house at a disadvantage. With health insurance underwriting, it's the house that always had the advantage. They accept your premiums only when the data tells them it's a good bet.

A TOUGH INSURER HIRES A REFORMER

WellPoint, the insurer that rejected Mary, traced its roots to those schoolteachers in Dallas who signed up for hospital insurance under the Blue Cross brand in 1929.

From that quiet start, insurance plans from Blue Cross and Blue Shield, which was launched in the 1930s as insurance covering doctors' care, began to proliferate through the first half of the twentieth century. The Blues, as they were called, were the leading source of private, employer-sponsored insurance.

As the plans began shooting up across the country, the originators of the first Blues formed an association that claimed the Blue Shield and Blue Cross trademarks and logos as their intellectual property. They then licensed them to newcomers in other states and regions, so there would be only one Blue in each place. There would be no competing Blues in any region. The association itself remained a nonprofit organization, although most of the insurers licensing the Blue name soon transitioned into large profit makers.

By 2007, having recently merged with another Blue licensee called Anthem, which dominated California, WellPoint had become the country's second largest health insurer, insuring one in every nine Americans and recording more than $60 billion in revenue and $5 billion in pre-tax income.

The company was known among industry regulators as one of the tougher, more consumer-unfriendly industry giants.

Mary Fowler was certainly no fan.

Which caused a bit of embarrassment for her daughter Liz during Liz's first day at her new job in 2007—at WellPoint, where she had become vice president for public policy.

Bob and Mary Fowler had come to visit Liz in Washington that day. When Mary, making small talk, told one of Liz's coworkers that she was now living in Nevada, the coworker gushed, "That's great. We're the leading insurer there. You should buy our policy."

"I tried and you rejected me," Elizabeth's mother shot back.

· · ·

FROM THE START, Liz Fowler had been concerned that WellPoint might not be a good fit.

That was because before arriving at WellPoint, Fowler, who by then was forty, had spent her career pushing healthcare reform. She had evolved into a moderate on the subject, because she thought moderate reform, as opposed to a single-payer-style upheaval, was all that was likely to be achievable, if that. But at WellPoint—which in 2007 was fiercely (and successfully) leading the fight against Arnold Schwarzenegger's Romney-style proposal for California—even moderate change was to be resisted at all costs.

Fowler had come to WellPoint from a senior position working on healthcare for Max Baucus of Montana, the senior Democrat on the powerful Senate Finance Committee. She had decided to make a career change because Baucus had lost a lot of his friends among Democrats after he supported President George W. Bush's 2003 legislation to extend prescription drug coverage to people on Medicare, a program called Medicare Part D. The rank and file Democrats' objection to the Bush law was that while it did extend a benefit to seniors, the benefit was not enough, mostly because there was a huge gap in their coverage, later dubbed the "doughnut hole." Besides, the law was a budget buster, a completely new and unpaid-for entitlement that was aimed, the Democrats charged, at currying favor for the Republicans with seniors while creating huge deficits for the next president.

Worst of all, the Democrats saw the law as an enormous handout to the pharmaceutical companies and their lobbyists, who fed so much money into Republican campaign coffers; the law prohibited Medicare from negotiating discounts with the drug companies, even though private insurers routinely negotiated such discounts.

Fowler thought her boss's role in creating Part D was honorable and even right on the merits because the new law provided important aid to seniors. However, she also knew that the fallout would limit his clout on Capitol Hill, at least for the next few years.

So why not take a breather from the Hill and earn more money with less frustration?

When she decided to leave Baucus, Fowler resisted offers to become a lobbyist. WellPoint told her that she would advise broadly on policy, not lobby her old colleagues. She would not make nearly the money she could make as a lobbyist, but she would earn more than if she stayed in government, and, she thought, she could feel good about her work.

"Healthcare policy is what I know," she later told me. "If I can't do that and need to stay in Washington [where her husband works as a lawyer], what am I going to do? Open a doggy day care center? . . . I didn't want to be a lobbyist and call my old friends and colleagues and say 'Hey, I have this thing I want to come talk to you about.' But I was okay with doing broad policy analysis."

STILL, WELLPOINT WAS a long way from where Liz Fowler had started.

As the daughter of a family practitioner in Minnesota, Fowler had always been interested in healthcare, so much so that she was a premed student when she enrolled at the University of Pennsylvania. Her interest in being a doctor waned as she began to hear more from her father about how his practice had become less satisfying because of all the Medicare rules, insurance paperwork, and other distractions that had come to dominate his workday.

Fowler's focus shifted completely when she took a class in healthcare policy as a sophomore. She had vaguely understood that some of her father's patients had faced crushing medical bills, which had contributed to her father's overall unhappiness with his practice. But she was amazed to learn that most developed countries around the world had figured out how to provide affordable healthcare for all or most of their people. Fowler was stunned, as only a twenty-year-old college sophomore could be, that there was something her country was not best at and, in fact, in her professor's estimation had become one of the worst at.

She was soon determined to be part of changing that. She liked what she had learned in class about the Swedish system so much, she recalled, "that I even tried to take Swedish."

After graduating from Penn in 1989, Fowler went to work as a policy analyst at Medicare. Two years later, she left to get a doctorate from the Johns Hopkins School of Public Health. While at Hopkins she worked as a researcher for Gerard Anderson, a leading healthcare economist. (Though a highly regarded academic, Anderson's view of healthcare in America boiled down to this blunt prescription: "The prices are all too high.")

Fowler also spent a summer working at the mecca of single-payer advocates—the English National Health Service. Established after World War II and funded through general taxes, the NHS generally provides all medical care for free to all residents. Healthcare spending as a percent of England's gross domestic product is about half of what it is in the United States, while healthcare outcomes are generally better.

Fowler had then followed a man she was serious about back to Minnesota, where she decided to enroll at the University of Minnesota Law School.

After graduation and following an unhappy stint at a prestigious Washington law firm, she took her first job on Capitol Hill in 1999. By 2005 she had become Baucus's chief Democratic counsel for healthcare on the Senate Finance Committee.

BY THE END OF 2007, Fowler, too, could see the stars aligning. She had watched from a vantage point that made her uncomfortable—a huge insurance company fighting reform—but she could see momentum building. Costs and coverage had become such a burden for people like her mother that the forces for reform were stirring again. Healthcare was suddenly getting attention as a big issue in the coming presidential election—an election that seemed likely to put the Democrats back in charge.

Meantime, the businessman Republican governor of Massachusetts seemed to have gotten together with Ted Kennedy to cook up a plan that had produced bipartisan praise and, in fact, seemed to have revived a spirit of bipartisan comity. That was the kind of environment in which Max Baucus could do his best work.

Maybe it was time to go back.

CHAPTER 3

MAX, BARACK, HILLARY, BILLY, AND THE GATHERING CONSENSUS

March–May 2008

BY MARCH 2008, LIZ FOWLER HAD RETURNED TO THE SENATE FI-nance Committee. With the Democrats having retaken the Senate majority in the 2006 elections, her boss, Max Baucus, was now chairman.

Baucus told Fowler and the rest of his staff that he was determined to set the stage for systemic healthcare reform in 2008. Mindful of the precedent set by Romneycare, he thought he could pull it off whether a Democrat or Republican was elected that November. Baucus, a conservative Democrat, prided himself on doing deals with Republicans. He considered himself the ultimate doer–deal maker, not a partisan barn burner.

When Baucus, then sixty-six, met with his staff to discuss healthcare, he often talked about Lester Skramsted, whose picture Baucus kept on his desk. Eight years before, Baucus had befriended Skramsted in a living room in Libby, Montana, at a gathering of people stricken with asbestosis, a chronic and often deadly lung disease. Extensive litigation had proven that their illness was the result of an environmentally unsafe mining operation operated in Libby by W. R. Grace, the giant chemical and materials company. Even family members of workers like Skramsted had been infected when the miners carried the asbestos dust home every night on their clothing. Their children sometimes fell ill just by sitting on their fathers' laps. "It was so sad," Fowler recalled.

Settlements of liability claims against Grace were not sufficient, in Baucus's view, to cover the medical care necessary over the duration of their often-terminal illness; and Baucus had long cited the struggle of Skramsted (who died in 2007) and his family in talking about the need to give Americans better healthcare protection.

A graduate of Stanford and Stanford Law School, Baucus had worked in Washington for the Securities and Exchange Commission before returning to Montana to practice law. He was elected to the state legislature in 1973, the U.S. Congress in 1974, and the U.S. Senate in 1978.

At first impression, Baucus's genial demeanor, punctuated by a habit of bursting into a grin even after he hears or says something serious, often make him seem less intelligent or substance-oriented than he is. Yet, Fowler recalled, "Max was really serious about healthcare. He wanted to do something big and thought this was the time."

"So did I," Fowler continued. "This was the best opportunity in one hundred years of people talking about doing something."

During that one hundred years, Fowler added, from Theodore Roosevelt to FDR to Truman to Clinton and to Romneycare—the proposals had kept moving further to the right, with the Democrats moving closer to the Republican position. "If we waited any longer, who knew what we would end up with?"

Baucus decided that the smartest way to proceed would be for Fowler and the rest of his staff to plan a series of hearings on healthcare reform that would culminate in a bipartisan Capitol Hill "summit" late in the spring of 2008. That would, in turn, produce draft legislation or, failing that, a "white paper" summarizing the myriad healthcare-related policy issues and the chairman's take on them.

"IS THERE ROOM FOR OLD TEDDY?"

About a month before Fowler and her team started putting together those hearings, Barack Obama had received the call he had been hoping for since his campaign had begun a year earlier.

"Is there still room on that train for Old Teddy?" Senator Edward Kennedy asked Obama on January 28, 2008.

According to his widow, Vicki, who was with Kennedy during the call, and to a top Obama campaign aide, Kennedy did not make support of healthcare reform or anything else a quid pro quo during the call, which came to be considered a pivotal moment in the Obama campaign. But Kennedy did mention his career-long cause, saying words to the effect of "Oh, by the way, you know how I feel about healthcare and I really appreciate your commitment to reform."

Hillary Clinton was furious about the Kennedy endorsement. Had she been in the room during that call hearing Kennedy remind Obama of the Massachusetts senator's devotion to healthcare reform, she would have been still more beside herself. For the principal issue Obama had found to separate himself from Clinton during the 2008 primary season had to do with healthcare.

"SHAME ON YOU, BARACK OBAMA"

As she had in Las Vegas at the beginning of the campaign, Clinton had continued to tout the individual mandate as a key part of a reform package. Ted Kennedy had championed the mandate from the time he had sung its praises in the 2006 Romneycare law.

Obama had not simply continued to exclude a mandate from his plan. His campaign was now distributing flyers in battleground states attacking Clinton for wanting "to make you buy health insurance you can't afford." The flyers didn't mention that the Clinton plan—in fact, the most expensive and core element of the Clinton plan—called for government subsidies for those who could not afford the insurance.

On February 23, 2008, less than a month following Kennedy's Obama endorsement, Clinton held a press conference in Ohio, where she did not hide her fury at the man who was now her sole opponent. It produced probably the angriest news clips of the Democratic primary.

"Time and time again," Clinton thundered, holding up an Obama campaign flyer, "you hear one thing in speeches and then you see a campaign that has the worst kind of tactics, reminiscent of the same sort of Republican attacks on Democrats. . . . Since when do Democrats attack one another on universal health care? I thought we were trying to realize Harry Truman's dream. I thought this campaign finally gave us an opportunity to put together a coalition to achieve universal health care. That's what Senator Edwards and I talked about throughout the campaign. Just because Senator Obama chose not to present a universal health care plan does not give him the right to attack me because I did. . . . So shame on you, Barack Obama," she spat into the microphones, supplying a sound bite that made its way into every 2008 primary highlight reel.

Apart from their differences over the mandate—which Obama maintained was unenforceable and unnecessary because people would not need to be forced to buy affordable insurance—Obama had by that point developed a plan that was almost the same as Clinton's and Romneycare: Employers would be required to keep providing insurance; exchanges would be set up so that people without employer coverage could buy in the individual market in a competitive environment, with subsidies given to families who couldn't afford the premiums; and insurance companies would not be allowed to discriminate against anyone on the basis of preexisting conditions.

As with the other candidates, Obama had now met enough people on the campaign trail whose stories he could use to punctuate his plea for universal coverage. Within three months of his Las Vegas flop, he began speaking powerfully about the Chicos family, small business owners in Decorah, Iowa, struggling to pay monthly insurance premiums that had swollen to $1,000 a month because Mr. Chicos had had cancer.

But Obama never mentioned a mandate.

Gruber, the MIT professor and Romneycare co-inventor, was a Democrat. But he had not signed on with Obama, Clinton, or anyone else during the primary campaign. He had met with Obama in 2006 when Obama was on the verge of entering the race, and found him "interested in the issue and fairly knowledgeable," he recalled. "But I thought Hillary was likely to win, and, in any event, because of my relationship with Romney"—who was running for the Republican nomination—"I decided to stay out."

But to Gruber and most other economists, including some on Obama's campaign team, as well as the entire insurance industry, the difference between a mandate and no mandate was crucial: If people didn't have to buy insurance but could instead sign up when they became ill, the resulting wait-until-you-need-it dynamic, which the economists called adverse selection, would cripple the entire scheme. Insurers, faced with insuring a disproportionate number of people who knew they needed it while not collecting premiums from the young and others who thought they didn't, would have to raise rates to cover the added risk. The inflated rates would, in turn, exacerbate the problem in a vicious downward spiral by discouraging all but the truly ill from signing on to pay the still-higher premiums.

That logic didn't cut it with Obama's political team. They had polled a mandate and thought it was a loser. "People hate health insurance companies," one Obama political aide told me. "So now we're going to tell healthy people they have to buy insurance from them? Are you kidding?"

Ted Kennedy was unworried by Obama's position. "Teddy was focused on electing Obama, who he thought represented the kind of new generation his brother did," recalled senior Kennedy healthcare aide John McDonough, who had run a Massachusetts healthcare reform advocacy group that had helped lay the groundwork for Romneycare. "And he knew that that would be the best way to produce healthcare reform. . . . And knowing Teddy," McDonough added, "assuming he cared about Obama's position on the mandate, I bet he always figured Obama would come around to the mandate once he was elected, because he would see the logic as the [legislative] process ran its course."

AN UNUSUAL SENATE ALLIANCE

As the 2008 primary campaign continued, Kennedy and Baucus formed an alliance to lay the groundwork for healthcare reform. Although both were Senate Democrats, they each chaired committees that shared—and often fought over—turf when healthcare was on the agenda. So their willingness to work together was, in itself, seen by Capitol Hill insiders as a sign that the issue was gathering momentum.

Kennedy's Committee on Health, Education, Labor, and Pensions—called HELP—was stocked with some of the Senate's leading liberals, including Iowa's Tom Harkin, and Bernie Sanders, the Brooklyn-born Vermont senator who called himself an independent but caucused with the Democrats. The Finance Committee, on the other hand, had more moderate Democrats, such as Baucus and North Dakota's Kent Conrad.

Among the many reasons the Clinton healthcare reform push had died on Capitol Hill in 1993 was that the Finance Committee, then chaired by New York centrist Democrat Pat Moynihan, had stiff-armed Kennedy and his HELP Committee. Moynihan's committee had jurisdiction over anything having to do with raising money. Because Moynihan had no enthusiasm for tackling major changes in healthcare, he froze the process of getting a coherent bill to the Senate floor.

Baucus and Kennedy and their staffs were determined that this time would be different.

"The two staffs really got along," recalled Kennedy staffer McDonough. "Liz [Fowler] gets along with everyone. . . . And we all remembered the Clinton years. So early on we met—and then Baucus and Kennedy met—and planned how we would work together."

The plan was for each committee to write, or "mark up," its version of healthcare reform and then negotiate the differences. "We knew that their bill would be more liberal than ours," Fowler explained. "But because we're the Finance Committee, ours would have the fees or taxes in it that would raise the money, while theirs would have more liberal reforms."

On the other side of the political divide, the Republicans in the 2008 presidential primary weren't talking much about broad healthcare reform— except for Romney, who touted his success in Massachusetts. Still calling his mandate "the ultimate conservative approach," Romney declared at a debate in Simi Valley, California, that "A lot of people talk about health care. I'm the only one that got the job done. I got health insurance for all our citizens. . . . I'm proud of what we accomplished."

Other than occasionally attacking Romney's mandate as an assault on freedom, GOP front-runner and eventual nominee John McCain said little on the subject.

"BILLY"

By April, Barack Obama had turned healthcare into one of his favorite topics. The issue became a way to promise a big idea that would touch people's lives while also demonstrating that, unlike Clinton, he was not a Washington insider and was not going to go to the White House to play the inside-the-Beltway game. Thus, one of Obama's strongest TV spots used his promise of healthcare reform to attack a Louisiana politician who seemed a real-life parody of a Beltway insider doing the bidding of the special interests that wrote him checks.

The Obama campaign called the ad "Billy."

The spot opened with Obama, in shirtsleeves, speaking at a campaign reception. "The pharmaceutical industry wrote into the prescription drug plan that Medicare could not negotiate with drug companies," he began. "And you know what? The chairman of the committee, who pushed the law through, went to work for the pharmaceutical industry making $2 million a year. Imagine that!"

Obama was referring to former congressman Wilbert Joseph Tauzin II, whom everyone calls Billy.

The bare facts of the Billy story were even more gasp worthy than Obama could get across in a thirty-second ad. A lawyer and member of the Louisiana legislature from the small town of Chackbay, Tauzin was elected to the House of Representatives as a Democrat in 1980. Though more conservative than most congressional Democrats, Tauzin, who is part-Cajun, deployed a combination of small-town charm and sharp elbows that served him well in Washington. Repeatedly elected with little or no opposition, he eventually worked his way up to majority whip and chair of the powerful Energy and Commerce Committee, becoming the most powerful conservative Democrat in the House.

When the Republicans took over the House following the 1994 elections, Tauzin was unbowed. He switched parties.

He was rewarded for jumping ship with the same Energy and

Commerce chair he had had as a Democrat, making him the first member of Congress to achieve a leadership position in both parties. Voters back home didn't care; they kept reelecting him.

It was when he was chairing Energy and Commerce for the Republicans, in 2003, that Tauzin had engineered the drug benefits bill that Obama referred to in the ad. It funded Medicare to buy drugs for seniors but did not let the agency try to negotiate discounts from the drug companies. It was the same bill that Baucus had supported, to the consternation of many fellow Democrats.

And, yes, just as Obama had told his campaign rally, soon after that, Tauzin had quit Congress and taken a $2 million a year job as the pharmaceutical industry's lead lobbyist.

The ad closed with Obama adding a few more lines linking Billy to the larger mess he was going to clean up: "That's an example of the same old game playing in Washington. You know, I don't want to learn how to play the game better. I want to put an end to the game playing."

In Tauzin's telling, there was one complication to his story that the Obama ad didn't mention. In the year before he took the $2 million Pharmaceutical Manufacturers Association of America (PhRMA) job, he had been diagnosed with what he told me was colorectal cancer. His doctor had initially said he had a 1 percent chance of surviving. But he was saved by a newly developed drug. "I'm alive because of the pharmaceutical industry and its ability to invest in new drugs," is how he put it. "So that was a big part of my decision."

Nonetheless, Tauzin was not upset by the Obama ads. "That kind of stuff just rolls off my back," he later explained to me, chuckling.

In fact, by the time the "Billy" ad ran, its namesake was already thinking about the kind of deal he might make for the drug companies with a new president, even Obama. Tauzin was becoming convinced that a Democrat, probably Obama, was going to be elected and that healthcare was going to be high on the new administration's agenda. In that case, his members' profit margins would no doubt become a prime target.

"Billy liked to say that if you're not at the table, you're going to be on the menu," recalled the CEO of one of the largest drug companies who was on the PhRMA board's executive committee. "He said we should think about making a deal and get to the table first, so we could minimize the damage. The Democrats were talking about some things that were life threatening to our industry."

INSURANCE COMPANIES AT THE TABLE

At the leading insurance company lobby—America's Health Insurance Plans (AHIP)—executive director Karen Ignagni was thinking the same thing in the summer of 2008. She, too, did not want to be on the menu.

Ignagni, who was fifty-four in 2008, was considered one of Washington's most effective lobbyists, though in an un-Billy way. She was a good, solicitous listener. She didn't pull her punches, but she didn't try to fast-talk her way through a pitch with over-the-top rhetoric or hollow arguments, either. Ignagni also had an interesting pedigree for someone representing one of the Democrats' favorite big business targets. The daughter of a Rhode Island fireman, she was a Democrat who had worked on healthcare issues for the AFL-CIO before being recruited to AHIP in 1993.

As early as 2006, as Romneycare was being hammered out in Massachusetts, Ignagni had begun coaxing her insurance trade association to get on the healthcare reform train instead of in front of it by articulating its own reform proposals.

Like Tauzin, Ignagni sensed the political momentum building for reform. However, she and the insurance company executives who were her bosses were also aware that the status quo wasn't working for them, either. Unlike Tauzin's pharmaceutical manufacturers, who seemed to enjoy record profits year after year, the insurance industry was not what it used to be.

Large employers were increasingly saving money by self-insuring—setting aside their own money to pay their share of their workers' healthcare bills and leaving the big insurance companies the lower margin job of simply vetting and processing the bills for them.

The individual market was in deeper trouble. In fact, it was in danger of drying up completely. In states such as Mary Fowler's Nevada, where insurers were allowed to reject applicants who had preexisting conditions or charge them high prices, people were increasingly going uninsured. Worse, a few states, like New York, had done what Obama was now proposing: force insurers not to discriminate but without an accompanying mandate that everyone had to buy insurance. As a result, insurers in New York—fearful of the adverse selection dynamic, in which only the sick would buy policies—had jacked up premiums to $15,000 to $25,000 a year for families of four. The prices were so out of reach that the market had dwindled almost to extinction. In New York, twenty-six thousand individual policies would be sold statewide in 2010.

Ignagni and her members feared that the country might soon be beset with New York–style "reform."

So in June 2008, Ignagni convinced her members to put together a more detailed reform proposal than the one AHIP had first espoused about six months earlier. Along with cost-cutting initiatives, such as electronic medical records and tort reform to curb medical malpractice suits that were thought to encourage doctors to practice expensive defensive medicine, Ignagni's plan called for universal coverage that would include "limits" on excluding people with preexisting conditions, accompanied by a mandate that everyone had to buy insurance.

Moreover, federally financed subsidies would be offered to people who needed help paying the premiums. In other words, there would be universal coverage, with taxpayers helping people pay their insurance bills. It would be a Romneycare-like win for advocates of universal coverage. And a win for Ignagni's members.

ANOTHER ACCIDENT OF HISTORY

With the Democratic candidates pushing reform, and even the drugmakers and insurers thinking about how to support it, only one event threatened the building momentum in mid-2008. As with the Watergate scandal that derailed Nixon's reform push, it was an unrelated accident of history.

In May 2008, Ted Kennedy suffered a seizure and was diagnosed with a brain tumor. Suddenly, reform's most ardent and effective champion, the master of Capitol Hill deal making, was likely going to be sidelined.

Kennedy had brain surgery in June, an operation that did not reverse the grim diagnosis his doctors had given him. However, he instructed his staff to begin meetings among themselves and with stakeholders so that they could keep working in parallel with Baucus's people. They needed to have a plan ready for the newly elected president.

The group Kennedy's staff assembled, mostly HELP Committee staffers and friendly healthcare reform policy advocates, were all Democrats. But they had been directed by Kennedy to come up with a package that could pass a Senate with Republican votes. Democrats had only fifty-five votes in 2008, even assuming the support of their most conservative members, plus the presumed vote of independent Bernie Sanders. Getting something through the Senate would require a sixty-vote margin to survive a filibuster.

At the same time, Fowler and her staff—pushed by Baucus in meetings that seemed to happen every other day or so—charted a more public course. As Baucus had instructed, they organized witnesses to testify at Finance Committee hearings in the late spring. Those hearings would be the lead-up to what Baucus envisioned as an unusual show of momentum and consensus: a daylong bipartisan "summit" that Baucus and his senior Republican colleague on the committee, Chuck Grassley of Iowa, would convene in June.

Grassley and Baucus were good friends and had worked together to produce numerous Finance Committee legislative initiatives. The Democratic and Republican staffs also got along. "I remember going to one of the Finance staff meetings on health," recalled one Kennedy staffer, "and you couldn't tell the Democrats from the Republicans." Their summit, organized by the staff to include participation in marathon panel sessions by everyone who was anyone in healthcare policy, was going to be a big deal.

CHAPTER 4

"THIS IS WHAT I THOUGHT THE SENATE WOULD BE LIKE"

June 2008

"I HAVE BEEN MARRIED FOR A VERY, VERY LONG TIME," IOWA SENA-tor Chuck Grassley began. "I have long since given up thinking I can get what I want, when I want it, and how I want it.

"It is called compromise in any venue," the senior Finance Committee Republican continued. "We all have to be willing to listen to each other, recognize strengths, improve upon weaknesses, and find a common ground that best serves our nation. The opportunity is coming. . . . I challenge you to make a difference and improve our health care system, as you expect Senator Baucus and me to make a difference and to improve our health care system."

Grassley was addressing the opening session of the June 16, 2008, healthcare summit that Baucus and Fowler had organized on Capitol Hill in an ornate auditorium at the Library of Congress. About three hundred members of Congress, staffers, lobbyists, and healthcare policy specialists were gathered to hear experts speak on subjects from cost control to insurance to preventive care to medical high tech. Including Baucus and Grassley, sixteen senators in all—half Democrats, half Republicans—would chair the various panels.

THE MOON SHOT

Before he introduced Grassley, Max Baucus had likened the job ahead to President John Kennedy's effort to land a man on the moon: It was a seemingly insurmountable goal that could be achieved only if everyone pulled together. In fact, Baucus had given the summit a title reminding everyone of the pioneering, patriotic days of the moon shot: "Prepare to Launch."

Baucus used a review of the hearings his committee had held in the days immediately before the summit to outline the urgency of the work ahead. He cited the testimony of Raymond Arth, who, he said, owned a small Ohio manufacturing company. "His company's premiums have increased rapidly for several years because many of his employees have stayed on the job and have aged," Baucus said. "Even after he switched his employees to a high-deductible plan, his premiums jumped thirty-two percent in one year because one of his employees has an expensive medical condition. Just one sick employee can make coverage unaffordable in the small group market."

Arth, whose company specialized in making faucets for recreation vehicles, later told me that in 2008 his premiums had not only increased by 38 percent, but that the policy's deductibles—the amount his employees had to pay before insurance kicked in—had jumped from $500 per family to $5,900.

The panels that followed presented an encyclopedic catalog of the problem. The more they talked, the more the senators seemed to come together. Grassley's plea for teamwork seemed not at all out of the question.

The first speaker was Ben Bernanke, the Republican-appointed chairman of the Federal Reserve Board. In June 2008, Bernanke was, of course, grappling with the impending collapse of the American economy. Yet he had come to the summit, he explained, because "the decisions we make about health care reform will affect many aspects of our economy, including the pace of economic growth, wages and living standards, and government budgets, to name a few."

Bernanke proceeded with a litany of the threat posed by healthcare's skyrocketing costs; government spending just for Medicare and

Medicaid, he pointed out, would consume half of the entire federal budget by 2050 if changes weren't made, up from an already-ruinous 25 percent in 2008.

Baucus then asked the Fed chairman a question that produced an extraordinary answer—and a stunning reaction from his Republican counterparts.

"Some people suggest," Baucus began, "that because the American system is so complex and because it is so tied to the political pressures in all different segments, whether it be pharmaceuticals, insurance companies, consumers of health care, and whatnot, that perhaps we should look at some kind of a Federal health board, somewhat patterned after the Federal Reserve system, to help solve some of these problems."

Bernanke allowed that creating an independent board to control health costs might not be a bad idea. He even offered as an analogy the way elected officials had shielded themselves from politically unpopular yet necessary decisions related to closing military bases by setting up an independent commission to choose which would be the unlucky cities and towns that suffered the shutdown of such large employers. Congress then had to vote the plan up or down, with no changes.

What was more surprising was how Grassley, a Republican, seemed to warm to the idea of an independent panel of Washington experts making cost cuts affecting the healthcare people would receive: "We know . . . that Congress does not seem to have the political guts to do anything about it now," Grassley told Bernanke. "So I do think . . . that trying to find some mechanisms . . . might be the way to go forward."

Later in the day, even conservative senator Mike Crapo, a Republican from Idaho, said he thought that "having some type of a base closure type approach to this" was a "good idea."

"NO ONE WANTS TO TALK ABOUT COST"

Following Bernanke was a panel that included MIT's Jonathan Gruber. He pointed to Romneycare's success in expanding coverage, while conceding that costs had exceeded the state's budget projections.

Picking up on the subject of costs, Craig Barrett—the CEO of Intel, who had formed a business-labor coalition with Andy Stern and his service employees union to push healthcare reform—offered this indelible description of the problem: "Medical costs go up by how much each year? One Iraq war. The U.S. increases its health care costs by one Iraq war per year."

The Intel CEO's frustration had mounted as he had listened to the discussion, Barrett said, because it seemed to focus only on coverage, not costs. "I always come back to the issue of cost. . . . No one wants to talk about cost because that's tough," Barrett said. "As a bigger employer, we are very happy to provide health care costs. As our health care costs approach a billion dollars a year in a couple of years, it's going to be increasingly an economic disincentive to do business in the United States."

Other panels covered root causes of the crisis—obesity, smoking, lack of access to routine checkups—and the need to deal with them. Everyone agreed. Who wouldn't? Likewise, everyone seemed to agree that any reform would have to include easier access to preventive care, such as mammograms to catch breast cancer early. No one spoiled the party by dwelling on the complications, such as whether certain preventive tests created so many false alarms that they raised both costs and anguish, much less whether the special interests that profited from those tests would ever allow Congress to scrutinize them or exclude them from the list of easy-to-access, subsidized preventive care. (Would hearing tests count? What about prostate cancer screenings of questionable value?)

A LESSON IN POLITICAL SCIENCE

Among the most thoughtful panelists was Peter Orszag, then the head of the nonpartisan Congressional Budget Office, or CBO. He summarized the obstacles involved in eliminating what he said was the $750 billion a year (at the time, almost exactly the same as the entire defense budget) that America wastes on excessive healthcare spending.

"The political scientists will say," Orszag said, "that a common problem is, you're not in a good situation when there's a concentrated interest, [where] someone's income is being affected, and diffuse benefits." In other words, reform will be difficult because it would mean taking money away from those who directly benefit from it—people who sell healthcare, and will be motivated to hire lobbyists—in order to benefit the more general population who, because of insurance, won't get the direct benefit of the healthcare savings.

If that hurdle could be overcome, Orszag added, the best ways to cut costs would be to use information technology to judge and act on the comparative effectiveness of drugs, medical devices, and other treatments.

Moreover, the system had to be overhauled to pay doctors and hospitals based on their results, not on the fee-for-service basis of how many times a doctor saw a patient or how many tests the doctor ordered. This was a favorite theme of Orszag, an economist with degrees from Princeton and the London School of Economics.

There was unanimous agreement that something had to be done about fee-for-service, too.

But when it came to specifics, it was a lot easier to focus on providing more care to more people than on where to cut costs in order to pay for that care.

Jon Kingsdale's testimony crystallized the coverage-cost dichotomy, and the differing degree of political difficulty associated with each. Kingsdale, a veteran manager of health insurance plans, had run Romneycare from the beginning. He clearly convinced the senators and their staffs that Romneycare's three-legged stool—no exclusions for preexisting conditions, an individual mandate to buy insurance, and subsidies to buy it for those who needed help—had worked to spread insurance coverage in Massachusetts.

But midway through his appearance he echoed Orszag's political science lesson about spreading coverage being a lot easier than tackling costs: "I think politically . . . which is something you have to think a lot about, that we made the right choice. We went for coverage, frankly, before we went for specific cost containment. Though there is broad agreement on the need for containment, any particular cost containment idea means reducing revenue flow to somebody, and there is always stronger opposition from even a smaller party than there is broad depth of broad support. So, I think that's the right order. . . . So we're now wrestling with cost containment."

In other words, Intel's Barrett was right: "No one wants to talk about cost because that's tough."

One discordant note was sounded by Jeanne Lambrew, a professor at the Lyndon B. Johnson School of Public Affairs, who had worked on healthcare in the Clinton administration. A champion of Medicare and Medicaid, Lambrew disagreed with those touting the private marketplace as the prime solution, noting, "It is hard to imagine a private system that functions without public programs filling in those gaps. . . . I think the interesting part about public programs that we often underestimate is they are standard setters. They are critical to leveraging the types of reforms that we would like to see in our health care system."

That point of mild debate notwithstanding—and with thirty-two panelists, plus dozens more experts asking questions from the audience, there were many such differences—by the end of the day, Baucus's summit had the "Kumbaya" feel of a university commencement.

Or, as Nebraska Democrat Kent Conrad put it, "I want to say this: When I came here twenty-two years ago, this is what I thought the United States Senate would be like." Pausing while the audience laughed, Conrad added, "Boy, has this been a rare experience. I want to applaud Chairman Baucus and Senator Grassley. This is what it should be like."

Baucus ended the day on the same upbeat note. "There is more agreement than there is disagreement," he said. "I find that very, very encouraging. . . . The stars, I think, are aligned about as well as they are going to be for us to really move, and we have an opportunity in the next administration, whoever it might be, to tackle this."

Three weeks later it seemed that the most likely next administration was, in fact, not going to move.

CHAPTER 5

A NEW PRESIDENT COMMITS, AND HIS CAMP DIVIDES

July–November 2008

Until Hillary Clinton had conceded the Democratic nomination to Barack Obama nine days before the Baucus summit, on June 7, 2008, Neera Tanden had been the Clinton campaign's chief domestic policy adviser. In fact, she had been in charge of debate preparation the night Clinton outshined Obama in Las Vegas the year before.

By 2008, she was a hardcore Clinton loyalist, having worked on Hillary Clinton's Senate staff and Senate campaign, and, before that, as deputy domestic policy adviser in the Bill Clinton White House.

In between the Clinton White House and the Hillary Clinton Senate race, Tanden had worked at the Center for American Progress, the left-of-center think tank full of Clinton administration alumni that had organized the 2007 Las Vegas debate.

Tanden, who was thirty-eight in 2008, had a classic only-in-America résumé: The child of parents who emigrated from India, her mother had been forced to go on welfare and food stamps after Tanden's father left when she was five. By the time Neera was twenty-six, she had graduated from UCLA and Yale Law School and gone to Washington, where she quickly moved up the ladder through a variety of staff positions.

Jason Horowitz, in a memorable 2011 profile in *The Washington Post,* described Tanden's D.C. persona this way: "At 5 feet 2 inches tall, with an infectious laugh and impatience for ineptitude, Tanden brims with a moxie that can shift to sarcasm. Critics and allies alike describe her as an effective molder and messenger of intricate policy, as well as an expert practitioner of in-house politics. Friends say she is remarkably well-rounded: a model wife and mother, ideal company for a glass of wine, a perfect partner for spontaneous office dancing."

Tanden had hesitated at the offer to join the Obama campaign as senior domestic policy adviser. She was close and fiercely loyal to Hillary Clinton. However, now she wanted Obama to win, badly.

So by the end of June she and her artist husband and two young children had moved to Chicago to join the campaign.

A few days later, Tanden attended her first meeting with the new boss and his senior staff. Sitting around a conference table were Obama, campaign manager David Plouffe, and senior campaign adviser David Axelrod, as well as the pollsters who worked for Axelrod. The group began to run through how the campaign was going to deal with various policy issues. When healthcare came up, an Obama pollster seemed to shrug it off. His data showed, he said offhandedly, that while healthcare reform might have been a good issue in a Democratic primary, it didn't score well in a general election. In fact, pushing it might scare off independents. "We should forget it," he said.

Axelrod and Plouffe nodded in agreement.

"What the f——," Tanden thought to herself. "I just moved my family out here and was told I could concentrate on healthcare while the others did the economy."

But then Obama broke in. "If I become president, I'm going to try to do healthcare fast. And I can't do it fast if I don't talk about it in the campaign. So we have to talk about it."

As they left the meeting, Obama took a relieved Tanden aside and casually said something that left her wondering whether to cry or laugh. "You know," Obama said. "I think maybe Hillary was right about the mandate. . . . I'm not going to talk about it in the campaign, but we may need it."

THE OBAMA STUMP SPEECH

Through the fall, Obama talked repeatedly about the healthcare crisis and how he was going to fix it.

His healthcare stump speech tended to stick to the basics, never mentioning a mandate and focusing on what the polls said was the best target—insurance companies.

"If I am president, I will finally fix the problems in our health care system that we've been talking about for too long," he promised a Miami campaign rally in October. "My mother died of ovarian cancer at the age of fifty-three, and I'll never forget how she spent the final months of her life lying in a hospital bed, fighting with her insurance company because they claimed that her cancer was a preexisting condition and didn't want to pay for treatment. If I am president, I will make sure those insurance companies can never do that again.

"My health care plan," he continued, "will make sure insurance companies can't discriminate against those who are sick and need care most. If you have health insurance, the only thing that will change under my plan is that we will lower premiums. If you don't have health insurance, you'll be able to get the same kind of health insurance that members of Congress get for themselves," he added, referring vaguely to how his planned insurance exchanges would gather people in large risk pools the way government employees' insurance did. "And we'll invest in preventative care and new technology to finally lower the cost of health care for families, businesses, and the entire economy. That's the change we need."

Beyond the fact that Obama was misstating or not remembering his mother's fight with her insurance company correctly and would be caught on that in a book published four years later,[2] the statement in the stump speech that people would be able to keep the insurance they had (but would pay less for it) would later come back to haunt him.

However, in the fall of 2008, healthcare turned out to be a winner,

---

2. In a 2012 biography of Obama's mother, Stanley Ann Dunham, journalist Janny Scott reported that Ms. Dunham's fight with an insurance company was about whether a preexisting condition nullified her disability insurance, not the coverage for her cancer treatment.

in large part because his Republican opponent's stance was so weak and tin-eared.

The McCain answer to the healthcare crisis wasn't the Romneycare solution created by the Republican opponent he had just vanquished in the primaries. Instead, McCain took half of the original Heritage Foundation solution—not the mandate, but the elimination of the tax exemption given to everyone who got health insurance from an employer. With the billions in extra taxes that this would yield every year McCain promised to provide a $5,000 voucher for every family to buy its own health insurance from the incumbent insurers. Now everyone would have the cost-cutting incentive they lacked when their employers bought them insurance. They would become savvy, hard-bargaining customers in the healthcare marketplace because they would have "skin in the game," as proponents of the plan put it. And with that $5,000 voucher, everyone could go into the market.

To the extent that McCain's plan was understood by voters at all— and that was questionable, given how McCain de-emphasized healthcare on the stump—it was a loser on multiple counts. It portended exactly the kind of mass disruption that people instinctively feared because everyone with a job might lose their insurance. It constituted a tax increase for those Americans for whom the current tax exemption might be worth more than a $5,000 per family voucher. It still put people with preexisting conditions at the mercy of insurance companies. And it put everyone up against the challenge of trying to buy insurance using a voucher that was not likely to cover the full cost.

What mattered more than the details, according to polling done at the time that showed McCain overwhelmingly on the losing side of this debate, was that McCain's plan threatened to upend the employer-based system that most Americans were used to.

TRANSITION INFIGHTING

Obama did not mention healthcare in his victory speech in Chicago's Grant Park on Election Night, 2008. Given the history of the occasion and the fact that the country had been plunged into an economic crisis, that was no surprise.

But beginning the next day and through the early days of the transition, a dynamic played out that was similar to what Neera Tanden had gone through in her first meeting with Obama and his staff in July. Most of the Obama people, including newly appointed chief of staff Rahm Emanuel, didn't want to bother with healthcare in the early days of the administration. They were focused on an economy in free fall, and were leery, even dismissive, of any distraction—least of all a distraction that would engage the most powerful lobbies in Washington.

Rattling those cages anytime was a huge risk, as the Clintons had discovered. That was a memory especially indelible to Emanuel, who had worked in the Clinton White House. Why launch some big healthcare proposal in the middle of a financial crisis when Congress was going to be asked to act quickly on a huge economic stimulus bill?

Ironically, some of the people being asked to frame Obama's economic package disagreed—particularly Peter Orszag, the head of the Congressional Budget Office, who had testified at the Baucus summit in June about the need for, and difficulty of, tackling health costs. Orszag was involved in the transition and was about to be appointed as the head of the White House Office of Management and Budget.

As his testimony before Baucus's group had suggested, Orszag was consumed with the idea that healthcare was the economy's Achilles' heel. Some of his friends considered him a fanatic about it, even linking it to the lanky economist's obsession with diet and exercise.

Orszag and other economists working on the transition argued to Obama that, while of course they had to push ahead with the financial stimulus package, fixing the healthcare system was, as Bernanke had told the Baucus panel, a key ingredient in fixing the American economy. Healthcare costs threatened both job growth and the deficit, they reminded Obama.

For Obama, this economic angle was a handy argument to use against aides such as Emanuel, political guru David Axelrod, and Phil Schiliro, who was about to be put in charge of congressional relations. But, Obama later told me, his mind was already made up. "We didn't have the luxury of working on just one big issue—the times demanded more," he recalled. "I believed that reforming our health care system wasn't a side project, but a vital part of rebuilding our economy. . . . It was clear that we couldn't address the problem of the middle class falling behind in the long term, without taking on health care in the short term. And we had a once in a generation chance to do it."

"He was really into healthcare, all the nuances and details," recalled Tom Daschle, the former Senate majority leader and healthcare policy aficionado who had become an Obama confidant. "He told me about all the people he'd met on the [campaign] trail with healthcare stories," added Daschle, recounting a conversation he said he had with the president-elect early in the transition. "And he said he was going to do it now."

Obama's plan for getting it done sooner rather than later involved Daschle. Within days of being elected, Obama started talking to Daschle about taking over the fight for healthcare reform, either as a healthcare "czar" in the White House or as secretary of the Department of Health and Human Services (HHS).

Daschle had a better idea. He would do both.

Having been heavily involved in healthcare in his years in the Senate, Daschle had seen the kind of unwieldy, territorial bureaucracy the Department of Health and Human Services could be. In fact, the agency within HHS known as the Centers for Medicare and Medicaid Services (CMS), that dispensed the hundreds of billions of dollars for those programs, was itself a behemoth that resisted oversight even from its HHS parent. Daschle knew that together the two agencies had been perpetually turf conscious, even secretive, when it came to letting a president and his White House staff get a handle on what was going on at the HHS building a few blocks from the White House, or at the CMS headquarters outside Baltimore. A czar in the White House wouldn't be nearly as effective, Daschle thought, as a czar who could be in the White House when necessary yet also encamped at and directly in control of HHS, too.

Obama liked the idea. He knew that Daschle, perhaps singularly, had the political smarts, the Capitol Hill credibility, the deep grounding in healthcare policy and passion for reform, and the experience with all the relevant bureaucracies to make this work. Plus, Obama knew Daschle was good at finding smart people to help him; three of Obama's top staffers had first worked for Daschle.

But for Daschle one hesitation lingered through the November transition: Was Obama really going to stick to his plan to push health-care reform, despite the warnings of so many of his top aides to deal with the economy first?

The two had one final conversation about that in about the third week in November. "He completely convinced me," Daschle recalled. "He was even a bit annoyed that I kept asking."

ADDING ORNAMENTS TO THE HOOD OF A JALOPY

When Daschle began working at the Obama transition team's Washington office in November he brought Jeanne Lambrew with him. Lambrew was the University of Texas professor who, at the Baucus summit, had pushed back on the notion that the private sector could always be the answer; she was enamored of public healthcare providers, such as Medicaid and Medicare. With her writings and experience as a public health advocate in the Clinton administration she was a highly respected policy wonk, thought to come at most issues from the left. Lambrew had also co-authored a book with Daschle on healthcare reform. A key suggestion in the book had been to establish the kind of independent Federal Reserve–like board to regulate wasteful health spending that Baucus's summit panel had seemed to warm to.

There were others with health policy experience joining the transition team, but Lambrew, as Daschle's deputy and writing partner, was clearly the senior policy staffer. Lambrew might have been inclined to push for a more radical overhaul. However, political realities— combined with the lessons learned in the Clinton years, along with Obama's own campaign platform—dictated that the system was going to be reformed, not scrapped. "We were going to build on the house we had, not knock it down and rebuild a new house," recalled one senior Obama adviser. "Sometimes that's messier and harder, but that's the reality we had to work with."

That made sense for those focused on the realities of Washington. However, to those working in the trenches, it sidestepped a different reality.

When I began my reporting for the special issue of *Time* about medical costs, I approached a doctor friend for an introduction to healthcare economics. He sent this email summarizing his view of his world:

> You are attempting to investigate and understand a miasma of convoluted, dysfunctional, poorly integrated systems. It's like a car built in 1965. In its early years it performed well even though it was misused and abused. The warranty was up decades ago and never renewed. No parts are around anymore to fix it. It's time to abandon it and, with great care, buy a new car.

This was a doctor who practiced in the Bronx, not on Capitol Hill.

Resigning themselves to stick with the old house, or jalopy, threatened to limit what the Obama team could do about costs for the same reason that scrapping the system wouldn't fly politically. As Princeton healthcare economist Uwe Reinhardt liked to say, "Cutting healthcare costs means cutting someone's income"—income that represented close to a sixth of the economy and, therefore, wielded unequaled power in terms of money and breadth.

THE LEFT-WING WONK AND THE KNOW-IT-ALL

True to Orszag's notion, to which Obama had agreed, that healthcare reform was intrinsic to economic reform and recovery, the gathering economic team thrust itself into the deliberations of the domestic policy transition team that was responsible for figuring out a healthcare reform plan. The economics group was led by former Treasury secretary Larry Summers, who was to become the president's head of the National Economic Council in the White House, as well as Orszag. They were backed up by two younger men who had trained as physicians and had immersed themselves in healthcare economics and policy.

One was Bob Kocher, who had been a partner at McKinsey & Company. Kocher, thirty-nine, had led the giant consulting firm's healthcare economics research team. A Harvard-trained internist, Kocher was a walking encyclopedia of healthcare markets data who had an uncanny ability to turn it all into eye-opening PowerPoint presentations illustrating the dysfunction of the American system. Summers put him on the National Economic Council staff.

The other was Ezekiel Emanuel, a cancer specialist and former associate professor at Harvard Medical School who was chairing the National Institutes of Health's Department of Bioethics, which he had founded.

With an MD and a PhD (in political philosophy) from Harvard, a master's from Oxford, and a position teaching oncology at the Dana-Farber Cancer Institute in Boston, Zeke Emanuel was the most academically credentialed of the trio of brilliant Emanuel brothers. There was Ari, the Hollywood agent who had become an entertainment mogul and was supposedly the model for the profane hyperagent in the HBO series *Entourage*. And, of course, there was Rahm, the Clinton aide who had become a fast-rising congressman from Chicago, and was about to become the president's chief of staff. Zeke, who at fifty-one in December 2008, was the oldest of the Emanuel brothers, was also the brashest—which was clearing a high bar.

As soon as Zeke knew that Rahm was going to be chief of staff he had petitioned his brother for a job working on healthcare. The Emanuel brothers are fanatically loyal to one another, but they spare no niceties when talking among themselves. "Rahm told me to go f——myself," Zeke recalled. "But he knew I was right and talked to Orszag about getting me a spot through him." As Orszag moved into his job as head of the Office of Management and Budget, he arranged for Zeke to be loaned to the OMB from the National Institutes of Health while staying on the NIH payroll.

Zeke had the brains, cunning, and biting persona of his two brothers, the Hollywood deal maker and Washington pol. But he was ready, willing, and able to layer it with the self-righteousness of a guy who treated cancer patients. When it came to healthcare issues, at times Zeke Emanuel had taken positions that others may have agreed with but thought too edgy to articulate. In particular, his take on healthcare economics—informed by what he had studied in philosophy, had seen as a cancer doctor, and had confronted as a bioethicist at the National Institutes of Health—had sometimes found him flirting with topics such as whether patients near the end of life should be encouraged to forgo painful, expensive care.

Almost immediately an awkward divide became clear, separating the Lambrew camp and the economics folks. In particular, Lambrew and Zeke Emanuel seemed to those who observed them to have developed a dislike for each other almost from the start.

Lambrew treated Emanuel as if she thought he was a know-it-all who couldn't stand not to dominate the conversation and wouldn't hesitate to use his academic and medical credentials to pull rank on anyone who disagreed with him.

To Emanuel, Lambrew was the naïve, left-wing policy wonk who wanted unlimited healthcare for everyone, even if the taxpayers had to pay for it and even if the care being provided was unnecessary.

But, according to three senior Obama advisers, Lambrew was fast gaining an ally that neither Zeke nor Rahm Emanuel had counted on—Valerie Jarrett.

THE REAL CHIEF OF STAFF

Jarrett was coming to the White House with the title of senior adviser to the president. In 1991, just before Michelle Obama had married the future president, Jarrett had hired the future Mrs. Obama to work at city hall in Chicago, where Jarrett was a deputy chief of staff to the mayor. Since then, Jarrett, who was fifty-three during the transition, had been a big sister of sorts to both Obamas, giving them career advice, introducing them to power players around town, and ultimately encouraging and guiding Barack Obama's ascent from community organizer to state senator to U.S. senator to president.

Through the campaign and the transition, Jarrett had assumed an outsized role as the person closest to both the president and First Lady. In fact, according to five of the highest ranking White House officials, through the Obama presidency, no senior Obama aide regardless of title or stature—not Rahm Emanuel nor any future Obama chief of staff, nor Tom Daschle, let alone any other cabinet member—would ever be senior to Jarrett when it came to having the president's ear or his confidence. As a practical matter, these Obama advisers maintained, Jarrett was the real chief of staff on any issues that she wanted to weigh in on, and she jealously protected that position by making sure the president never gave anyone else too much power.[3]

Reporters would begin to catch on to her influence later in the administration; the press began quoting anonymous White House staffers as calling Jarrett the night stalker because she, alone, would go up to the first family's living quarters in the evening, after all the issues of the day had supposedly been hashed out, and provide the last word.

Asked about the assessments of those five senior officials that Jarrett was "the real chief of staff," Obama declined comment.

It wasn't so much that Lambrew was a Jarrett favorite, though the two did get along well. Rather, it was a matter of Jarrett almost immediately not liking the idea of Rahm Emanuel being in charge. Although the soon-to-be-former congressman was a Chicago politician, he had not traveled in her circles. And, as a former Bill Clinton aide, he had, in fact, remained neutral in the Hillary Clinton contest with Obama. It was understandable that the more genial Obama wanted the take-no-prisoners Emanuel to be the chief who could keep the rest of the staff in line and make deals on Capitol Hill. But his hard-charging style and portfolio had to be kept in check, Jarrett told another senior Obama adviser. Now, the sudden arrival on the scene of Rahm's even more rambunctious brother seemed like part of a Rahm power play.

Besides, to the extent she had delved into the issue, Jarrett thought that extending coverage should, indeed, win out over fights about cost control that the new administration was likely to lose. That was exactly how Lambrew and the domestic policy staff saw it. For Lambrew and those working with her, healthcare reform had always been about extending coverage, something they knew the president-elect had be-

---

3. Jarrett, as is her practice, declined to be interviewed.

come impassioned about as he met the uninsured or underinsured on the campaign trail.

Summers, Orszag, Kocher, Zeke Emanuel, and the rest of the economic team, however, saw reform in terms of their turf. They were determined to try to go after healthcare costs and spending as a tool for economic recovery—something the boss had also become impassioned about.

Yet Orszag was also the one who had told the Baucus summit how difficult attacking healthcare costs would be politically. And Jon Kingsdale, who ran Romneycare, had conceded at the same forum that in Massachusetts they had decided to go for expanded coverage first and deal with costs later because "politically" that was "the right choice."

Now, in the first weeks of the transition, Jonathan Gruber, who had designed Romneycare, delivered a message to both sides that neither wanted to hear. Although Gruber was not officially on the transition team, he was talking to the people who were, and he gave them his blunter version of Kingsdale's concession. "I told them," he recalled, "that you can either try to expand coverage or you can try to do something to control costs. But trying to control costs too much dooms whatever you do, because the lobbyists will kill you. That's what happened to Hillary in 1993."

The industry will happily allow universal coverage, Gruber explained to the transition people, "because that creates more customers. What it won't allow is cost control."

Which meant that the industry's idea of reform would be for the government to create more customers who would, through insurance subsidized by the government, Romneycare-style, pay the same sky-high prices for hospital care, drugs, and medical devices that everyone was already paying.

"Then the question becomes," Gruber continued, "what's the most we can do about cost control in a coverage bill without going too far and rolling the whole thing over the edge?"

Lambrew was fine with that prescription. Expanding coverage was the priority.

The transition economic team heard Gruber, but they were determined to prove him wrong.

When it came to healthcare, Daschle was senior enough—and seasoned enough—to have a foot in both the economic and healthcare reform camps. He, too, was confident the new Obama team could go further than Gruber thought without going over the edge. And he thought he could handle any friction with Lambrew, his protégé coauthor. Nor was he worried about Jarrett.

Meantime, the Senate was moving ahead, not waiting for how the Obama camp might resolve these conflicts.

CHAPTER 6

EVERY LOBBYIST'S
FAVORITE DATE

November–December 2008

Max Baucus had continued with even more hearings after his June summit. Liz Fowler and the Finance Committee staff, including those working for Republicans as well as Democrats, had continued meeting with as many experts—in academia, think tanks, and trade associations—as they could find. Baucus himself met with seventy of his ninety-nine colleagues, one-on-one or in small groups, to get their thoughts and create still more momentum.

Baucus was on a mission. Despite his willingness and ability to forge compromises, during a thirty-year career in the Senate Baucus had produced no truly landmark legislation. In fact, as one of the most conservative Democrats who had often voted with Republicans, he was not regarded even in his own party as a standout lawmaker. It was clear to his staff that he intended to change that. The senator from Montana was certain the time for comprehensive healthcare reform had finally come and that he could be the one to make it happen. He was determined to make his moon shot.

"He was chairman of a powerful committee, and it was near the end of his career, so he wanted to do something big with that power," is how one staff member put it.

It was no surprise, then, that Baucus wasted no time making sure his favorite issue was on the president-elect's agenda before the Obama transition team could even find their desks. On November 6, 2008, two days after the election, the Senate finance chair sent Obama a letter telling him that "next week I will present to you and to the country my plan to move forward on health care reform in the early days of the 111th Congress and of your administration."

That was followed on November 12 by a Baucus white paper, "Call to Action: Health Reform 2009."

Its public release was the first sign of an odd twist in what history might have predicted would be the dynamics of the relationship between a president elected with much fanfare and high expectations and the members of his own party on Capitol Hill. Baucus was poised to take the lead, and the incoming president and his transition team, even with the campaign now over, were willing to follow. This was not going to be anything like Franklin D. Roosevelt's first one hundred days, when the new president sent proposals to Congress to be passed, quickly.

Instead, Baucus's staff sent their white paper to the Obama transition team as a courtesy, and incorporated minimal suggestions. It wasn't that the two camps differed; by now most Democrats in Congress and on the presidential campaign trail had settled on the same core ideas, modeled after Romneycare. It was just that the lead came from a different end of Pennsylvania Avenue. Baucus, after all, had decided when he had rehired Fowler in early 2008 to push for reform, no matter which party won the White House.

The white paper—drafted by a team of seven, headed by Fowler—covered the healthcare landscape on ninety-eight small-print, heavily footnoted pages. It began with the overview that had stunned Fowler as a sophomore in college: "The U.S. is the only developed country that does not guarantee health coverage for all of its citizens."

LOTS OF DETAILS, BUT DOZENS OF BILLION-DOLLAR QUESTIONS

Baucus had wanted to draft actual legislation. Fowler convinced him not to. Proposing legislation would make for too specific a target because the Congressional Budget Office—the nonpartisan agency that

projects the costs of any proposed legislation, a process called scoring—
would have to score it. That would invite attacks about provisions that
might or might not make it into a bill to be negotiated with Republicans and with the House of Representatives and the White House.

Baucus agreed. Besides, he wasn't fully wedded to everything in
the plan; he just wanted to keep things moving. So he went with
Fowler's white paper approach.

However, Baucus was sure of one thing. He wanted to present a
moderate plan from the start—a plan that could attract bipartisan support and send a signal to more liberal Democrats that this time a law
was going to be drafted that could actually survive the gauntlet to
come of lobbyists and conservative opposition. That meant he was
going to stake out one clear position from the outset: This law would
not provide for the government-run, single-payer insurance system
that the more liberal members of his party argued was the only solution to spreading coverage while cutting costs.

Baucus came down squarely on the Romneycare model of reforming rather than scrapping the current system by using the three-legged
stool: no more exclusions for preexisting conditions; a mandate that
everyone have insurance, which they could buy on a "national health
insurance exchange" if they could not get insurance at work; and subsidies for what his white paper said were the "90 percent of uninsured
individuals" who could not afford to buy policies. Those below the
poverty line would go into an expanded Medicaid program; everyone
else would get subsidies to buy on the exchange. In addition, all non-
small businesses had to offer insurance to their workers or pay a penalty.

Those were the basics, which might have been enough for the campaign stump or for senators presiding over hearings. But actual healthcare reform—especially the type that was proposed to be jerry-rigged
onto a patchwork of thousands of pages of existing laws and regulations and dozens of different funding and delivery systems—was all
about the details. And those details would now be picked through by
armies of lobbyists representing not just the usual-suspect heavy hit-
ters, such as the drug or insurance companies, but special interests
from every imaginable corner of medicine—from urologists to leuke-

mia victims to private equity firms that had invested in ambulance services.

Fowler and her team had spent multiple all-nighters teasing out those details.

The section about universal free access to preventive care said that everyone, even the uninsured, would be given a "RightChoices card" to get a menu of preventive services to be defined by an "Independent Health Coverage Council." That sounded like the independent board Fed chairman Bernanke, as well as Baucus and Grassley, the Iowa Republican, had warmed to during Baucus's summit.

The same Independent Health Coverage Council, whose members would be appointed by the president and confirmed by the Senate, would define "coverage" and "affordable" for a provision requiring employers to offer workers affordable coverage. It would also define "adequate" for the section requiring insurance companies on the exchange to sell only "adequate" coverage.

Money would be saved by the funding of "Comparative Effectiveness Research," that would advise Medicare (and private insurers) about what the most cost-effective drugs, devices, and treatments were.

An initiative that Grassley had pressed Baucus to include was also something Zeke Emanuel was obsessed with: doctors' conflicts of interest in accepting consulting and speaking fees or lavish trips and other perks from drug companies or device makers whose products they prescribed. The Finance Committee had heard testimony that these companies now had some kind of financial relationship—from providing free samples to paying consulting fees—with 94 percent of all practicing physicians, and that drug companies spent $7 billion a year on visits to physicians by salesmen, who provided the doctors with $18 billion worth of free samples. There would now have to be full disclosure of those relationships, and it would be available on a national database.

In perhaps Baucus's furthest lean to the left, his "Call to Action" proposed that anyone from the age of fifty-five to sixty-four be able immediately to buy into Medicare instead of paying far higher private insurance premiums, though this option would be available only during a transition period in the year or two before his insurance exchange kicked in.

BUT THESE AND HUNDREDS of other details weren't really details at all in the larger scheme of things. They were placeholders for the fights to come. In Washington, legislation about something this broad—Baucus was proposing, after all, the equivalent of reforming the entire economy of France—requires hundreds if not thousands of pages, not ninety-eight.

For example, the section on the mandate said that it would be enforced "possibly through the U.S. tax system." How would that work? And, if as in Massachusetts, where the state tax system had imposed a tax penalty on people who did not get insurance, how much would that penalty be?

"One option" for financing start-up costs for the health insurance exchange was "a small assessment on [insurance] premiums," the white paper noted. How small? On all premiums for all health insurance, or just on the policies sold on the exchange?

"The ability of insurance companies to [charge] on the basis of age would also be limited," the Baucus paper said. How limited? How much less could an insurer charge a twenty-four-year-old compared to a sixty-four-year-old? The insurance industry and their lobbyists would certainly be homing in on that detail.

Comparative effectiveness research sounded great. But who would appoint the researchers? Who would control what they studied? And what would it take for their research to see the light of day, much less be used by Medicare or private insurers to restrict use of a drug or device based on these experts' determinations of cost-effectiveness? Experimental drugs that these experts might consider worthless or long shots not worth paying for were coveted by people suffering from different diseases.

Victims of serious illness, be it cataracts or lymphoma, now had their own highly effective lobbying organizations, typically supported by the drug companies whose products treated those ailments. Would they tolerate letting bureaucrats tell patients what treatments they could get? How would Billy Tauzin—the head of the drug industry lobby who said he was saved by a miracle drug—react to this?

Baucus, perhaps channeling Gruber's warning about "going over the edge," tiptoed around these questions in his "Call to Action."

Similarly, the paper's litany of how Americans overpay for MRIs, CT scans, drugs, and administrative costs compared to other countries was instructive. Yet there was nothing specific about what Baucus wanted to do about it.

The paper envisioned authorizing Medicare to try experiments in which hospitals and doctors saved money by providing "bundles" of services. They would be held accountable for, and paid based on, whether the patient got well rather than how many treatments he had. How would that work? Would the doctors and hospitals get to keep some of the savings for themselves? What if the patient's doctor or hospital didn't want to participate? Hadn't this been tried in the 1990s with little success?

The "Call to Action" promised that there would be premium subsidies to make insurance affordable for all. But what did "affordable" mean? How high would a family's income have to go before it didn't qualify? Would income levels account for regional wage and cost of living differences, so that a family earning $100,000 a year in Manhattan could get a subsidy while a family with the same income in Baucus's Montana wouldn't?

States would be given grants to experiment with tort reform pilot projects that might cut the practice of defensive medicine, such as overtesting and overtreating, thought to be the result of doctors and hospitals fearing malpractice suits. How much would be spent on this? What kinds of projects? The trial lawyers and their beneficiaries in the Democratic Party would be all over that one.

On the next-to-last page there was an attempt to finesse an issue that was a political hand grenade: After declaring that John McCain's approach of eliminating the tax exclusion for employer-based health insurance premiums "goes too far because it would cause widespread disruption," Baucus declared that "more targeted reforms of the exclusion might make the incentive more equitable." He suggested that this could be done by capping the benefit to be excluded from taxes based on the value of the benefit, or on a person's income. In other words, lavish plans that provided complete coverage but little contribution from the worker might be taxed—or people with high incomes might be taxed—for the value of the insurance. But who would be taxed and how much?

In fact, Baucus and his team had wanted to go further. They had hoped that by eliminating much of the tax break by taxing people making more than $100,000 a year for the insurance benefit, they could get back some $300 billion over ten years. It was the largest component of their back-of-the-envelope strategy for financing all of their plan's expanded coverage and other reforms.

But when the Baucus people touched base with the president-elect's gathering transition staff immediately after the election and showed them a draft of the "Call to Action," the Obama people asked Fowler to scale back this provision and make it vague. Obama had promised that there would be no new taxes for the middle class. Taxes on health insurance benefits of those with incomes of more than $100,000 would violate that promise. Thus, the major revenue source for financing reform became another detail to be worked out later.

Baucus's "Call to Action" might not have presented a fully baked plan for the Congressional Budget Office to score for the costs of all this expanded coverage, and for the programs envisioned to promote wellness and preventive care. And it might have been more a handwringing exercise than a battle plan when it came to dealing with how much more the country was paying, compared to other countries, for worse health-care results. Nonetheless, it was a huge red flag waved in front of a thousand bulls. It presented so many lightly penciled-in details and was full of so many i's to be dotted and t's to be crossed—each potentially affecting billions of dollars and millions of patients—that, recalled a Baucus staffer who helped Fowler write the draft, "We quickly became everybody's favorite date. Every lobbyist in town wanted to see us."

KENNEDY'S LOWER-KEY PUSH

Ted Kennedy's HELP Committee was in touch with Fowler's group through the 2008 summer and fall. However, they had stuck to their own, lower-key effort to prepare their senators to mark up a bill. Beginning in October, the staffers, all Democrats, began convening meetings of representatives of doctors, hospital executives, insurers, drug companies, and large employers, as well as reform advocates and academics.

According to an account in a book written by senior Kennedy staffer John McDonough about these congressional deliberations,[4] the group quickly discarded both a radical single-payer approach that eliminated employer-paid insurance and a piecemeal approach that would expand coverage incrementally to various groups (such as more children) and enact limited insurance market reforms. Instead, they, too, focused on the Romneycare approach—broad reform but within the borders of the current system. That, of course, had also been the Clinton, Edwards, and (except for the full mandate) Obama framework, and it was where both the Baucus white paper and the Obama transition team had landed.

The HELP group also acknowledged in their internal discussions— more than Baucus's "Call to Action" did and more than the Obama economic team was willing to—what the Romneycare chief had told Baucus's summer summit: This approach was about going for broad coverage immediately and putting cost control aside for another day.

By November 19, 2008, Baucus had organized a meeting with the ailing Kennedy and four other senators, two Democrats and two Republicans. They included Grassley, the senior Republican on Baucus's committee, and Chris Dodd, the Connecticut Democrat and close Kennedy friend whom Kennedy has asked to fill in for him as his illness increasingly forced him to the sidelines. The meeting, which was in Kennedy's memento-festooned Capitol hideaway just off the Senate chamber, was friendly enough. The senators agreed to expand the group to eleven and instructed their staffs to prepare a summary of their areas of agreement and disagreement.

But one issue loomed that might spoil the good cheer: Kennedy had insisted that the Democrats hold open the possibility of trying to pass healthcare reform in the guise of legislation related mainly to

4. *Inside National Health Reform,* published by University of California Press in 2011.

taxes and finance. That kind of bill enabled a Senate process called budget reconciliation. Under Senate rules, budget reconciliation bills required only 51 votes, not the 60 needed to override a filibuster. The November 2008 elections had just boosted the Senate Democratic vote tally to 58 (including the independent Bernie Sanders of Vermont). Still, 58 was not 60, and two Senate Democrats, Kennedy and Robert Byrd, were now so ill they soon might not be able to get to the floor for a vote. Reconciliation was not an ideal way around a Republican roadblock because much of the envisioned healthcare reforms might not pass the financial issues—only smell test. But Kennedy and other Democrats considered it an important card to hold.

The following week, a meeting of all eleven senators and their staffs broke up over the reconciliation issue. They agreed to try again in January. However, with the need for an economic package to get through Congress becoming more urgent every day, no one now thought healthcare was going to happen in the first months of the new administration. Ted Kennedy was especially frustrated. He wasn't sure how much time he had.

CHAPTER 7

PUNTING TO CAPITOL HILL

January–March 2009

AN OFFICIAL OF THE TEN-DAY-OLD OBAMA ADMINISTRATION TOLD the press it was "a stupid mistake" but that it would not derail Tom Daschle's nomination to be secretary of health and human services. That was the cabinet post he was about to assume, in addition to a role as the White House czar in charge of healthcare reform.

Daschle had not reported as income on his tax returns the use of a car and driver that had been provided to him over a three-year span after he had left the Senate as part of his job as an adviser to a private equity fund. It was supposedly worth $182,000. As a result, he owed $100,000 in back taxes, which he immediately paid once the Senate committee staffers vetting his finances in preparation for a sure-thing Senate confirmation vote brought it to his attention.

However, with incoming Treasury secretary Timothy Geithner having already suffered the disclosure of his own embarrassing $34,000 back taxes problem, Daschle's "stupid mistake" became a big mistake.

Five days later, on February 4, 2009, Daschle withdrew from consideration for both posts. The man who might have been able to finesse the differences in the White House between the healthcare reform team and the economic team, who might have strengthened the White House's hand on Capitol Hill, and who might have been able to manage the HHS bureaucracy if a law was passed and had to be implemented, was now off the stage.

Rahm Emanuel saw the sudden talent and leadership gap as one more reason to question whether the new president ought to push ahead so soon with an ambitious reform plan, especially because with every passing day the challenge of getting an economic stimulus bill passed seemed to mount. But Obama insisted on moving ahead. "I am going to do this," he promised Orszag. He instructed his chief of staff to find a new White House healthcare reform leader, and to begin a search for a new HHS secretary. He also made sure that more than $600 billion in expenditures for creating universal healthcare was put in a budget message he would send to Congress at the end of the month. The money was a placeholder; no specifics had been worked out for how it would be spent or how it would be paid for.

On March 2, 2009, Obama announced that Kathleen Sebelius, the second-term governor of Kansas, would be Daschle's replacement at HHS.

The daughter of a former governor of Ohio, Sebelius was a seasoned politician and former state insurance commissioner, which gave her some healthcare policy experience. She was regarded as an effective governor, and, in fact, had been on the short list of possible Obama picks for vice president in 2008.

A governor's executive experience is usually valuable in Washington cabinet jobs. But Sebelius had nothing like Daschle's experience in Washington and with the HHS bureaucracy. More important, she would never have Daschle's clout in the White House. Unlike Daschle, the former Senate majority leader, she had no significant relationship with Obama and was not simultaneously going to be a senior White House adviser with easy access to him. Daschle would have been the one person responsible for conceiving, passing, and implementing a healthcare reform law. Without him, there would be no one in charge.

Also in February, Rahm Emanuel found the other half of Daschle's replacement. Nancy-Ann DeParle would be counselor to the president and director of the White House Office of Health Reform. DeParle, who was fifty-two at the time of her appointment, had run the agency that oversaw Medicare and Medicaid in the Clinton administration, after which she had joined a private equity firm specializing in health industry investment.

A Rhodes scholar and graduate of Harvard Law School whose mother died of lung cancer when she was a teenager, DeParle grew up in Tennessee. Following a few years of practicing law there, she entered government service in her early thirties as the commissioner of the Tennessee Department of Health and Human Services. DeParle knew Rahm Emanuel and Lambrew from her Clinton administration days.

Friends regarded DeParle as a seasoned manager and savvy infighter when she had to be, and she certainly had the right résumé. But she, too, was no match for Daschle. Yet Obama took an almost instant liking to her, as did Valerie Jarrett. Zeke Emanuel would soon tell a friend that he thought the president was "mesmerized by her; maybe it's that they both lost parents early on, or something."

While Rahm Emanuel worked at replacing Daschle, the economics staff plugged away at staying involved in the healthcare debate, though they feared that with Daschle gone almost all of the initiative had been ceded to the Senate. They worried, presciently, that they would be reduced to playing at best an editing role in Congress's writing of sweeping healthcare reform.

Eight days before the inauguration, Zeke Emanuel and Bob Kocher, the former McKinsey partner working for Larry Summers, had sent Lambrew a spreadsheet of possible provisions the administration could ask for in a reform bill that would start to bend the inexorably rising curve of healthcare costs. "Bending the cost curve" had become a mantra for reformers such as Orszag, Summers, Zeke Emanuel, and Kocher.

Kocher and Zeke Emanuel had been working on the spreadsheet since December. Their projected savings totaled more than $300 billion over ten years, to be gained by reforms ranging from requiring doctors to use electronic medical records, to cutting Medicare payments for oxygen and wheelchairs, to penalizing hospitals that had high rates of patients who were discharged and then readmitted within thirty days.

They got no reply from Lambrew.

However, the economic team hedged their bets on their continuing relevance by injecting one of those ideas into the $800 billion economic stimulus package being put together for more immediate action: Nearly $20 billion was allocated to provide incentives to doctors and hospitals that invested in scaling up to "meaningful use" of electronic records.

The other way Kocher, Zeke Emanuel, and their colleagues made themselves useful was by sharing much of their thinking about cost cuts with the Baucus and Kennedy staffs.

PEP RALLY IN THE EAST ROOM

On March 5, 2009, a few days before DeParle was officially to start work, about 150 legislators, union leaders, patients' advocates, corporate CEOs, representatives of small business, doctors, healthcare industry executives, and seven people whom a White House press release called "Everyday Americans" were invited for an all-day meeting on healthcare reform.

Obama began the day by declaring to the group assembled in the East Room of the White House, "We have tried and fallen short, stalled time and again by failures of will, or Washington politics, or industry lobbying. . . . I know people are afraid we'll draw the same old lines in the sand, give in to the same entrenched interests, and arrive back at the same stalemate we've been stuck in for decades. But I am here today," Obama insisted, "because I believe that this time is different. This time, the call for reform is coming from the bottom up, from all across the spectrum—from doctors, nurses and patients; unions and businesses; hospitals, health care providers and community groups."

With that send-off, each attendee was assigned a room in the White House or the Executive Office Building, where breakout sessions were to be moderated by White House staffers to address two questions: "What are the best ideas for getting all Americans covered?" and "What are the best ideas for bringing down costs?" Tellingly, there were two moderators for each session: typically, one from the economic staff and one from the domestic policy staff.

Lambrew, White House Domestic Policy Council chief Melody Barnes, and the White House congressional liaison staff had carefully chosen and invited potentially cooperative Republican legislators to be paired in the rooms with legislator friends from the other side of the aisle. They also stocked the room with a balanced group of industry and union leaders. Junior White House aides took notes to catalog the ideas discussed.

At four o'clock, everyone gathered back in the East Room, where the president was to conduct what the White House called "A Town Hall" meeting. First, Obama introduced a surprise guest: the ailing Senator Ted Kennedy.

Kennedy had missed all of the earlier sessions that day, and his presence for the wrap-up in the East Room had been uncertain until the last minute. Looking gaunt and walking unsteadily with a cane, he smiled broadly as he entered the room. The crowd, which included Republican minority leader Mitch McConnell, Republican senators Chuck Grassley of Iowa and Orrin Hatch of Utah, and a mix of Republican House members, gave Kennedy an ovation.

"It is thrilling to see you here, Teddy," Obama began, before thanking him, Baucus, and Grassley for "the extraordinary work" they had been doing. "My understanding is that we have had an extraordinarily productive set of sessions," the president continued.

Not really. Of the thirty-six people I later asked about the meeting, including some members of the president's own staff, none could remember hearing any new ideas. Instead, they all agreed on the goals of expanding coverage and cutting costs. They praised apple-pie initiatives such as electronic medical records and more funding for wellness and prevention, and otherwise espoused positions that could have been predicted based on their politics or the interests they represented. Billy Tauzin, representing the pharmaceutical lobby, talked about the need to make sure nothing was done to dampen the profits necessary to encourage his employers to spend on the research and development of trailblazing new drugs.

The Republicans worried about deficits and the government interfering in the industry. The Democrats urged universal coverage as the top priority.

One group, whose moderators were Valerie Jarrett and Zeke Emanuel, barely got beyond opening statements because Emanuel so dominated the conversation, one participant told me.

Yet the sessions were friendly if inconclusive. As with Baucus's summit—though that was far more substantive—there seemed to be a general feeling among participants in the various breakout meetings that they could agree to disagree today and somehow work out their differences down the road.

Even Chip Kahn was in an agreeable mood. Kahn, who now ran a hospital industry lobbying group, had created the insurance lobby's "Harry and Louise" advertising campaign that had torpedoed Hillary-care in the early 1990s. According to a White House summary of the breakout session that Kahn joined, he had declared to those in his group "that times are different and 'it's time for action.'"

"It was all friendly," PhRMA's Tauzin told me. "Nothing new, but it did have the feel of a pep rally, especially when Teddy appeared."

The only point of sharp disagreement in the sessions was over what reformers called the "public option." During the Democratic primary, the leading candidates, including Obama, had tempered their calls for subsidies to be provided to people to buy private insurance with proposals that the government would also set up a nonprofit insurer that would compete alongside the private companies.

It was the candidates' fallback from the Medicare-for-all, single-payer alternative pushed unsuccessfully by Democrats from the Truman era through the 1980s and insisted on by the liberal Democrat Dennis Kucinich in the 2007 Las Vegas forum. The government wouldn't take over everyone's healthcare but would instead provide, as a consumer "option," a government-run insurance plan that consumers could choose instead of private insurance.

The details of this alternative varied, depending on who was proposing it. In some versions, the public option's nonprofit insurer would by law pay the same low prices Medicare pays to doctors and hospitals—which would effectively eliminate private insurance companies because they pay so much more than Medicare pays and, therefore, would have to charge much higher premiums than the public insurance company. In other versions, the government nonprofit insurer wouldn't have any pricing advantage at all over the other insurers, which many thought made the idea pointless.

Obama had never been specific on the campaign trail about which version he favored, although, like the other leading Democratic primary candidates, he had said, generally, that he favored including some kind of public option. But the insurance companies, hospitals, doctors, drugmakers, and every other industry sector opposed even the seemingly weaker version, as did Republicans and other free market supporters. For them, the idea of a government insurer competing, with or without a pricing advantage at the start, with the private sector and doing whatever it could to drive down prices was a nonstarter.

Baucus agreed. His white paper had no public option. However, other Democrats, particularly liberals in the House led by California congressman Henry Waxman, were staunch proponents, as were many Democratic senators, including some on Kennedy's HELP Committee. To them, the public option—even, somehow, the mild version—was a path toward getting rid of private insurance and moving to a single-payer system.

When the public option came up in the East Room, Obama waffled. He called on Grassley to offer some comments about the day's events, and the Iowa Republican began by stressing that "Max Baucus and I have a pretty good record of working out bipartisan things— I think [there have been] only two bills in eight years that haven't been bipartisan. . . . And we expect to work on this in the committee in June." However, Grassley continued, "The only thing that I would throw out for your consideration—and please don't respond to this now, because I'm asking you just to think about it—there's a lot of us that feel that the public [option] . . . is an unfair competitor and that . . . we have to keep what we have now strong, and make it stronger."

"I'm not going to respond definitively," Obama answered, whereupon he deftly summarized both sides of the argument and his eagerness to navigate between them:

> The thinking on the public option has been that it gives consumers more choices, and it helps . . . keep the private sector

honest, because there's some competition out there. That's been the thinking.

I recognize, though, the fear that if a public option is run through Washington, and there are incentives to try to tamp down costs . . . that private insurance plans might end up feeling overwhelmed. So I recognize that there's that concern. I think it's a serious one and a real one. And we'll make sure that it gets addressed, partly because I assume it will be very hard to come out of committee unless we're thinking about it a little bit. And so we want to make sure that that's something that we pay attention to.

More generally, Obama was careful to stress that for him health-care reform was about costs as much as it was about extending coverage—that he was firmly in both the policy camp personified by Lambrew and the economics camp led by Orszag and Larry Summers. He noted that when his staff selects ten sample letters for him to read out of the forty thousand he gets every day, "out of the ten, at least three every single day relate to somebody who's having a healthcare crisis."

Therefore, the president added, "There is a moral component to this that we can't leave behind. Having said that," he continued, "if we don't address costs, we will not get this done. If people think we're simply gonna take everyone who's not insured and load them up into a system . . . the federal government will be bankrupt. State governments will be bankrupt. I'm talking to you liberal bleeding hearts out there," he added. "Don't think that we can solve this problem without tackling costs. And that may make some in the progressive community uncomfortable but it's gotta be dealt with."

Of course, to many of those progressives, the best way to tackle both costs and coverage was the single-payer Medicare-for-all system that everyone else acknowledged was a pipe dream politically—which Grassley had just confirmed by objecting to the far milder public option alternative.

Otherwise, the president stressed his open-mindedness. "During the campaign," he said, "I put forward a plan for health care reform. I thought it was an excellent plan, but I don't presume that it was a perfect plan or that it was the best possible plan. . . . If there is a way of getting this done . . . entirely through the market, I'd be happy to do it that way. If there was a way of doing it that involved more government regulation and involvement, I'm happy to do it that way, as well."

To some in the East Room, Obama's flexibility was disappointing. He was saying he would follow, not lead. He and his staff—both the Lambrew faction and the economics group—seemed to have their act together only in so far as they wanted to fulfill the president's mandate that healthcare remain a priority. They had not decided on any specifics of their own.

"Remember, this was a few weeks after the inauguration," recalled one industry representative. "Obama was still walking on water. He could do no wrong. But he has no plan for what he calls a national crisis? I was shocked. Can you imagine Lyndon Johnson not having a ten-point plan and telling the group in front of all those TV cameras, 'Here's my plan'? Who would have opposed him? Instead he farms this out to the Senate and House, just the way he farmed out the stimulus to Nancy Pelosi so she could turn it into a Christmas tree for the Democrats on the Hill."

The Obama administration and its supporters saw it differently.

Phil Schiliro, Obama's newly appointed head of congressional relations, was a longtime senior congressional staff person and a veteran of getting difficult bills through Congress. To him, a piece of legislation had to pass through a filter that represented all the different opponents who could derail it.

The problem, as Schiliro saw it, was that in 2009 the House and Senate had different filters. The House had a strong Democratic majority that would demand a more liberal bill than the Senate. So if the president had tried to send up a bill meant to please both, each side would have blocked it with its own filter. The only practical path was to let the two branches pass their own bills and negotiate the differences.

And then there was recent history. White House chief of staff Rahm Emanuel and other alumni of the Clinton White House remembered the disaster that had ensued when they presented a fully baked plan to Congress, albeit a monstrously complicated one, eighteen months after Bill Clinton took office.

Others believed that the vacuum created by Daschle's sudden exit dictated this course. Besides, with all of the work Baucus and Kennedy and their staffs had done, the Senate had already stolen the show and seemed to be making great progress. Baucus and Kennedy had sent Obama a letter the day after Daschle dropped out, urging him to continue to make healthcare reform a priority. But they weren't waiting.

And then there was the math. With only fifty-eight Democratic votes in the Senate (counting the independent Sanders of Vermont), Republicans such as Grassley would have to sign on to get reform past a filibuster. An Obama-branded bill seemed unlikely to get over that hurdle. There was nothing in the Constitution about a filibuster and the need for sixty Senate votes to pass legislation. Yet by 2009 that hurdle was accepted as a given.

Ted Kennedy agreed with Max Baucus not only that compromise was required, but that the real action was going to have to come from the Senate, not the White House. In fact, they had made a date to meet at Kennedy's Georgetown home the day after the East Room gathering to pin down what they thought was possible and to reaffirm that this time their two committees were not going to let turf fights derail things.

Fowler and Baucus would arrive the next day for a lunch with Kennedy, his wife, Vicki, and David Bowen, Kennedy's top health adviser. It lasted more than two hours, and included a tour of the house and a full display of the ailing Kennedy's charm. Kennedy seemed to want to make sure that Baucus understood he was handing the torch to him.

"A SEAT AT THE TABLE"

The first nonlegislator Obama called on at his East Room town hall was a surprised Karen Ignagni, who, Obama happily noted, "represents America's Health Insurance Plans."

The insurers' lead lobbyist thanked Obama and pledged her support: "We understand we have to earn a seat at the table," Ignagni said, channeling her and Tauzin's determination not to be on the menu. "You have our commitment to play, to contribute, and to help pass health care reform this year."

"Karen, that's good news," Obama said. The crowd applauded.

The only semi-sour note was sounded by Mitch McConnell, the Republican Senate minority leader. When Obama called on him, McConnell politely urged the president to shift his priorities to worrying about the deficit and entitlement spending, including not only Medicare and Medicaid but also Social Security.

Obama dispatched the Republican leader with a promise to work with him on the problem, then pivoted to call on Henry Waxman, the liberal congressman from California.

OBAMACARE ON THE REPUBLICANS' DINNER MENU

Obama had made only two brief mentions of healthcare in his inaugural address seven weeks before. As with his speech on Election Night, this was not surprising given the economic crisis and the historic ascension of the nation's first African American to the presidency.

However, healthcare had been high on the agenda at a dinner held the night of the inaugural in a private room at Washington's Caucus Room restaurant. And the discussion wasn't nearly as polite as McConnell would be in the East Room seven weeks later.

Frank Luntz—the pollster who had helped then–House Speaker hopeful Newt Gingrich fashion the "Contract with America" platform to oppose President Bill Clinton—convened the dinner for leading Republicans. Ten from the House and ten from the Senate attended, along with about a dozen Republican strategists and lobbyists.

"The goal was to talk about what we could do about Obama, and healthcare was probably number one on the list," Luntz told me. "We knew we couldn't stop some kind of [economic] stimulus, but this we thought we could block—and we had to block it because it threatened to become another massive government takeover and entitlement. . . .

Newt insisted," Luntz added, referring to Gingrich, who also attended, "that this would ruin the country and in the short term ruin our party by giving something so big away to so many people."

This was a discussion among pols, not policy wonks. According to Luntz, only Gingrich touched on the substance of the kind of reform Obama had talked about during the campaign, and he did so only in general terms: Obama wanted to set up a whole new entitlement system to give everyone health insurance.

The politics, recalled Luntz, were "pretty clear." It was about both stopping anything the new president championed and also stopping another big-government program. No one mentioned that Obama was talking about a healthcare plan like the one Romney, and Nixon before him, had espoused.

Among the members of the House who dined with Luntz and Gingrich while the bands played on at the inaugural balls were then–minority leader Eric Cantor and then–budget committee chair Paul Ryan. On the Senate side Mitch McConnell was not there, but several of his top deputies were, including Tennessee's Bob Corker and John Kyl of Arizona, who as minority whip ranked just below McConnell.

To Luntz, the bipartisan approach to healthcare being entertained by some Republicans was just talk—a show destined to have a short run before it got the hook. "We knew some guys like Grassley were talking about working with the Dems," recalled Luntz. "The sense was that we'd let them play along but then come up with the arguments and polling that would get them to drop out."

BY THE TIME OBAMA convened his March 5, 2009, pep rally in the East Room, another, broader political wave was forming that would propel the opposition that Luntz and his dinner companions hoped to build. On February 19, Rick Santelli, a CNBC correspondent in Chicago, had let loose with an on-air rant about government bailouts that, he argued, would again promote the risky behavior that had caused the economic crisis. Santelli had concluded by suggesting that people in Chicago should stage their own "tea party" to protest the government's heavy hand.

Most political observers would later consider this the beginning of the Tea Party movement, the loosely organized assortment of grassroots groups of mostly conservative people that staged rallies across the country beginning in the spring of 2009 to protest all varieties of government interference and Washington crony capitalism.

By the summer of 2009, Washington's idea of healthcare reform would become the Tea Party's prime target. For as Santelli screamed into his microphone, a group of capital insiders representing multiple factions of America's biggest industry—healthcare—was negotiating exactly the kinds of secret deals that would have made Santelli scream louder had he known about them.

CHAPTER 8

DEAL TIME

FOR THE SENATE FINANCE COMMITTEE, THERE WAS A SILVER LINING in the collapse of Lehman Brothers that had accelerated the financial meltdown: Antonios "Tony" Clapsis, a bearded, wiry twenty-eight-year-old who loved crunching numbers.

When Lehman collapsed in September 2008, Clapsis had been working at the investment bank for about six years as a stock analyst concentrating on the healthcare industry. He managed to hang on for about six months, working for Barclays Bank, which had taken over many of Lehman's businesses. By March 2009, though, he had been let go with a generous severance package.

Clapsis's work for Lehman and Barclays involved what was called macroanalysis. His job was to keep track of policy changes emanating from Washington and predict how prospective legislative or regulatory changes might affect the earnings per share of various healthcare stocks, which, in turn, could be used to project the stocks' future prices. For example, how much might a new regulation governing how hospitals were to be paid by Medicare for kidney dialysis affect the stock price of one of the dialysis equipment makers?

To do that, he had struck up friendships with members of the Finance Committee staff, including Liz Fowler. Clapsis, who had worked in the Massachusetts state senate while attending Boston University, had not lost his interest in government. With his severance from Barclays, he figured he had enough money to take a public service job for a while.

In March, Fowler offered him an intriguing one. He would be the Finance Committee's best weapon in negotiating with the healthcare industry for givebacks in return for a healthcare reform law that would create millions of new customers for them—because he would be able to throw their own numbers back at them.

In the aftermath of Baucus's "Call to Action" white paper and even more so when it became clear that the White House was standing aside while Baucus (with Kennedy's committee working in parallel) plowed ahead, the Finance Committee staff had, indeed, become "everyone's favorite date." The most important suitors were the lobbyists from the key industry sectors who, as Tauzin had put it, wanted to sit at the table rather than be on the menu.

They each came offering deals—changes they would agree to that would help finance reform or otherwise further the goal of getting a reform bill passed. It was implicit, and it would gradually become explicit, that what they wanted in return was to avoid more radical reforms that would attack their bottom lines.

Clapsis became the black box that gave Baucus, Fowler, and the Finance Committee staff the information they needed in order to know how much to ask for—because in his prior life he had tracked how much expanding healthcare coverage was going to benefit each sector of the industry.

Getting the funds this way from the industry, rather than from a broader based tax, had become a priority for Baucus. Republican senator Olympia Snowe of Maine was insisting that she would support reform only if it were paid for without any such broader tax measures. Baucus was counting on Snowe, along with Grassley, as the two Republicans most likely to stick with him and give the bill bipartisan support.

Combining his own research with reports from stock analysts all over Wall Street that estimated how much of a boost Baucus's Romneycare-like plan to create so many new customers would give to each industry sector, Clapsis armed Fowler and the rest of the Baucus team with real numbers.

First to the table, beginning in early March, were the pharmaceutical companies, represented by several of Tauzin's deputies from PhRMA. These were preliminary talks; Tauzin and his board full of CEOs would come in later when a deal got close.

Clapsis had found analysts' reports estimating that universal coverage would bring the drugmakers more than $200 billion over the first ten years. The Baucus staff asked for $130 billion back, in the form of reductions in drug prices paid through certain parts of the Medicare and Medicaid programs, as well as a new tax on drug company revenues. In return, Baucus might be willing to forgo other reforms that would cut more deeply into their bottom lines.

One potentially devastating cut involved a reform long proposed by Democrats and resisted by Republicans that would allow Medicare to negotiate the prices it paid for prescription drugs. In what had become an enduring monument to the lobbying power of the drug companies, in 2003 Congress had prohibited Medicare, the world's largest drug buyer, from negotiating prices the way insurance companies were allowed to. Instead the government had to pay 106 percent of what the drugmakers reported to them was their "average wholesale price," a straitjacket that cost taxpayers $40 billion a year. PhRMA's highest priority, according to Tauzin, was preserving that law, even if it meant giving back some money to the federal government through discounts related to other Medicare and Medicaid payments.

A second potential killer was the perennially proposed, and perennially blocked, legislation that would allow consumers to buy drugs from Canada. Because Canada, like all other developed countries, enforced price controls on drugs, this could result in Americans buying the drugmakers' high-margin products at 30 to 50 percent off current prices.

Still another point of attack that worried the PhRMA people was the comparative effectiveness research Baucus had mentioned in his white paper. In their view, if comparative effectiveness was pushed too far, it could ruin sales of some of their most profitable products because some "expert" might decree they were not worth the price.

With all of those potential threats looming, the Finance Committee negotiators thought that it seemed reasonable that the industry give back $130 billion in return for avoiding those more radical reforms and for getting $200 billion in new revenue from all the new business generated by a law that would dramatically expand health insurance coverage.

Tauzin's people countered Clapsis's numbers by presenting an elaborate economic model of their own, prepared by their consultants. This analysis purported to demonstrate that expanding coverage would actually cost the industry money or be revenue neutral. Clapsis was amazed, even insulted, that such smart economists and their lobbyists had tried to sell him this stuff. He responded by pulling out his collection of analysts' reports that showed how reform would be a boon to the already-high-flying industry.

More than that, he referred to what CEOs had said in their conference calls with analysts, in which they tried to promote the value of their stocks: What they had seen and heard so far about the reform bills taking shape meant improved prospects for their bottom lines. Surely, their own CEOs must know what they are talking about, Clapsis argued. In fact, they would be violating securities laws if they were exaggerating these numbers in order to tout their stocks to the Wall Street analysts.

Clapsis, Fowler, and the others knew this was just PhRMA's opening volley. The drugmakers would come around because Clapsis's numbers were real, and because not making a deal would make them vulnerable on Medicare negotiation, importation, and a heavy-handed comparative effectiveness regime.

"Nothing concentrates the mind like a hanging," recalled one drug company executive involved in the negotiations. "A lot of what some of the Democrats were talking about was literally life threatening to us. So it made sense to deal with Max and his people."

By the second week in April, the Tauzin and Baucus staffs had reached a tentative deal. The drug industry would kick in givebacks worth $80 billion. The package included deeper discounts than those already provided for Medicaid's prescription drug coverage of the poor; a tax (which was called a fee) on all drug companies (to be calculated based on their respective market shares); and a subsidy for senior citizens when they reached the point (the "doughnut hole") where Medicare did not pay for their prescriptions.

A final element dealt with a complicated issue related to drugs called biosimilars, which are products derived from high-cost drugs known as biologics. Biologics are medicines created by living organisms, such as blood plasma, rather than by chemicals. The industry wanted their biologics to be protected from copying by biosimilars for twelve years—much the way patents protect drugmakers for a period of years from being copied with far less expensive generics. There was now no protection at all. However, because the legal issue was murky—it was possible copycats could be sued under existing patent law in some cases—even manufacturers of biosimilars had an interest in getting a law on the books, albeit with a far shorter time period for protection.

If you don't understand this description of the issue, understand this: Depending on whether you were liberal congressman Henry Waxman or PhRMA's Billy Tauzin, every year that biologics were protected involved billions in higher drug prices—or billions in the revenues necessary to finance the discovery of new miracle drugs.

Although most involved believed the biosimilars issue could be resolved, the deal on the $80 million in give-backs was not yet completely sealed. Tauzin and his board of drug company chief executives wanted to make sure the Obama White House was on board. In particular, they were worried about whether the president and Rahm Emanuel were committed to resisting opposition from the more liberal faction of the House, led by Waxman.

Waxman, a longtime industry nemesis, now chaired the House Energy and Commerce Committee, which shared jurisdiction over the bill. The drug lobbyists had been told by Baucus's people that Rahm Emanuel and Nancy-Ann DeParle, the new White House healthcare policy chief, had been kept up to speed and were supportive. But they wanted to be sure.

More generally, no one had seen a draft of an actual bill, because one did not exist.

Yet the deal seemed likely enough that on April 15, 2009, an unusual meeting took place in a conference room at the Democratic Senatorial Campaign Committee headquarters near the Capitol. Among those attending were the PhRMA lobbying team and representatives from some leading unions.

The meeting had been convened by Baucus chief of staff Jon Selib and White House deputy chief of staff Jim Messina. Messina had worked for Baucus and was now the president's chief political operative. (He would later manage the Obama 2012 reelection campaign.)

During their negotiations with the Baucus staff, the PhRMA people had talked vaguely about helping to get their $80 billion deal done by supporting a political action fund that would buy television ads supporting senators who favored reform and attacking those who didn't or were wavering. Messina and Selib, aided by political consultant Nicholas Baldick, were now calling in that promise. They outlined a plan for PhRMA to become the main financier of two political action committees that would buy those ads, but which, under the law, would not have to reveal their donors. The funds had the kind of innocuous-sounding names that Obama had made fun of on the campaign trail when attacking special interest money polluting politics: Health Economy Now and Americans for Stable Quality Care.

PhRMA ultimately contributed $70 million to the two funds, while the unions and other left-of-center groups chipped in relatively token amounts. The Service Employees International Union's Michelle Newar, who attended the April 15 meeting, explained the lopsided funding this way in an email to her colleagues, including SEIU boss Andy Stern: "They plan to hit up the 'bad guys' for most of the $. . . . They want us to put in just enough to be able to put our names on it—@ 100k."

"It seems like the right framework—a little from us and a lot from them," one of Newar's colleagues replied. "Okay with me," Stern chimed in.

Two weeks later, a solicitation letter went out to other groups seeking donations to buttress the cover story that the ads that would soon blanket the country supporting healthcare reform and pressuring senators who were on the fence were paid for by a broad-based collection of civic interests, not mostly by PhRMA.

Some of the PhRMA lobbyists, aware that they were the ad campaign's chief financiers, later groused in email exchanges that the political consulting company that Obama senior adviser David Axelrod had co-owned before taking his White House job was the firm placing the ads and getting the fees for doing so. When a Bloomberg reporter started calling around asking about the connection between the Axelrod firm and PhRMA, Bryant Hall, a top PhRMA lobbyist, emailed Nicholas Baldick, the political consultant managing the fund, that "this is a big problem." Baldick answered that he'd have a Health Economy Now press person talk to the reporter and deny any PhRMA connection.

"Yes, spin whatever," Hall replied.

Depending on one's view, this secret deal between Obama political operatives, PhRMA, staffers from the Senate Finance Committee who had just brokered a multibillion-dollar deal with PhRMA, major unions, and other liberal groups was proof that Washington was finally buckling down, coming together, and getting the peoples' business done; or it was Washington at its worst: liberal groups selling out to big business to accommodate all the groups' special interests.

Either way, with the secret meetings, cynical emails, and hidden contributions to political action funds, it was not the new way of doing business that Barack Obama had promised in his campaign. Then he had routinely vowed, as he put it during a town hall in Virginia, that in framing his healthcare reform bill, "We'll have the negotiations televised on C-SPAN, so that people can see who is making arguments on behalf of their constituents, and who are making arguments on behalf of the drug companies or the insurance companies."

Instead, he had given the Tea Party activists exhibit A in crony capitalism—if they ever found out about it.

THE NONPROFITS' PROFITS

The hospitals were next up at the Finance Committee negotiating table. More than 75 percent of America's 5,700 hospitals were officially nonprofit institutions. So, they have no shareholders and, therefore, no stock analysts following them and issuing reports that Tony

Clapsis could read. However, more than a thousand were run by for-profit companies, most of which had publicly held stocks that the analysts did follow. And Clapsis was attuned to one of the more surprising ironies of the American healthcare economy: The nonprofits—whether affiliated with universities, community charities, or spin-offs of religious organizations—typically had the same (or higher, when their tax-free status was accounted for) operating profit margins as the for-profits. So Clapsis could easily extrapolate information on the nonprofits from what the analysts said about how the for-profits would benefit from millions of newly insured customers, most of whom previously might not have come in for treatment or would be unable to pay their bills if they had.

The numbers were huge. Over the first ten years of universal coverage, Clapsis estimated that the hospitals would enjoy an extra $200 billion to $250 billion, maybe more.

When the lobbyists from the American Hospital Association began their meetings with the Baucus staff, Clapsis used not only these analysts' reports but also data from the AHA itself. In an effort to demonstrate its members' commitments to their communities, every year the hospital association publishes a "fact sheet" on uncompensated care. The association defines uncompensated care as the cost—not the chargemaster list prices, but the actual cost—of both the charity care that hospitals provided, as well as the cost of care given to patients who did not pay their bills.

The latest report, for 2008, had claimed $36 billion in uncompensated care. That represented only about 5 percent of all hospital revenue in 2008, but for Clapsis's purposes it was compelling. He pointed out that even ignoring healthcare cost inflation and projecting the same $36 billion over ten years would produce a total of $360 billion, most of which would seemingly now be paid by insurance. The hospital lobbyists countered that no reform plan was going to insure everyone and get rid of charity care or bad debt completely.

But the Baucus team had made their point. The hospitals were going to have to pay a big bill.

By April the two sides had settled on $155 billion in givebacks that would mostly take the form of reduced annual increases in Medicare payment rates to the hospitals, and penalties to be paid for bad, costly results, such as when Medicare patients were readmitted to a hospital within thirty days of having been discharged.

HOSPITALS, INC.

That same month, an aggressive suit filed in a western Pennsylvania federal court provided an unusually vivid picture, if Clapsis had needed one, of how nonprofit hospitals had become hard-charging big businesses.

On April 21, 2009, the West Penn Allegheny Health System, a group of hospitals in Pittsburgh, filed an antitrust complaint against the University of Pittsburgh Medical Center and Highmark, the region's dominant health insurer.

Known as UPMC, the University of Pittsburgh Medical Center had, by 2009, become a hospital industry phenomenon and—although officially a nonprofit, tax-exempt charity—the dominant business in western Pennsylvania.

UPMC was the state's largest employer. In fact, it had recently begun moving its managers and administrators into the top twenty-one floors (including a lavish penthouse suite of executive offices and conference rooms) of Pittsburgh's dominant downtown office tower. It was the skyscraper that had once been the headquarters of the company known since the Eisenhower era as the business face of Pittsburgh: U.S. Steel—the industrial giant founded by, among others, J. P. Morgan and Andrew Carnegie.

Following years of decline, U.S. Steel had been absorbed by an energy company. A much-slimmed-down version of its original self had then been spun off in 2002 and given back its old name. With most of its operations overseas, it now occupied only a few, lower, floors in its old tower. The big tenant was UPMC.

When the suit against UPMC was filed in April 2009, the hospital system was on its way to recording $7.1 billion in revenue for its current fiscal year—which at the time put it first among all U.S. hospitals in revenue—and more than $580 million in operating profit.[5] UPMC's chief executive officer Jeffrey Romoff was earning more than $4 million in salary and bonus. All of these numbers had been increasing rapidly year over year and would continue to do so.

By 2013, the Washington-based *National Journal* would discover the reality, and peril, of healthcare having replaced steel as Pittsburgh's dominant industry: "Unlike manufacturing, health care is generally not an export business," the Washington weekly observed. "Patient care is provided in the community and must be paid for with local resources. 'What you're doing is passing some money from one person to another,' said Martin Gaynor, a health economist at Carnegie Mellon. That imposes a wealth-based ceiling on every region's health sector."

CEO Romoff prided himself on being able to cope with that kind of challenge. Born in the Bronx, Romoff had worked for the hospital since 1973, when it was a small state-run psychiatric institution. A non-doctor, with a bachelor's degree from New York's City College and a master's in philosophy from Yale, Romoff had been given a job planning education programs because the hospital wanted to hire his wife, Vivien, who was the chief psychiatric nurse at Yale–New Haven Hospital.

Romoff soon began leading a charge to consolidate the psychiatric hospital with the university's other, larger, medical care facilities. Each step invariably ended up with Romoff's savvy, ambitious boss, who ran the psychiatric facility, in charge of what had been consolidated. Consolidations had then become outright mergers or purchases of other hospitals in the region—except for West Penn Allegheny, the hospital now suing UPMC.

Romoff, who became UPMC president in 1992 and CEO in 2006, liked to tell people that the secret to his and his hospital's success was

5. For the purpose of analyzing the financial performance of nonprofit hospitals, operating profit is defined as the excess of all revenue over all expenses, but with the accounting charge taken for depreciation (which is not a cash expense) added back. These numbers are derived from the hospital's report to the IRS covering the fiscal year beginning in July 2009.

that he always paid attention to "controlling as many variables and impediments as you can." The consolidations and acquisitions, he told me, "were just a step by step process of controlling the impediments"—which, the lawsuit now brought against him charged, meant eliminating competitors.

By the time Romoff was sued, UPMC controlled 55 percent of the market for hospital and outpatient clinical services in the region, with West Penn controlling 23 percent and losing market share rapidly.

However, the antitrust suit was not simply about UPMC's dominant share of hospital beds, doctors, and patients. It alleged an outright conspiracy between UPMC and the other defendant—Highmark, the insurance company—to control healthcare and healthcare prices in western Pennsylvania.

Operating under the Blue Cross Blue Shield banner, Highmark had an unheard of market share of the private health insurance sold in the region: between 60 and 80 percent depending on varying definitions.

It was how UPMC, as the provider of healthcare, and Highmark, as the insurer that paid for it, had teamed up that was at the core of the smaller West Penn Hospital's suit. Its complaint traced a fifteen-year history of UPMC and Highmark initially fighting with each other and then throwing in the towel and conspiring to create a two-pronged "super-monopoly."

First, UPMC had started its own health insurance company to compete with Highmark, because, as Romoff later explained to me, "We were worried about one insurance company being so dominant that they could squeeze what they paid us."

Then, Highmark had countered by providing hundreds of millions of dollars of financial support to allow the merger of a group of hospitals into what came to be called West Penn—the hospital system now suing UPMC and Highmark.

Still, the finances of the merged West Penn had continued a steep decline because of UPMC's growing dominance—and its increasingly aggressive hiring raids on the West Penn staff of doctors. (The complaint alleged that Romoff had repeatedly made statements that he

wanted to "destroy" West Penn and that he had used lavish bonus offers and inflated salaries to hire doctors away from his competitor that
UPMC did not need.)

With Highmark having been forced to offer cheaper insurance
packages to match competition from UPMC's insurance unit, and
UPMC tiring of the cost of competing with a Highmark-supported
West Penn, UPMC offered Highmark a truce in 1998.

However, Highmark turned it down, calling it, according to the
complaint, "an attempt to form a super-monopoly."

But in 2002, Highmark agreed to the deal. Under the agreement
UPMC scaled down its own insurance company to cover little more
than its own employees. Better yet, UPMC promised not to allow the
vast network of hospitals, outpatient clinics, and doctors' practices
that it now owned to be included in the network of any other insurance company. Only Highmark would be in the market selling insurance that provided access to UPMC. As a result, other big insurance
companies, such as Aetna and UnitedHealthcare, were unable to gain
a substantial customer base in the region.

In return, according to the complaint, Highmark agreed to pay
sharply increased prices to UPMC, which it would be able to do because it could raise premiums with no fear of competition. Highmark
also agreed to end the lower cost product lines it had created to compete with UPMC's insurance and which had been a key pipeline for
patients to West Penn.

The complaint summed up the charges this way: "Since the conspiracy's formation in 2002 . . . UPMC and Highmark have enjoyed
record profits—and an increasingly exploited Pittsburgh community
has suffered skyrocketing health care costs."

Although Zeke Emanuel would later push the issue to no avail in
White House deliberations on the healthcare reform law, stronger antitrust enforcement against rapidly consolidating hospitals like UPMC
was not mentioned in Baucus's "Call to Action" white paper. Nor had
it come up in any of the negotiations his team had with the hospital
lobbyists.

In fact, certain aspects of Baucus's plan, as well as what would become the White House economic team's focus on cost containment,

would actually encourage consolidation by promoting "bundled care." With bundled care, doctors, hospitals, and other providers got together to offer one price for attending to an illness rather than the traditional fee-for-service payment for each treatment or procedure. Obviously, the easiest way to bundle was to have all the players under the same roof, responsible for the same bottom line.

Thus, none of the reforms being talked about was seen by UPMC's Romoff as another "impediment." If anything, the opposite was true. Romoff might have to sacrifice some new Medicare revenue as part of the $155 billion in givebacks being negotiated in Washington by his trade group, the American Hospital Association, but he was likely to end up with much more from all the new paying customers the prospective new law promised. More important, nothing about the law seemed likely to impede his continuing plans to expand.

THE WARY INSURERS

Through the spring of 2009, Karen Ignagni, whose AHIP represented Highmark and all the other insurers, was also game to negotiate with the Baucus team. She had promised the president her cooperation at his East Room pep rally. However, both sides knew that figuring out this deal would be more complicated than lining up the quid pro quos for the drugmakers and the hospitals. Insurance, after all, was what the core of the reform law being drafted—universal coverage—was all about.

In discussions with Fowler and the Finance Committee staff, Ignagni and her team of lobbyists agreed that the insurers were about to get millions of new customers in the individual market, many if not most of whom would have their premiums paid in part by government subsidies. That was obvious. And because many of the insurance companies operated Medicaid plans serving the poor for the various states, there would be lots of new revenue there, too. However, the insurance lobbyists pointed out, the customers who would be buying on these new exchanges might present a risk profile different from the ones already in the individual market. No one could be sure what an exchange customer—or "life" in insurance jargon—was worth. Similarly, it was difficult to tell how much a new Medicaid life would be worth to an insurance company.

More than that, the question of what all this new insurance would mean to the bottom line for Ignagni's members depended on the details of what kind of insurance they would be able to sell.

Would there be any allowances at all for excluding any preexisting conditions, Ignagni and her team asked.

Could they at least charge people differing rates based on their age? This was called the age band question. The Baucus paper had mentioned that insurers would be able to charge older people more than the young. The industry needed to know exactly how much more. They wanted at least a five to one age band, or spread, to cover the higher costs of insuring people approaching Medicare age; but they knew the AARP (formerly the American Association of Retired Persons), which was hugely influential with Democrats on Capitol Hill, was already pushing for no more than a two to one ratio.

Could they charge more to people who were smokers and, therefore, much more at risk for a variety of health problems? If so, how much more? And how would they be able to make sure people told the truth about whether they smoked?

Exactly what kind of preventive care envisioned in Baucus's white paper would have to be provided with no deductibles or co-pays? The longer the list, the higher the cost to Ignagni's constituents and the less they should be asked to ante up to help finance reform.

Most important, the insurance lobbyists wanted details about the mandate. How was the requirement that everyone had to buy insurance going to be enforced? Would it have real teeth? How high was the monetary penalty going to be? Only something with real bite, they said, would get the insurers the customers—especially the younger, healthier ones—that they needed for this really to benefit them.

Finally, there was the question of the subsidies the government was going to provide to the poor and middle class to help them buy the insurance. This was going to be the prime government expense everyone was being asked to help finance. Would the subsidies be generous enough to allow enough lower- and middle-income families to buy insurance? If not, from the insurers' standpoint, the reform bill wouldn't be worth much.

Ignagni and her staff and Baucus and his staff agreed on the basics: AHIP would support getting rid of the ability to exclude preexisting conditions in exchange for the mandate and subsidies for lower income people to buy insurance. That had been AHIP's position since late 2007, and she and her board had no problem agreeing to say so publicly.

But before Ignagni and her members could commit to supporting an actual bill, much less agree to chip in money for those TV ads the way PhRMA had, they needed the details.

FROM PACEMAKERS TO WHEELCHAIRS

The fourth major player that Fowler, Clapsis, and the rest of the Baucus team focused on was the medical technology and device industry, which included makers of products ranging from simple blood sugar readers to MRIs and CT scans to pacemakers to wheelchairs. Its lobbying group, the Advanced Medical Technology Association, included some of the world's richest manufacturing companies (GE, Siemens), the diagnostic divisions of the major drug companies, and a catalog of relatively unknown firms that made billions selling products such as artificial knees and hips.

Many of these companies had profit margins that were the envy of corporate America. A 2011 survey for medical-industry clients by consultant McKinsey & Company would highlight device makers as the superstar performers in the booming medical economy.

A good example is Medtronic—which makes everything from neurostimulators inserted into the back to relieve pain, to defibrillators, to coronary stents, to surgical equipment. The Minnesota-based company had delivered an amazing compounded annual return of 14.95 percent to shareholders from 1990 to 2010. That meant $100 invested in the company in 1990 was worth $1,622 twenty years later. Medtronic's overall cost of making its products was about 25 percent of what it sells them for, yielding an unusually high gross profit margin of about 75 percent. The prospect of healthcare reform producing so many new customers to buy these products had to be appealing.

Yet the device lobby never bargained with the Baucus group or anyone else. It had no reason to. The government had no hook into their revenue the way it did with the other players. With the hospitals, for example, the government could tinker with Medicare reimbursement rates. But hospitals and doctors bought medical devices on their own, and if a Medicare patient was involved they simply billed Medicare the cost plus a markup.

"We knew we were just going to have to tax them straight up for all the new revenue they were going to get," recalled one member of Baucus's staff. "There was no indirect way to get them to pay." Clapsis penciled in $60 billion in medical device taxes over ten years as the device industry's contribution, which was about a 5 percent tax on its $120 billion to $130 billion in annual revenue from the U.S. market. They may not have been willing to negotiate, but they were going to have to chip in.

CHAPTER 9

BEHIND CLOSED DOORS:
WHITE HOUSE TURF WARS,
INDUSTRY DEALS, AND
SENATE WRANGLING

April–July 2009

Working in the White House on a Saturday afternoon had become routine for Zeke Emanuel and Bob Kocher. But they were usually able to leave at a decent hour. However, at 5 p.m. on Saturday, April 25, 2009, they were thrown into a state of near-panic. Emanuel, Kocher, and the rest of the staff from the Office of Management and Budget and the National Economic Council had been blindsided by the domestic policy crew.

White House healthcare reform policy chief Nancy-Ann DeParle had decided that it was time for the president to get up to speed on what Congress was cooking up. He needed to make some decisions on how the administration was going to weigh in on the various issues that loomed. So DeParle had asked Jeanne Lambrew, who was now running the health policy office at the Department of Health and Human Services, and Michael Hash, a DeParle deputy and veteran of the Clinton White House reform fights and of Ted Kennedy's health-care reform battles before that, to draft a briefing memo for the president. DeParle had then tinkered with it. Nearly three thousand words long, it was meant to prepare Obama for a meeting she had gotten on his calendar for the following Thursday.

Memos of this import and length don't just go to the president. As was standard practice, DeParle's office had submitted it to the White House staff secretary, who organizes the president's reading folder. As is also standard practice, the staff secretary then distributed it to others who had an interest in the subject before it would be sent off in the president's folder at eight o'clock that night. The idea was that if other members of the staff had any last-minute comments or suggested edits they could send them to DeParle's office for her to incorporate in a final version. Some staffers had already begun calling the process a "war of the pens."

It was only when the memo arrived just after 5 P.M. at Peter Orszag's and Larry Summers's in-boxes that Emanuel and Kocher saw it. Any hopes for an early departure that Saturday evening were gone.

To them, the memo leaned too far away from decisions aimed at containing costs or raising revenue. In some cases it used what they thought were incorrect numbers or pointed the president in one direction versus another with inaccurate or biased descriptions of his choices.

"These options have been presented to your senior staff, and we have developed a package that could plausibly offset the cost of reform," the DeParle memo began. The "we" certainly didn't include Zeke Emanuel or Kocher. The OMB–Economic Council team had only started to discuss those options with DeParle's group, and there wasn't, as far as they knew, any "package" yet that could "plausibly offset the cost of reform."

True, there were lots of ideas being talked about for new taxes and fees. Some, such as the money the drug companies were going to ante up, were by now pretty much signed off on by the Senate and White House staffs—though not by the House. However, others in the De-Parle "package" described in the pages that followed were simply ideas. No one had signed off on them. One example was a 10 percent excise tax on all sugar-sweetened beverages, which would generate $170 billion in new revenue. The economic team thought getting that through the Senate would be impossible. Other taxes the economic team liked—such as one on the sales of medical devices—were not included.

Imposing some kind of tax on employer-provided insurance, which the unions would oppose, was mentioned as a Baucus idea, but it was not included in the menu of options for the president. However, a 3 percent income tax surcharge on individuals with incomes above $500,000 and families with incomes above $1,000,000 was listed.

The memo acknowledged that some of these revenue-raising ideas "would be politically challenging." Emanuel and Kocher thought that to be an understatement bordering on fantasy. To them, there was no chance that any Republicans would agree to that 3 percent. They suspected DeParle's group had included it because they thought the president would like it.

Worse, from the standpoint of the economic team, the memo gave short shrift to what they thought were the real "game changers" when it came to costs.

Again, this was emblematic of the understandable tension between the two sides: The economic team wanted to use reform to bend the cost curve. DeParle and her healthcare reform policy team, including Lambrew at Health and Human Services, wanted to expand coverage. If some cost-cutting provisions helped to make coverage reform more fiscally palatable to Congress, that was a plus. But if any of the economic team's ideas were likely to face so much opposition from any sector of the industry that Congress would run for cover, that was a negative.

DeParle had included a half page describing three of Zeke Emanuel and Bob Kocher's cost-cutting ideas, such as promoting the "efficient use of technology" by, among other things, analyzing the cost-effectiveness of new medical technology, and data "registries" for all devices and drugs that would track the results they produced in one database in order to weed out those whose results did not justify their costs. That was the most far reaching—and, given the lobbying clout that would be arrayed against it—the most far-fetched idea that DeParle included.

However, DeParle had left out what the economic team considered to be some of the more important game changers, but ones that more left-of-center reformers had always been wary of: medical malpractice reform, tough penalties for hospitals with high patient read-mission rates, and a push to allow hospitals and doctors to consolidate their services into "bundled payments."

Emanuel and Kocher also wanted to add estimates of the savings that could come with each. DeParle and Lambrew refused.

Following frantic efforts by Emanuel and Kocher to get their edits into the memo, which, except for a few changes of words and phrases, were rebuffed by the domestic policy people, the revised seven-pager was sent to the president by the eight o'clock deadline.

According to three senior members of Obama's staff, Valerie Jarrett had been instrumental in establishing this messy process, which pur-ported to present a consensus from "your advisers," while not reveal-ing those advisers' points of disagreement. This was Obama's preference, or at least it was as expressed in a frequently voiced direc-tive from Jarrett: "Don't bring us your problems," she liked to say, according to these three advisers. "Bring us your solutions."[6]

Rather than laying out conflicting views for the president, the pro-cess frequently became a battle of whose views appeared over whose signature. Here, DeParle's views and signature prevailed.

This "war of the pens" also produced typographical errors, dis-jointed sentences, and other signs of a rush job to finish what at least had the virtue of being a crisp, complete picture of the state of the healthcare reform effort and the decisions that now needed to be made.

It began by walking the president through a summary of where things stood in the House and Senate. By now the House—where three committees shared jurisdiction—was settling on the big-picture issues much the way Baucus's and Kennedy's committees were. The core of their plans, too, was the Romneycare three-legged stool. But there were significant, looming differences in the details, which re-flected the more liberal nature of the House and the fact that none of the committee chairs there was worried about attracting Republican support.

6. Although Jarrett declined comment, assistant press secretary Eric Schultz denied this account offered by these senior Obama advisers, saying, "Valerie doesn't use this phrase and regularly reminds our staff that the president and our senior team don't like surprises, to further encourage staff to bring to their attention both problems and solutions."

The House's version of the coverage benefits that would be included in the baseline insurance policies that people would have to buy was more generous than the Senate's. That meant more expensive insurance and, therefore, more money for subsidies for lower income people to buy it.

The Senate, reflecting Baucus's post-election white paper, was talking about some kind of tax on employer-based insurance. The House, more sensitive to union reaction, didn't have that on its list.

The briefing memo reported that both the House and Senate were likely to include a public option—the setting up of a government-run nonprofit insurer to compete with private insurers that Senator Grassley had urged Obama to reject at the White House conference in March. The House's public option was more muscular and threatening to the insurance industry. The Senate version "attempts to minimize unfair competitive advantage with private plans" was the euphemism DeParle used to describe a Senate plan that would require the public insurance entity to pay doctors and hospitals the same prices that private insurers did, and would, therefore, likely have little impact.

DeParle's memo then walked the president through a series of trade-offs he was going to have to decide on at the big senior staff meeting she had scheduled for the following week.

More generous subsidies and subsidies to people higher up the income ladder would guarantee more coverage, but would obviously cost more. So would more generous benefits in the baseline insurance package.

Money could be saved by encouraging the insurance companies on the exchanges to offer less choice of the hospitals and doctors that would be in their networks; that way they could bargain for better discounts from the lucky providers in exchange for including them. However, noted DeParle, there is "some question about how this would relate to the fact that most public opinion research found that Americans highly value a choice of doctors." Obama knew that. His pollsters had successfully urged him to promise voters on the campaign trail that they would always be able to keep the doctors they had.

The most careful language was reserved for DeParle's description of the choices the president needed to make concerning the individual mandate. Here, she tried to ease Obama off his old campaign position—the one that had produced his attacks on Hillary Clinton for favoring the mandate.

"Your campaign plan," she began, "included a requirement for parents to cover children but not a similar requirement for adults, in part because you expressed concern about affordability of premiums for families. We have explored three alternatives to this approach."

In other words, DeParle was assuming Obama would agree to a different position. This was because people such as Rahm Emanuel and Neera Tanden—the Obama campaign policy adviser who was now working with Lambrew at HHS,[7] and who remembered what Obama had told her in July about how "maybe Hillary was right"—had assured DeParle that Obama was ready to move.

The three alternatives DeParle proposed were stacked in favor of the one listed last. First was a straight mandate, with no exceptions, which would require "generous subsidies so as not to pose an undue burden on the people being mandated." The second was something called automatic enrollment, in which people would be automatically enrolled but could then opt out and not pay any penalty the way they would if there was a mandate. DeParle noted that "experts in behavioral economics" believed this would work nearly as well as a mandate. However, she added, "others, including the MIT model we have been using"—meaning Jonathan Gruber—believed it would not work.

The final option was an "individual requirement with an exemption process." As in Massachusetts, those who could demonstrate that the premiums they would have to pay, even with subsidies, would take too much of a bite (such as more than 7 percent) out of their incomes would not have to pay the mandate's penalties. Others could claim an exemption for "special circumstances." That, of course, was the obvi-

---

7. Tanden would leave the Obama administration in early 2010 for the Center for American Progress, because, according to a *Washington Post* profile of her, she was "frustrated by the administration's insular culture."

ous choice—and, in fact, is exactly what Hillary Clinton had proposed when Obama attacked her for wanting to force people to "buy insurance they can't afford."

"GIVE THE HOUSE AND SENATE THE SPACE THEY NEED"

On April 30, 2009, a large group gathered with the president in the Roosevelt Room to review a PowerPoint about healthcare reform. This was the meeting that DeParle's April 25 memo had been meant to prepare the president for. But this time, the PowerPoint had been prepared jointly by the economic team and DeParle's healthcare policy people. Peter Orszag and Larry Summers had insisted on that. In fact, Kocher, who prided himself on his McKinsey-bred PowerPoint skills, controlled the document.

Unlike in DeParle's prior memo, in Kocher's PowerPoint slides the public option was never mentioned as something Obama even had to decide on.

By taking the pen from the healthcare reform team, the economic team was happily able to put up a bunch of real numbers. Thus, the first slide provided Kocher and Zeke Emanuel's full list of game changers, and declared in a bold box underneath the list that "For every 5% we can reduce healthcare growth over the next ten years we will save families $2,500." It was a nice thought, but it was also a turn of phrase that would come back to haunt the White House as it morphed into promises of $2 trillion in cost cuts and $2,500 a year per family in reduced spending on healthcare.

That was followed by a price list of coverage options and ways to raise money to pay for reform.

Generous insurance coverage with low deductibles? $1,120 a month in premiums.

Plain vanilla, "catastrophic" coverage: $420 a month.

Taxing employer-provided insurance for people in the 75 percent income percentile: worth $200 billion over ten years.

Taxing those benefits for all people in the 50th percentile or over: worth $325 billion over ten years.

The economic team was clearly on Baucus's side. They wanted to finance reform by taxing insurance benefits, something the unions and the healthcare reform team opposed.

The president started the discussion with one big, clear decision. The PowerPoint had laid out four possible reform plans, ranging from the most expensive, costing $1.2 trillion, to the least expensive, costing $600 billion. Each used a midpoint level of insurance coverage. The most expensive would include a mandate for all (with hardship exemptions), which would cost more because of the subsidies required to help people pay their premiums. The least expensive had no mandate. The president said he wanted to go for the big one.

Obama had now signed on to the mandate, though he would not go public about it until he was pressured by Baucus to write him a letter in early June saying he would "accept" it if legislators decided that that was the best course. (The draft of the letter would end up being negotiated between DeParle and an ever-reluctant David Axelrod, who still feared the political fallout, while Axelrod was on Air Force One traveling with the president to Egypt.)

Yet for all the specific numbers arrayed in the PowerPoint for various taxes and savings from givebacks by the hospitals and the drug companies, the rest of the conversation didn't focus on choosing those options. It was disjointed, rambling, vague.

Axelrod steered the group to a discussion about how to shape political strategy and messaging to keep things moving on Capitol Hill. Gene Sperling, the counselor to the Treasury secretary, gave a discourse on some of the finer points of the options for taxes listed on the PowerPoint, which now included an alcohol tax (worth $60 billion over ten years), a tobacco tax ($25 billion), and the income tax surcharge, which the economic team had raised from a $500,000 threshold to $1,000,000. None of these taxes would ever make it into any draft of a Senate bill.

Phil Schiliro, who was in charge of congressional relations, suggested that they defer making decisions on the taxes or the specifics of issues such as the nature of the penalty for enforcing a mandate. It was better to wait for Congress to come to grips with those details in the bills that would be drafted by each house, he explained—which was consistent with his view that the House and Senate were likely to come down on opposite sides of many of these issues and, therefore, that anything the president declared definitively would be opposed by one side or the other.

Obama was game for that. "We're committed to full reform," he said. "But we have to give the House and Senate the space they need," he added.

The meeting ended with no directive from the president other than asking Rahm Emanuel and Orszag to draft and give to Capitol Hill a list of "taxes we could support"—which at this stage seemed like everything on the list except the tax on employer-provided insurance.

CAPPING THE INSURERS' PROFITS

Another memo addressed to the White House and Department of Health and Human Services "health reform team" and signed by Jeanne Lambrew on May 2, 2009, also caught the economic team unprepared. It was about an arcane health insurance term called the medical loss ratio, or MLR.

The MLR is the ratio of claims insurers pay out to hospitals, doctors, and other providers of medical care compared to the premiums they receive from customers who buy their insurance. An insurance company that takes in $100 million in premiums and pays out $80 million to cover medical bills would have an MLR of 80 percent.

In fact, 75 to 80 percent was a typical MLR, which meant that 20 to 25 percent in costs to oversee claims and otherwise manage the company was par for the course—despite the fact that administrative costs to pay for healthcare in other countries were typically closer to 5 percent (meaning a 95 percent MLR), and Medicare's administrative costs were less than 1 percent.

However, on Wall Street a low MLR was a badge of honor. A 70 percent MLR meant that the company was keeping 30 percent of its revenue to cover all of its administrative costs and, yes, its profits and dividend payouts.

Conversely, among healthcare reformers, the MLR was viewed as a measure of community responsibility. The higher the MLR, the more generous the company was about paying claims as opposed to dividends or executive salaries.

In her memo, Lambrew zeroed in on the MLR in those terms, proposing that the reform package include a regulation, which had already been adopted in some states, that would require insurers whose MLRs dipped below a certain level in any given year to issue premium rebates to customers as a way of paying them back for that deficit. She did not propose specific benchmarks, but pointed to different proposals in the past that had targeted a 75 to 80 percent MLR for insurers in the small-group or individual market, and higher ratios for insurers in the large-group market—which served companies employing large numbers of workers, and where economies of scale lowered per-customer administrative costs.

In other words, if the limit was set at 80 percent and an insurer ended up with a 78 percent MLR, it would have to rebate 2 percent of its premiums to its customers.

Lambrew was careful to list the pros and cons, but on balance she made a good argument for including the rule in the reform package, noting that "increasingly fewer markets are competitive, as health insurance markets have become increasingly consolidated."

Lambrew was certainly on firm political ground. David Simas, an Axelrod aide who was already tasked with focusing on the politics of reform, had told Lambrew and DeParle that an MLR regulation that would force insurance companies to mail back refunds to consumers was a winner. In fact, it might end up being the single most politically appealing piece of healthcare reform.

The merits, though, were more debatable. At a meeting of his National Economic Council staff soon after Lambrew's memo circulated, Summers called it a "stupid idea," and told his people to try to kill it. It was "dumb for us to cap anyone's profits," he said, dismissing the idea much the way the legendarily blunt Summers might have taken down a freshman economics student at Harvard who said something in class that he thought was "dumb."

This kind of MLR regulation would create incentives for the insurers to load up on costs for medical care, Summers added. In the noncompetitive, concentrated markets that Lambrew had described, they would be motivated to worry less about getting deep discounts from hospitals, because the more they paid, the more they could keep for administrative costs and profits.

Worse, Kocher—the former McKinsey consultant—chimed in, they would engage in all kinds of games to shift expenses from the administrative category to the categories that counted on the "medical loss" side of the equation, which was supposed to include paying for care and paying for efforts to improve care through "quality improvements." A doctor at the insurance company, for example, whose job was to vet claims might have his or her role recategorized to include ascertaining that quality care was being provided. That would move his salary from administrative costs to claims costs, thereby raising the medical loss ratio. Some of the fees paid to pharmacy benefit managers—the big names were Caremark and Express Scripts—to manage prescription drug programs could arguably be called expenses related to insuring wellness or improving patient safety, which would also raise the MLR.

Whether Summers was right about the merits of the idea, the star Harvard economist was certainly on target about how insurers and those providing healthcare services would react to it. When the MLR provision would hit the health industry's radar in the months ahead as a likely part of reform, dozens of conferences would be convened around the country to go over the best ways to get expenses categorized as related to care and not management. Private equity firms evaluating investments would even try to gauge whether the service or product envisioned would be included on the good side or the bad side of the loss ratio calculation. The MLR regulation would turn that Wall Street badge of honor on its head, encouraging the insurers to shoot for higher MLRs.

Beyond that, there was an irony in Lambrew's MLR proposal that drove the economic team to distraction. Yes, insurance companies carried a lot of well-deserved baggage: infuriating customer service, incomprehensible Explanation of Benefits notices, arbitrary decisions denying care, and outsized salaries often paid to their top executives. (UnitedHealthcare's CEO had famously taken home more than a billion dollars in a severance package, before having to give back $486 million after he had left his job as part of a settlement with the SEC for having backdated his stock options.) Still, by 2009, most insurance companies were relative slackers in the healthcare ecosystem. Their tight profit margins were dwarfed by those of the drug companies, the device makers, and even the purportedly nonprofit hospitals.

That was because even in noncompetitive markets, insurers had to buy products from suppliers—hospitals, device makers, drug companies—that had been able in the past two decades to raise their prices with abandon.

That's not to say that the big insurers are managed well or that they haven't reacted to the corner they have been forced into by taking it out on their customers. But it does mean they are the only industry players who, however unsympathetic, are on the customer and tax-payer side of the divide. Like us, they *buy* healthcare. Yet the White House healthcare reform policy team thought they should be the only players to have their profits capped. They were the bad guys.

OBAMA LECTURES THE DRUGMAKERS

On May 10, 2009, President Obama had his first meeting with health industry executives meant to be a substantive bargaining session. Despite the groundwork that had been laid, and although they weren't from the insurance companies he had targeted during the campaign, the president treated them like bad guys, too.

A group of five pharmaceutical industry CEOs, accompanied by PhRMA's Billy Tauzin, trooped into the Roosevelt Room. With the president were DeParle, Rahm Emanuel, and deputy chief of staff Jim Messina, the political aide who had convened the meeting to get the drug companies to finance TV ads supporting reform.

"They made me bring some CEOs because they didn't want to meet with just a lobbyist," recalled Tauzin in an account confirmed by two others who were there. "We figured this was just to go over what we had agreed to—the $80 billion. Instead the president went off on biosimilars"—the issue having to do with how long high-priced biologic drugs would receive patent-like protection. "The Senate had already agreed to twelve years, and we knew we had the votes in the

House, too, although Waxman was at zero years," Tauzin added, referring to the liberal California congressman who had made allowing biosimilars to thrive a pet cause.

Obama insisted that it had to be seven years. "It was the only specific issue the president ever took a position with us on in all our conversations," recalled one industry executive who was in the room. "He just kept hammering away at it, lecturing us."

Tauzin figured Obama was putting on a show because he wanted word to get back to Waxman, whose support Obama needed, that he was working hard on Waxman's favorite issue. So he did not let the president's lecture bother him. But his CEOs, particularly Merck's Richard Clark, to whom Obama targeted much of his harangue, were surprised. They thought the meeting was about sealing the $80 billion deal.

A $2 TRILLION DEAL?

They were surprised still more the next day when they were called back to the White House with leaders of other healthcare industries to join an announcement by Obama that the industry as a whole had agreed to $2 trillion in cost cuts over the next ten years.

Aside from a goal of reducing "the healthcare spending growth rate" by 1.5 percent a year for the next ten years, there were few specifics in the "fact sheet" that the White House press office distributed proclaiming the "historic" agreement to cut trillions from health spending. Each of the befuddled industry leaders standing next to Obama simply said he would try.

The drug executives were now more nervous. Was their deal really a deal? Where had that $2 trillion number come from? Two trillion dollars was a long way from $80 billion. How much of the $2 trillion were they expected to chip in? Hadn't they been assured by Baucus's people that the White House was on board?

The signals were, at best, confusing. Five days earlier, on May 6, 2009, one of the industry lobbyists had emailed a colleague about "our frustration with the lack of direct discourse inside the White House." However, she continued, "Rahm's calling Nancy Ann [DeParle], and knows Billy [Tauzin] is going to talk to Nancy Ann tonight. Rahm will make it clear that PhRMA needs a direct line of communication, separate and apart from any other coalition."

But the May 10 and May 11 White House meetings, coming as they did just after that email exchange, had only exacerbated the problem. Even as the ads they had financed began running across the country, the PhRMA people were nervous.

On the evening of May 14, an article for the next day's edition of *The New York Times* was posted online and generated a frenzy of panicked emails among the drug industry lobbyists. Veteran healthcare reporter Robert Pear's front page report quoted officials from various state and national hospital associations and Ignagni from the insurance lobby as charging that "Obama had substantially overstated their promise earlier this week to reduce the growth of health spending. . . . They say they agreed to slow spending in a more gradual way and did not pledge specific year-by-year cuts."

To add to the confusion, Pear quoted DeParle as having called him to say, " 'The president misspoke' when he described the industry's commitment." However, Pear reported in the same paragraph, DeParle had then called him back "an hour later to say 'I don't think he misspoke. His remarks correctly and accurately described the industry's commitment.' "

This fiasco had been orchestrated by the economic team, proving that neither side—neither DeParle's health policy group nor the Orszag-Summers staff—had a monopoly on clumsiness. Orszag and Summers were anxious to get the president fully out front on costs and thought that by expressing the goal—which the president had articulated before on the campaign trail as allowing for a reduction in insurance costs of $2,500 per family—they would move things along.

THE DRUG INDUSTRY GETS ITS DEAL

"Buckle up for tomorrow," emailed lobbyist Rick Smith to his colleagues at PhRMA, referring to the Robert Pear *New York Times* article. "This is unbelievable. . . . I suggest we strictly stick to a short script . . . something along the lines of 'We will respect the confiden-

tiality of our discussions with other associations working on this positive initiative. . . . We also look forward to working with the
Administration and members of Congress toward passage of a bipartisan health reform bill.' "

Bryant Hall, the senior PhRMA lobbyist on Tauzin's team with
the strongest ties to the Democratic side, saw danger: "Perfect timing
to cut our deal [with] the White House as this is swirling," he replied
sarcastically.

By the next afternoon the PhRMA people were under what Hall
described in an email as intense pressure to knock down the *Times*
scoop by signing a joint statement with the other industry sectors reaf-
firming their commitment to cut costs. Although the statement was
bland, Tauzin did not want to sign it. He relented only after his deputy emailed him that "Rahm is already furious. The ire will be turned
on us."

Actually, the ire was soon turned on everyone involved in these
closed-door deals, as the press—its appetite whetted by the back-and-
forth between industry officials and the White House coming out of
the May 11 $2 trillion pledge—began asking what, if anything, had
been pledged and to whom and by whom in what settings. Liberals on
Capitol Hill, especially in the House, also wanted to know.

On June 3, 2009, when some members of the House and Senate
began talking openly about lifting the ban on buying drugs from Canada as part of the reform package, Nancy-Ann DeParle emailed
PhRMA's Hall to reconfirm that she and her White House colleagues
had decided, "based on how constructive you guys have been, to oppose importation in this bill. It is my understanding that this is being
conveyed [to Capitol Hill]—let me know if this is not the case."

But at another White House meeting with drug executives and
lobbyists, on June 10—which included Rahm Emanuel, Messina, and
DeParle, as well as Clapsis and Fowler from Baucus's staff—the drug
industry heard a tougher message. DeParle upped the ante from $80
billion to $120 billion. The Obama people were worried about a revolt
in the House, led by Waxman, if they let the drugmakers off too easy.
If they couldn't get $120 billion, the more life-threatening reforms
cutting into PhRMA's revenues would be thrown into the package.

Tauzin didn't budge. He knew they could never get sixty votes in the Senate if the drugmakers switched sides and began financing a different set of ads, and he said so.

Within days DeParle and Emanuel sent out word that in an upcoming Saturday radio address, the president was going to call for radically more expensive cuts in how Medicaid and Medicare pay for drugs than were included even in her $120 billion demand. Tauzin still refused to cave, and his people pushed the Baucus staff to bring the White House on board, which is what they had promised was already the case.

Finally, the drug lobbyists met with the Baucus Finance Committee staff and got back to the $80 billion deal, accompanied by what the Baucus people promised was really and truly the White House's blessing. The next day Tauzin wrote to Messina at the White House that his "five principal CEOs have accepted the terms we discussed with the Committee yesterday."

THAT DAY, JUNE 15, 2009, Obama took to the stump, telling an American Medical Association convention that "we will keep this promise to the American people: If you like your doctor, you will be able to keep your doctor, period. If you like your health care plan, you'll be able to keep your health care plan, period. No one will take it away, no matter what."

Both DeParle's shop and the economic team were nervous about those pledges. They knew that to make a mandate truly work to ensure that Americans had adequate insurance coverage, the reform bill was going to have to outlaw many of the policies like the one Emilia Gilbert in Connecticut had had when she arrived at the emergency room—which were cheap, and which people may have "liked" until they realized how badly they were protected. And, as the PowerPoint presentation to the president just two weeks before had made clear, insurers were going to be allowed, even encouraged, to create "narrow networks" that limited patients' choices of doctors and hospitals in order to keep premiums low.

However, the policy and economic teams didn't write the president's speeches and their comments about the drafts they saw were ignored. The speechwriting and politics staff told them these were technicalities—footnotes—that could not be fitted into an effective speech.

Notably, the June 16 speech contained none of Obama's campaign trail attacks on the drug companies or insurers. Instead, the president promised savings that could come through better electronic medical records, more efficient use of prescription drugs, and more coordinated care overall. All the players in healthcare were going to be asked to chip in, Obama said. But he didn't criticize any of them. A deal was in the air.

Three weeks later, on July 7, 2009, the drug company CEOs met in the White House with Rahm Emanuel, DeParle, and Baucus and shook hands on the deal. PhRMA's public relations team then began drafting talking points for its members so that the drug industry could describe the deal without letting on exactly what they had gotten in return—how they had averted the "life-threatening" reforms the executives had feared. There would be no prescription drug importation. Medicare would not be set loose to negotiate drug prices. There would be no draconian cuts in Medicaid payments. And, yes, there would be twelve years of protection for biologics rather than Waxman's zero years or Obama's seven. However, the talking points, which went through multiple drafts, wouldn't mention all of those dodged bullets. Rather, they would describe only what the drug companies had agreed to contribute in terms of new discounts for Medicaid and to reduce the Medicare doughnut hole.

When the White House press office announced the PhRMA deal on July 20, it was called an agreement between Baucus's Senate Finance Committee and the drugmakers. It, too, omitted the bullets PhRMA had been allowed to dodge.

But Waxman knew. He soon attacked the deal and said it would not fly in the House.

In early August, PhRMA got wind that *The New York Times* was preparing a story about a provision Waxman had drafted in his version of a reform bill that would allow Medicare to negotiate drug prices. The reporter was saying that PhRMA had told him that the drug companies had gotten a promise from Baucus that there would be no such provision. However, the reporter was also saying that no one at the White House was responding to his question about whether the Obama administration supported or opposed what it was still calling the Finance Committee deal. Other papers, including the *Los Angeles Times,* had already reported the same thing and were demanding to know what deals had been made or not made and whether the White House felt bound by them.

The prior month an item had appeared in *Congress Daily* in which Waxman had claimed that the White House was not bound to honor any deals made by the Senate. That reporter had written that he had gotten a "no comment" from the White House. When that story appeared, a lobbyist for Novartis, the giant drug company, had emailed Bryant Hall, the Democratic-connected lobbyist at PhRMA, to ask if the White House was backing out of the deal. But he and other drug lobbyists had been satisfied when Hall emailed back that he had spoken directly to Rahm Emanuel after the story appeared and had been assured that Waxman's claim was not true—that, of course, there was a deal.

Now PhRMA wanted the Obama people to take a public stand. "Send the reporters to me," White House deputy chief of staff Jim Messina replied in an email to Hall at PhRMA. The next day this story appeared, in which the White House finally came clean:

> Pressed by industry lobbyists, White House officials on Wednesday assured drug makers that the administration stood by a behind-the-scenes deal to block any Congressional effort to extract cost savings from them beyond an agreed-upon $80 billion.
>
> Drug industry lobbyists reacted with alarm this week to a House health care overhaul measure that would allow the government to negotiate drug prices and demand additional rebates from drug manufacturers.
>
> In response, the industry successfully demanded that the White House explicitly acknowledge for the first time that it

had committed to protect drug makers from bearing further costs in the overhaul. . . .

"We were assured: 'We need somebody to come in first. If you come in first, you will have a rock-solid deal,'" Billy Tauzin, the former Republican House member from Louisiana who now leads the pharmaceutical trade group, said Wednesday. "Who is ever going to go into a deal with the White House again if they don't keep their word? You are just going to duke it out instead."

A deputy White House chief of staff, Jim Messina, confirmed Mr. Tauzin's account of the deal in an e-mail message on Wednesday night.

"The president encouraged this approach," Mr. Messina wrote. "He wanted to bring all the parties to the table to discuss health insurance reform."

This crisis might have been averted, PhRMA lobbyist Hall speculated to DeParle in an email, had White House operatives consulted more with the House leaders in the first place. DeParle didn't buy it. "Maybe we would have never gotten anywhere if we had," she replied. "I know this is tough for you guys," she added. "It's tough for us, too. I'm the one walking the halls in [the House office buildings] getting yelled at by members."

Meantime, an updated Goldman Sachs analyst's report on how drug companies were likely to fare if the law passed was circulating on Wall Street. It confirmed Tauzin's strategy: "Cost side of equation meaningfully offset by benefit from increased coverage," the report was headlined.

THE HOSPITALS GET THEIR DEAL

To the Obama administration, hospitals apparently did not carry the baggage that the drug companies did. On July 8, 2009, Vice President Biden announced the $155 billion agreement with the hospitals. The White House, and certainly Biden, had had little to do with negotiating the hospitals deal; most of the bargaining sessions had been with Fowler, Clapsis, and the rest of the Baucus team, not at the White House. Yet, unlike the PhRMA deal, this one merited a White House imprimatur.

Tellingly, the $155 billion in givebacks had to do with the hospitals accepting lower increases in Medicare payment rates, plus the penalties on readmissions. The hospitals did not agree to the kind of systemic reforms that the economic team coveted. "Kocher and Zeke kept talking about bundled payments," said one member of the Senate negotiating team, "but we and the hospitals had trouble seeing that there was any there there."

By now conservative groups were getting wise to what was going on and were beginning to push back. Even the Heritage Foundation, which had provided the intellectual underpinning for the core of the reform package now taking shape, was manning the opposition barricades. *USA Today* reported that "Dennis Smith, a health care expert at the conservative Heritage Foundation, said hospitals will end up making money from a health care overhaul that costs the government $1 trillion. 'These savings are really a mirage,' he said. If Obama's plan is enacted, 'hospitals are likely to get more revenue than what they are pretending to give up.'"

GETTING THE SIXTIETH SENATE DEMOCRAT

Biden had done something important to advance healthcare reform beyond this ceremonial role in the hospitals deal. At the end of April, he had been instrumental in persuading Pennsylvania Republican senator Arlen Specter—a longtime friend and former Senate colleague facing a tough primary fight from a conservative challenger—to switch to the Democratic Party.

On July 7, 2009, Specter's switch became that much more important when Al Franken—the *Saturday Night Live* comedian turned Democratic Senate candidate in Minnesota—was sworn in following a recount battle that had lasted nine months.

With the Democrats able to count on Vermont independent Bernie

Sanders, they now had the sixty votes needed to get healthcare past a filibuster, provided they could corral all the Democrats.

Senate majority leader Harry Reid immediately turned his attention to making sure that happened. Baucus, however, still wanted a bipartisan deal. He was worried about some of the most conservative Democrats. Besides, Max Baucus loved doing bipartisan deals in his Finance Committee.

There was also great concern that there would soon be one less Democrat. Ted Kennedy had been told in late May that he had maybe three or four months to live.

Baucus's bipartisan spirit was not in evidence in mid-June when the other Senate committee concerned about healthcare—Kennedy's Health, Education, Labor and Pensions, or HELP, Committee—began to edit, or "mark up" the draft bill that Kennedy's staff had circulated. With Kennedy now ailing, he had designated Chris Dodd of Connecticut, a close friend, as his stand-in on the committee to pull the bill together. But Dodd had been unable to duplicate Kennedy's legendary ability to bring Republicans along. By the end of the spring, the HELP meetings had become exclusively Democratic staff conversations.

Their draft included the three-legged Romneycare stool and generous subsidies for people to buy insurance in compliance with the mandate. However, there was no public option. There were also no provisions for the financial givebacks negotiated with the hospitals or insurers or for any proposed taxes on the device makers or on insurance benefits provided by employers; that would all be the province of the Finance Committee, which had jurisdiction over all of the bill.

Beginning on July 17, 2009, the HELP Committee members met in sometimes-marathon sessions to mark up their bill. Dodd was constantly on the phone consulting Kennedy, who was confined to his Cape Cod home. Seven hundred and eighty-eight amendments were offered, "three quarters of which were filed by the ten Republican members," according to an account in the book written by Kennedy aide John McDonough. Of those, McDonough wrote, 161 were adopted in whole or part.

The final product added a mild version of the public option, the kind that—because it purportedly would not allow the new government-run insurance provider to have any price advantages over private insurers—seemed pointless to harder-line reformers. The House's bill, which had emerged three weeks earlier after the three House committees with jurisdiction successfully merged their drafts, had a far stronger public option and included a new tax on millionaires.

Both the HELP and House bills also set the "age band" at two to one, meaning that the oldest people could be charged only twice what the youngest would be charged for insurance.

Insurers routinely charge a five to one age band, because older people had so many more healthcare needs than the youngest beneficiaries. Lead insurance lobbyist Ignagni and her insurance company members had told Fowler that there was no way she could agree to that. They would either be forced to charge older people so little that they would lose money, or charge the youngest so much that they would not enroll, creating a pool of mostly old, high-cost customers, which would negate the goal of getting lots of people contributing into the risk pool. Fowler assured her that the Finance Committee bill would try to fix the age band.

A MASTER LOBBYIST WORKS HIS MAGIC

One of the more dramatic confrontations in both Henry Waxman's House committee and in the HELP Committee during their July markup sessions involved that arcane multibillion-dollar issue of how long to protect biologics from biosimilars.

In both the House and Senate committees, the result featured a virtuoso display of lobbying by representatives of one giant biologics company—Amgen, a Thousand Oaks, California–based creator of medicines targeted at treating serious illnesses, from cancer to kidney disease to rheumatoid arthritis.

Amgen deployed the kind of muscle on Capitol Hill that had become standard: More than $1.1 million in contributions from individuals associated with the company and its lobbyists had been doled out to the members of the Senate Finance and HELP committees in just the

2008 election cycle (with higher totals on the way for the 2010 cycle). Amgen also spent lavishly on lobbyists, deploying dozens (including some who had worked for Baucus) from multiple firms. Its total lobbying bill from 2007 through 2009 alone was more than $38 million.

But Amgen had more than that. The company had David Beier, its senior vice president for global government affairs.

As Beier prowled the halls of the Capitol in July 2009, his company was being investigated by fifteen state attorneys general for conspiring to provide kickbacks to hospitals and clinics by overfilling Medicare-paid-for vials of an anemia drug so that the overfill could then be sold separately, giving the hospitals and clinics a secret bonus for using its product. The company would later settle that case along with at least two others that also involved illegal sales and marketing tactics.

However, despite Amgen's run-ins with the law, Beier was not the fast-talking, unscrupulous influence peddler that had become a Washington prototype in the popular press.

For starters, everyone seemed to like and respect him, and not because he had Tauzin-like charm. A lawyer and former chief domestic policy adviser in Vice President Al Gore's office, Beier, who was sixty in 2009, was soft-spoken, didn't argue, and, in the view of members and staffs on both sides of the aisle, always presented the other side of an issue so they would not be blindsided. He tried to make sure that the lobbying team he directed was willing and able to do the same. Fascinated by the regulatory and intellectual property issues a company like Amgen faced in Washington, he even ran bootcamps for the team to train them on Amgen's issues.

Beyond that, Beier seemed to know everyone, be everywhere, and know everything in a way that stunned some of those who dealt with him. During the frantic deliberations on healthcare through 2009 and into 2010, some members of the White House staff sometimes found themselves calling him to find out what had happened at a House or Senate meeting. Staffers on the Hill often used him to find out what the White House was up to.

Henry Waxman was Beier's chief nemesis on biologics. Waxman thought Amgen and the other drug companies should get zero years of protection—that makers of biosimilars should be turned loose to copy Amgen's products immediately. Because biologics could not be patented, Waxman thought, they didn't deserve patent-like protection to preserve the drugmakers' outrageous profits.[8]

Beier had worked hard to turn this into a broader Silicon Valley debate about entrepreneurship, innovation, and protecting valuable (and lifesaving) inventions. He had enlisted the support of Democrat Anna Eshoo, the congresswoman representing Silicon Valley, while broadening that base with support from groups representing patients with diseases treated by products invented by Amgen and other biologic companies—groups that were often, though not always, funded by the drug companies.

Beier had another argument. Since biologics had come on the healthcare scene there had been a stalemate over biosimilars; contrary to Waxman's view, the law didn't specify whether they could be copied or not following any period of protection or no period, and therefore many companies feared the uncertain legal consequences of making them. Thus, Beier's side argued, some deal—like his twelve-year deal—would save money by allowing for the production and marketing of cheaper biosimilars under a clear set of rules, something his own company wanted to do.

Chairmen don't often lose a vote in their own committees; if they think they might lose, they use their prerogative to avoid the vote. So Waxman was stunned when Beier won a twelve-year provision in Waxman's committee 47–11. In the HELP Committee on the Senate side Beier first orchestrated the defeat of a seven-year bill sponsored by Sherrod Brown, a liberal Ohio Democrat. Then he won a twelve-year provision. Both votes were bipartisan: 17–5 in favor of Amgen.

KENNEDY GETS HIS BILL, WHILE BAUCUS ROMANCES SNOWE

With Ted Kennedy happily watching the proceedings on C-SPAN from his Cape Cod home, the HELP Committee voted on July 14,

---

8. The simplest explanation for this legal argument, which the U.S. Supreme Court agreed to in an unrelated and not exactly similar case in 2013, is that because biologics are derived from living organisms, not chemical formulas, they cannot be patented.

2009, to send the fully marked-up bill to the Senate floor, which, of course, would not actually happen until it was reconciled with the bill Baucus was working on.

No Republican on the HELP Committee voted yes. A *New York Times* report noted Kennedy's absence, which the paper wrote "has been especially painful to Mr. Kennedy . . . who has spent much of his career trying to expand health coverage." The *Times* story then quoted Republican Orrin Hatch as saying "It is a very one-sided, very liberal bill. I know that Ted would not have done that had he been able to be here." But Kennedy and his staff, as well as other Democrats, regarded that as a convenient excuse from a party that seemed to be drawing the line against any reform bill, even one modeled after Romneycare.

Despite repeatedly promising DeParle, Rahm Emanuel, and Obama himself that his committee, too, would begin a markup, Baucus had been holding off. Meanwhile, the list of Republicans willing to entertain the prospect of a bipartisan deal was gradually shrinking— almost as if the Republican political leaders who had attended the Frank Luntz inauguration night dinner were giving them the hook, one by one. The original bipartisan gang of eleven senators from the Finance and HELP committees had become a Gang of Seven, all from Finance. It now included only three Republicans: Grassley, Mike Enzi of Wyoming, and Olympia Snowe of Maine. Baucus's staff suspected Enzi was really there to report back to Republican leader McConnell.

Baucus insisted to the White House people and other worried Democrats, including Senate majority leader Harry Reid, that if he worked on Grassley and Snowe a bit longer he could bring them along. Everyone else on the Democratic side wanted to get the bill voted on before the August recess.

"Timeline is slipping, but Baucus and Grassley are going to cut a deal today, we think," wrote someone who took notes of a July 13 White House meeting of healthcare reform staffers. By now Obama had joined the team courting Grassley. "He must have called me half a dozen times on my cell phone, usually out of the blue," Grassley would later recall. "He said he was just checking in and hoping I was working things out with Max [Baucus]."

Still, Grassley did not sign on.

Later on July 13, the president met with Reid, Baucus, and House Speaker Nancy Pelosi to resolve who should get subsidies to help them buy insurance on the exchanges: Should it be families with incomes up to 400 percent above the poverty level (about $92,000 for a family of four) or 300 percent above poverty (about $72,000)? The difference was tens of billions of dollars in federal outlays, but limiting the subsidies to 300 percent would likely put insurance out of reach for millions of families. As it was, the formulas being developed by Gruber (who was now consulting for the Department of Health and Human Services) and others were likely to put good coverage out of the range of even many families making up to 400 percent.

Obama chose 400 percent and the group agreed, though Baucus was worried that Republicans Snowe and Grassley would object.

Reid and his staff were more worried about getting something ready for a vote that would pass muster with what were now fifty-nine Democrats, plus Vermont's Sanders. Through July, Baucus kept on promising he was on the verge of winning over Grassley and/or Snowe, yet he seemed never able to get either Republican over the goal line. Reid and his staff had especially little use for Baucus's romancing of Snowe, with whom Reid had a frosty, often dismissive relationship. When Baucus was heard one morning complimenting Snowe on her perfume, people on Reid's staff and even Fowler and her colleagues thought the effort was getting ridiculous.

Still, Baucus persisted. His effort was complicated by the fact that Snowe was thought by some around the Senate to be difficult to work with—hard working (she carried around thick briefing books that she constantly pored through), but stubborn, painstaking, and sometimes inconsistent. "Yes, I carried around thick books," she later told me. "Because I thought I was sent here to do real work. A lot of people thought being here was about broad strokes—talking points—to appeal to a base, not legislating. When you're rejiggering sixteen percent of the economy [going to 19 or 20%], the details actually count."

By midsummer, Fowler had counted seventeen items or tweaks that Snowe had insisted on. Some made good sense, like tightening a provision for penalizing hospitals with high infection rates. Others—including a separate program for small businesses to buy insurance for their employees on separate exchanges—seem overly complicated and not worth the trouble. Nonetheless, Baucus put all of them into the bill. Still the Maine Republican would not commit. She kept coming back with more asks and looking for more details. She was particularly concerned about seeing exactly how the premiums and subsidy formulas would work—details that she told me she never got to her satisfaction.

GRASSLEY CLAMPS DOWN ON "NONPROFIT" HOSPITALS

Grassley, too, persuaded Baucus to make dozens of changes in the draft that Fowler and her team were working on. Most of what the Iowa Republican suggested strengthened the bill. For example, he persuaded Baucus to remove a provision allowing Medicare to establish a billing category for doctors to bill patients for counseling on end-of-life and hospice decisions. Grassley told Baucus that having even a mention of that in the bill would allow opponents to scare people by charging that the government was trying to save money by having people agree to die sooner than later.

Grassley had long been focused on accountability and transparency among nonprofit institutions, particularly hospitals, that enjoyed tax exemptions from the IRS. He often cited a study demonstrating that the tax-exempt hospitals provided charitable care representing less than 5 percent of their fast-rising revenues, which was barely higher, if at all, than the for-profit hospitals provided. So he inserted a provision requiring hospitals, as a condition of keeping their tax-exempt status, to issue annual public reports detailing the charitable care and other "community benefits" they had provided in the prior year, which the IRS would review.

Emilia Gilbert—the woman who fell in her Connecticut backyard and then had to pay off Yale–New Haven Hospital's exorbitant chargemaster fees under a court order in $20 weekly increments—would have appreciated another of Grassley's changes. The Iowa Republican added a requirement that before nonprofit hospitals could hand over their overdue bills to lawyers or debt collectors, they had to use aggressive methods to solicit patients to determine if they needed financial aid. Most important for Gilbert and hundreds of thousands, maybe millions, of patients like her, Grassley added a provision allowing the IRS to take away a hospital's tax exemption if it tried to charge patients who needed financial aid more than the average amount paid for those services by insurance companies and Medicare. In other words, hospitals would not be able to make people like Gilbert pay their inflated chargemaster prices.

Baucus's efforts to accommodate Grassley and Snowe seemed to be working. Even DeParle thought so. In mid-July, the White House health reform chief met with Grassley. He seemed friendly, even encouraging. He mused about going back to his farm in Iowa, which DeParle took as a possible sign that he might retire rather than run for another term in 2016. That boded well in the sense that he might want to add bipartisan healthcare reform to his legacy.

DeParle also met with Snowe, with whom she and Fowler had formed something of a bond. Snowe, too, seemed on the verge.

Still, as the Senate's summer recess loomed, neither Republican had signed on to Baucus's bill. Obama met again with Baucus and Reid on July 23, 2009. "Sad mood," is how one White House staffer summarized everyone's exasperation in a journal entry.

A "BOMBSHELL" FROM THE BEAN COUNTERS

Despite the stall, the staff—and even Obama himself—were now heavily engaged in the nuances of the various drafts of bills circulating on Capitol Hill. A lot of the effort involved scrounging for money. Should they lower the subsidies being drafted in the Baucus bill? Could they raise the penalties on employers who didn't provide health insurance?

Sixty people from the White House and the Department of Health and Human Services attended a July 15, 2009, "innovation" meeting that Summers's and Orszag's people considered a bust, because it was mostly taken up with the HHS and Medicare people explaining why they couldn't make better use of data and didn't have the computer systems that could implement bundled payments.

The economic team also met with officials from the Justice Department and Federal Trade Commission to explore one of Zeke Emanuel's pet issues: better antitrust enforcement against hospitals that were gobbling up neighboring hospitals, doctors' practices, clinics, and laboratories and then raising prices in the less-competitive market. The regulators rebuffed them, saying this was a complicated problem that needed lots of further study before anything might be done. Besides, there was another Washington process obstacle in their way: meddling with antitrust laws would require the involvement and approval of the Senate Judiciary Committee and its turf-conscious chairman, Patrick Leahy of Vermont.

On July 17, the Congressional Budget Office announced what one of Obama's healthcare aides called "a bombshell," when he interrupted another of those meetings to report it. The CBO had just scored the House bill and declared that it would not result in any significant long-term healthcare savings.

Orszag, the former CBO director now running Obama's Office of Management and Budget, and Nancy-Ann DeParle "rushed up to Capitol Hill to reassure them that it would save money, but it's not really true," wrote a White House aide in a journal.

Orszag and Larry Summers and their staffs had been lobbying the House and Senate staffs to include something that they argued would be a real cost cutter: provisions that would allow Medicare to make decisions based on comparative effectiveness. But so far they had been rebuffed not only by the legislative staffs but by the White House healthcare policy people.

They were also pushing to have the status of an independent agency called MedPAC, which was already in place advising Medicare on cost savings, upgraded so that if costs increased more than a set amount in a given year, the agency's determinations would be binding. "MedPAC on steroids" was how they referred to it. This was basically the kind of independent control board that the Republicans and Democrats at Baucus's June 2008 summit had warmed to—and which they had said could be like the independent agency that decides which military bases to close.

But none of those cost savers had made it into the House bill, and the CBO had noticed.

Worse, the CBO did not score savings that might come from broad-brush reforms where specific metrics could not be predicted. It was one thing to predict that X number of people would have to pay this or that tax, or that a government agency could save X dollars if it moved to cut this or that category of costs. It was quite another to guess at what some broad change in policy might save or cost. Thus, all of the provisions in the bill encouraging bundled care in place of fee-for-service billing—and even giving the HHS secretary the right to require certain bundling programs for Medicare services after they had been successfully tested—had not been scored as savings.

Rahm Emanuel, Orszag, Valerie Jarrett, and Summers quickly convened a meeting with Treasury officials to deal with the CBO crisis. According to notes kept by one member of the staff, they all agreed that what *would* "score," and score big, would be a tax on the health insurance provided by employers to their workers. But Gene Sperling, a counselor to Treasury secretary Tim Geithner, objected that the tax would be "horrible," because it would "go after teachers, firemen, and other unions."

The press quickly picked up on the CBO report that the House version of reform would cost over a trillion dollars and be only partially offset by new taxes and unspecified cost savings. This was not the "budget neutrality"—the principle that offsets would cover all the costs—that Obama had repeatedly promised. That news piled on to pundit coverage of Baucus's stalled progress, which came on top of all the coverage speculating about backroom deals being negotiated with the drug companies and other industry sectors.

POSITIONING OBAMA BETWEEN
HEALTHCARE'S TWO "EVIL PLAYERS"

It added up to bad news from the White House polling operation. David Simas—the Axelrod aide now directing healthcare polling and messaging full-time—reported that approval ratings for reform were quickly dropping into negative territory.

Two economics aides—Summers deputy Jason Furman and Treasury's Gene Sperling—began working on a slimmed-down, fallback reform plan.

But Obama was still fixated on the big plan. "Why can't I explain that this is about costs and not just coverage?" Obama complained to his senior staff on July 28, 2009, during another meeting about bending the cost curve. "I'm a good communicator and did a prime-time news conference and still couldn't get through."

The reason, as one healthcare staff person put it in a journal entry, was that Obama was being pulled in two different directions: "Obama wants to cut costs, but really can't say it," because Simas's polling was telling him that the message had to be something else.

A fastidious dresser who had a habit of licking his fingers and then polishing his shoes with them, Simas, then thirty-nine, liked to boil his data down into stories that smacked of deep insights. The story here, he explained at a July 23 meeting, was not about costs, but about what he called the two "evil" players in healthcare: "insurance companies" and "government bureaucrats" whom the public fears want to stop them from getting the care they need. The "proven message" Simas told the healthcare team (both the policy and economic groups) at the meeting, could be summarized in a simple diagram he put on a whiteboard: On the far left side of a line were the insurance companies, whom he labeled "evil." On the far right side were the bureaucrats, whom he also labeled "evil." In the middle was Obama, who had to be portrayed as protecting the people from the two evils. Get that message across, Simas assured the group, and "we gain twenty points." On the other hand, if Obama is seen as one of the bureaucrats trying to cut costs, they would lose.

WORDS THAT WORK: "GOVERNMENT TAKEOVER"

Frank Luntz—the pollster who had convened the group of prominent Republicans the night of Obama's inauguration—had a different take on the same idea. While running a focus group in St. Louis following the January dinner, he heard an offhand comment from one of the participants that immediately energized him. "We don't want a government takeover of our healthcare," a woman in the group had said quietly, almost to herself.

"Government takeover." That was it. Luntz had made his reputation for being the master of, as he liked to put it, "words that work." He had coined "death tax" as a way for Republicans to describe taxes on wealthy people's estates. Now he had a new winner.

"Government takeover" would become the prime phrase he featured in a "words that work" memo he distributed to Republicans to use in fighting healthcare reform. Other phrases touted in his memo included "protect the sacred doctor-patient relationship" and "We will oppose any politician-run system that denies you the treatments you need when you need them."

Simas was right. Bureaucrats were regarded as evil. But if Luntz had his way, Obama was going to become the "evil" bureaucrat in chief. This label would stick, despite the fact that, from the Democrats' perspective, Obama's plan was the opposite of a government "takeover" of healthcare. Rather, it was all about the government, through premium subsidies, giving everyone money to buy healthcare from the same private insurers who would pay the same high prices to the same private drug companies, doctors, device makers, and "nonprofit" but profitable hospitals to provide it.

TARGETING THE NEW ENEMY

On July 29, 2009, Simas's messaging was ready for Obama to roll out at a "town hall" organized by the AARP, the powerful membership organization for people fifty years and older that was a key reform supporter.

The event was viewed in healthcare circles as likely to be pivotal in Obama's effort to reverse all the negative summer momentum, so much so that Karen Ignagni and her colleagues at the health insurance lobby she ran turned on a television to watch it live.

They did not like what they heard. Suddenly, the president was talking about "health *insurance* reform," not healthcare reform.

"The idea behind reform," Obama declared, "is: Number one, we reform the insurance companies so they can't take advantage of you.

Number two, that we provide you a place to go to purchase insurance that is secure, that isn't full of fine print." A public option would be included in the exchanges to compete with the private insurers, Obama added, taking a position that had not been hashed out in any of his White House meetings.

When it came to cutting costs, that, too, was going to come by taming the insurers. The high profits they make from administering certain Medicare programs would be cut, Obama explained, before retelling the incorrect story of his mother having been threatened with a denial of coverage because her insurer had decided her cancer was a preexisting condition. "That happens all across the country," he added. "We are going to put a stop to that." However, he promised, "If you have insurance that you like, then you will be able to keep that insurance."

Ignagni was upset although not surprised. "In politics, when things get tough, the best thing to do is to find a good enemy," she told her staff. "For the White House, that's now us."

"They definitely reorganized and seized on what they considered to be the most vulnerable player as their target," recalled Stephen Hemsley, the president and CEO of UnitedHealth Group, the country's largest health insurer. "If you look at our profit margins," he added, "it didn't make sense. We're the only industry in the healthcare sector that wants to advance their goals of cutting costs by making the system more transparent and efficient. But we are a good target."

Speaker Nancy Pelosi picked up on the message the next day, calling the insurance industry the "villains" in the fight for reform.

True, the insurers had not yet signed on the way Tauzin's pharmaceutical executives and the hospitals had, but they had squarely backed the basics of the Romneycare three-legged stool sooner and more vocally than any of the other industry players. How could they be expected to go further yet? All the core variables were still unresolved: how much more they could charge older people than younger consumers, how high the penalties would be for those who did not obey the mandate, what coverage would be required in the plans sold on the exchanges, or what preventive care would be required to be covered with no deductibles and no sharing of costs by the patients.

Nonetheless, the irony was that Ignagni's industry had the most to gain from the reform taking shape. They stood to get all those new customers that would now come into an individual market that was otherwise dying. Plus they would get the safety net being offered for their larger employer-based business by the requirement that employers would have to keep buying (or start buying) insurance for their workers.

They also had the most to lose if reform collapsed, for surely Obama would seek as a politically popular fallback a prohibition against excluding people with preexisting conditions that did not include the mandate that would come with broader reform.

That logic was so compelling that it seemed that the insurers might not have minded playing the role of the enemy, if that was what it took to get reform done. Or at least they didn't mind being dubbed the enemy until they could bargain for and get comfortable with all the unresolved variables they were worried about.

Meantime, the five big for-profit insurers—Aetna, Cigna, Humana, United, and WellPoint—hedged their bets. Following Obama's pivot to "insurance reform," they quietly agreed to contribute a total of $86 million to a U.S. Chamber of Commerce political action committee that would fund anti-reform ads if that became necessary. According to Princeton historian Paul Starr's book, *Remedy and Reaction,* the companies gave the money to Ignagni's AHIP, but she gave it to the Chamber because she did not want AHIP to run the fund and do the attack ads directly.

With the Chamber of Commerce involved, the healthcare industry now had a hat trick. A *Politico* survey of Washington, D.C., insiders asking who had the most effective lobbyists would later report that the top three lobbying teams were housed at PhRMA, at America's Health Insurance Plans, and at the Chamber of Commerce.

A RETAIL SALE AT THE SENATE

Following the launch of Obama's new insurance reform campaign everyone at the White House was digging in for a final push. They were monitoring what was going on in the Senate, where, for example,

they learned one afternoon that furious lobbying from the soda industry and retailers had convinced Baucus to take the soft drink tax off
the table.

It seemed like every day some senator or another added something
new to Baucus's working draft or took something out. Evan Bayh, the
Indiana Democrat, wanted the medical device tax reduced; some of
the device companies were headquartered in his state. Democrat Ben
Nelson of Nebraska wanted to make sure that the states, or at least his
state, paid no share of the cost of expanding Medicaid. Michael Bennet of Colorado and Barbara Mikulski of Maryland wanted something
added so that seasonal workers, even those working long hours during
the months they worked, would not be considered full-time employees for whom companies had to provide health insurance. Bennet was
concerned about Colorado ski resorts; Mikulski was looking out for
Maryland crabbers.

With every Democratic vote necessary to reach sixty, no one could
be ignored. It was a retail sale, one by one, requiring the Baucus draft
to grow every day, quickly becoming a monstrous document. "This
was healthcare, not some narrow subject," Fowler realized. "Everyone
had some personal policy priority and/or pet issue around healthcare."

Baucus, too, had priorities and pet issues, and they all made it into
his draft, including a provision to provide healthcare for people suffering from asbestosis. He had not forgotten his friend Lester Skramsted
or the people back in Libby, Montana.

And everyone, it seemed, had lobbyists. Unlike most big pieces of
legislation, where there is a clear divide between who's for it and who's
against it, the lobbying was splintered, covering a range of interests as
broad as an industry that on its own is larger than the economies of all
but five countries.

"The pressure was just so intense," recalled a woman who handled
healthcare for one of the Finance Committee Democrats. "And the
lobbyists were everywhere. The insurance lobby. The cancer patients'
lobby. The tanning bed lobby." (One proposal afoot was a tax on tanning salon revenues.) "The insulin lobby. The ambulance lobby. You
name it. And everyone was watching who we were talking to in the
halls."

STANDING TALL ON ALL FOURS AT THE WHITE HOUSE

The internal fights at the White House continued. Orszag and his team infuriated Lambrew by contradicting numbers she had prepared for a presentation to be given to the president detailing the revenues and costs of the various plans everyone was still considering.

On August 5, 2009, they focused on provisions for allowing the continuation—called grandfathering—of those insurance policies already out in the market that had annual limits on payouts or other coverage gaps that would not meet the reform law's new requirements. How long could people who had a policy like Emilia Gilbert's that covered only $2,500 of her $9,400 trip to the emergency room in Connecticut be allowed to keep these policies? What kinds of offending limits would be so bad as to require the policies to be withdrawn from the market immediately? In other words, they were wrestling with the exact issue that contradicted Obama's promise, repeated just a week earlier at the AARP town hall, that "if you like your insurance you can keep it."

Lambrew wanted no insurance policies to be grandfathered at all once the exchanges were launched. She hated the insurance companies, she told one meeting, and especially hated the insurers who sold those skimpy, often useless policies. Consumers needed to be protected. Period.

The same day, August 5, Rahm Emanuel reported, according to notes of a staffer, that he had had a "great meeting with the Gang of Six,"—the Baucus-led Senate group whose Republican members now included just Grassley and Snowe, with Enzi of Wyoming having dropped out. "But no fucking leaking," Emanuel warned his people.

Four days before, Emanuel had told the staff, according to the same staff member's notes, "Never does a man stand so tall as when he is on all fours kissing a congressman's ass." Now the chief of staff seemed unusually upbeat after having apparently stood tall with Grassley. He didn't want any leaks that might scare off the Iowa Republican.

Not even Emanuel could anticipate what Grassley and other members of Congress would find waiting when they arrived home for the August recess.

CHAPTER 10

THE TEA PARTY SUMMER,
"I'M FEELING LUCKY,"
AND "YOU LIE"

August–September 2009

I T BEGAN IN PHILADELPHIA ON AUGUST 11, 2009, WHEN THE CABLE and network news shows led with footage of Arlen Specter getting heckled at a town hall meeting. Specter, a courtly twenty-eight-year veteran of the Senate, seemed stunned. He had switched to the Democratic Party in April thereby supplying (with Al Franken of Minnesota, following a recount there), the critical sixtieth vote to overcome a potential filibuster. But that shouldn't have been a problem in Democratic Philadelphia, especially for Specter, who had begun his political career there.

What had inflamed the crowd was healthcare reform, which was now starting to be called Obamacare. The crowd had been organized by one of the Tea Party groups that had sprung up following Rick Santelli's CNBC rant in February. They were fed up, they proclaimed, with bailouts, crony capitalism, secret deals, and the government relentlessly trying to interfere with their lives. To them, Obamacare epitomized all that.

The next day, in Adel, Iowa, Chuck Grassley got booed off the stage by hecklers holding "You're fired" signs. Their principal complaint, too, was the purported government takeover of their healthcare.

Other Grassley town halls that day were more polite, but no less hostile. "I had seen some of this at a town hall I held in July," Grassley later recalled. "But this was different. Usually, about forty or fifty people showed up and we met in a library. Now there were three or four hundred, and we had to move the meeting out onto the lawn."

The veteran Iowa Republican promised that he would never vote for a public option because "government is a predator." That was a nuance lost on the crowd. The public option seemed like Washington jargon, a detail.

They were more concerned about the backroom deals that had by now gotten so much press, and about the kind of government intrusion that they thought healthcare reform threatened—particularly the "death panels" that former Republican vice presidential candidate Sarah Palin had been saying were part of the proposed law.

Indeed, "death panels" had become the watchword of that government takeover.

To the extent that Palin was referring to anything in the proposed law remotely resembling death panels, she might have been talking about provisions for independent medical panels to report on the comparative effectiveness of one treatment or drug compared to another—the provisions that the White House economic team thought were so weak in the drafts they had seen so far as to be toothless. Or she might have been thinking about the independent panel that the Obama economic advisers had so far fruitlessly tried to strengthen so that in the event of intolerable medical inflation it could recommend spending cuts that Congress would have to vote up or down. In other words, it was the arrangement akin to the one used to close military bases that Grassley had supported at Baucus's summit.

Or Palin could have been trying to pin the death panel label somehow onto a provision that simply allowed Medicare to code for billing purposes the time a doctor spent counseling a patient about hospice care—a provision Grassley had already convinced Baucus to delete because just the idea of doctors talking to patients about preparing for the end of life might scare people.

Nancy-Ann DeParle, who had been deeply involved in the White House courtship of Grassley, turned on the TV on the evening of August 12 to see Grassley respond to a question by telling the crowd that he, too, was against the Obamacare death panels, or, as he put it, "a government program that determines you're gonna pull the plug on Grandma." He did not mention that there was nothing in any pending bill that would pull any plugs on anyone's grandma.

By the time Grassley got back to Washington in September, he had declared on Fox News that he was against another element of the "government takeover"—the individual mandate that he, like Romney, had celebrated as an essential element of individual responsibility. "The town halls helped me to realize that there were constitutional issues with the mandate," is how Grassley later explained it to me. "It's one thing for a state to require you to buy something. But it's another for the federal government to."

There was predictable overplay of what was going on by the media. Covering town halls that were not raucous, which was most of them, wasn't good television. Colorado Democrat and Finance Committee member Michael Bennet, a moderate former businessman facing a tough election fight, used an elaborate PowerPoint to walk his constituents through the basics of the pending reform proposal. Bennet got lots of questions, some hostile, but there were no eruptions. And no video coverage.

Yet politicians of every stripe were getting the message. On the Sunday talk shows on August 16 White House officials began to waver on the public option, which caused former Vermont Democratic governor and presidential candidate (and physician) Howard Dean to squawk. Without the public option, Dean said, the proposed law wasn't worth passing.

On August 18, Grassley told Baucus and DeParle that he was bowing out of the negotiations. Even if the Democrats accepted every change he wanted he could still not support a bill, he said. By now no one on the reform side was surprised.

Obamacare was becoming a political third rail.

During August conference calls, the drug company executives and Karen Ignagni's insurance industry bosses signaled that they had gotten the message, too. PhRMA's board of drugmaker CEOs toyed with pulling out of their deal. The insurers gave the go-ahead for the

Chamber of Commerce to start funding those opposition ads. In both camps, the media coverage of the town halls was hitting home. A view was forming that maybe the political climate had changed so much that, once again, healthcare reform could be killed altogether. Maybe they wouldn't have to make any compromises to avoid the more dire reform provisions, the threat of which had brought them to the table in the first place.

"WHAT'S MY NAME?"

Obama met with his senior staff just before departing to Martha's Vineyard for his end of August vacation. Some were shell-shocked by the town hall clips they had seen during what the reformers would soon be calling the Tea Party summer. They counseled that the effort was lost, that they should try to craft a radically slimmed-down package and move on to other domestic policy issues. Jarrett said nothing, as was her habit in large meetings with the president.

Phil Schiliro, who was in charge of congressional relations, wasn't so sure the game was over. Schiliro prided himself on being able to give the president definitive predictions based on being able to see a clear path to getting a bill over the finish line. In this case he certainly couldn't do that. However, he could see a path that might work. As the discussion among Obama's top advisers continued, Schiliro interrupted.

"Mr. President," he said. "Do you feel lucky?"

"Phil, where are we?" Obama answered.

"In the Oval Office, sir."

"Phil, what's my name?" Obama continued.

"President Obama, sir," Schiliro replied.

"Of course, I'm feeling lucky," Obama answered.

"Well, if we get lucky, there may still be a way we can do this," Schiliro continued.

Obama insisted that they keep at it.

President Obama's edict when he took office was that, with some exceptions, his administration was not going to hire lobbyists. This upset the usual way that Schiliro, a veteran congressional aide, would have staffed up his White House congressional liaison shop. Traditionally, this was done by hiring lobbyists, who were typically former congressional staffers. Now, because of Obama's edict against hiring lobbyists, Schiliro's only choice had been to hire *current* staffers.

That turned out to be a blessing in disguise, Schiliro later told me. He had been able to recruit some of the most effective, senior people from Capitol Hill, eager to join the team of a newly elected president who projected so much promise. Thus, Schiliro now had a group that was much closer in touch with the legislators they had to herd to the finish line.

Valerie Jarrett went into high gear, too, something she did not receive much credit for in the press. Since the early days of the administration she had been helping Schiliro with his and his team's incessant outreach to legislators, interest groups, the business community (with mixed results), and anyone else who could help the president's health reform cause.

Like Schiliro, Jarrett advised the president that they could survive the Tea Party summer. Obama had survived much worse to get to that desk in the Oval Office, she reminded him.

Now, Jarrett redoubled her efforts, while serving, Schiliro thought, as someone who would buck up the president whenever the rest of the staff suggested he stand down. It wasn't that Obama needed bucking up; he never seemed to waver. But it was nice, Schiliro thought, that if he ever started having second thoughts Jarrett would be up there in the White House living quarters that evening to talk him out of it.

Wall Street thought there was a path, too. A Goldman Sachs analyst speculated in an August 25 report that healthcare reform was still possible and would boost the earnings of the for-profit hospitals, even with the hospitals' $155 billion in givebacks. Those givebacks "do not look onerous," the analyst reminded his clients.

The next day Zeke Emanuel was confident enough that he began looking ahead to when the law would be on the books. On August 26, 2009, he told his brother, who had asked him to start working on a scaled-back plan to extend coverage only to more children and other special populations, that he wanted Rahm to make him the head of CMS—the agency inside the Department of Health and Human Services that would implement the big healthcare reform law if it passed. "I can't make you anything, you're my brother," Rahm Emanuel yelled at him. "Forget it."

Besides, the chief of staff added, "Obama and Valerie love Nancy-Ann [DeParle]." If someone was going to run Obamacare it was going to be her.

Undeterred, Zeke Emanuel began drafting a memo outlining what he would do if put in charge.

"WHAT MY GRANDPA CALLED THE CAUSE OF HIS LIFE"

The day before, August 25, 2009, Ted Kennedy died.

At the Boston memorial service for Kennedy, Obama eulogized him as a man who "Through his own suffering . . . became more alive to the plight and suffering of others—the sick child who could not see a doctor."

One of Kennedy's grandchildren cited "what my grandpa called the cause of his life . . . that every American will have decent quality healthcare as a fundamental right and not a privilege."

After the service, which took place during a furious rainstorm and was attended by a who's who of American politics, Obama got first-hand exposure to a relatively tangential issue that threatened to complicate the law he and Kennedy championed. One of the Catholic bishops in attendance bent his ear about abortion: The president risked the opposition of the church (and, by inference, legislators, particularly conservative Democrats in the House) if he didn't make sure that no one got subsidized premiums to buy insurance that included coverage for abortions. There was even, he was told, strong opposition to insurance that paid for birth control.

Yet one of Obama's favorite stump lines had been his promise that insurance reform would mean that women no longer paid higher premiums than men—a difference that was largely attributed to the insurers' desire to account for the additional expense risk that women posed because they could become pregnant and accumulate bills for family planning, childbirth, or, in some cases, abortion.

PLAYING THE CBO GAME

September 2, 2009, brought more evidence of the Obama team's desperation. It involved something called the SGR, one of those only-in-Washington acronyms. It stood for "sustainable growth rate" and was a monument to D.C. dysfunction.

In 1997, Congress had become concerned about the exploding costs of Medicare, and decided that the best way to do something about it was to go after doctors, who made more money the more services they provided and billed for—the fee-for-service problem that Orszag was obsessed with.

Under fee-for-service, Medicare had established "relative value units," which specified how much a doctor would be paid for different categories of care, from a routine office visit to brain surgery. So to hold down Medicare expense growth, Congress passed a law that stipulated that if, based on the prior year's Medicare expenses, Medicare's costs were projected to increase at a rate exceeding the percentage increase in the gross domestic product—or a "sustainable growth rate"—then the fee associated with every relative value unit would be cut proportionately to make up for the overage. If, for example, Medicare inflation exceeded the growth in gross domestic profit by 2 percent, every relative value unit (how much the doctor would be paid for a given treatment) would be reduced by 2 percent.

In other words, doctors—whose incomes had never increased during the recent decades of the healthcare boom the way earnings for hospital administrators, drug executives, or CT scan equipment salesmen had—were assumed to be the prime drivers of costs, and they would, therefore, have to pay for driving them too high.

If you are having trouble following the logic, it's because there is no logic. Even assuming that a doctor is engaging in a fee-generating activity to enrich himself and not to help a patient, the idea that any one of the 700,000 American physicians would cut his own fee-generating activities for fear that his 1/700,000 contribution to Medicare's doctor bills would result in a cut in that value unit for him and all other doctors is absurd. If anything, a doctor who was worried that his fees for each service might be cut would be motivated to bill for more services in order to get himself back to even.

The scheme, of course, didn't work. Medical inflation continued to outpace growth in the gross domestic product. That's why every year there would be news stories about an emergency "doc fix" on Capitol Hill, in which Congress would relent and restore the money to the relative value unit so that doctors' fees from Medicare weren't cut to the point where they would be so low as to drive physicians out of business or force them to stop treating seniors on Medicare.

For years, this annual doc fix fire drill had generally kept the doctors' payments from being reduced, typically freezing them with little or no upticks for inflation.

In return for getting support for Obamacare from doctors and their main trade group, the American Medical Association, the Obama administration, Kennedy's staff, and Baucus's staff had all promised the AMA that a permanent doc fix would be included in the healthcare reform law. No longer would doctors have to worry about last-minute congressional action to save their livelihoods.

However, now, on September 2, with Obamacare in such trouble, the Baucus people and DeParle's White House team had agreed that they would leave the doc fix out of the bill. Why? Because the Congressional Budget Office had scored its cost at $200 billion over ten years. Jettisoning it would instantly bring healthcare reform $200 billion closer to the deficit neutrality they had promised. They would tell the doctors they would do a permanent fix in a separate bill, something Washington had failed to do for more than fifteen years. Sure, the CBO would still score that separate bill at $200 billion if and when such a bill was drafted, but that wouldn't count against Obamacare.

That decision was emblematic of two important dynamics.

First, the doctors—the players in the healthcare economy who, with nurses, actually provide healthcare—had seen their influence evaporate compared to the big-money industry stakeholders such as the drug companies, insurers, and hospitals. As a result, they could be trifled with in a way that would have been unimaginable in the Truman era, when they had almost single-handedly torpedoed reform. They just didn't have that clout any more.

Frantic emails from AMA lobbyists to the White House when the AMA got wind of the switch were shrugged off. The AMA was already on record supporting the reform plan because of the coverage it would give to so many millions of Americans. They couldn't be seen as changing positions for a reason related to money. They had to settle for the promise that they would get this permanent fix in in a separate bill.

Second, the doc fix gambit made it clear that the Congressional Budget Office scoring process was more a game to be played than it was a precise measuring device to be read like a thermometer.

Every start-up enterprise has to make projections and get them validated by outside parties. As someone who has started several businesses (some that succeeded, others that have failed), I have made countless projections of costs and revenues for potential investors to review. As the guy seeking the money to start the business, I am naturally optimistic. Otherwise, why would I want to do it?

It's the job of the potential investors to review those projections—in effect, to "score" them in CBO parlance—after which they typically come up with a best case, a worst case, and a case in the middle.

A government enterprise is different. First, those designing the enterprise don't present, or score, anything. They just give the package of provisions in the proposed law to the CBO—a congressionally established group of nonpartisan, independent economists and analysts—to figure it all out. Someone vetting an investment for a private equity firm would consult broadly around the industry looking for clues about the projections that, again, the entrepreneur would have presented. CBO's turf-conscious economists treasure their independence and work wholly on their own.

The projections CBO had to make regarding the Obamacare enterprise involved three buckets of money.

First, CBO had to figure out what everything in the proposal—such as the subsidies for people to buy insurance or the cost of setting up the insurance exchanges—would cost.

Second, how much government money could be saved by the reform measures in the program, such as Medicare reducing its payments to hospitals or to drug companies?

Third, how much could be brought in from new fees, taxes, or penalties, such as the new tax on drug company revenues, or the penalties to be paid by individuals who ignored the mandate to buy insurance?

Many of these variables interacted; a higher penalty for ignoring the mandate would bring in more money, but would also attract more people to the exchanges where they would require more subsidies.

Baucus and the White House team were focused on one thing when it came to the CBO: Would the sum of the second and third buckets—savings and new revenues—equal the first bucket of costs and, therefore, make the enterprise budget neutral?

Scoping out how the CBO would deal with all this was easier than usual in this case because the Democrats in the Senate and at the White House had enlisted Jonathan Gruber as a consultant to try to use his black box to project the CBO's black box. Jeffrey Liebman, a Harvard professor now at Orszag's White House Office of Management and Budget, developed his own shadow model. Moreover, when he ran the CBO, Orszag had had the agency score some hypothetical reforms that were now part of the bill being drafted.

So the reformers were able to make a lot of good guesses about where the CBO would come out. But they were only guesses, and they were often wrong. The CBO's scoring results were unpredictable and often maddening to the staffers and legislators on the receiving end of its work.

Sometimes the frustration came because the CBO worked on its own schedule with its own inexplicable priorities. At times during the summer of 2009 the Senate staffs would be in the midst of a heated debate over some key provision, waiting desperately to get the CBO's score of how much the overall numbers would be changed by a tweak of some proposed tax rate or in the penalty to be paid by employers who didn't provide insurance. But the CBO would come back instead with a score of some change they had long since stopped caring about.

Other times, the scores just seemed wildly off, or a revision would emerge from the CBO staff (often in a matter-of-fact heads-up email to someone on the congressional staff) that turned a positive score into a negative one.

Most of the time, the CBO numbers seemed to err on the conservative side. In part this was because—as the White House people had been reminded when their proposals for broad but untested changes (such as bundled payments) were scored at near zero—the CBO wouldn't attach much of a positive score to something where there was not sufficient analogous data to back it up. Put differently, the CBO would have had trouble scoring Google's ad revenues over its first ten years from something called an Internet search, because it would have had no precedents to compare it to. So its default score would have been zero or something close to that.

Moreover, the numbers crunchers at the CBO seemed to prefer that whatever mistakes they made would be mistakes that projected that some initiative would cost more than it might or that some tax or fee would bring in less than it might. That way, if they ended up being wrong, it would be good news for the country's bottom line.

That, too, was not how real-world projections were done. True, no business wanted to miss its targets. But if every investor habitually projected costs too high or revenue too low, there would be no investments.

Nonetheless, the other extraordinary thing about the CBO was that its scores were accepted as the last word by everyone. The experts drafting the law might complain to the point of hysteria, yet it did no good. The CBO score was *the* score.

Accordingly, the CBO process was seen as something not to respect but, as with the decision to put the doc fix aside while still promising it as part of reform, to game as best one could. In short, CBO was an only-in-Washington institution—an independent body whose only virtue was its independence. Which meant not only freedom from political influence but also freedom from having to do its job the way people in the real world did.

THE DEMOCRATS AND THE TRIAL LAWYERS

In the same meeting in which the White House staff decided to take the doc fix out of the bill, they discussed another issue that the doctors cared about: medical malpractice tort reform.

Like many healthcare and legal policy analysts, the economic team believed that trial lawyers were abusing the courts by suing doctors too often for bad outcomes rather than bad treatment. Making it harder for doctors to be sued successfully would cut spending because it would lessen the practice of defensive medicine.

Doctors would no longer have the reason, or the excuse, to order extra blood tests or MRIs or CT scans as a way of demonstrating in a courtroom that they did everything they could to prevent whatever adverse event they might be sued for. For example, doctors in the United States order 70 percent more CT scans per capita than German doctors do (and the bill per test is four times as high). And emergency room doctors will tell you that it has become routine to order one or more CT scans for almost any complaint—either because the tests are so profitable or because they are practicing defensive medicine, or both.

Some healthcare experts estimated that malpractice reform could save as much as $70 billion a year (5 percent of hospital and doctor expense). Even a 1 percent cut in doctor and hospital costs would yield $14 billion in savings or $140 billion over ten years, including about $40 billion in federal Medicare and Medicaid cost savings that the CBO could score.

The economic team was not the only constituency pushing tort reform. Initiatives designed to curb meritless suits against physicians and hospitals had also been promised to the American Medical Association in return for the doctors' support.

Yet now, someone on the domestic policy team reported in the September 2 meeting, the president had been told by Harry Reid that Reid would not bring any bill up for a vote that included tort reform. Pretty much every Washington Democrat knew that Reid, himself a former lawyer, was forever mindful of the fact that trial lawyers (along with the unions) were the most reliable source of big-money support for his Senate Democrats.

The White House group decided that the best they could do was ask the president to talk to Reid and try to persuade him at least to include some kind of test programs. They were not hopeful.

"THE CHARACTER OF OUR COUNTRY"

When Ted Kennedy was told in May that he had little time left, he wrote a letter to Obama and asked his wife to give it to the president after he died. On September 3, 2009, Vicki Kennedy fulfilled his wish.

The letter might surprise those who are cynical about politicians or liberals or Kennedys in particular—who think they don't care about anything except their careers. Written when Kennedy had zero to gain, when he wasn't running for anything and had only months to live, it began by thanking the president "for your repeated personal kindnesses to me." Then, it was all about healthcare:

> When I thought of all the years, all the battles, and all the memories of my long public life, I felt confident in these closing days that while I will not be there when it happens, you will be the president who at long last signs into law the health care reform that is the great unfinished business of our society. For me, this cause stretched across decades; it has been disappointed, but never finally defeated. It was the cause of my life. And in the past year, the prospect of victory sustained me—and the work of achieving it summoned my energy and determination.
>
> There will be struggles—there always have been—and they are already underway again. But as we moved forward in these months, I learned that you will not yield to calls to retreat . . . I saw your conviction that the time is now and witnessed your unwavering commitment and understanding that health care is a decisive issue for our future prosperity. But you have also reminded all of us that it concerns more than material things; that what we face is above all a moral issue; that at stake are not just the details of policy, but fundamental principles of social justice and the character of our country. . . .
>
> And while I will not see the victory, I was able to look forward and know that we will—yes, we will—fulfill the promise of health care in America as a right and not a privilege. . . .
>
> So, I wrote this to thank you one last time as a friend—and

to stand with you one last time for change and the America we can become.

Obama was so moved by the letter that, with Vicki Kennedy's permission, he decided to use quotes from it as the centerpiece of a nationally televised speech to Congress on the evening of September 9 that he hoped would counter the storm from the Tea Party summer.

"What we have . . . seen in these last months is the same partisan spectacle that only hardens the disdain many Americans have toward their own government," Obama told Congress. "Instead of honest debate, we have seen scare tactics. . . . And out of this blizzard of charges and counter-charges, confusion has reigned."

Obama then walked America through his plan, spelling out what it would do and what it would not do, including be a "government takeover." And then he brought up "our beloved friend and colleague, Ted Kennedy," quoting liberally from Kennedy's letter, and playing off of Kennedy's description of reform as being about "the character of our country."

"I've thought about that phrase quite a bit in recent days—the character of our country," Obama said. "One of the unique and wonderful things about America has always been our self-reliance, our rugged individualism, our fierce defense of freedom, and our healthy skepticism of government. And figuring out the appropriate size and role of government has always been a source of rigorous and, yes, sometimes angry debate.

"For some of Ted Kennedy's critics," Obama continued, "his brand of liberalism represented an affront to American liberty. In their mind, his passion for universal health care was nothing more than a passion for big government. But those of us who knew Teddy and worked with him here—people of both parties—know that what drove him was something more. . . . His friend Chuck Grassley knows that. They worked together to provide health care to children with disabilities.

"On issues like these," Obama concluded, "Ted Kennedy's passion was born not of some rigid ideology, but of his own experience. It was the experience of having two children stricken with cancer. He never forgot the sheer terror and helplessness that any parent feels when a child is badly sick. And he was able to imagine what it must be like for those without insurance; what it would be like to have to say to a wife or a child or an aging parent—there is something that could make you better, but I just can't afford it. That large-heartedness— that concern and regard for the plight of others—is not a partisan feeling. It is not a Republican or a Democratic feeling. It, too, is part of the American character—our ability to stand in other people's shoes."

Polls following the September 9 prime-time speech to Congress were positive. And Schiliro and his congressional liaison team thought it had worked to reenergize Obama's immediate audience of Capitol Hill Democrats, especially in the House.

However, what received most of the attention was an outburst from South Carolina Republican congressman Joe Wilson, who seemed unmoved by Obama's celebration of Ted Kennedy's "large-heartedness."

"You lie," Wilson shouted when the president promised that un-documented aliens would not be covered by Obamacare. Obama was telling the truth. No version of the pending draft covered people who were in the country illegally. Nonetheless, Wilson's outburst hogged much of the attention.

What got almost no attention was something else Obama said— that "the plan I'm proposing will cost around $900 billion over ten years." That was $200 billion to $300 billion less than the CBO was estimating would be the outlays (before offsetting savings and taxes designed to make it deficit neutral) for the House and Senate plans being debated, and $300 billion less than the plan Obama had chosen from the PowerPoint options given to him in April. Instead, it was the reduced back-of-the-envelope estimate that Obama had instructed the domestic policy and economic teams to come up with during the late spring and summer—which was the ongoing cause of all those tense, contentious White House meetings since the spring, in which they debated changes in various subsidy formulas and other aspects of the package. It was also why the doc fix had been thrown overboard.

There was something even more surprising to those working in the weeds on the various proposals. Obama had referred to "my plan."

What plan? The White House had never issued a proposal, continuing to prefer, as Obama had told the staff at the April 30 meeting, "to give the House and Senate the space they need."

CHAPTER 11

SNOW JOBS, POISON PILLS,
AND BOTOX

September–December 2009

A WEEK AFTER OBAMA'S SPEECH TO CONGRESS, ON SEPTEMBER 16, 2009, Baucus gave up on a bipartisan bill. He had sent Republicans Grassley and Snowe a final version of the 223-page draft that Fowler and her team had assembled summarizing his proposal. After hearing nothing back from them, he circulated the draft to the entire Finance Committee as his own.

Baucus's proposed law was Romneycare, USA:

- The three-legged stool: an individual mandate, no exclusion of preexisting conditions, and subsidies for buying insurance for those who needed it.
- Online exchanges for people to compare insurers' offerings before deciding what to buy.
- The same Romneycare arrangement of insurance offerings to be sold on those exchanges: The least expensive plan would be the "bronze plan," offering the minimum people would have to buy to fulfill the mandate. More expensive "silver," "gold," and "platinum" options would provide more generous protection.

Subsidies for people to buy the mandated insurance would be pegged to the cost of the second lowest priced silver plan offered.

People with incomes at 100 percent of the official poverty line (about $24,000 for a family of four) and up to 300 percent above it (about $72,000) would not have to pay above certain percentages of their incomes for that silver plan. Any higher costs would be picked up by the government subsidies. (For now, Baucus had decided to be less generous than the Obama people, who wanted subsidies for people earning up to 400 percent of poverty.) Buyers on the exchanges could use the same subsidies calculated based on the silver plan's cost to buy the cheaper bronze plan or the more expensive gold and platinum packages.

Those living below the poverty line would be given Medicaid for free.

From the left, Baucus's plan drew criticism because the subsidies seemed so stingy that premiums would be unaffordable for many families, especially those in the lower middle class. In fact, the subsidies were less generous than those in the Romneycare plan. On this core provision, Baucus had come out on the right of the Republican governor.

The left was also unhappy because, unlike the House proposals and the one already voted on by the Senate HELP Committee, Baucus's draft had no provision for a public option—the government-run insurer to compete with the private insurers. Instead, the government would help finance nonprofit cooperatives to sell insurance, although few experts saw that as a meaningful alternative.

From the right, of course, Baucus's plan was attacked as a government takeover.

The Obama staff knew Baucus's draft was coming but did not know all the details until just before he released it.

TAXING BROKERS AND BOTOX

The main concern at the White House was revenue.

True to his white paper pronouncement Baucus had included a tax on employer-paid health insurance that was the largest single contributor (worth as much as $300 billion over ten years) to the new revenues his plan projected in order to achieve budget neutrality.

Obama's staff had hotly debated this tax since the summer. The White House health reform and political staffs were against it because of the political flack it would get from the unions. That would surely cause some Democrats to break away, endangering not only one or more of the crucial votes in the Senate but even the Democratic majority in the House.

More than that, as senior political adviser David Axelrod had constantly reminded the group, Obama had spent tens of millions of dollars on campaign ads attacking John McCain for wanting to remove the tax exclusion on workers' healthcare benefits. Axelrod had even prepared a brief video reel of the ads to show at one meeting.

Predictably, the economic team had a different view. This was a huge revenue raiser, and it might be the only way to pay for reform. In July, they had even invited three outside economists, whom Emanuel and Kocher carefully rehearsed, to come in and explain to the president why it was a good idea.

The numbers had been tempting, but by the summer the policy and political teams had prevailed. Obama had attacked the idea on the campaign trail and promised not to raise any taxes on the middle class at all. He was not going to go back on that.

With Obama poised to oppose Baucus's biggest money raiser, his staff and senior Treasury Department officials began in September to go over a new list of taxes or penalties to take its place. Summers suggested taxing health insurance brokers' fees. Someone else suggested a tax on Botox and other plastic surgery expenses. A tax on diagnostic tests such as MRIs or CT scans was talked about for a while. Only the plastic surgery tax would make it into the draft, but just the fact that all of them were put on the table and discussed with staffers on Capitol Hill set off fire alarms for whole new squadrons of lobbyists. Even a highly technical suggestion for Medicare to save money by changing the way it paid for kidney dialysis, which was worth "only" a few billion dollars over ten years, got David Beier of Amgen and his team fired up, because Amgen would have been on the receiving end of that one.

At one September 22 meeting, Gene Sperling from Treasury suggested six other revisions to Baucus's draft that could raise money. But, recorded one of the participants who was taking notes, "NAD"— Nancy-Ann DeParle, who, with Jeanne Lambrew, was the main communications link to the Baucus staff—"was inattentive."

The same day, DeParle got wind of a plan by Republicans to torpedo the bill by backing a more radical reform being proposed by Oregon Democrat Ron Wyden, a Senate Finance Committee member. Wyden had made healthcare reform a pet issue, but his views about it differed significantly from Baucus's. He was going to propose an amendment in the committee that would allow employers to stop providing insurance and instead give tax-free vouchers to their employees to buy insurance on the new exchanges. It was a variation on the old McCain plan that the unions and many Democrats in the Senate would hate. All the Republicans and some Democrats were likely to vote for it, meaning it could become a poison pill making the overall law intolerable to most Democrats.

"Reid is going to call Wyden and tell him to go to hell," is how the notes taken by one of DeParle's colleagues described the strategy for sidelining Wyden.

ON SEPTEMBER 22, 2009, the Senate Finance Committee started its debate on Baucus's draft.

Tony Clapsis, the young refugee from Lehman Brothers who had done the math that helped win concessions from the drug and hospital industries, was amazed and impressed that for four weeks the senators waded so deeply into the details.

True, they often focused on heavily lobbied constituent issues, such as whether Blanche Lincoln's tanning bed manufacturers back home in Arkansas would face a new tax, or whether Michael Bennet's ski resorts in Colorado would have to count seasonal waiters and instructors as full-time employees.

But they dug into nuances related to the heavier policy issues, too. Barbara Mikulski of Maryland was deep into the kinds of preventive care that would have to be included for free in the basic insurance package. She, along with several other senators, mostly women, demanded, for example, that the Senate should ignore a just-issued report questioning the advisability of women getting mammograms before reaching age fifty. Mammograms for women over forty were kept in, despite the new evidence that the tests at that age produced so many false positives, compared to lifesaving diagnoses, that they caused more expense, more needless treatment, and more scares than they were worth.

These were the kinds of costly compromises with medical science that drove doctor-reformers like Zeke Emanuel crazy. Of course, the lobby for the companies that made mammography equipment got into that fight, too.

The senators grilled Fowler and the staff over thousands of details, and proposed 564 amendments, of which 135 were voted on.

The White House healthcare policy and economic teams were constantly sending in critiques of the amendments and even new ideas. Zeke Emanuel made a list of six new cost-cutting possibilities. They went nowhere.

A public option amendment proposed by New York Democrat Charles Schumer was voted down, with three Democrats, including Baucus, voting no. A second version was also rejected.

But on October 14, the night before the final vote, Schumer told Baucus that he and the still-agonizing Olympia Snowe wanted to offer another amendment related to the mandate. Baucus, making a joke of how everyone was still romancing Snowe, interrupted. "You mean the Snowe-Schumer amendment, right, Chuck?" he said to Schumer, a notorious show stealer.

Their amendment passed. That panicked Gruber and everyone else who thought the individual mandate was pivotal. Under the amendment, there would be no penalty at all in the first year and the penalty would be only $95 in the second year, and go up slowly after that. "You've got to tell them to vote no," Gruber pleaded to Fowler and anyone else on Capitol Hill or at the White House he could reach.

"No senator is going to vote against a lower penalty in a straight-up vote," one staff person told him. "Schumer knows that."

Schumer's strategy was simple. From the start he had been skeptical about going for sweeping reform amid the economic crisis, and he was worried, in the aftermath of the Tea Party summer, that health-care reform was going to hurt Democrats in the upcoming 2010 congressional elections. If Obama and Baucus, to whom he was not close, were going to insist on pushing ahead, he would at least make sure the bill had the mildest penalties possible and the most goodies (which is why he had also pushed for more generous subsidies and a broad package of free preventive care). For Schumer, keeping the penalties low, not to mention not having them even kick in until after the 2014 midterm elections, was a no-brainer.

So, too, was the issue of who would get subsidies, something that Schumer and Senator Bob Menendez of New Jersey were focused on. Baucus's idea to limit them to people making up to 300 percent above the nationally measured poverty level might make sense in Montana and other relatively low-cost, low income states. However, 300 percent of poverty for a family of four was only about $72,000. A family earning at that level in New York or New Jersey had to have a subsidy. Baucus agreed to raise the ceiling to 400 percent.

TAXING THE RICH—QUIETLY

During the nearly four-week markup, staffs from the White House, Treasury Department, and Finance Committee had been in constant touch about how to deal with the Obama administration's opposition to getting rid of the tax exclusion on employee health insurance benefits because it violated the president's campaign promise. They had finally come up with a solution that was in part suggested by Massachusetts senator John Kerry. They would not tax all benefits, just the value of insurance benefits that were overly generous. And the employers would pay, not the workers.

Businesses would pay a 40 percent excise tax on any premiums it paid on behalf of its workers exceeding $27,500 per family. It was called a "Cadillac tax." However, a $27,500 premium was likely to be more Buick than Cadillac. The cost of insuring workers, especially for employers subject to contracts negotiated by strong unions, was likely to exceed the benchmark in the coming years.

The Cadillac tax was a way to skirt Obama's promise not to raise taxes for the middle class because the employers, not the workers, would pay it. Yet the more union leaders heard about it, the more they complained, knowing it would encourage employers to cut back on generous benefits and force employees to pick up more of the cost of their insurance.

To the economic team, though not to the political advisers in the White House, that was a significant plus: Businesses would put more pressure on insurers to design less expensive packages, and employees might be more careful about what they spent because their deductibles and co-insurance payments would be driven higher. All of that could moderate the rising cost curve.

The expected revenue impact—estimated at about $110 billion over ten years—was far less than the $300 billion Baucus's more direct plan had originally been projected to raise. But the Finance Committee staff and the Obama administration came up with a solution that filled that new gap, plus all the old gaps they had been dealing with. They bulked up on a plan to tax high earners, though not with an income tax boost. More than $300 billion would be raised by a .9 percent Medicare payroll tax on families earning more than $250,000, plus a new 3.8 percent tax on income from capital gains, dividends, and other non-job-related income. It was a hefty tax increase. However, because it did not tamper with basic income tax rates it did not attract nearly as much attention.

At 2 A.M. on October 16, 2009, the Finance Committee voted 14–9 in favor of the marked-up bill. Olympia Snowe joined the Democrats in voting yes. "I thought the committee process had been really great," she later explained. "I was hoping for the same open, full debate on the Senate floor."

MORE CBO GAMES

The CBO scored the bill as deficit neutral. Pivotal in that calculation was yet another element of how unreal the CBO process was. It involved an issue that had been an obsession of Ted Kennedy's: providing a safety net for the elderly who could not afford nursing home care or at-home assisted living.

Medicare does not provide for long-term assisted living. Every year as people continued to live longer, they were forced to spend or shed assets until they were so poor that they could qualify for the bare-bones support that Medicaid offers to the poor. Kennedy's father had needed care for eight years following a debilitating stroke in 1961. His mother had suffered a stroke, too, and was in a wheelchair for nine-teen years until her death. Of course, his family was wealthy enough to pay for all of that. However, Kennedy had been working on the issue for decades.

Now, under a provision Kennedy championed called the CLASS Act (Community Living Assistance Service and Supports), Americans would be able to buy insurance at a young age that would go into a fund to provide them assisted living later on. It was to be a govern-ment program, but Kennedy had had to accept as a compromise that it would be voluntary. That meant that people could self-select—the exact danger that proponents of an insurance mandate feared in fash-ioning the broader health insurance plan. To counter those fears, the secretary of health and human services would be required to certify that the plan would be fully self-supporting before it could be imple-mented.

But there was this CBO catch: Because the insurance premiums would have to be paid in for five years before anyone could get any benefits paid, and because no benefits could be paid until someone had a "qualified disability," CLASS was certain to take in much more money in its first ten years than it would pay out, even if it was des-tined to become insolvent. So despite the fact that CLASS was meant not to be a tax or a revenue raiser in any way, under CBO's accounting rules it was going to be a big profit maker in the ten-year period from 2010 to 2020. In fact, CBO gave it a positive score of $70 billion.

Within two years, on October 11, 2011, CLASS would be "indefi-nitely suspended" by Kathleen Sebelius, then secretary of health and human services, before it had even been launched, because it was deemed financially unsustainable. Yet in 2009, it was the CBO score—a positive $70 billion—that counted.

"The whole thing was a fiscal masquerade," Olympia Snowe would later tell me. "It was obvious."

On October 7, 2009, CBO blessed the Finance Committee bill while the senators were still completing their markup, scoring it not only as deficit neutral but as projected to produce a slight decrease in the deficit over the ten-year period.

THE PRESIDENT GETS A "SNOW JOB"

"Larry said Peter [Orszag] had misled POTUS [President Obama] on the intensity of the cost controls," a member of Obama's staff wrote in a diary. The staffer was describing an October 20, 2009, memo that National Economic Council head Larry Summers had written to Rahm Emanuel about what budget office director Peter Orszag had told Obama about how the Finance Committee bill would affect overall healthcare spending. "Peter gave the President a snow job."

"Larry was right," the staffer later explained to me. "Peter overstated to the president how great the bill was on costs and Larry called him on it."

By now the economic team was growing so frustrated that they were fighting not just with the healthcare reform policy people, such as DeParle and Lambrew, but among themselves. And the more they examined the Senate bill the angrier they got. They had gotten in a provision for an independent payment advisory board to suggest Medicare cost-cutting measures if healthcare inflation exceeded the growth of the gross domestic product by a certain amount. However, Tauzin and the PhRMA lobbyists were all over that one and had gotten the senators to weaken the trigger.[9] Worse, the hospital lobby had succeeded in excluding the biggest expense—Medicare hospital payments of any kind—from the board's purview until 2019.

Similarly, the malpractice reform pilot projects that they had pushed for had been whittled down to almost nothing.

And the plan to start a real comparative effectiveness program to measure the costs versus benefits of devices and drugs had been gutted. Now the panel could research comparative effectiveness but vari-

9. As of the fall of 2014, the board had never met and, in fact, no members had been appointed to it.

ous amendments had been inserted specifically prohibiting the research to be used by Medicare to limit or even advise on the use of any drug or other treatment. The researchers could discover that drug A, which cost ten times what drug B cost, was less effective, but Medicare could not respond by refusing to pay for drug A.

"Healthcare reform continues to evolve, and we're paying close attention," Amgen CEO Kevin Sharer told stock analysts on a conference call the next day (October 21) to discuss his drug company's 23 percent jump in earnings per share for the third quarter of 2009.

FIVE BILLS, ONE LAW

On Saturday evening, November 7, 2009, the House of Representatives voted on the bill that Speaker Nancy Pelosi and her staff had hammered together by merging the versions passed by the three House committees that shared jurisdiction. It had been an agonizing process, enabled by Pelosi's determination to make it happen. Although House members were mostly moderate to left of center, there was a large contingent of conservative Democrats, called the Blue Dog Coalition, who came from what in 2009 were swing districts. Following the Tea Party summer, the Blue Dogs understandably feared a healthcare reform bill would be used to attack them from the right.

One of their key concerns was abortion, the issue Obama had gotten an earful about from a bishop at Ted Kennedy's memorial service and which the church had increasingly complained about since. Federal subsidies should not be used to pay for insurance that covered abortion—and maybe not even contraception, some of the Blue Dogs insisted.

Other Blue Dogs were worried about more basic issues. They didn't want any kind of public option, for example—a provision that Pelosi's liberal members insisted on. In the end, a public option was included, but Pelosi had to yield on abortion, disappointing many of her members, by allowing a provision requiring that no subsidies would pay for abortion coverage. Women would have to buy it separately with their own money, which was arguably an accounting sleight of hand since those women could use the subsidies they were getting for their overall insurance to help pay for it.

Just as the three House versions had now been merged and passed, the newly approved Senate Finance Committee bill now had to be combined with the version passed by Kennedy's HELP Committee. After that a final Senate bill would have to be reconciled with that final House bill, then voted on again by both bodies and given to the president to sign.

At a White House meeting of the healthcare reform team during the second week in November, the group speculated that getting the bills merged in the Senate was likely to be so difficult that the Senate vote on the final law might not come until just before Thanksgiving, about two weeks away. The same group had predicted a Baucus deal with Grassley, which had never come, by early July. This time, they would be only a month off.

With Harry Reid and his staff in charge of the process, the pressure intensified. To get past a Republican filibuster, the bill was going to have to get all fifty-nine Democrats (plus independent Bernie Sanders) on board, or at least fifty-eight, if Snowe could be counted on to back up her yes vote for the Finance Committee bill with the same vote on the Senate floor.

Some of the liberal Democrats wanted to use the process of merging the HELP and Finance Committee drafts to revive the public option. They threatened to oppose a bill that didn't include it. Sanders, the Vermont independent, was making the same noises.

"Why aren't we jumping up and down about that, telling them how stupid it is?" Summers asked his White House colleagues on October 21, referring to the public option, according to notes taken by someone who was at the meeting. "Would it reassure you to know that they don't care what we think?" Jason Furman from Treasury shot back.

What Reid did care about was corralling all of his Democrats. And Joe Lieberman, the Democrat from insurance-industry-friendly Connecticut, told Reid he would not vote for a bill that had a public plan of any kind. Yet the liberals were threatening from the opposite direction, and the House bill, which would have to be reconciled with whatever Reid produced, had the public option.

On November 19, 2009, Reid presented his bill merging the Finance Committee and HELP versions. It included:

- Schumer's and Snowe's lower penalties;
- the Cadillac tax;
- the new Medicare payroll tax on high earners and a tax on their capital gains and dividends;
- a tax on elective plastic surgery;
- a device tax approximating the $60 billion (over ten years) that Tony Clapsis had first sketched out;
- a $102 billion tax (again over ten years) on insurance companies, based on their revenues;
- fifty state insurance exchanges instead of the House's simpler national exchange;
- the drug and hospital givebacks that had been negotiated;
- and a public option, but one that each state could choose to opt out of.

Just before Thanksgiving, the Senate cast sixty votes to begin debate on Reid's bill. Snowe voted no; she wanted her colleagues to wait until after the New Year to vote, she said. However, she didn't take a position one way or the other on how she might vote after the debate on the floor.

THE VOTE TO MOVE the Reid bill to the Senate floor was only the starting bell for another round of hand-to-hand combat. As the Senate came back from Thanksgiving recess and began what would be three weeks of debate mostly featuring predictable, partisan speeches, Reid was running one-on-one bargaining sessions behind closed doors in his office. Every Democrat had something more he or she wanted from Reid, and they were all given an audience with the majority leader to demand it. Reid had decided he needed somehow to mollify all of them, because his instinct was that Snowe was going to cave.

Since her yes vote in the Finance Committee, Snowe had become even harder to read. But the Democrats and their staff knew she had been ostracized by the other Republicans since that vote. She was shunned when she showed up at lunches of the Senate Republican caucus. It seemed to be getting to her, they speculated, which was why she had voted no on beginning the floor debate.

Snowe told me she thought the treatment by her Republican colleagues was "more funny than troubling."

Although Baucus still wanted to win her over, Reid didn't care. He could get it done with his fifty-nine Democrats and Sanders—thanks to Ted Kennedy.

Besides writing that letter to Obama, Kennedy had done something else for the cause as he was about to die. He had convinced Massachusetts governor Deval Patrick to get a bill passed in the state legislature allowing for the immediate appointment (by Patrick, a Democrat) of a replacement in the event his seat became vacant. Patrick had quickly appointed a Democrat, which is what gave Reid his filibuster-proof margin immediately and presumably in the foreseeable future, because a Democrat was assumed to be a sure winner in the election for the vacant seat now scheduled for January.

Still, sixty votes meant sixty votes, not fifty-nine or fifty-eight. Which gave every Democrat in the Senate a veto over this enormously important bill.

Evan Bayh of Indiana still thought the tax on his medical device companies back in Indiana was too high. The companies had refused to negotiate any givebacks with Baucus's people, but their lobbyists had been all over Capitol Hill presenting a consultants' study full of charts and calculations purporting to demonstrate that the tax would kill tens of thousands of jobs—despite the new patients the law would produce who would be buying the companies' high-margin products with their new insurance. Reid agreed to cut the tax in half, which was also a favor to the newly seated Al Franken from Minnesota, where other device makers were headquartered.

Within days, an analyst from Wall Street's Bernstein Research reported that "as we previously anticipated, the medical [device] industry tax was reduced," because of the industry's lobbying efforts.

"The impact of the reduced tax looks manageable to us," the analyst concluded, "especially when offset by the benefits of expanded coverage."

Blanche Lincoln of Arkansas wanted a change that would ease the penalty on employers who did not provide health insurance by allowing them to delay coverage for three months for new employees after a one-month orientation period. (Walmart, among other home-state businesses, was concerned.) Lincoln got it. But she gave up her opposition to a tax on tanning bed services, even though many of the beds were made in her state, because Reid wanted to placate the lobbyists for the dermatologists, the drug companies that sold Botox, and the plastic surgeons. They were objecting to the proposed tax on elective cosmetic surgery that had been dubbed the Bo-tax. So Reid dropped the Bo-tax and substituted in the tanning bed tax.

The draft of the merged bill required the federal government to pay the entire cost for states to expand Medicaid to all people below the poverty line for the first three years and then 90 percent after that. Ben Nelson of Nebraska thought that wasn't generous enough. Reid gave Nebraska—only Nebraska—100 percent forever. At the Republicans' urging, the press came to call that deal the "Cornhusker Kickback."

Mary Landrieu wanted hundreds of millions more in federal aid for her Louisiana Medicaid recipients. She got it. That provision was quickly dubbed the "Louisiana Purchase."

The last bargain was with Joe Lieberman. The Connecticut senator finally got rid of the public option, including a version that allowed individual states to choose to implement it or not. Lieberman also shot down an alternative that would have allowed people fifty-five years old or older to buy into Medicare so they could be protected but pay lower premiums from 2010 until 2014, when the exchanges, with their premium subsidies, would kick in.

"This is essentially the collapse of health reform in the United States Senate," Howard Dean, the former Vermont governor and Democratic presidential candidate, told the Vermont public radio station when he heard about the elimination of the public option and the Medicare buy-in.

Zeke Emanuel and others at the White House wanted, among other priority items, that the comparative effectiveness provisions be toughened up and that the tort reforms be turned into something real. Reid gave them none of that.

"The Administration will put its foot down in Conference," one aide wrote in a journal, referring to additional opportunities to make changes during the closed-door negotiations in which a bill passed by the Senate would be merged with one passed by the House. The House and the Senate bills each included language encouraging the bundling of care as an alternative to fee-for-service, but "the design of the bundled payment program will have almost no effect on the payment system and practices of physicians," one memo circulating among the staff conceded, before listing five bundling provisions that they had to push for in the anticipated conference.

Meantime, Reid moved not only to lock in votes with any amendments necessary to keep his Democrats on board, but also to head off some Republican mischief. In December, the Republicans hatched a plan to launch a poison pill that would cause the drug companies to walk away from the deal and launch an attack reminiscent of the "Harry and Louise" ads that had scuttled Hillarycare fifteen years earlier. They were going to vote for an amendment sponsored by liberal Democrats to allow for consumers to buy drugs from Canada. This was the dreaded importation provision, the threat of which was one of the reasons Tauzin and PhRMA had come to the table in the first place.

Of course, Republicans, more beholden than Democrats to PhRMA, had always led the charge to block importation. Yet suddenly they had become consumer advocates. Their plan was to support the amendment, which, because it was amended to a pending bill, only needed a majority vote to pass. If that happened, Tauzin would have to call in enough favors from moderate Democrats to doom the entire law's prospects for getting the requisite sixty votes. The whole thing would be dead.

On the merits, most Democrats loved importation. It would save consumers—and cost the drug companies—$400 billion over the next ten years.

Jay Rockefeller, the West Virginia Democrat, summarized the awkward choice that the Republican scheme had forced on him. "I don't think that's going to get my vote," he told *The Huffington Post,* explaining that even though he had been a supporter of importation, he was concerned that if it passed it would blow up the overall deal. "I'm not messing around with anything without 60 votes. Nothing," he said. "And I'm a co-sponsor of the amendment."

Reid spared Rockefeller and others the dilemma of voting against something they favored. He refused to let it come up for a vote at all.

"I'M GONNA GO SEE TEDDY"

On December 19, 2009, Reid introduced a "manager's amendment" to the final bill that incorporated all of the deals he had made, meaning that all fifty-nine Democrats and Sanders would vote for it because even if they thought something like the Cornhusker Kickback or the reduction in the device tax was wrong, there was another nugget in there especially for them.

Reid would later be hailed by healthcare reformers as a hero for keeping the Senate in session day and night through the week leading up to Christmas as he carefully introduced the amendments that were in the package of the deals he had negotiated but blocked all others.

But Snowe was disgusted, she told me, that the most important piece of domestic legislation in decades was being rammed through that way. Nonetheless, expanding health insurance had been an issue she had worked on since serving in the Maine state senate. So she was still on the fence for the final vote.

On December 23, Snowe traveled through a morning blizzard in Washington to meet with the president. It was the eighth time they had met one-on-one about healthcare reform.

Snowe sat down and quickly told the president she couldn't vote yes—yet.

"I urged him to take a breather, and let us have a hiatus over the holidays and then have a full, open debate—not the closed process that Harry [Reid] was running," Snowe recalled. "I told him the opposition was only going to grow if he passed a bill this way by ramming it through with no Republicans. But he told me that the heat would subside. He compared it to how the opposition to his surge in Afghanistan had subsided once it started."

On Christmas Eve morning, in a moment of high drama, the Senate passed the bill with no Republican votes.

Liz Fowler was sitting with Baucus and Dodd on the Senate floor when the sixtieth vote was recorded at about 7 A.M. After the tally was announced, Dodd turned to them and said, "I'm gonna go see Teddy." He got up and left to go to Arlington National Cemetery, where Senator Kennedy had been buried in August.

CHAPTER 12

NEW TROUBLE,
THEN MOUNT EVEREST

December 2009–March 2010

Wᴴɪʟᴇ ᴀᴛᴛᴇɴᴛɪᴏɴ ᴡᴀs ꜰᴏᴄᴜsᴇᴅ ᴏɴ ᴛʜᴇ Sᴇɴᴀᴛᴇ ᴅᴇʙᴀᴛᴇ ᴀɴᴅ Harry Reid's retail sales skills, a different debate was percolating in the White House that seemed to spell trouble for the reform push, no matter the Senate vote.

The optimists on Obama's staff had begun looking ahead to how they would implement the new law—including the setup of the on-line health insurance exchanges with all of its varieties of bronze, silver, gold, and platinum plans. Now the split between the healthcare reform policy team and the economic team began to take a different turn. They began skirmishing over who would be in charge of making the law work.

On December 14, 2009, Zeke Emanuel and Bob Kocher—the McKinsey alumnus and physician who worked for Larry Summers—wrote Summers and Orszag a memo warning how difficult implementation was going to be. They urged that Summers and Orszag lead an effort to make sure the White House got it right by looking to the private sector for leadership.

"When health insurance reform legislation passes, there will be two important consequences," they wrote. "First, the federal government will be viewed as having responsibility and accountability for much of the health care system. Indeed, changes in the health care system, for good and bad, will become associated with reform. Second, implementation of a complex piece of legislation in a very short timeframe poses significant challenges, and will become a dominant public policy issue."

They proceeded to identify issues to be decided in the conference that they expected would be held to resolve the differences between the bills that had now been passed by the House and Senate that would affect the challenges of implementing the law—for example, whether the insurance exchanges would start in 2013 or 2014. Similarly, they highlighted the necessity of sticking with the House's plan to have one national online exchange rather than risk the chaos of operating fifty-one exchanges, one for each state and the District of Columbia, as was called for by the Senate bill.

Then they issued this warning about the difficulty of launching even one online marketplace: "The tasks of creating and operating an Exchange are monumental," requiring, they wrote, eight key challenges, from developing contracts with each insurer, to building the software for people to select insurance, to having the right amount of subsidies paid to the insurers through the Treasury Department after the IRS verified what people seeking subsidies reported about their income.

It was going to require "a whole new technology system," they warned. That could only be accomplished if the program operated under a "strong central authority" with one leader, and "if the Exchange can have the flexibility of the private marketplace rather than the government contracting system."

By now, Zeke Emanuel had told his brother he was thinking of himself as that strong central authority. But Kocher had been talking to another potential leader working in the Obama administration with stronger credentials for the job. Todd Park, who was thirty-six in 2009, had been recruited to be the chief technology officer of the Department of Health and Human Services (HHS). When he was twenty-four he had cofounded Athenahealth, which became one of the country's trailblazing healthcare information technology companies and made him a multimillionaire. A Phi Beta Kappa graduate of

Harvard, Park had then helped start other healthcare-related technology ventures, some for profit, others nonprofit.

Everyone seemed to like Park. He was modest and soft-spoken, yet as with Athenahealth, he usually seemed to have a new idea that was practical and ended up working.

Park seemed like a natural for this job.

One would have thought that as the Department of Health and Human Services chief technology officer, or CTO, he was actually going to be in the line of fire, anyway. Why wouldn't the HHS CTO be responsible for the launch of the high-tech insurance exchanges? After all, however the organization chart turned out, HHS was going to be the agency where the exchanges would reside.

That was not how the management of technology worked in Washington. A CTO at a federal agency had a great title but didn't have a line-of-fire job. Park was involved in setting his agency's broad technology policy, not implementing anything.

In fact, those most likely to be in charge of implementing technology at HHS didn't even report to Park; most worked at the Centers for Medicare and Medicaid Services (CMS), a unit of HHS, where responsibility for the health insurance exchanges would likely be placed. And they reported to their own CMS chief technology officer, who reported to the head of CMS, not to Park.

Moreover, the people doing procurement, who would issue the contracts to those building the website, didn't really report to any of them; they were career civil servants who were supposed to be independent in order to prevent corruption.

Kocher still hadn't come to appreciate the culture of the bureaucracies in his new hometown or the rigid organizational charts that governed them. He only knew from his McKinsey days that Park was reputed to be a superstar. So he began meeting with him, sometimes over lunch, to talk about how to get the project going.

Shouldn't they bring in a seasoned healthcare executive from the outside as the CEO? Kocher asked Park. And shouldn't that executive then be allowed to outsource the building of the e-commerce exchange—or exchanges if the calamitous Senate version allowing for individual state exchanges prevailed—to one of the Silicon Valley e-commerce companies that really knew how to do this?

Park thought that seemed like a good idea. The two agreed that there was no way the technology piece could be done in the usual Washington way, with the usual-suspect government contractors, who, both men agreed, were better at using their influence and their skill at dressing up bid proposals with extravagant promises to get contracts than they were at fulfilling those contracts.

However, whatever sharp elbows and ambition Park might have been born with had long since been softened after he had made his first millions. He told Kocher that he thought that someone who had run a much bigger organization than he had—perhaps a CEO from one of the insurance companies—would be better for the job.

Kocher also talked with the U.S. chief technology officer at the White House, Aneesh Chopra, about the need to do the healthcare reform project differently. Chopra heartily agreed.

Two weeks later, at the urging of Kocher and Emanuel, David Cutler, a Harvard economics professor and universally recognized healthcare expert, had weighed in with a memo of his own to Larry Summers, urging that the new law required a structure and management team worlds away from what he knew HHS or CMS were capable of. And it had to be run by a seasoned business executive.

Nearly five years later, President Obama would tell me he agreed: "In hindsight," he told me, "there should have been one central person in charge, a CEO of the Marketplace." But in late 2009, as the sweeping new law moved closer to passage, Obama and his team rejected that approach, choosing instead to parcel the work to the usual players eager to protect the turf that came with their titles.

Nancy-Ann DeParle wrote her own implementation memo to Rahm Emanuel, with a copy to Valerie Jarrett. DeParle's version of how Obamacare would happen was not complicated: She would run the program from the White House. She was, after all, head of the Office of Health Reform and had run CMS in the Clinton years.

In DeParle's memo, an HHS Office of Consumer Information and Insurance Oversight would oversee the exchanges, the CMS Office of

Information Services (the in-house tech team) would build them, and the CMS Office of Public Information would work on marketing them. It would all be overseen by Jeanne Lambrew, who would supervise day-to-day implementation from HHS. Lambrew, too, had the right title: head of the Office of Health Reform at HHS. DeParle, in turn would supervise Lambrew.

When Kocher and Zeke Emanuel got wind of DeParle's memo they pushed Summers and Orszag to talk to Rahm Emanuel about the problem. The chief of staff's response, according to what his brother later told me, was that he didn't want to have to deal with this "bureaucratic crap" now. They could worry about all that after they got a law passed.

A CANDIDATE TAKES A VACATION

Meantime, on December 9, 2009, a Massachusetts woman named Martha Coakley decided to go on vacation with her family. Like Richard Nixon getting caught up in Watergate, Wilbur Mills's companion wading into the Tidal Basin in Washington, Tom Daschle becoming ensnared in a tax controversy, or Ted Kennedy getting brain cancer, this became another curve ball from out of nowhere that threatened to block the reformers.

Coakley, the Massachusetts attorney general, was the Democrat running for Ted Kennedy's seat to replace the temporary stand-in appointed by the governor following Kennedy's death. She was heavily favored to win. However, her Republican opponent, an attractive state senator named Scott Brown, seemed to be gaining more traction than anyone had expected—running, in fact, on a platform that included a promise to block Obamacare.

Frank Luntz's "words that worked" seemed to be working for Brown in his race to replace Kennedy, the icon of healthcare reform.

Coakley's widely publicized decision to leave town little more than a month before the January 19 election was regarded by political pundits as a major blunder.

The Democratic Senate candidate was, of course, Harry Reid's sixtieth vote. Without Coakley, the conference bill that had to be negotiated and blended into one bill that the House and Senate would then have to approve in a second vote would fail. Reid would never get it past a Senate filibuster.

Nonetheless, by the first week in January, the House and Senate staffs—by now only Democrats, because there were no Republicans who were going to vote for anything they came up with—were meeting with the Obama advisers to negotiate the differences in the two bills, plus consider any new details the White House people wanted to add. They divided into groups to consider how to resolve the gaps in various aspects of the two massive bills.

The meetings were long and tedious. Progress was slow. Shouting matches sometimes erupted. Many of the House members and their staffs clearly hated the Senate bill. For them it was far too stingy. They complained that there was no public option, and that having fifty state exchanges, which the more conservative Senate had written in to make the law as much like Romneycare as possible, was absurd. The Cornhusker Kickback and Louisiana Purchase were an embarrassment to the country, they argued. And the Cadillac tax was a nonstarter because of union opposition.

We need all that or we lose our sixty votes, the Senate side insisted. "Bullshit," the House negotiators shot back more than once.

Occasionally, one or both sides stormed out of the room amid profanity-laced arguments.

There was an arcane legal debate that seemed to meander endlessly about how to set up the now-weakened comparative effectiveness panel so that it could be independent but still part of the executive branch. The economic team was horrified when DeParle told them that if they couldn't solve that one in the next day or two, they should just forget the whole comparative effectiveness thing.

The Democratic negotiators spent the entirety of January 12, 2010, getting through thirty-five pages of what was going to be a more than nine-hundred-page bill. Zeke Emanuel was kicked out of the room for arguing too much.

The next day a column in *The New York Times* by David Leonhardt argued that CMS needed new, strong leadership to implement reform and that the lack of that leadership "suggests that The White House is not giving attention to what will happen once Mr. Obama signs a bill." The policy team was sure Zeke Emanuel had instigated the article, which he indignantly denied.

Obama became involved in trying to break the stalemate. He convened three sessions of his own with the Democratic leaders in the Cabinet Room. The House side, led by Speaker Pelosi, said it could not get a bill passed with so many of the offending provisions that were in the Senate version. The Senate side, led by Reid, countered that Reid couldn't afford to lose even one of his senators, and that going along with the House would surely do just that.

Though they seemed slowly to be making progress, there was still no agreement through the first half of January.

The groups were working on the Sunday before Election Day in Massachusetts when one negotiator said out loud what many had begun to think, based on news reports coming from the Bay State. "Aren't we wasting our time? Are you watching the polls in Massachusetts?"

Still, the teams continued through Tuesday, January 19, 2010—until just after 8 P.M. Then, the election returns came in, declaring Republican Scott Brown the winner. The negotiators immediately put their pens down. One group adjourned to a bar near the Capitol to have farewell drinks and watch Brown claim his victory. Their sixtieth vote was gone. So was Obamacare.

THE "POTBELLY" ALTERNATIVE

The next day, Karen Ignagni called one of her contacts at the White House. Ignagni's insurance lobby had been officially critical of the bill since the summer, when Obama had pivoted to calling it insurance reform and when the details emerged that Ignagni's insurance industry employers disliked so much—the low penalty, the narrow age bands, what they viewed as inadequate subsidies, and, then, the $102 billion tax. And her five largest members had contributed to a Chamber of Commerce political action committee that was now funding ads that blasted the bill.

Yet now Ignagni, seemingly betraying her fear that simple insurance reform outlawing preexisting condition exclusions but with no mandate to buy insurance might become the Obama administration's fallback, was asking what she could do to help get things back on track. Her White House contact told Ignagni she would get back to her when they figured out what they were going to do.

In fact, someone on Nancy-Ann DeParle's staff was preparing a memo for the president suggesting exactly that fallback. Forbidding exclusions for preexisting conditions would cost nothing yet arguably yield nothing—except, as had happened with that "reform" in New York, a nationwide evaporation of the individual marketplace because of skyrocketing premiums resulting from only the sick wanting to buy insurance.

The same day, Liz Fowler began thinking about her future. Her thoughts stretched so far beyond healthcare reform that she went on-line to see how much it would take to open a franchise for Potbelly, a sandwich shop she liked. The up-front investment was $275,000. Not likely.

The next day, January 21, Ignagni emailed one of Valerie Jarrett's aides asking that Jarrett be given the message that "Leader Reid's office said we are done with health care for the year." Wasn't there something Jarrett or the president could do?

STILL "FEELING LUCKY"

But by January 22, there was hope in the air in some quarters. That night Zeke Emanuel was seated at a dinner next to Supreme Court justice Antonin Scalia. The conservative Scalia kidded Emanuel about the apparent collapse of Obamacare. Zeke offered to bet him that they would get Obama's reform package through, somehow.

At Rahm Emanuel's behest, his brother and others on the Obama team had begun playing with a drastically scaled-back proposal that might extend coverage to more children or go after the insurance companies the way Ignagni feared. However, Obama had told the staff that he had not given up yet. He was still "feeling lucky." And determined.

"When the going got tough," Obama recalled when I asked why

he persevered, "thinking of those Americans [he had met with health-care coverage problems] and what they were going through is what kept me going." To Phil Schiliro, the Scott Brown election posed less of a challenge than what they had faced during the Tea Party summer. Reform bills had already passed both the House and the Senate, and he and his congressional liaison team were already mapping out an idea to turn them into one bill that could become law despite the apparent loss of the sixtieth Senate vote that seemed to be needed to pass a House-Senate conference version.

Schiliro, as well as some of the political people at the unions and other interest groups promoting Obamacare, had begun thinking about that idea when the polls in Massachusetts started signaling trouble in the weeks running up to Election Day. In fact, Schiliro had told Obama about it the night of the Scott Brown election.

It boiled down to this: Why not just have the House pass the Senate bill? Then they would not need another Senate vote on a negotiated conference bill, requiring the now-impossible sixty-vote margin. There would be no conference and no conference bill, just the Senate bill that had already passed.

The problem, of course, was that most House Democrats hated the Senate bill, as evidenced by the hostile, agonizing, and mostly fruitless negotiations that had preceded the election debacle in Massachusetts. House members would never agree to pass the Senate's version of healthcare reform. They hadn't even agreed to meet the Senate halfway. The White House had had lots of problems with the Senate bill, too.

But there was a way the House could get some changes in the Senate bill that the Senate could agree to without needing sixty votes. It had to do with the procedural rule called reconciliation, the rule Ted Kennedy had refused to tell the Republicans he would not try to use. From the grave Kennedy was still keeping healthcare reform alive.

Under the Senate rules, if a bill was predominantly about finance—raising taxes and spending them—a majority of senators could vote to limit debate and force a vote. It did not take the sixty votes to cut off a filibuster that other legislation did.

If the House and Senate Democrats could negotiate changes in the

Senate bill, those changes could be introduced in the Senate as an entirely new bill to supplement the bill already passed. If those changes could pass the test of being mostly about financial matters, then Harry Reid would need only fifty-one votes to pass this new Senate bill, which would actually be a bunch of amendments to the first bill that had needed, and gotten, sixty votes.

The first hurdle, though, was negotiating those changes. Negotiating was exactly what the House and Senate Democrats had been unable to do before the Scott Brown Massachusetts victory, and now the House at best could only tweak a Senate version that a large contingent of House Democrats detested.

PhRMA's Billy Tauzin thinks that the freak election of Scott Brown is the one accident of history in healthcare reform annals that worked the other way, to help reform. In his view, it provided the path to save the reform effort because it eliminated the House's ability or willingness to fight with the Senate. For Speaker Nancy Pelosi and her House Democrats, it was now the Senate bill—with whatever relatively minor finance-related tweaks they could get—or nothing.

There could be no more arguments from Pelosi that Reid had to put in a public option or her members would walk away, or that there had to be one national exchange instead of the unwieldy fifty state exchanges the Senate had provided for. It was crunch time, and the Senate had all the leverage. Scott Brown had called the House Democrats' bluff. And they could rationalize folding by blaming it on Brown (and Martha Coakley's decision to take a vacation).

Tauzin's theory made sense to many of the other troops in the battle when I later asked them about it. Then again, that assumes that both sides would otherwise have let their disagreements kill reform after all the work that had been put into it—and knowing that Bill Clinton's failed healthcare reform effort was thought to have turned the House over to the Republicans in 1994.

Either way, the Scott Brown election did get the House Democrats back to the table, though with so little leverage that the only question left was whether they would, indeed, swallow their pride (and put aside their strong beliefs) and let Max Baucus and Harry Reid prevail.

"THANKS FOR NOTHING"

Which brings us to Pelosi, then the House Speaker. Initially, the San Francisco liberal told the president when he asked her about it immediately after the Brown election that there was no way she could get her Democrats to vote for the Senate bill. But within days, her anger and disappointment morphed into determination to get it done.

Soon, Pelosi had no qualms about taking whatever she could get. She wanted to pass a law, not win a debating contest with the Senate.

She was fierce about it. Yes, they would do the best they could to get whatever changes to the Senate bill they could negotiate into a reconciliation bill requiring only fifty Senate votes. But at the end of the day, they were going to pass the Senate's bill, no matter what they could get. She and other senior House Democrats began whipping their members into line.

"I got you elected and now you won't do this? Thanks for nothing," she spat at one reluctant Democrat as a stunned Nancy-Ann De-Parle looked on. The congressman soon changed his mind.

"We will go through the gate," Pelosi told reporters on January 28, 2010. "If the gate is closed we will go over the fence. If the fence is too high, we will pole-vault in. If that doesn't work, we will parachute in."

A much more publicized Pelosi statement would come a few weeks later, when on March 9 she was quoted telling a national convention of county officials that "we have to pass the bill so that you can find out what is in it." Her comment was seized on by reform opponents as proof of the proposal's monstrous complexity and its supporters' disregard for the democratic process.

In fact, Pelosi was simply promoting what she thought were the bill's benefits, which, in her view, had not been discussed enough because the political fight over passing it was dominating the cable news networks. What Pelosi actually said was, 'You've heard about the controversies, the process about the bill . . . but I don't know if you've heard that it is legislation for the future—not just about health care for America, but about a healthier America. But we have to pass the bill so that you can find out what is in it—away from the fog of the controversy."

Obama supplemented Pelosi's efforts with his own wrangling of House Democrats, something he had not done nearly as avidly as most of his predecessors.

On February 4, the day Scott Brown was sworn in as a senator, Obama told an audience at a fund-raiser that he was planning to continue the fight. A *New York Times* article about the speech was skeptical. Referring to the possible strategy of using the Senate bill with a few amendments to be passed in a new bill, it reported that "it is no longer clear that Senate leaders could muster even 51 votes to make fast-tracked changes to the Senate-passed health bill, let alone the 60 votes it would take to approve a revised measure under the normal rules. In the House, Ms. Pelosi, too, now faces an uphill climb."

The climb got easier a few days later when WellPoint, the insurance company where Fowler had worked and that had rejected her mother because of her preexisting condition, announced an increase in premiums of as much as 39 percent throughout California. Jubilant Democrats seized on it as proof that the insurance companies had to be reined in.

"To do this at that moment, someone at WellPoint must have been trying to sabotage their company and us," a senior Republican staff person later told me. "Could they actually be that stupid?"

Karen Ignagni at America's Health Insurance Plans had a similar reaction. She quickly convened a staff meeting to try, fruitlessly, to think of ways to put out the PR fire ignited by her second biggest member company. It didn't matter that WellPoint's profit margin for 2010 would be less than 5 percent (and would decline further in 2011)— far less than the margins enjoyed by the hospitals, drug companies, and device makers, whose bills the insurer paid.

Meantime, Obama helped keep the battle alive with a head fake. On February 25, he convened a televised session with Republican and Democratic legislators at Blair House across from the White House. It was billed as a bipartisan summit to discuss ways to resolve the health-care deadlock. It really was a way for Obama to buy time while Reid and Pelosi worked far from the cameras on a solution that was anything but bipartisan: getting Obamacare through the House and Senate without a single Republican.

Earlier that week, Obama had issued—finally—what he said was his own plan. But it was only the list of changes that he said would improve the Senate bill. In fact, most were the amendments that were coming into focus as ones that the House wanted and that Reid would agree to.

It was a small list. Obama's "plan" would, among other things, eliminate the now widely ridiculed Louisiana Purchase and Cornhusker Kickback deals that Reid had made; provide more generous subsidies for people to buy insurance; and scale back the Cadillac tax on generous insurance plans and not have it kick in until 2018.

The unions wanted that last change badly. As a result, the Cadillac tax—which would have yielded $300 billion over ten years in Baucus's original bill and would have, in Orszag's view, done the most to encourage lower healthcare spending—was now scaled back to about $39 billion.

Among the changes added to make up for the lost money was a reversal of what Charles Schumer and Olympia Snowe had done to minimize the penalty for ignoring the mandate. It would now apply in the first year. More important, to the relief of people such as Ignagni and Gruber, it was stiffened significantly; it would now be the *higher* of $95 or 2 percent of a family's income, and both benchmarks would rise year by year. The employer penalty for not providing insurance was also increased, angering businesses, especially those with part-time hourly workers. Now it would apply to all employees working thirty hours or more a week, not forty. The Chamber of Commerce, the National Retail Federation, and the Republicans said that this would be a job killer.

Other proposed changes, such as a strengthening of the Senate's abortion restrictions, were ruled out of order in an arduous, arcane hearing before the Senate parliamentarian. He decided they were not sufficiently linked to budgetary issues and, therefore, could not be included in a reconciliation bill that required only fifty-one votes. To appease conservative Democrats in the House, Obama agreed to issue an executive order purporting to do the same thing once the bill passed.

"FISCAL FRANKENSTEIN"

Once the House and Senate had agreed on the amendments that were to be included in what would be called the sidecar bill, which needed only fifty-one Senate votes, there was a final problem. It epitomized the hostility between the House and Senate and the general atmosphere of distrust in Washington. To make the deal work, the House first had to vote for the Senate's original bill. Only then could the House and Senate vote for the sidecar bill to amend it to be more to the House's liking. But what if the Senate Democrats reneged? Many House Democrats didn't trust the Democrats in the Senate to keep the deal and vote for the sidecar amendment once the House had voted for their bill.

To solve that, Pelosi had Reid get a letter signed by fifty-one senators promising to vote for the amendments.

On Sunday, March 21, 2010, Pelosi wrangled a 219–212 vote for the Senate bill. Thirty-four Democrats voted against it.

"The American people are angry. . . . This body moves forward against their will. Shame on us," said then–House minority leader John Boehner just before the vote on a bill that Republican Paul Ryan, the future Republican vice presidential nominee, called a "fiscal Frankenstein."

"This isn't radical reform," Obama said in a televised victory statement from the White House, "but it is major reform."

The Senate quickly kept its end of the bargain, voting 56–43 for the sidecar amendments.

Whether Ryan was right about the new law being a "fiscal Frankenstein," it certainly was a drafting Frankenstein. One had to read the 55-page sidecar bill full of the agreed-upon amendments alongside the original 906-page Senate bill to understand what was really in it. Worse, the rush to finish off the deal had produced some sloppy drafting from the Senate Office of Legislative Counsel, an obscure group of career lawyers who put the Senate staff's long legal drafts into actual legislative language. Beyond the usual typos there were some significant inconsistencies.

The most important drafting mistake seemed to say that insurance bought on the exchanges run by the federal government and not by the states (if a state decided not to set up its own exchange) would not qualify for subsidies at all, although elsewhere the language did, as was clearly intended, include the exchanges run from Washington.

That error—which would become the subject of litigation in the federal courts in 2014—was the result of a last-minute change as the Senate bill was being passed early in the morning on Christmas Eve. Fowler and her staff had always intended that the federal exchange would be a backup in states that could not or would not mount their own exchanges so that people in those states could get the full benefit of Obamacare. The CBO had scored the bill based on this unambiguous intention. However, someone had mistakenly cut and pasted language from a provision in an earlier draft that referred only to state exchanges and used it in one place, though not elsewhere, as a boilerplate reference to the exchanges in one of the clauses describing how the subsidies would work.

Normally, these and other slipups, once discovered, would be corrected in a routine "fix" that would get a unanimous vote. However, with Republicans already talking about repeal, no unanimous vote on anything related to Obamacare was likely.

"ASSUMPTION THAT PASSAGE = EXECUTION, WHICH IS WORRISOME"

The night of the House vote, Obama gathered his staff on the Truman Balcony for a champagne celebration. Obama toasted his team, although he noted that "now we all have to get to work."

One member of the group, while sharing everyone else's near delirium, later recalled that there was something slightly troubling about what Obama said next. The president seemed more focused on the work ahead involving getting people to sign up on the exchanges, rather than on executing all the steps that had to be completed—the regulations, the software, the rules for the insurance companies—to get people to the stage where they could sign up. "Assumption that passage = execution, which is worrisome," is how this healthcare staffer shorthanded it that night in a journal that this person kept.

There was none of that concern two days later, on March 23, 2010, when Barack Obama signed the Affordable Care Act in an elaborate East Room celebration. As the ceremony began, Vice President Biden said to the president—and into a mike that, unknown to him, was turned on—"This is a big f——king deal."

Biden was right. Barack Obama, alone among more than a century of presidents, had scaled what has been called "the Mount Everest" of American domestic policy challenges.[10]

Insisting on not giving up on multiple occasions when the fight looked hopeless, or at the least like a reckless gamble of his political capital, Obama had gotten a law passed that in theory could provide every American with health insurance coverage.

"AN AMAZING PERSON"

Zeke Emanuel, who had fought hard and mostly without success for more cost-cutting provisions, went around collecting autographs from the legislators and other dignitaries in the room.

Liz Fowler was one of two members of Baucus's staff invited to the event (along with his chief of staff, who had convened that meeting eleven months before to raise the secret fund from PhRMA to pay for pro-reform ads). Fowler didn't collect autographs, but she was given a signing pen by Obama.

The next week Baucus took to the Senate floor to make an unusual speech. "I wish to single out one person," he began. "Her name is Liz Fowler . . . my chief health counsel. . . . Liz Fowler worked for me many years ago, left for the private sector, and then came back when she realized she could be there at the creation of health care reform, because she wanted that to be, in a certain sense, her professional life-

10. For the origin of the "Mount Everest" metaphor, please see "Methodology and Source Notes" in the back of this book.

time goal. She put together the White Paper last November 2008—which became . . . the blueprint from which almost all health care measures in all bills on both sides of the aisle came. She is an amazing person. She is a lawyer; she is a Ph.D. She is just so decent. She is always smiling. She is always working. Always available to help any Senator, any staff. I thank Liz from the bottom of my heart."

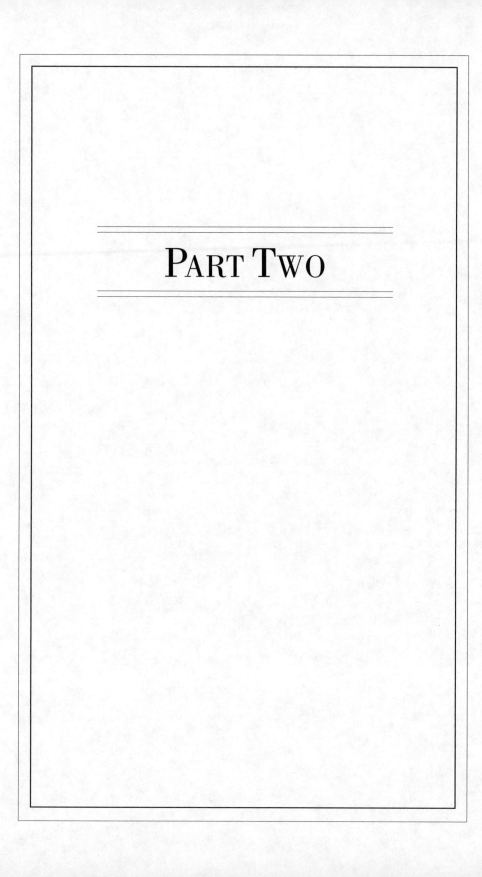

PART TWO

CHAPTER 13

IN WASHINGTON
"EVERYTHING IS SLIPPING,"
BUT NOT IN KENTUCKY

April–December 2010

THE CELEBRATORY SIGNING CEREMONY HAD NOT COMPLETELY DIS-
tracted the White House political team from the challenges it faced.
Polls measuring what people thought of the reform law were negative
from the start. The messy narrative of backroom deals, Tea Party rallies, claims of a government takeover, and the partisan vote had taken
their toll.

Hoping to recover quickly, Obama and his team staged a campaign-
style rally in Iowa two days after the East Room ceremony. The president's appearance featured the woman who had been with him for a
healthcare speech during the Iowa primary campaign three years
before—Amy Chicos, whose husband's cancer care bills had threatened to bankrupt her because the premiums to cover his preexisting
condition were so high.[11]

Another aspect of the attempt at political recovery was, to para-
phrase Nancy Pelosi, an effort to get people to realize the benefits that

---

11. When I reached Chicos in early 2014, she declined to talk about whether the Affordable
Care Act had helped her situation, saying that she had been made "uncomfortable" about
being thrust into the limelight, adding "I have since come to realize how much the corpo-
ratocracy influences and controls these things, and keeps the rest of us busy writing letters
and articles, happy to let us think we are making a difference."

were in the bill, by giving them some of those benefits as quickly as possible. This involved issuing regulations for those provisions of the new law that could be implemented immediately because they did not need the long planning and building process that creating the insurance exchanges required.

The person in charge was Nancy-Ann DeParle, the head of the White House Office of Health Reform. With Valerie Jarrett's help and her widely viewed status as one of the president's pets, DeParle had so far been able to shrug off efforts by Summers and Orszag to bring in someone from the outside to take over.

DeParle had expressed a desire to go back to her private equity firm in 2010, after which she wanted Jeanne Lambrew to run the effort. However, Obama had persuaded her to stay and, in the process, hinted that she might be getting a promotion to a position higher up in the White House hierarchy.

DeParle delegated much of the work to Lambrew, the former Texas professor and expert on healthcare programs for the poor, who was in charge of the Department of Health and Human Services Office of Health Reform. Lambrew's ability to get those regulations written—a tortuous process in the federal bureaucracy in the best of circumstances—would soon be seen by the economic team as not nearly as strong as her desire to control the process of writing them.

The initial implementation meeting of the staffs from the Domestic Policy Council, the Office of Management and Budget, and the National Economic Council who were assigned to work on healthcare didn't happen until April 8, more than two weeks following the passage of the law.

The first issue on the agenda was "grandfathering"—how long people who had insurance policies that now offered insufficient coverage under the new law would be allowed to keep them. Lambrew wanted to get rid of all the offending policies as soon as possible and certainly by the time coverage was to be offered on the exchanges. Someone asked if she or someone on her staff had checked with Ignagni at AHIP, the health insurance trade association. "We haven't because we don't trust them," Lambrew answered matter-of-factly, according to the notes of someone at the meeting.

It made sense politically to try to get a regulation targeted at the insurers out the door first. Insurance reform had worked for Simas and the political team. Besides, this was basic consumer protection; these were mostly lousy policies that offered inadequate coverage when people really needed it. Stephanie Cutter, a top Obama political aide who had been assigned to direct the marketing of Obamacare, chimed in that grandfathering sounded like a loophole to her. It would be good to go after those policies head-on. The less grandfathering, the better.

However, as the White House team would later learn, on this issue Cutter had a political tin ear. This was a regulation that would be viewed as victimizing people who already had insurance policies—the policies Obama had promised they could keep if they liked them.

Not talked about at all in the first month of meetings were the regulations that might have the most immediate impact and be the simplest to issue—the ones to implement the provisions Senator Grassley had inserted restricting what hospitals could charge needy, uninsured patients such as Emilia Gilbert, the school bus driver sued by Yale–New Haven Hospital. The subject would not come up until late May, at which time someone on Lambrew's team said, vaguely, that the IRS "is working on that."

By April 21, 2010, every deadline the team had set for issuing regulations had been extended. All of the myriad categories of regulations they needed to write now seemed more complicated than anticipated. They were eager to throw another dart at the insurers by writing the rules for that medical loss ratio—the MLR, which required insurers to spend a stipulated percentage of their premium revenues on paying out claims as opposed to administrative expenses and shareholder dividends. But that job had gotten bogged down in debates over how to define administrative expenses.

On top of that, the insurers were already lobbying furiously at the White House, at HHS, and on Capitol Hill, which had oversight responsibility for the regulations and could make life tough for the administration. They were focused on what another set of regulations would say about what would be included in "preventive services" that they had to provide for free and about the "essential services" that had to be covered in every insurance plan.

At another April session, the head of the IRS told the team that verifying the subsidies people buying insurance on the exchange were entitled to based on their prior year's tax returns would be a "nightmare" requiring platoons of his best people. Larry Summers agreed, calling it "a new frontier for the IRS—140 million tax returns with new attachments," according to notes taken at that meeting.

Meanwhile, Aneesh Chopra—the U.S. chief technology officer—sent an email to people on the domestic policy staff offering to help oversee what was happening with the website build. "STOP!" was the only reply he got.

At an April 29 meeting that DeParle chaired there was a consensus, according to one note taker, that "Everything is slipping."

The original deadline for releasing the first set of regulations had been set for the next day, April 30.

That day, none were issued. In fact, the first set—by far the easiest ones to write, pertaining to a provision allowing children under age twenty-six to be covered in their parents' policies—wouldn't come out until May 13. A month into the law, the team was two weeks behind schedule.

HAPPY TALK AT THE WHITE HOUSE

On April 30, 2010, the day they missed their first deadline, DeParle issued this report on the White House blog: "Just over a month ago, President Obama signed the Affordable Care Act into law. . . . The day of that signing the President made one thing clear—he expects his Administration to deliver the benefits of reform to the American people as effectively and expeditiously as possible. As the President said, 'we need to get this right.' Over the last month, we've begun doing that. We've made significant progress in implementing the new law and making reform a reality for millions of Americans."

By early May, DeParle and Lambrew were giving biweekly memos to the president reporting that there was excellent progress on all fronts. The only exception was the building of the website for the exchanges, which had not started because the Department of Health and Human Services' CMS unit was going through the usual process of drafting a statement of work that would serve as a document for soliciting proposals to do the job from government contractors. The president even started receiving a "dashboard"—a chart appearing on his computer or tablet screen—with color-coded grids showing the progress on all the tasks. Everything was green. No yellows or reds.

"THE PRESIDENT LIKES TO HEAR SOLUTIONS, NOT PROBLEMS"

In May, Kocher and Zeke Emanuel convinced their bosses, Summers and Orszag, that they had to do something. Summers and Orszag began by talking to Rahm Emanuel about the need to bring in someone with real experience running a private-sector insurance and/or e-commerce business to be in complete charge. Emanuel told them to talk to the boss, but warned that Obama "loved" Nancy-Ann, and so did Valerie Jarrett.

One of them talked to Jarrett, starting with the problems they already could see coming. "The President likes to hear solutions, not problems," she reportedly replied, according to someone who was told about the conversation. "If there are problems, bring them to Nancy-Ann [DeParle]; she is the one the President put in charge." Of course, to them, DeParle, along with Lambrew and the dysfunctional HHS technology procurement process, were the problems. So, according to four people on the White House staff, Orszag wrote the president a memo urging him to bring in someone to supplant DeParle. He got no answer.[12]

When I later asked the president whether he remembered the Orszag memo, all he would say was, "At this point, I am not so interested in Monday Morning quarterbacking the past."

"The president doesn't like confrontations," one of his former senior advisers later explained to me, in a conversation echoed by three other senior White House alumni. "The 'no-drama' Obama stuff you

---

12. Neither Summers nor Orszag would be interviewed or quoted for attribution; each refused to confirm or deny the existence of the memo. I have not seen the memo. DeParle agreed to be interviewed but declined to have direct quotes attributed to her. She did convey the impression that she remembered such a memo, but said she was not certain of its existence.

always read about starts with him. Sometimes if you confront him with something like this he'll just stare at you silently, as if telling you to change the subject. Or, he'll say 'You guys work it out.' And, you know, in so many other instances things did work out for him, so I guess we all kind of thought, this, too, would work itself out."

"He had never run anything before," added another former close adviser who was in the White House at the time. "And I think he was feeling his way about how much detail to get into, how much attention he should pay to this stuff. It was always 'You guys figure it out.'"

"If you tried to talk to Obama about Valerie having too much influence and undercutting the chief of staff on stuff like this, you would just get a cold stare," added a third Obama confidant. "It was really troubling."

1,492,000 MAN-HOURS OF PAPERWORK

The first eighteen pages of what, according to *The Washington Post,* would be 9,625 pages of regulations covering Obamacare were published in the *Federal Register* on May 13, 2010, in a printed volume and on the *Register*'s website. Included in the notice, with no trace of appreciation for the irony, was a statement that "the collection of information contained in these regulations has been reviewed and approved by the Office of Management and Budget in accordance with the Paperwork Reduction Act of 1995." As a result, the notice continued, the Office of Management and Budget estimated that it would take 1,492,000 man-hours to complete the paperwork required to comply with just these eighteen pages of regulations related to one provision of the law.

By the time of a June 7 White House meeting, DeParle's team was focused on the prospect that many more states than they had anticipated might not create their own exchanges.

The House bill had provided for one national exchange run by the federal government. The Senate bill that prevailed after the Scott Brown election in Massachusetts allowed each state to set up an exchange, with the federal government providing an exchange for states that opted not to run their own.

A major technology challenge that Kocher and Zeke Emanuel had worried about in their December memo to Summers and Orszag was the one associated with the need for the federal government's Treasury Department and IRS to connect with fifty state exchanges to provide payments to the insurers and vet subsidy requests by the consumers. Now it also looked like the backup federal website they thought they would need in case a few states opted not to create their own could become an e-commerce site that had to provide state-specific exchanges for dozens of states, all emanating from one central federal website.

A "PENALTY," NOT A "TAX"

The reason their prognosis had changed so much for the worse was simple: The vituperative politics of Obamacare hadn't subsided following its passage. Quite the opposite. It had intensified. Repeal had become a Republican rallying cry for the 2010 midterm elections. And twenty-eight different state attorneys general, all Republicans, were on their way to court to have the law declared unconstitutional.

The reform team had received their first briefing on that litigation from White House counsel Robert Bauer in late April, when there were already nine active suits. The chief claim against the law was that the penalty for not complying with the individual mandate was an overreach of the authority given the government in the Constitution's Commerce Clause to regulate commerce. This wasn't regulating commerce; it was penalizing people for not engaging in commerce by refusing to buy insurance from some private company.

It was an argument conservatives had not raised when the Heritage Foundation had championed the mandate, but it had a certain ring to it. Yet Bauer, taking the view that most legal academics had already espoused, said he was confident the courts would not interfere with Congress's judgment that this was a penalty necessary to regulate and improve the health insurance market, which, of course, was commerce.

"We think we're in a strong position," Bauer reported, according to notes of the meeting taken by one of the participants.

Unmentioned in the discussion (although it was always mentioned in the government's briefs) was that had Congress called the penalty a tax, there would have been no case at all. The Constitution gave broad taxing power to Congress. And the nation's tax collector, the IRS, had been charged under Obamacare with collecting what anyone who ignored the mandate owed. Yet no politician on Capitol Hill or in the White House wanted to be associated with raising taxes if he or she could avoid it. Many, like David Axelrod and Charles Schumer, were wary of the penalty as it was.

Months before, in the early stages of drafting the bill, someone on the Finance Committee staff had mentioned the possibility of calling it a tax because he had heard a Republican staffer say something about the Commerce Clause. However, he was quickly shot down. The issue hadn't come up since—until the lawsuits started flying. Still, Bauer did not mention the possibility of calling the penalty a tax as a defense. He was confident about the Commerce Clause. Insurance was commerce, and the mandate was simply a necessary way to regulate that commerce by strengthening the insurance market.

As various federal trial courts and intermediate appeals courts came down on different sides of the Commerce Clause question about the mandate, the case would take two more years to reach the Supreme Court, during which time the Republicans' argument would increasingly pick up steam among legal and political pundits.

A POLITICAL FIRESTORM HIDING IN PLAIN SIGHT

On June 17, 2010, the regulations governing grandfathering were published in the *Federal Register*. The insurance companies noticed them and immediately pushed back. Ignagni complained to the White House and Baucus's staff that this would cause chaos when most people with plans that no longer met the adequacy test were cut off at the end of 2013.

But to Lambrew, for whom this was a pet issue, these regulations were already a compromise. Except for plans that had lifetime limits, the sale of which would be banned within months, she had allowed a transition period extending to the end of 2013 for plans with impermissible annual limits and plans that otherwise provided inadequate coverage. That way, those people could buy new insurance on the exchanges, which would have been launched by then.

"I hate that company," she said during one staff meeting, referring to a prominent marketer of inexpensive insurance. "They're bottom feeders. But I guess we need them to stay in business until 2014."

Hiding in plain sight—if anyone other than those in the industry had read the *Federal Register*—was this matter-of-fact prediction that Lambrew's team had included in the *Federal Register* notice: "Reliable data are scant, but a variety of studies indicate that between 40 percent and 67 percent" of the fourteen million policies in effect in the current individual market would have to be canceled under these regulations. That seemed to mean that five to ten million people would be notified in the fall of 2013, just as the Obamacare exchanges were launching, that their insurance policies would be canceled on December 31.

AN EARLY TECH WIN

On June 30, 2010, the Department of Health and Human Services launched an Obamacare-related website that suggested that anyone worried about the agency's digital proficiency was crying wolf. The site, envisioned as a forerunner to the exchanges, allowed visitors to review all the current insurance plans offered in the individual marketplace, broken down by the zip code where a consumer wanting to do comparison shopping lived.

Monthly premiums were listed, as were deductibles and other details of each plan. Although those details were complicated and difficult to understand, because health insurance is inherently complicated and difficult to understand, the presentation, on a website designated HealthCare.gov, was clear, simple, and smart. It was a promising step toward President Obama's promise that Obamacare was going to make buying health insurance like buying an airplane ticket from Orbitz or Expedia.

But this was not an e-commerce site. You couldn't buy anything yet, or find out what your subsidies would be.

The man behind this quick win, launched just three months after the law had been signed, was Todd Park, the Department of Health and Human Services chief technology officer who also held the title of "entrepreneur in residence." Park was the person Bob Kocher had talked to about running the Obamacare implementation.

Just after the president had signed the bill into law, Park had quickly and quietly put a team together to design and build HealthCare.gov.

How did Park do that amid all the bureaucracy around him? First, he persuaded the people at Health and Human Services working on the technology for the "real" Obamacare website that this one was simply an informational tool, a PR project. As such, it was not something the HHS technology procurement people, let alone the technology office at its CMS unit working on the real website, had to worry about. Then, because it was an informational offering that involved a minor software project, he persuaded the staff at the HHS Office of Public Affairs, which usually ran all PR projects, to let him take that burden off their hands.

And then he had proceeded as if doing one of his start-ups—not by procuring a contractor, but by gathering a small team of coders who worked with him.

In fact, one of the people he had "contracted" to help design and code the easy-to-navigate home page was someone Park had met by responding to a tweet from a Web designer in New Jersey who had tweeted to his followers a description of his idea for Park's site. Someone had then retweeted his message to Park.

Yes, Park's version of government procurement was a tweet.

KENTUCKY ENTERS THE DERBY

Also in June 2010, a similarly modest effort to get in on the Obamacare action began in Frankfort, the state capital of Kentucky. Carrie Banahan, a career civil servant, who was then fifty and had worked her way up to executive director of Kentucky's Office of Health Policy, began writing a grant application to the federal government to pay for Kentucky to begin planning its Obamacare exchange.

Banahan had read a lot about Obamacare, including its provision to fund an expansion of Medicaid to all of the poor in any state. She was hoping Governor Steven Beshear, a Democrat, was as enthusiastic about the new law as she was. In addition to having one of the nation's highest poverty rates, Kentucky had some of the absolutely worst healthcare rankings: 43rd in sedentary lifestyles, 44th in annual dental visits, 49th in heart disease, 49th in poor physical health days, 50th in cancer deaths, and 50th in smoking. Anything that might provide Kentuckians with more medical care seemed to Banahan like a great idea.

However, Kentucky was also not a place where a politician might want to launch something called Obamacare. In 2008, Barack Obama had lost Kentucky to John McCain 57 to 41 percent, and his popularity was perceived to have been sinking since, in significant part because his environmental initiatives so threatened the state's dominant coal industry.

Governor Beshear, a former lawyer and state attorney general, is glib and charismatic and can excite a room with a speech. Banahan is much the opposite—blond but hardly glamorous, soft-spoken, and modest. But both are strong-minded. And it turns out that they shared a determination to get behind Obamacare, including launching their own killer exchange.

By August 31, Banahan had submitted Kentucky's grant request for $1 million to begin planning the exchange. It included all the precise timelines and expense detail that the government required, including the fact that the grant would cover 25 percent of Banahan's $100,000 salary to supervise the planning. Banahan got the go-ahead from Washington just a month later.

"We were the first to get a grant," Beshear later told me. "And after that we applied for everything we could from Washington. But we kept it as our program."

Even the name was Kentucky-bred. To Kentuckians this would be "Kynect," not Obamacare.

Other governors took the opposite approach. In Minnesota, Republican Tim Pawlenty, preparing for a 2012 presidential race, announced that he would turn down all grants and any other money from Washington. In fact, he issued an executive order to all state agencies telling them not to participate in any aspect of the new law.

CHAPTER 14

AN *OFFICE* BECOMES
A *CENTER*—AND IT MATTERS

January–June 2011

"Once OCIIO became CCIIO, implementing [Obamacare] became pretty much impossible."

Huh?

That was the explanation that was later offered to me by a senior Obama administration official as troubles with the rollout of the law started making headlines. He thought I'd get it immediately. Which, of course, I didn't because I was not steeped in the interplay of Washington bureaucracy and politics.

Here's what he meant. Bear with me. The story of this mind-numbing parade of acronyms actually matters.

The original setup was that the Centers for Medicare and Medicaid Services—CMS, the unit of the Department of Health and Human Services cabinet agency that runs Medicare and Medicaid—was going to run Obamacare. Jeanne Lambrew, the head of the CMS *Office* of Health Reform was to oversee things there, and Nancy-Ann DeParle was to oversee her from the White House.

At CMS, Lambrew was going to work with the *Office* of Information Services (the technology people), the *Office* of Acquisition and Grants Management (the procurement people), and the *Office* of Consumer Information and Insurance Oversight. The acronym for that last one is "OCIIO."

OCIIO's job was to coordinate all of the insurance companies' participation in the exchanges. That included making sure the policies they put on sale met the law's standards (which OCIIO was supposed to promulgate), that the pricing and subsidy calculations for buying the policies would work, and that all the other rules and processes for selling insurance on the exchanges produced information that was clear to the consumer. They also had to make sure the exchanges provided seamless, real-time connections between the insurance companies and the consumers visiting the site, as well as connections to the government agencies that had to calculate subsidies and vet citizenship or legal immigration status.

In other words, OCIIO was really the hub, the center of the action. And the other *offices*—such as technology and procurement, as well as the *Office* of Communications, which was worried about marketing—were spokes, feeding their work into what OCIIO was responsible for. However, because all of those players were *offices,* too, the organization was multiheaded and convoluted. For at CMS, no head of an *office* could order around the head of another *office.*

Then, as the midterm election returns came in on November 2, 2010, the confused structure became worse. OCIIO, the hub of the wheel, was quickly demoted.

The night the Republicans took back the House of Representatives, they vowed to repeal Obamacare or at least kill it as a practical matter by cutting off the funds to implement it. The key funding ingredients of Obamacare had been written into the bill and could not be taken away, except by new legislation. But other smaller yet important funding categories for the personnel necessary to run the exchanges and oversee all the new insurance rules remained part of the regular annual appropriation process that the House controlled. This included the money for OCIIO.

Worried not only about that, but also about the baggage Obamacare now seemed to present going into the president's 2012 reelection campaign, the administration went into a full defensive crouch. The bureaucratic upshot was that the *Office* of Consumer Information and Insurance Oversight, or OCIIO, would now have to become the *Center* for Consumer Information and Insurance Oversight, or CCIIO.

Why? Because a *center* could be buried deep within the bowels of CMS where it would need no independent funding from the newly Republican House of Representatives the way an *office* would.

Whoever ran the key division meant to implement Obamacare had now been demoted to running a *center*. That meant that at CMS he would rank below those running the *offices* responsible for procuring the necessary work from contractors to build it all for him and then for making sure the technology worked. At CMS rank meant everything, which was one reason that between 2010 and 2014 four different frustrated men would rotate through the job of being head of the newly demoted *center*.

The shift from *office* to *center* also meant that a man named Henry Chao, who had been made director of technology for the *Office* of Consumer Information and Insurance Oversight—where he was supposed to oversee the technology build for the federal exchange—now had to be put back in his old position as deputy director of technology in the *Office* of Information Services. Chao was still supposed to work on the federal exchange, but he, too, lost clout. And there was no senior person in the new *center*—which, again, was supposed to be the hub of the entire effort—who had any responsibility for the technology.

Yes, it all seems like a game of who sits at which table in the high school cafeteria. But in Washington this is high-stakes stuff.

There were other bureaucratic shuffles soon after Election Night, 2010. Larry Summers left as head of the National Economic Council. Orszag, too, told colleagues he was on his way out to a banking job in New York. That left Zeke Emanuel and Bob Kocher without the bosses who had been able at least to try to insinuate them—and their preoccupation with costs and, now, management—into the implementation meetings run at the White House by DeParle. By the late spring and early summer of 2011 they, too, would be leaving.

At the same time, Nancy-Ann DeParle was promoted to White House deputy chief of staff for policy. To fill her spot, DeParle brought

Jeanne Lambrew from HHS to the White House as the new head of the Office of Health Reform. The former professor was now the White House person in charge of overseeing the launch of Obamacare, including the complicated e-commerce website and all the rules and technology powering it.

DeParle later told me she was uninvolved in implementing Obamacare after that, because Lambrew's office was put under the purview of the Domestic Policy Council, headed by Melody Barnes. Unlike DeParle, Barnes, a highly regarded lawyer and former adviser to Ted Kennedy on legal and civil rights issues, had no experience in healthcare policy or the HHS and CMS bureaucracies.

Three other members of the White House staff told me, however, that DeParle stayed involved in Obamacare from her perch as deputy chief of staff, where, as a practical matter, she was Barnes's boss. Notes kept by two White House staff members and a journal kept by one White House staff person indicate that DeParle chaired multiple meetings about Obamacare implementation through 2011.

Liz Fowler had left Baucus's office in July to work on implementing the law at HHS. In December, she, too, moved to the White House. She was going to work on those aspects of the launch affecting issues under the purview of the National Economic Council and the Treasury Department. Although she had always been friendly with Lambrew, Fowler would soon grow disaffected. Lambrew had sharp elbows and guarded her turf so jealously that there was little for Fowler to do.

Stephanie Cutter—the political operative in charge of Obamacare marketing—had been talking to the reform staff in the spring, according to notes kept by a staff member, about sending out "SWAT Teams" across the country to "tell the story of Obamacare." But she all but abandoned her operation following the midterm elections. The only visible sign of activity from Cutter was a message she posted on the White House blog touting the issuance of the medical loss ratio (MLR) rules, which had taken until November 22 (six months behind schedule) to be completed.

To the extent that the president talked about Obamacare following the midterm blowout it was mostly about how, in addition to kids now being able to stay on their parents' policies until age twenty-six, the insurance companies were going to be brought to heel. They could no longer exclude people with preexisting conditions or cancel their insurance. Most important, the coming exchanges would save consumers money by forcing insurance companies to present their products clearly in one place where people could compare prices. It was all about competition driving prices down—when, in fact, as Obama and his team knew, what was actually going to drive prices down were the subsidies. The projections were that 75 to 80 percent of those buying online would be middle-class and lower-middle-class families who could get an average of more than half of their premiums paid for by Uncle Sam.

These generous subsidies were never stressed. "Millions of Americans Are Paying Less for Obamacare Than Cable" is how a headline on the *Vox* news website would read, accurately, when the subsidies were tallied after the initial Obamacare enrollment period in 2014. In 2011, there were no news stories like that.

Millions more living below the poverty line would get healthcare, via Medicaid, for free, because under Obamacare the federal government was paying the states to extend it to everyone living in poverty. Before Obamacare, states set their own rules, and many states had especially severe restrictions that limited their programs to people living at a fraction of the poverty level or just to families with children.

In fact, although the Obama team never stressed it and the press mostly missed it, the Congressional Budget Office projected that 16 million Americans who were going to get insurance under the new law by 2019 were going to get it from Medicaid—that is, poor people getting something for free—rather than through the exchanges. That was 50 percent more than the 10.6 million Americans receiving federal welfare when Ronald Reagan ran against welfare in 1980, or the 10.9 million getting welfare checks in 1997 when President Clinton compromised with the Republicans and reformed the program.

Put simply, between the subsidies and Medicaid expansion, Obamacare was a massive income redistribution program providing health insurance to those who could not pay for it—something Democrats in a different time might have been proud, rather than afraid, to acknowledge.

But heading into the 2012 reelection campaign, it was better to trumpet Obamacare as a modern innovation that would force another hidebound industry to be more competitive. "Expedia for health insurance" was a more winning bumper sticker than "Money for the poor," let alone "Money for the poor so they can buy the same product everyone else does at the same prices that make everyone in the healthcare industry so rich."

Which made a successful build of that cool new online insurance exchange that much more important.

WHO? HOW? WHAT?

Through the summer of 2011, the White House and HHS and CMS staffs, along with people from the Labor Department and the Internal Revenue Service, met and struggled with who was going to do what to make those exchanges work.

Labor had to deal with implementing the mandate that employers provide workers with insurance. What kind of reporting would be required? How would it be verified? How would Labor coordinate with CCIIO at CMS?

The law called for insurers who ended up with an unusually sick population to be compensated from a fund paid for with contributions from insurance companies who had ended up with unusually healthy populations. (The goal was to make sure insurers weren't incented to try to discourage sick people from signing up.) What were the funding rules for that going to be?

What would be the process for vetting claims from people who said that a hardship should exempt them from the mandate?

How would people who did not have Internet access be able to buy insurance on the exchanges? That would require another contract for a vendor to process paper applications—a $114 million job that would not be awarded until July 1, 2013, more than two years later.

At a June 11 meeting, the White House healthcare reform and economic staffs and representatives of the multiple agencies involved in the launch worried that it was now clear that the procurement process was going much too slowly. On top of that, the man who had run the

OCIIO had resigned because he didn't want to run a CCIIO. So the work was lagging there, too.

Yet someone had to decide what was needed to build the exchange website and support services before a contractor could be chosen to deliver on those requirements. What capacity or security requirements should they require? How could rules be written to spell out exactly what was needed in terms of the look of the website and its customer friendliness? The CMS procurement team—with input from the other CMS *offices* and the demoted *center,* yet insisting that it had the final say—slaved all summer over a dense statement of work that would have to spell all that out for contractors who wanted to bid on the project.

"WORLD CLASS IT SERVICES" AND "A FIRST CLASS CUSTOMER EXPERIENCE"

Finally, on September 30, 2011, the CMS procurement office announced that a company named CGI Federal had been chosen to build the federal insurance exchange—the one intended as the backup for states that did not build their own. This "backup" would end up being the exchange for thirty-six such states, evidence that "Obamacare" had become a dirty word in red states and was seen as an implementation challenge even in some blue states. With the target date for the launch set at July 1, 2013, CGI had less than two years to deliver on the contract it had just won.

No one in the White House or in any senior capacity at the Department of Health and Human Services or its CMS unit had anything to do with the choice of CGI. Non–civil servants are walled off from choosing contractors as a protection against cronyism or corruption. Rather, a team of civil servants at the CMS *Office* of Acquisition and Grants Management—part of a corps of more than twenty-six thousand government contracting officers—had made the decision. They chose CGI from among a half dozen government contractors who were on a list of those who were prequalified to fulfill what was called an indefinite-delivery, indefinite-quantity (IDIQ) task.

An IDIQ contract produced a hunting license for companies seeking work from the government. Getting on the list was a process that took lots of time and money and, therefore, made sense only for companies focused on trolling for government contracts. It was not something that more entrepreneurial enterprises, especially those outside Washington, were likely to bother with.

Even if the CMS procurement people had been inclined to cast a wider net, which they usually weren't, they became compelled to use this prebaked list because they had missed their deadline for issuing a Request for Proposals and had not gotten it out until the end of June. That delay required a shortened process that could consider that IDIQ group only.

CGI had delivered the best response to CMS's fifty-nine-page statement of work, which listed everything that would be required to complete the job. There were thousands of details, but broader requirements, too, including "world class IT services," "a first class customer experience," and "seamless coordination" between multiple government databases. The contract was set at $93 million. It would later become $293 million.

THE USUAL SUSPECTS

The blurb at the top of the government contracts page of the CGI website proclaimed, "Trust us: Technology is not the hard part." By which, the firm explained, it meant that CGI knew the technology cold, but that the real value it added was in designing and building user-friendly, efficient technology systems and websites for complicated government programs.

The other teams working in the administration on Obamacare were assured by the CMS procurement officials that CGI was the smart choice. The firm had handled other CMS contracts well and had won high marks for its work creating a database to monitor the massive spending associated with the economic stimulus program in 2009.

What they were not told was that CGI—a Canadian-based company—had purchased another Washington-area contractor whose work on several government projects had resulted in a variety of mishaps and disputes, and that CGI had bungled a healthcare-related project in Canada.

While CGI's bona fides may have been unclear, what was clear by now to Aneesh Chopra, the chief technology officer at the White House, and to Todd Park, who had that title at HHS, was that CGI was one of those usual-suspect government contractors that, as they had discussed nearly two years earlier, should not be used on a project like this.

Moreover, CGI wasn't really in charge. CMS was signing dozens of other multimillion-dollar contracts—ultimately there would be fifty-five of them—to complete various tasks other than building the elements of the federal website for which CGI would be responsible. For example, a firm called QSSI, which was a subsidiary of a subsidiary of giant health insurer UnitedHealthcare, got a $68 million contract to connect the website to the various federal agency databases to verify income, citizenship, and other elements of the application process.

In a situation like this, where there are multiple contractors, the lead contractor—in this case, CGI—would usually be designated as the general contractor to be in charge of all the others. Or a wholly different company would be hired to supervise everyone else—and bear the blame if all that work didn't mesh. However, Henry Chao and the staff at the CMS Office of Information Services had decided that *they* would be the general contractor. To Chopra and Park, the White House and HHS chief technology officers, that was the biggest threat to the launch.

Chopra and Park tried to talk about all that to Sebelius and to Marilyn Tavenner, a former Virginia secretary of health and human resources, who was about to be appointed the acting administrator of CMS. They were told that everything was in hand, that CMS was used to doing big data projects.

However, the big data that CMS handled had to do with vetting and paying masses of Medicare bills. It didn't involve a complicated e-commerce offering containing hundreds of various insurance products and requiring a spaghetti plate full of connections to those insurers and to government agencies. CMS, in fact, did not even have a website that handled inquiries about Medicare claims or allowed people to sign up electronically.

Chopra and Park tried to go to meetings about the project, the government's biggest consumer technology undertaking ever. Lambrew told the two chief technology officers they weren't needed, that everything was on track. DeParle backed her.

Having fought off the efforts by the economic team to bring in seasoned executives to run the launch, Lambrew and DeParle were now firmly in charge. Bob Kocher and Zeke Emanuel—left without their rabbis Summers and Orszag, who had resigned—were similarly excluded. They, too, soon left the White House for jobs outside government.

For her part, Kathleen Sebelius, the former Kansas governor who had been appointed health and human services secretary when Daschle had to bow out, devoted whatever time she spent on the launch mostly to looking in on the process of drafting the rules that would govern the insurance sold on the exchanges and to encouraging the large insurers to participate. This, rather than technology or e-commerce, was a natural focus for a former state insurance commissioner.

Nonetheless, according to notes taken at a July 1, 2011, White House meeting convened by DeParle, "the insurance companies were going bananas" because of the delays in issuing the regulations governing the products they would have to create, run through their actuarial models, establish prices and marketing messages for, and then launch into the exchange market by July 1, 2013—which in the summer of 2011 was still the target launch date.

When a set of preliminary insurance rules for the industry to comment on was finally issued on July 15, 2011, the launch date had been changed to October 1, 2013.

By the end of 2011—after the "comment" period on the preliminary rules had to be extended because the insurers complained about so many ambiguities, gaps, and impractical provisions—the process for getting the vitally important final insurance rules out the door would be severely, perhaps irredeemably, behind schedule.

CHAPTER 15

MEANTIME, OUTSIDE
THE BELTWAY . . .

January–December 2011

The struggles and internal battles in Washington during the summer of 2011 over launching the exchange played out under the radar. And with the Obama administration now in a defensive crouch when it came to Obamacare, there was no sign of Stephanie Cutter's "SWAT Teams" out there telling the story of the new law's glories.

But outside the Beltway, fixing healthcare had not become any less of an issue for millions of Americans for whom the law promised great relief—if the work to implement it could get done.

STEVEN AND ALICE'S DEATH PANEL

In early January 2011, a patient I'll call Steven D. learned the hard way what being underinsured means.

Soon after he was diagnosed with lung cancer on January 3, Steven and his wife, Alice, who lived in Northern California, knew that they were only buying time. The question was how much was the time worth. As Alice, who was making about $40,000 a year running a child care center in her home, explained, "[Steven] kept saying he wanted every last minute he could get, no matter what. But I had to be thinking about the cost and how all this debt would leave me and my daughter."

Sarah Palin's attacks aside, there was no Obamacare "death panel" that governed that decision. Steven's wallet did.

By the time Steven would die at his home in Northern California the following November, Alice had collected bills totaling $902,452.

$77 FOR GAUZE PADS

The family's first bill—for $348,000, which arrived when Steven got home from Seton Medical Center in Daly City, California—was full of all the usual chargemaster profit grabs: $24 each for nineteen niacin pills that are sold in drugstores for about a nickel apiece, and four boxes of sterile gauze pads (available on Amazon for $5.38 each) for $77 a box.

None of that was considered part of what was provided in return for Seton Medical Center's facility charge for two days in the intensive care unit at $13,225 a day, twelve days in the critical care unit at $7,315 a day, and one day in a standard room. The room charges totaled $120,116 over fifteen days. There was also $20,886 for CT scans and $24,251 for lab work.

I asked Alice how she felt about the obvious overcharges for items like the gauze pads: "Are you kidding?" she responded. "I'm dealing with a husband who had just been told he has stage-four cancer. That's all I can focus on. . . . You think I looked at the items on the bills? I just looked at the total."

Hospital billing people typically consider the chargemaster to be an opening bid. They use it to negotiate with insurance companies and often even with the uninsured if a patient without insurance is willing to negotiate a quick cash payment. But Steven and Alice didn't know that. No medical bill ever says "Give us your best counteroffer."

The couple knew only that the bill said they had maxed out on the $50,000 payout limit on a UnitedHealthcare policy they had bought through a community college where Steven had briefly enrolled a year before.

That insurance policy, with that $50,000 claims limit, was exactly the kind that Obamacare, under Jeanne Lambrew's regulations, would now outlaw, despite the president's promise that if "you like your insurance you can keep it."

Alice and her husband had, indeed, liked their plan, she had told me—until they realized how little $50,000 buys at an American hospital.

"We were in shock," Alice recalled, remembering the moment she opened the envelope containing the first bill. "We looked at the total and couldn't deal with it. So we just started putting all the bills in a box."

Robert Issai, the CEO of the Daughters of Charity Health System, which owned and ran Seton, declined to respond to requests for comment on his hospital's billing or collections policies.

Senator Grassley's provisions in the Obamacare bill that prohibit tax-exempt hospitals from charging chargemaster rates to patients needing financial aid would have restricted the Daughters of Charity in this situation. That part of the law was intended to take effect immediately once Obama signed the bill and his administration wrote the regulations to implement it. However, although the more complicated and arguably less important (though politically easier to market) MLR rules that Stephanie Cutter blogged about had been completed, these hospital billing regulations still had not been written when Steven D. fell ill, nearly ten months after the East Room signing ceremony.

A PAKISTANI RUG MARKET

Four months into her husband's illness, Alice by chance got the name of Patricia Stone of Menlo Park, California. Stone was one of fifty to a hundred "medical billing advocates" who by 2011 had made a cottage industry out of helping people deal with one of the abiding ironies of America's largest consumer product: completely inscrutable health-care bills and equally opaque insurance company Explanations of Benefits.

In talking to a half dozen of them while researching the *Time* article, I discovered that the advocates had settled on two basic strategies, neither of which spoke well for the sophistication of the biggest industry in the world's most celebrated free market economy.

First, in dealing with insurance claims, they had found that if they called an insurer and got an unsatisfactory answer, they could wait and call the same insurer back again with the same question—and often get a different, more favorable answer. There was no consistency. Everything was so complicated that they often could get the response they needed just by calling the customer service line a few times and finding someone who had a different read on the same issue. One billing advocate in Connecticut told me how she got a better response, worth nearly $10,000 to her client, simply by re-calling an insurer's customer service line twenty minutes after her first call.

Second, when dealing with a hospital chargemaster, the advocates would treat the process like the proverbial Pakistani rug market. They would call and offer to pay 30 to 50 percent of the bill. The hospital would settle for 50 or 60 percent in a matter of minutes, maybe 70 or 80 percent if it had a hard-nosed billing department. One advocate told me that it was so easy to get a $15,000 emergency room bill down to $10,000 with one call that she often kept clients waiting a week or two to make it seem like it had been harder for her to earn her $300 or $400 fee.

The advocates' effectiveness was more illustrative of the market in which they worked than it was any kind of a global solution to the market's dysfunction. Each seemed to handle forty to seventy cases a year for the uninsured and for those disputing insurance claims. That would be only about five thousand patients handled by all of the advocates in a year, out of what must have been millions of Americans facing these issues—a gap in help dealing with these bills that had to be part of the reason why 60 percent of the personal bankruptcy filings the year Obamacare was passed related to medical bills.

$902,000 FOR ELEVEN MONTHS OF LIFE

Advocate Patricia Stone's typical clients are middle-class people having trouble with insurance claims. Stone felt so bad for Steven and Alice—she saw the blizzard of bills Alice was going to have to sort through—that, Alice told me, Stone "gave us many of her hours," for which she usually charges $100, "for free."

Stone was soon able to persuade Seton Medical Center to write off most of its $348,000 portion of Steven's overall $902,000 bill. Her argument was simple: There was no way Steven and Alice could pay it all now or in the future, though they would immediately scrape together $3,000 as a show of good faith and promise to pay the rest of the written-down amount later.

But other bills would keep piling up. Sequoia Hospital—where Steven was an inpatient, as well as an outpatient—sent twenty-eight bills, all at chargemaster prices, including invoices for $99,000, $61,000, and $29,000. Sequoia is part of the giant, ostensibly nonprofit Dignity Health hospital chain, which had more than $9 billion in revenue in the year Steven was treated.

Doctor-run outpatient chemotherapy clinics wanted more than $85,000. One outside lab wanted $11,900.

Stone organized these and other bills into an elaborate spreadsheet—a ledger documenting how catastrophic illness in America unleashes its own mini gross domestic product.

The spreadsheet produced the family's own death panel sessions. "We started talking about the cost of the chemo," Alice would later tell me. "It was a source of tension between us. . . . Finally the doctor told us that the next [chemotherapy session] scheduled might prolong his life a month, but it would be really painful. So he gave up."

Alice would end up paying out about $30,000. Even after all the deals she got because she was lucky enough to find a billing advocate, she would still owe $142,000 one year after her husband's death. Ultimately, she would have to sell a family farm she inherited to pay it all off.

When the Obamacare insurance exchanges, with their premium subsidies, took effect in 2014, Steven and his wife could have bought a plan with no limits on how many treatments he could have had and, of course, no accounting for his preexisting condition. Because of the subsidies offered to people with low incomes, they would have paid less than the $400 a month Steven had paid for his now-inadequate insurance that Obamacare was going to cancel.

Nonetheless, if Steven was healthy at the time and if he didn't know about the subsidies—polls would show that most people didn't[13]—he might have complained that Obama was breaking his promise by taking away the insurance Steven liked and forcing him to buy something else that was more expensive.

PENNSYLVANIA TURF WARS

If more evidence was needed of how the marketplace that forced Alice to sell the family farm seemed to operate as if in its own universe, it was provided by a suit filed in federal court in western Pennsylvania just as Steven and his wife were staring down those hundreds of thousands in bills for treatment of his terminal cancer.

The suit accused the giant University of Pittsburgh Medical Center (UPMC) of using deceptive advertising to sell its own health insurance product.

As explained on page 103, UPMC and Highmark were the dominant hospital system and insurer respectively in western Pennsylvania. They had been sued for an alleged antitrust conspiracy in 2009 by a smaller hospital chain called West Penn Allegheny Health System. West Penn had charged that the two had formed a "super-monopoly" to crush West Penn and, at the same time, keep other insurance companies from intruding into Highmark's market.

Now, little more than two years after that 2009 suit from West Penn, UPMC (the giant hospital system) and Highmark (the insurer) had turned on each other, and their fight had made its way into court, with Highmark suing UPMC.

UPMC's chief executive—Jeffrey Romoff, the man who told me he prides himself on his ability to see and remove "impediments"—had apparently decided that his alleged co-conspirator, Highmark, had become another impediment. So Romoff had stepped up the marketing of his own UPMC insurance company—a venture whose ac-

13. In fact, in September 2014, a Kaiser Family Foundation poll reported that of those who actually signed up on the exchanges and received subsidies, nearly half did not know they were getting the subsidies.

tivities and marketing he had dialed down during the time of his alleged conspiracy with Highmark. He was spending millions on ads comparing UPMC's insurance to Highmark's and urging people to switch to UPMC.

Highmark's suit, filed on July 13, 2011, claimed that the UPMC ads were misleading. The major element of the deception, Highmark charged, was that UPMC was "scaring" Highmark's customers into thinking they could no longer have access to UPMC's dominant facilities and doctor networks, or would soon lose access, when, in fact, Highmark's network contract with UPMC extended through 2013.

How did it happen that these two healthcare giants, who had been accused in a compellingly documented complaint of conspiring with each other, were now litigating against each other?

According to court documents and what Romoff, himself, later told me, here is what had happened since that 2009 suit was filed accusing them of being joined-at-the-hip partners in an antitrust plot.

First, investigators from the Justice Department had started looking into the 2009 charges filed against UPMC and Highmark by the smaller West Penn hospital system. The feds were sounding like they, too, were going to conclude that the UPMC-Highmark arrangement seemed too cozy.

Both sides became nervous.

UPMC told Highmark that the hospital might have to strike a more competitive pose by revving up its own subsidiary insurance company—the company that the 2009 antitrust suit accused UPMC of agreeing to let die as part of its conspiracy with Highmark.

Equally bad for Highmark, if not worse, UPMC was going to have to let other, competing, insurers have access to the vast UPMC network of hospitals and doctors, opening the way for them to sell insurance at competitive prices to patients, most of whom were used to being treated at UPMC and would not buy insurance from another insurer if they couldn't continue to be treated there.

Along with that, UPMC was going to have to raise Highmark's rates after their current contract expired, so that Highmark would be forced onto a level playing field with the other insurance companies now allowed into the network.

Highmark, in turn, told UPMC that it might have to protect itself by helping the West Penn hospital system by sending it more patients. In other words, Highmark was going to try to revive the competitor that Romoff had thought he had vanquished.

The rationale for everything was the government investigation and the West Penn antitrust suit—which the two defendants were able to get dismissed because of these moves.

It was then that UPMC had unleashed the ad campaign for its revived insurance subsidiary, which was what Highmark targeted in this July 2011 suit.

But Highmark had more in its arsenal than a complaint about unfair advertising. In a move that infuriated Romoff, four months after filing the false advertising suit, Highmark announced a deal not just to try to send West Penn more patients, but to buy West Penn—yes, the same West Penn that had sued Highmark only two years before. If UPMC could own an insurance company, why couldn't Highmark own a hospital chain?

That announcement would be followed in 2012 by an even more explosive suit, this one brought by UPMC.

UPMC's 2012 suit would charge that Highmark had conspired with, and propped up, West Penn in order to drive UPMC out of business. The idea that UPMC could be driven out of business seemed far-fetched, yet UPMC CEO Romoff is one of those people who believes that if you are not moving up you are on your way down. Still more unusual was that Romoff's complaint essentially admitted the prior conspiracy with Highmark, although it said UPMC had been forced into it.

"Highmark has maintained a stranglehold on Western Pennsylvania's health insurance market," the 2012 UPMC suit would charge, "through a course of unlawful, malicious, and unabashedly anticompetitive conduct . . . to destroy UPMC as a negotiating entity, starve UPMC Health Plan [the UPMC insurance company] of the revenues necessary to emerge as a significant insurance competitor, and stifle competition from other insurers."

One of the central elements of this "unabashedly anticompetitive conduct," Romoff's 2012 suit would charge, was Highmark's alleged strong-arming of UPMC into the conspiracy that had led to the 2009 suit by West Penn against the two of them. Romoff's complaint would put it this way: "Bowing to both financial reality and the crushing public pressure fomented by Highmark, in June 2002, UPMC capitulated to Highmark's demands."

That was one way to look at it. Another was that by the time of the West Penn antitrust suit and the follow-on federal investigation, UPMC was so dominant that it no longer was worried about West Penn. Therefore, it didn't need any agreement with Highmark, and the federal investigation offered a convenient reason to end it. It could then weaken Highmark by inviting in other insurers and charging everyone a high price, while keeping prices low for its wholly owned insurer.

But then Highmark had fought back by adopting West Penn, which now presented a new "impediment" to Romoff and UPMC. With Highmark's financial power behind it, West Penn might be able to become a real competitor for UPMC's patients.

By mid-2014, both sides would have dropped their suits, but the battle among them would continue on a new front. UPMC—whose market share of hospital beds and doctors' practices was stronger than ever—was still threatening to throw Highmark out of its network, which would cripple Highmark.

The governor of Pennsylvania had intervened to mediate an agreement to extend their contract to the end of 2014, but beyond that there was little he could do. Hearings were held in the state capital, but there was little the legislators could do, either.

Through the summer of 2014, UPMC's advertising for its own insurance company touting its superior access (because of its status as an arm of UPMC) to the best doctors and hospitals would fill airwaves and adorn billboards all over Pittsburgh—except for the space taken up by competing Highmark ads promising, somehow, even greater availability of doctors and facilities. Patients, the vast majority of whom had to rely on Highmark for their insurance and on UPMC for their care, would be caught in the middle. They couldn't be sure what to believe was going to happen to their healthcare at the end of 2014.

At a hearing of a state house of representatives committee held as

the stand-off was looming, the always-blunt Romoff told one legislator, "Let me agree that UPMC and Highmark are both monopolies."

THE MEDICARE ALTERNATIVE

The same day—July 13, 2011—that Highmark sued UPMC over the
hospital's advertising, a patient a few hundred miles away in southern
New Jersey got a radically different look at American healthcare.

An eighty-eight-year-old man whom I'll call Alan A. collapsed
from a massive heart attack at his home outside Philadelphia. He survived and spent two weeks in the intensive care unit of Virtua Marlton
Hospital. Virtua Marlton was part of a four-hospital nonprofit chain
that, in its 2010 federal filing, had reported gross revenue of $633.7
million and an operating profit of $91 million. Alan then spent three
weeks at a nearby convalescent care center.

Alan had been covered by Medicare for twenty-three years. Medicare pays hospitals based on the average cost of treating each coded
category of illness, plus an allocation for overhead. The Medicare
number crunchers—the data and technology people overseen by
CMS's Henry Chao, who was going to be tasked to build the Obamacare federal exchange—do that by averaging the cost of every hospital's treatment of the same malady. Then, they account for differences
in overhead (such as labor costs and rent), based on region, on whether
the hospital spends money training upcoming doctors, and on other
factors. About 3 percent is added in for operating profit. The result is
what Medicare will pay when someone like Alan shows up at Virtua or
at the convalescent center where he was transferred.

Medicare made quick work of Alan's $268,227 in chargemaster bills
from the hospital and convalescent center, paying just $43,320. Except
for $100 in incidental expenses, Alan paid nothing because 100 percent
of inpatient hospital care is covered by Medicare.

The ManorCare convalescent center, which Alan later told me
gave him "good care" in an "OK but not luxurious room," got paid
$11,982 by Medicare for his three-week stay. That amounts to about
$571 a day for all of Alan's physical therapy, lab tests, and other ser-
vices. As with all hospitals in nonemergency situations, ManorCare

did not have to accept Medicare patients and their discounted rates. But it did accept them. In fact, it welcomed them and encouraged doctors to refer them.

Healthcare providers may grouse about Medicare's fee schedules, which they claim they lose money on. But Medicare's payments must have been producing profit for ManorCare. It was part of a for-profit chain owned by the Carlyle Group, a blue-chip private-equity firm.

$48.50 FOR LIFESAVING TREATMENT

About a decade before his July 2011 heart attack Alan had been diagnosed with non-Hodgkin's lymphoma. He was seventy-eight, and his doctors in southern New Jersey told him there was little they could do. Through a family friend, he got an appointment with one of the lymphoma specialists at the Memorial Sloan Kettering Cancer Center in New York. That doctor told Alan that he was willing to try a new chemotherapy regimen on him, but he warned that he hadn't ever tried it on anyone Alan's age.

The treatment worked. A decade later, Alan was still in remission, traveling up to Sloan Kettering every six weeks to be examined by the doctor who saved his life and to get a transfusion of Flebogamma, a drug that bucks up his immune system.

With some minor variations each time, Sloan Kettering's typical bill for each visit was the same as or similar to the $7,346 bill he received during his visit there in the summer of 2011 (just before his heart attack). It included $340 for a session with the doctor. His actual out-of-pocket cost for each session was a fraction of that. For that $7,346 visit, it was about $50.

The transactions related to Alan's Sloan Kettering care represented the best the American medical marketplace had to offer—and a regime that for people over sixty-five will not be altered by Obamacare. First, obviously, there's the fact that Alan was alive after other doctors gave him up for dead. Then there's the fact that Alan, a retired chemist of average means, was able to get care that might otherwise be reserved for the rich but was available to him because he had the right insurance.

Medicare, of course, was the core of that insurance, although Alan—along with 90 percent of those on Medicare—had a supplemental private insurance policy, usually called a Medigap policy, that kicked in and generally paid 90 percent of the 20 percent of the costs for doctors and other outpatient care that Medicare does not cover.

Here's how it all computed for Alan, using that summer 2011 Sloan Kettering bill for $7,346 as an example.

Not counting the doctor's separate $340 bill, Sloan Kettering's bill for the transfusion was $7,006.

In addition to a few hundred dollars in miscellaneous items, the two basic Sloan Kettering charges were $414 per hour for five hours of the nurse's time for administering the Flebogamma and a $4,615 charge for the Flebogamma.

According to Alan, the nurse generally handled three or four patients at a time. That would mean Sloan Kettering was billing more than $1,200 an hour for that nurse. When I asked Paul Nelson, Sloan Kettering's director of financial planning, about the $414-per-hour charge, he explained that 15 percent of these charges was meant to cover overhead and indirect expenses, 20 percent was meant to be profit that would cover discounts for Medicare or Medicaid patients, and 65 percent covered direct expenses. Assuming that just three patients were billed for the same hour at $414 each, that would still leave the nurse's time being valued at about $800 an hour (65 percent of $1,200). Pressed on that, Nelson conceded that the profit is higher and is meant to cover other hospital costs such as research and capital equipment.

Medicare—whose patients, including Alan, are about a third of all Sloan Kettering patients—bought into none of that math. Its cost-based pricing formulas yielded a price of $302 for everything other than the drug, including those hourly charges for the nurse and the miscellaneous charges. Medicare paid 80 percent of that, or $241. That left Alan and his private insurance company together to pay about $60 more to Sloan Kettering. Of that, Alan paid $6, and his supplemental insurer, Aetna, paid $54.

Bottom line: Sloan Kettering got paid $302 by Medicare for about $2,400 worth of its chargemaster charges, and Alan ended up paying $6.

THE CANCER DRUG PROFIT CHAIN

It was with the bill for the transfusion that the peculiar economics of American medicine took a different turn—a dynamic that in no way will be changed by Obamacare, thanks to the bargain struck by Billy Tauzin and PhRMA.

By law—the law Tauzin and PhRMA fought to protect in their negotiations with Baucus and the Obama administration—Medicare has to pay hospitals 6 percent above what Congress calls the drug company's "average sales price." That is supposedly the average price at which the drugmaker sells the drug to hospitals and clinics. Under the law, Medicare cannot control what drugmakers charge or even try to negotiate a price based on what a giant buyer it is. The drug companies are free to set their own prices.

Applying that formula of average sales price plus the 6 percent premium, Medicare cut Sloan Kettering's $4,615 chargemaster charge for Alan's Flebogamma to $2,123. That's what the drugmaker told Medicare the average sales price was, plus 6 percent. Medicare again paid 80 percent of that, and Alan and his insurer split the other 20 percent—10 percent for him and 90 percent for the insurer. That made Alan's cost $42.50. With the $6.00 Alan paid for his share of the other hospital charges, his total cost for his treatment at Sloan Kettering was $48.50.

In practice, the average sales price for Alan's Flebogamma does not appear to be a real average. Two other hospitals I asked reported that after taking into account rebates given by the drug company, they paid an average of $1,650 for the same dose of Flebogamma, well below the $2,123 Medicare paid Sloan Kettering. And neither hospital had nearly the leverage in the cancer care marketplace that Sloan Kettering does. One doctor at Sloan Kettering guessed that it was paying $1,400.

Nelson, the Sloan Kettering head of financial planning, told me that the price his hospital paid for Alan's dose is "somewhat higher" than $1,400, but he would not be specific. Even assuming Sloan Kettering's real price was "somewhat higher" than $1,400 (say, $1,600), the hospital would have made about 33 percent profit from Medicare's $2,123 payment. So even Medicare was contributing mightily to hospital profit—and drug-company profit—when it bought drugs.

The hospitals and PhRMA had struck a good bargain when they negotiated Obamacare.

SALARIES IN A WORLD OF THEIR OWN

In its latest report on file with the IRS when Alan had his summer 2011 treatment, Sloan Kettering had an operating profit of $406 million even after everything it spent on research and the education of a small army of young cancer doctors.

The cash flow came from more than just drug markups. There was also the high pricing enabled by a deservedly great brand.

Insurance companies negotiated discounts off Sloan Kettering's chargemaster prices, but chief operating officer John Gunn told me that his hospital can drive a hard bargain because insurers want to make sure Sloan Kettering is in their network.

That brand power produced not only lavish cash flows, but also lavish incomes for the non-doctors who worked to generate it. Sloan Kettering had six administrators making salaries of more than $1 million.

When I looked at this list of salaries for the *Time* article, I discovered that compared with their peers at equally venerable nonprofits, these executives were comfortably ensconced in a medical ecosystem that was in a world of its own. For example, Sloan Kettering had two development office executives, or fund-raisers, making $1,483,000 and $844,000. Another New York nonprofit that mines the same field for donors—the Metropolitan Museum of Art—paid its top development officer $345,000. Harvard paid its chief fund-raiser $392,000.

Asked why salaries at Sloan Kettering are so much higher than those at equally wealthy nonprofits such as the Met and Harvard, Gunn replied, "All of us hospitals have the same compensation consultants, so I guess it's a self-fulfilling prophecy."

Compensation consultants advise clients on what the market-based salary is for executives in a given peer group—CEOs or chief fund-raisers at hospitals of a certain size, for example. So if the same hospital compensation consultants set high salaries for a large portion of the people in each hospital peer group, then those salaries are destined to stay high while still being deemed consistent with the "market."

Whatever the rationale for the compensation rates, the prospectus that Sloan Kettering's bankers and lawyers used to sell the bonds that helped finance its incessant expansion (including opening satellite clinics in New York's suburbs) struck a tone that seemed at odds with the daily sight of men and women rushing through the halls of this great cancer center doing God's work. The halls were sprinkled with cheerful posters aimed at patients, but the prospectus was sprinkled with phrases such as "market share," "improved pricing," and "rate and volume increases." Then again, the same prospectus described the core of the business this way: "higher five-year survival rates for cancer patients as compared to other institutions."

Indeed, if I had needed cancer treatment instead of heart surgery, I would have fought to get into Sloan Kettering (which was across the street from New York–Presbyterian, where I had my operation). I wouldn't have cared how much they paid their fund-raisers or anyone else.

A 460 TO 800 PERCENT MARKUP

The business at the beginning of the Flebogamma supply chain did even better than Sloan Kettering when it came to Alan's care.

Made from human plasma, Flebogamma is a sterilized solution intended to boost the immune system. Sloan Kettering likely bought Alan's Flebogamma from a Barcelona-based company called Grifols.

In the company's 2011 annual report, worldwide sales of all Grifols products were reported to be up 7.7 percent, to 2.3 billion euros. Despite the continuing worldwide recession, net profit was up 10.1 percent. In its half-year 2012 shareholder report, "Growth in the sales . . . of the main plasma derivatives" would be highlighted, as would the fact that "the cost per liter of plasma has fallen."

A Grifols spokesman would not discuss what it cost Grifols to produce and ship Alan's dose. But he did say that the average production for its bioscience products, Flebogamma included, was approximately 55 percent of what it sells them for. However, a doctor familiar with the economics of cancer care drugs told me that plasma products typically have some of the industry's higher profit margins. He estimated that the Flebogamma dose for Alan—which Sloan Kettering seemed to have bought from Grifols for $1,400 to $1,600 and sold to Medicare for $2,123—can't cost more than $200 or $300 to collect, process, test, and ship. That would be a 460 to 800 percent markup.

In Spain, as in the rest of the developed world, Grifols's profit margins on sales are much lower than they are in the United States, where, thanks to PhRMA's vigilant efforts, the company can charge much higher prices. Aware of the leverage that drug companies—especially those with unique lifesaving products—have on the market, most developed countries had, by the time Obamacare was passed, regulated what drugmakers could charge, limiting their profit margins. In fact, the drugmakers' securities filings routinely warned investors of tighter price controls that could threaten their high margins—though not in the United States.

The difference between the regulatory environment in the United States and the environment abroad is so dramatic that McKinsey & Company researchers found that overall prescription drug prices in the United States were "50% higher for comparable products" than in other developed countries. Yet those regulated profit margins outside the United States remain high enough that Grifols, Baxter, and other drug companies still aggressively sell their products there.

By 2012, more than $280 billion would be spent each year on prescription drugs in the United States. If Americans paid what other countries did for the same products, they would save about $94 billion a year.

As you would know from talking for five minutes to Billy Tauzin, the pharmaceutical industry's common explanation for the price difference is that U.S. profits subsidize the research and development of trailblazing drugs that are developed in the United States and then marketed around the world. Apart from the issue of whether a country with a healthcare-spending crisis should subsidize the rest of the developed world—not to mention the question of who signed Americans up for that mission—the companies' math doesn't add up.

According to the securities filings of major drug companies, in the last few years their R & D expenses have generally been 15 to 20 percent of gross revenue. In fact, Grifols spent less than 5 percent on R & D in 2011. Neither 5 percent nor 20 percent is enough to have cut deeply into the pharmaceutical companies' bottom-line *net* profits. This is not *gross* profit, which counts only the cost of producing the drug, but the profit *after* those R & D expenses are taken into account.

In 2011, Grifols made a 27.4 percent net operating profit—after all its R & D expense, as well as sales, management, and other expenses, were tallied. In other words, even counting all the R & D across the entire company, including research for drugs that did not pan out, Grifols made stellar profits.

All the numbers seemed to tell one consistent story: Regulating drug prices the way other countries do would save tens of billions of dollars while still offering profits that would encourage the pharmaceutical companies' quest for the next great drug. But the deal-making dynamics of Washington hadn't allowed for the healthcare reformers to do that. Instead, Obamacare sent more customers into this high-profit market, most of whom had government subsidies to pay insurance premiums that were inflated by these high drug prices.

A $0.33 BILL = BILLIONS IN WASTE

The mound of bills and Medicare statements Alan showed me for 2011—when he had his heart attack and continued his treatments at Sloan Kettering—seemed to add up to about $350,000. His total out-of-pocket expense was $1,139, or less than 0.4 percent of his overall medical bills. Those bills included what seemed to be thirty-three visits in one year to eleven doctors who had nothing to do with his recovery from the heart attack or his cancer.

In all cases, Alan was routinely asked to pay almost nothing because Medicare and his supplemental insurance covered so much of it. He had paid $2.20 for a check of a sinus problem, $1.70 for an eye exam, and $0.33 to deal with a bunion. When he showed me those bills he chuckled.

A comfortable member of the middle class, Alan could easily have afforded the burden of higher co-pays that would have encouraged him to use doctors less casually or would at least stick taxpayers with less of the bill if he wanted to get that bunion treated. However, the AARP (formerly the American Association of Retired Persons), and other liberal entitlement lobbies opposed these types of changes early on in the debate over healthcare reform. Their support was crucial, and no reforms requiring those who could afford it to pay a higher share of the Medicare bills ever made it into any Baucus drafts or any other. As with doing something to control drug prices, that was more reform than the process would allow.

Medicare spent more than $6.5 billion in 2011 to pay doctors (even at the discounted Medicare rates) for the service codes that denote the most basic categories of office visits. From looking at Alan's bills and the near-free ride he got for any type of treatment, it seemed clear that a provision in Obamacare asking people like Alan to pay more than a negligible share, could have recouped $1 billion to $2 billion of those costs yearly, and probably saved billions more on needless tests generated by all of those office visits.

THE DOCTORS PARADE IN

Another bill, for which Alan's share was $0.19, illustrated why Peter Orszag was so fixated on fee-for-service.

It was one of fifty bills from twenty-six doctors who saw Alan at Virtua Marlton hospital or at the ManorCare convalescent center after his heart attack, or read one of his diagnostic tests at the two facilities. "They paraded in once a day or once every other day, looked at me and poked around a bit and left," Alan recalled. Other than the doctor in charge of his heart attack recovery, "I had no idea who they were until I got these bills. But for a dollar or two, so what?"

The "so what" was that although Medicare deeply discounted the bills, it—meaning taxpayers—still paid from $7.48 (for a chest x-ray reading) to $164 for each encounter.

"One of the benefits attending physicians get from many hospitals is the opportunity to cruise the halls and go into a Medicare patient's room and rack up a few dollars," explained a doctor who has worked at several hospitals across the country when I asked about all the traffic trooping in and out to have a look at Alan. "In some places it's a Monday morning tradition. You go see the people who came in over the weekend. There's always an ostensible reason, but there's also a lot of abuse."

With the kind of "bundled" pricing Orszag favored, Alan would likely not have been as popular with all of those doctors. The hospital and its doctors would have been paid a set price for treating him successfully, not for how many times how many doctors looked in on him. But the bundles Orszag, Kocher, and Zeke Emanuel managed to wedge into the final bill involved limited pilot projects. They might ultimately lead to reforms, but they were far from revolutionary.

AN INSURANCE COMPANY IN SILICON ALLEY?

"I was just told that a company that I would like to start would be impossible," tweeted twenty-six-year-old Joshua Kushner on December 11, 2011. "The harder an idea is to execute the bigger the opportunity," he added. "We want you to call us. We want you to take your medicine. Free calls, free generics."

Kushner was tweeting about starting a health insurance company. His inspiration: Obamacare and the coming insurance exchanges.

Kushner was not an insurance company type. Two weeks after this tweet, *Forbes* would choose him—along with HBO's *Girls* creator and star Lena Dunham—as one of its "30 under 30" future superstars. As a junior at Harvard four years earlier, Kushner had founded what had become the largest online gaming service in Latin America. He had since raised $200 million for a private equity firm called Thrive Capital, which became an early investor in Instagram.

Kushner was rich before those successes. His father had been a wealthy New Jersey–based real estate developer and investor. His brother, Jared, now ran the firm, which had expanded into Manhattan. Both brothers, while unfailingly polite (as if their parents would take away the car keys if they didn't behave like gentlemen), cut high profiles in New York's fast lane. Jared had bought the *New York Observer,* a Manhattan weekly that lost money yet was a favorite in New York media and real estate circles. And he was married to Donald Trump's glamorous daughter, Ivanka. Josh, too, was regularly found in the gossip columns that kept tabs on the models he was dating.

Although Joshua Kushner was not your usual health insurance executive, he was an insurance customer, which is how he got the idea that he had started talking to friends about.

Kushner, who had just graduated from Harvard Business School, had been reading a lot about Obamacare when he happened to get an Explanation of Benefits from his insurance company, purporting to explain why the insurer had paid only a portion of a recent bill. Kushner couldn't understand it, no matter how many times he read it. Yet as a Harvard College and Harvard Business School graduate, he considered himself a pretty smart guy. Maybe the fault was theirs, not his.

It was a thought a lot of us have probably had. Only Kushner, who was vaguely aware that Obamacare was going to allow for the sale of health insurance in a competitive online exchange, saw the baffling insurance bill as an opportunity rather than a frustration. And, as his tweet about his friends' reaction revealed, he was too naïve to realize how impossible it would be. That his friends dismissed the idea just spurred him on. He was an entrepreneur, not a realist.

Following the tweet, Kushner would find himself incessantly "jamming the idea with my friends," he later recalled. "That's how you do something like this; you find your smartest friends."

Before long he would recruit Mario Schlosser, then thirty-two, and Kevin Nazemi, then twenty-nine, and set up an office at his venture firm's headquarters in lower Manhattan. Kushner had met Schlosser at Harvard Business School, and they had started the Latin American gaming service together. Schlosser had also worked at a hedge fund developing trading models and as a McKinsey consultant working on healthcare analytics.

Kushner also knew Nazemi from Harvard Business School. He had an undergraduate degree from MIT and had run a bunch of consumer businesses for Microsoft. Nazemi would focus on designing and marketing their venture.

As they began to put together a business plan and lure investors, they developed the shorthand description, or elevator pitch, for their idea: "A health insurance start-up that is using technology, design, and data to help humanize and simplify healthcare."

CHAPTER 16

WAITING FOR OBAMACARE

January–December 2012

THE CLOSER IT GOT TO ELECTION DAY 2012, THE MORE THE OBAMA healthcare and political teams seemed to want to avoid doing anything to call attention to the president's signature domestic policy initiative, including issuing the rules necessary to implement it.

Through the first quarter of 2012, there were still no regulations telling the insurers exactly what they could or could not sell on the exchanges and how they could sell it.

Little details were missing, too, such as how an extra charge for smokers, which the final version of the law had allowed, would work.

There was also the question of how each insurer's deductibles, co-pays, and network limits could be displayed on the exchange websites. Would people be able to see all of that information before they clicked through to an insurer-specific page? How much leeway would the state-run exchanges have to be different?

For Karen Ignagni's insurance companies, these were paralyzing unknowns. They usually took years to bring new products to market once they had a grip on details like these.

THE STALL

These were complicated issues, and in Washington even the simplest rulemaking required a five-step approval process culminating in a sign-off by the Office of Management and Budget. OMB often took months to move drafts of regulations off its many desks.

But there was more to this slowdown than Washington bureaucrats mired in the usual quicksand. It was also deliberate. Two CMS officials would later tell me that beginning in January 2012 they were told by their superiors that the already-slow rule-making process had to be slowed still more. They could take their time sending drafts to the White House for approval, they were told, because the White House was only going to stall before sending whatever the rule was over to OMB, which would stall even more. They did not want to make any waves before the election.

In a third case, a White House staffer told me that a member of Obama's political team had said that there was no need to rush any-thing out the door, though he rationalized it by explaining that for now "the person in charge of Obamacare is John Roberts." He was referring to the chief justice of the United States and the fact that the constitutionality of Obamacare was on its way to being argued before the Supreme Court in late March 2012.

"WE DIDN'T KNOW WHAT WE DIDN'T KNOW"

The technology build didn't need anyone's interference to gum up the works. The now-demoted Henry Chao, working under his old dep-uty director title in his old *office,* was still waiting for the procurement people in another *office* to finish signing up the dozens of contractors whose work he would be in charge of cobbling together with what the main contractor, CGI, was supposed to produce.

Chao had experience managing Medicare and Medicaid data sys-tems. But those systems had long since been built. Chao had never built a new one from scratch. CGI was already telling Chao that with-out the other contractors signed up and working—and without the

rules spelled out for how the insurance would be offered and sold—
the October 1, 2013, launch deadline was in danger of being missed.

Although a poor communicator, who often left non-techies wondering how to translate what he had just said, Chao was a well-
respected, hard-driving civil servant. He prided himself on the CMS
data machine and the team that ran it. One colleague told me, "Henry
exuded confidence as habitually as you and I breathe."

Through the end of 2011 and into 2012, Chao assured his boss, CMS
head Marilyn Tavenner, that he and his team would be able to get the
project done on time.

"We hadn't ever built anything like this," Tavenner would later tell
me. "We didn't know what we didn't know."

$474,000 FOR PNEUMONIA

As 2012 began, another couple I met while examining medical bills for
the *Time* report, whom I'll call Rebecca and Scott S., seemed to have
carved out a comfortable semi-retirement in a suburb near Dallas.
Scott had successfully sold his small industrial business and was working part-time advising other industrial companies. Rebecca was running a small marketing business. Both were in their late fifties.

On March 4, 2012, Scott started having trouble breathing. By din-
nertime he was gasping violently as Rebecca raced with him to the
emergency room at the University of Texas Southwestern Medical
Center. Both Rebecca and her husband thought he was about to die.

Scott was in the hospital for thirty-two days before his pneumonia
was brought under control.

Rebecca told me that "on about the fourth or fifth day, I was sitting around the hospital and bored, so I went down to the business
office just to check that they had all the insurance information.

"Even by then, the bill was over eighty thousand dollars," she recalled. "I couldn't believe it."

The woman in the business office matter-of-factly gave Rebecca
some additional bad news: Her insurance policy, from a company
called Assurant Health, had an annual payout limit of $100,000. Be-

cause of some prior claims Assurant had processed, Rebecca and Scott were already well on their way to exceeding the limit.

It was another of those insurance products that the new law would eliminate, beginning in 2014.

Just the room and board charge at Southwestern was $2,293 a day. And that was before all the real charges were added.

When Scott checked out, his 161-page bill was $474,064. Scott and Rebecca were told they owed $402,955 after the payment from their insurance policy was deducted.

The top billing categories were:

- $73,376 for Scott's room.
- $94,799 for "resp services." That mostly meant supplying Scott with oxygen and testing his breathing, and included multiple charges per day of $134 for supervising oxygen inhalation, for which Medicare would have paid $17.94.
- $108,663 for "special drugs," which included mostly not-so-special drugs such as "sodium chloride .9%." That is a standard saline, or salt water, solution, probably used intravenously in this case to maintain Scott's water and salt levels. (It is also used to moisten contact lenses.) You can buy a liter of the hospital version (bagged for intravenous use) online for $5.16. Scott was charged $84 to $134 for dozens of these saline solutions.

Then there was the $132,303 charge for "laboratory," which included hundreds of blood and urine tests ranging from $30 to $333 each, for which Medicare either pays nothing because it is part of the room fee or pays $7 to $30.

Through a friend of a friend, Rebecca would soon find Pat Palmer, another of those billing advocates.

The best Palmer would be able to do for Scott and Rebecca was get Texas Southwestern Medical to provide a credit that still left them owing $313,000. By early 2013, the nonprofit hospital would offer to cut the bill to $200,000 if it was paid immediately, or it would allow the full $313,000 to be paid in twenty-four monthly payments. "How am I supposed to write a check right now for two hundred thousand dollars?" Rebecca told me. "I have boxes full of notices from bill collectors. . . . We can't apply for charity, because we're kind of well off in terms of assets," she added. "We thought we were set, but now we're pretty much on the edge."

By January 1, 2014, Scott and Rebecca—who had not been able to find any new insurance following Scott's hospitalization in 2012 because he had a preexisting condition—would be protected through an insurance plan that they were able to buy thanks to Obamacare. Scott's preexisting condition could no longer be used to deny him coverage.

Because Scott and Rebecca's income was too high to qualify them for subsidies, they didn't have to buy insurance on the Texas version of the federal exchange. (Subsidies can only come via the exchanges.) They bought it directly from Blue Cross Blue Shield of Texas. However, under the new law, all policies—not just those on the exchanges—had to comply with the new rules, such as not discriminating based on Scott's preexisting condition. The insurance was expensive—$700 a month. However, they were now protected from bills like the ones they got in 2012, even as the hospital persisted in trying to collect on that old bill.

By the time Rebecca focused on their new insurance, she had become a sophisticated consumer, having learned about those policies with annual limits the hard way. As a result, she had a major complaint about Obamacare. She thought the Obama administration had been too lenient in dealing with inadequate insurance policies. After Lambrew issued her rules allowing policies like Scott's Assurant policy to be continued, or "grandfathered," until January 1, 2014, Rebecca complained to me that the insurers had obviously "gotten" to someone in the administration. They should never have allowed those policies to continue being sold even that long, she said.

A $132,000 SINKHOLE

Other than putting Scott and Rebecca in a situation where their new insurance company would no doubt get a discount off the chargemaster bills they received, there is nothing in Obamacare that addresses the costs, and cost structure, that Scott's near-fatal illness triggered.

The best example in their case was what may seem the most surprising medical care sinkhole, because everything about it is an afterthought for most patients: seemingly routine blood, urine, and other laboratory tests. Scott was charged $132,000 for them, or more than $4,000 a day.

About $65 billion would be spent on these tests in the United States in 2012, the year Scott was rushed to the hospital.

Cutting the over-ordering and overpricing of these tests might have easily taken $20 billion a year out of that bill. But that was one giveback the hospitals were not asked for in their negotiations over whether they would support reform. True, the pilot projects in the law meant to encourage a bundled price for services—rather than the fee-for-service orgy spread across Scott's 161 pages of bills—might help cut this overage some. But the lab test sinkhole was never attacked frontally.

Much of that over-ordering involves patients like Scott, who require prolonged hospital stays. Their tests become a routine, daily cash generator.

"When you're getting trained as a doctor," said a physician who was involved in advising on healthcare policy early in the Obama administration, "you're taught to order what's called 'morning labs.' Every day you have a variety of blood tests and other tests done, not because it's necessary but because it gives you something to talk about with the others when you go on rounds. It's like your version of a news hook. . . . I bet sixty percent of the labs are not necessary."

The country's largest lab tester is Quest Diagnostics, which would report revenues in 2012 of $7.4 billion, and operating profit of $1.2 billion, or about 16 percent of sales. Like the hospitals, labs like Quest have a chargemaster. If your doctor sends your blood to Quest for testing and the company is not in your insurer's network, you must pay the entire bill or face a bill collector and an endangered credit rating. But if Quest is in your network, $400 in charges becomes $20 or $30.

However, companies like Quest, which mostly pick up specimens from doctors and clinics and deliver test results back to them, are not where the big profits are. The real money is in healthcare settings that cut out the middleman—the in-house venues, like the hospital testing lab run by Southwestern Medical that billed Scott $132,000. Hospital-affiliated in-house labs accounted for about 60 percent of all testing revenue in 2012. Which means that for hospitals, they were vital profit centers.

In fact, by the time Obamacare became law, labs were also increasingly being maintained by doctors who, as they formed group practices with other doctors in their field, financed their own testing and diagnostic clinics. These in-house labs have no selling costs, and as pricing surveys repeatedly find, they can charge more because they have a captive consumer base in the hospitals or group practices.

They also have an incentive to order more tests because they're the ones profiting from the tests, the ultimate extension of Orszag's fee-for-service problem. *The Wall Street Journal* would report in April 2012 that a study in the medical journal *Health Affairs* had found that doctors' urology groups with their own labs "bill the federal Medicare program for analyzing 72% more prostate tissue samples per biopsy while detecting fewer cases of cancer than counterparts who send specimens to outside labs." It was a way for some doctors to do something other than sit on the sidelines while every other player in the healthcare economy cashed in.

"THEREFORE, YOU CAN MAKE PEOPLE BUY BROCCOLI"

The Supreme Court's hearing on the constitutionality of Obamacare began while Scott was still in the hospital and his wife was worrying about how to deal with the bills that were piling up. Beginning on March 27, 2012, the hearing stretched over three days, not the conventional single day, and each hearing was two hours a day, instead of the usual one.

What was more unusual was the unmasked hostility from what seemed to be a majority of the justices. Five of the nine seemed ready to reject the idea that the Constitution's Commerce Clause could be used by Congress to force people to buy something from a private company.

Justice Antonin Scalia, the sharp-tongued conservative, ridiculed the notion that because everyone ends up using healthcare, everyone could be made to buy insurance: "Everybody has to buy food sooner or later, so you define the market as food. . . . Therefore, everybody is in the market. Therefore, you can make people buy broccoli."

The usually more moderate chief justice John Roberts offered the similar spin that approving the individual mandate requiring everyone to buy health insurance would be like allowing a requirement that people had to buy cell phones so that they could reach first responders quickly in the event of any emergency.

Justice Anthony Kennedy—a Ronald Reagan appointee thought likely be the swing vote in tight cases because he was seen as sitting in the middle between the Court's Republican-appointee conservatives and Democratic-appointee liberals—complained to the government's lawyer, Solicitor General Donald Verrilli, that "you are changing the relationship of the individual to the government."

What was additionally discouraging to Obamacare supporters—including Liz Fowler, who was in the chamber on the second day—was that Solicitor General Verrilli let the hostility knock him off-balance. His arguments were not nearly as tightly drawn and effective as those of his opponent, Paul Clement, a former solicitor general in the George W. Bush administration, who was carving out a specialty as the conservatives' star appellate lawyer.

Clement fared so well and Verrilli struggled so mightily that by the last day of the three-day high-court drama, many respected legal pundits were predicting doom for Obamacare.

By the Obama administration's own account in its brief, doom is what now would come if the Court struck down the mandate that everyone had to have insurance. Gone were the qualms Obama and his staff had had during the campaign, the transition, and through the winter of 2009 about the mandate. Forgotten was how Obama had used Hillary Clinton's support for a mandate as his point of attack against her. Gone was the political team's reliance on some of the economists and behavioral scientists who had said that a mandate wasn't necessary—that a "death spiral" of higher premiums would not necessarily come if people could wait until they were sick to buy insurance but insurers could still not exclude them for preexisting conditions. Now, the coming death spiral was all over their brief.

Meanwhile, Mitt Romney, the father of the mandate, was running in the opposite direction.

Through the Republican primary contests of 2012, the former Massachusetts governor had been put on the defensive by opponents who charged that the reviled Obamacare was the offspring of Romneycare. Tim Pawlenty, the Minnesota governor who had ordered every agency in his state to have nothing to do with the new law, had taken to calling Obamacare O'Romneycare. Rick Santorum, the former Pennsylvania senator who would finish second to Romney in the primary race, said Romney's history on healthcare disqualified him for the nomination because he could never confront Obama on what should be the main issue of the general election campaign. How could Romney attack Obamacare, he argued.

Romney certainly tried. On the 2012 campaign trail he promised to repeal Obamacare on the first day of his presidency. What he had done in one state, he asserted, did not justify Obama's "one-size-fits-all" for all states, and he attacked a federally imposed mandate as an assault on liberty that would not work.

Jonathan Gruber, the MIT economist who had helped Romney create Romneycare and then worked on Obamacare, had sat out the 2008 election. Now, he happily allowed himself to be interviewed at every opportunity confirming that Obamacare was modeled exactly from Romneycare and, like Romneycare, was going to work fine.

CASH FOR CANCER CARE

About a week before the Supreme Court argument, Sean Recchi, a forty-two-year-old from Lancaster, Ohio, was told that he had non-Hodgkin's lymphoma. His wife, Stephanie, decided that she had to get him to MD Anderson Cancer Center in Houston.

Stephanie's father had been treated at the famed cancer center ten years earlier, and she and her family credited the doctors and nurses there with extending his life by at least eight years.

Because Stephanie and her husband had recently started their own small technology business, they had been unable to buy comprehensive health insurance. For $469 a month, or about 20 percent of their income, they had been able to get a policy that covered just $2,000 a day of hospital costs.

This was another policy that would not qualify under Obamacare as adequate insurance in 2014.

At MD Anderson in 2012, it already didn't qualify. "We don't take that kind of discount insurance," said the woman at the Houston cancer center when Stephanie called to make an appointment for Sean.

Stephanie was then told by the billing clerk that the estimated cost of Sean's visit—just to be examined for six days so a treatment plan could be devised—would be $48,900, due in advance. Stephanie got her mother to write the check. "You do anything you can in a situation like that," she later told me when I spoke with her for the *Time* report.

The Recchis flew to Houston, leaving Stephanie's mother to care for their two teenage children.

On the morning of the second and most heated day of the Supreme Court Obamacare argument, Stephanie had to ask her mother for $35,000 more so Sean could begin the treatment the doctors had decided was urgent. His condition had worsened rapidly since he arrived in Houston. He was "sweating and shaking with chills and pains," Stephanie recalled. "He had a large mass in his chest that was . . . growing. He was panicked."

Nonetheless, while the justices grilled Solicitor General Verrilli, Sean was held for about ninety minutes in a reception area, because the hospital could not confirm that his mother-in-law's check had cleared. He was allowed to see the doctor only after he advanced MD Anderson $7,500 from his credit card.

The hospital would later tell me that there was nothing unusual about how Sean was kept waiting. According to an MD Anderson spokeswoman, "Asking for advance payment for services is a common, if unfortunate, situation that confronts hospitals all over the United States."

The total cost, in advance, for Sean to get his treatment plan and initial dose of chemotherapy was $83,900.

The first of the 344 lines printed out across eight pages of his hospital bill—filled with the chargemaster's indecipherable numerical codes and acronyms—seemed innocuous. But it set the tone for all that followed. It read, "1 acetaminophen tabs 325 mg." The charge was only $1.50, but it was for a generic version of a Tylenol pill. You can buy 100 of them on Amazon for $1.49 even without a hospital's purchasing power.

On the second page of the bill, the markups got bolder. Recchi was charged $13,702 for "1 rituximab inj 660 mg." That's an injection of 660 milligrams of a cancer wonder drug called Rituxan. The average price paid by all hospitals for this dose is about $4,000. However, MD Anderson probably gets a volume discount that would make its cost $3,000 to $3,500. That means the nonprofit cancer center's paid-in-advance markup on Recchi's lifesaving shot would be 300 to 400 percent.

When I asked MD Anderson to comment on the charges on Recchi's bill, the cancer center released a written statement that said in part, "The issues related to health care finance are complex for patients, health care providers, payers and government entities alike. . . . MD Anderson's clinical billing and collection practices are similar to those of other major hospitals and academic medical centers."

The hospital's hard-nosed approach pays off. Although it is officially a nonprofit unit of the University of Texas, MD Anderson has revenue that exceeded the cost of the world-class care it provides by so much that its operating profit for the fiscal year 2010 (the most recent annual report it had filed with the U.S. Department of Health and Human Services when Sean Recchi arrived there) was $531 million. That was a profit margin of 26 percent on revenue of $2.05 billion, an astounding result for such a service-intensive enterprise.

Rituxan is a prime product of Biogen Idec, a company that had reported $5.5 billion in sales in the year before Sean Recchi fell ill. This was not an enterprise suffering through the Great Recession. Its

CEO, George Scangos, was paid $11.3 million in 2011, a 20 percent boost over his 2010 income.

When Obamacare would go into effect, the Recchis would be able to get real health insurance coverage, rather than the $2,000 a day variety that would do little more than get Sean a few blood tests and x-rays in his first hour or two at MD Anderson. Preexisting conditions would be no problem. And they would qualify for generous subsidies, making the cost the same or less than the $469 a month they had paid for their relatively useless prior policy.

However, Sean would not be able to use any of his new coverage to go to MD Anderson. Insurance that would be offered to Recchi in Ohio would have provider networks that, depending on the price, would restrict his choice of hospitals even within the state. There was no way any of these so-called narrow networks were going to include coverage for the blue chip cancer hospital in Texas.

Nor would Obamacare do anything to curb the prices that the pharmaceutical company could charge a hospital, or that any hospital could charge to Recchi—or, actually, now to his government-subsidized insurer—for the drug he needed to stay alive.

THE "ASS" IN THE EMERGENCY ROOM

One of the toughest debates in the White House and among Democrats on Capitol Hill as they were framing the new law had to do with not only how generous the subsidies to help people pay their premiums would be, but also what portion of medical bills people could be asked to pay once they got insurance. This involved deductibles (the amount in bills the patient has to pay before insurance kicks in), co-pays or co-insurance (the amount chipped in, such as $25 per doctor's visit, or 20 percent, once the deductible has been reached), and what is called the maximum out of pocket (the total a patient can be asked to pay in deductibles and co-insurance in a given year).[14]

14. I am reminding readers of these terms even though most have health insurance, because polls consistently report that many consumers of health insurance don't understand the jargon. In fact, most buy based solely on the premium and may not even be aware of the precise amount of the deductible or out-of-pocket limits.

Beyond the subsidies that helped everyone earning up to 400 percent above the poverty line pay their monthly premiums, people with incomes closer to the poverty line were given a second subsidy that limited their total out-of-pocket exposure. However, the amount that better-off, middle-income consumers buying insurance on the exchanges might have to pay out of their pockets in deductibles or co-insurance was formidable for the typical "silver" and "gold" plans—as much as $12,700 before an out-of-pocket limit kicked in.

Those high burdens on people with insurance not obtained on the exchanges had become part of the larger American landscape as employers sought to limit soaring insurance premiums by asking their workers to chip in more.

With so much of the bill being shifted from insurers to patients, by 2012 hospital bill collecting from individuals even with insurance was becoming a big business.

On March 23, about a week after Sean Recchi checked into MD Anderson, Bruce Folken, sixty-three, went to the emergency room at Fairview Ridges Hospital, just outside Minneapolis in Burnsville, Minnesota. There, he got a firsthand look at how far hospital bill collecting had come.

Folken had chest pains. The bill for determining that this was a false alarm and that at worst Folken had indigestion was $4,355.10, including two CT scans for $2,911.

Folken's insurance covered all of it, and because the Fairview Ridges Hospital was in the insurer's network, his insurer would get that $4,355 discounted to $1,967.

Folken's policy had a $1,000 deductible. At the time he went to the emergency room, Folken had paid out $507 in 2012 toward that $1,000. That meant that he had $493 more of potential liability before his insurance kicked in.

Typically, this would mean that the hospital would bill the insurance company the $1,967 (the full amount of the discounted bill), and the insurer would then pay the hospital that $1,967, less Folken's share remaining on his deductible ($493)—or $1,474. Folken would then be billed by the hospital for the balance of $493.

But that isn't how things worked in the emergency room at Fairview Ridges.

About halfway through Folken's stay in the ER, as he reclined on a bed with an IV tube in his arm, he was approached by a woman with what he recalled was a hospital insignia on her vest. What happened next, he told me, "was kind of scary." The woman explained that the hospital had already checked online with his insurance company—"because I had apparently signed some form when I came in allowing them to," he explained—and knew that he had $493 left on his deductible. "She told me that the charges were certain to exceed that amount, then looked down at me and asked, 'So would you like to pay the $493 now?'

"I hesitated," Folken recalled. "I usually like to read bills before I pay them, but she kept looking at me, so I decided I did not want to upset things in the middle of them examining me for a heart attack. So, I said, 'Sure, I'll pay, but I need to get my wallet,' which was in my pants, hanging on a hook where I could not reach it. So she smiles and says, 'Can I get your wallet for you, so you can pay now?' I was so nervous that I gave her the wrong credit card, not the credit card that is tied to my medical payments account."

A few weeks after Folken's visit to the emergency room, he read an article in the Minneapolis *Star Tribune* reporting that the state attorney general was investigating billing practices at the nonprofit Fairview chain of six Minnesota hospitals. The major charge, as later outlined in a suit brought by the Minnesota attorney general, was that Fairview was using employees of a firm called Accretive Health to ask patients getting treatment, even in the emergency room, for payment. Asking for advance payment in these emergency situations violated state regulations because it was impermissibly coercive, the attorney general charged.

According to the suit, "Accretive prepared a document [explaining how the company works], called the 'Accretive Secret Sauce.' The cover states: 'You've never seen ASS like ours!' and 'Check out our ASS!' The Secret Sauce states that typical hospitals do not collect money in the emergency room but that one of Accretive's Secret Sauce ingredients is to make bedside collections visits in the emergency room to extract money from patients."

Accretive, which was the creation of a private equity firm, put a not-terribly-different spin on its strategy: "Accretive Health is a built-for-purpose company founded in 2003 with the sole focus of generating significant, sustainable improvements in revenue cycle outcomes," its website explained.

When Folken read about the suit against Fairview and Accretive, he contacted the attorney general's office and became one of her many sample cases. He even volunteered to allow his name to be used and ended up in local news stories and on a segment of NBC's *Rock Center* newsmagazine.

Accretive would later settle the attorney general's suit by agreeing to pay a $2.4 million fine, some of which would be distributed to the allegedly intimidated patients, including Folken. The firm did not deny that it had designed the hospital bill collection strategies and tactics (which, its lawyer later told me, also included having people available to help patients fill out financial aid applications). Nor did Accretive dispute that it deployed employees at client hospitals to supervise these collection strategies. However, the Accretive lawyer did deny that the woman who had approached Folken in the emergency room was its employee.

With healthcare revenues continually outpacing other sectors of the economy, Accretive was by now one of many popular private equity investments in medical bill collecting.

THE $28,000 AMBULANCE

A few months after someone in a Minnesota emergency room fetched Bruce Folken's wallet for him so that he could pay before he was treated, David Cramer, a graduate divinity student at Baylor University in Texas, was in a serious rollover accident on a highway in Bourbon, Missouri. He would later provide this account of how his emergency treatment turned out:

> I was flown 60 miles by helicopter to a major hospital, where I received treatment for serious, but not life threatening, injuries. Despite being a doctoral student on a meager sti-

pend, I was fully insured with both auto and health. My medical bills were all negotiated significantly so that I only had to pay around $4000 out of pocket for all of my treatments combined.

However, after my health and auto insurance paid a combined total of nearly $9,000 to the medical helicopter company, they refused to settle the remainder and thus are requiring me to pay nearly $20,000, which is near my entire annual salary (which covers living expenses for myself, my wife, and our two young children).

After doing some research, I learned that the helicopter company is for profit. . . . Still, after I explained to them that I literally live at or below the poverty line for a family of four, and that I had no ability to refuse their services, they nevertheless continue to insist on me paying the total remaining balance, even suggesting that I put it on credit cards.

By the time Cramer wrote to me, he had delved into the company that had provided his air ambulance—Air Methods Corporation—and discovered a conference call that CEO Aaron Todd had hosted for stock analysts a few months later. Todd reviewed his company's good fortunes amid the lagging recovery from the recession and provided this information that Cramer had not mentioned: "Net cash provided from operating activities for 2012 increased to $151 million compared with $95 million in the prior year period," Todd told the analysts. "Looking forward to 2013 and beyond," the ambulance company CEO added, "as always our budget objective is to grow revenue by 10% or greater and to grow earnings per share by 20% or greater."

"Air Methods Is Poised to Fly Higher Thanks to Obamacare," a columnist for the stock-pick website Seeking Alpha would declare in 2014.

The Air Methods website also touted a unit that helped hospitals with in-house ambulance services maximize revenues and collections. "Many hospital billing services immediately write off all rejected claims or place patients in collections," the website declared. "Many volunteer EMS [emergency medical service] agencies don't have the personnel or the time to follow up on complex reimbursement claims with Medicare or private insurance claims."

As Cramer found out, Air Methods had mastered the use of those bill-collecting resources. As of October 2014, the young divinity student and the lawyer he had been forced to retain were still fighting with Air Methods over the nearly $20,000 that the high-flying ambulance company—whose stock was up about 500 percent since Obama signed the healthcare reform law—insisted he owed.

"I feel like I'm living in a Kafka novel," Cramer wrote.

Cramer had fallen victim to a loophole in his and pretty much everyone else's insurance coverage big enough to fly an Air Methods helicopter through. The insurance company that Baylor used for students such as Cramer, Blue Cross Blue Shield of Texas, paid for ambulance services, but paid only what it thought was reasonable and customary—in this case, $4,000. Hardly peanuts for a quick helicopter ride, but not what Air Methods had in mind. And while many states prohibit balance billing for ambulance services (charging the patient the difference between what an insurer will pay and what the charge is), many others, including Missouri, allow it.

As for Obamacare, while the new law requires insurance companies to insure emergency services, it requires only that out-of-network providers be paid what the in-network provider would have been paid by the insurer. And it does not prohibit balance billing for the remainder. "The ambulance guys have a very strong lobby," a Senate staffer told me. "And lots of our members, especially in rural areas, love the ambulance companies and want to support what they do."

As a result, Obamacare provides the ambulance companies with the assurance that with the new law they would always be cushioned by having many more of their patients have insurance that would pay a reasonable fee, yet they would not be limited from being able to charge more if they could collect it.

THE CHIEF JUSTICE'S "BETRAYAL"

Liz Fowler sat with Max Baucus in the front row of the spectator seats as the justices filed in on June 28, 2012, to announce whether twenty-eight Republican state attorneys general and a group of private party plaintiffs had prevailed in their effort to strike down Obamacare. Fowler, who had not liked what she had seen when she attended one of the hearings in March, feared the worst.

At first, it seemed that the law had been struck down. Roberts, reading the Court's controlling opinion, ruled that the Commerce Clause did not, in fact, allow Congress to mandate that people buy insurance. It looked like Obamacare was going to be over before it started.

However, as the chief justice read on, he declared that the mandate could be allowed, because although the Obama administration had not called it a tax, the penalty for people who did not buy insurance was, indeed, a tax.

It was an argument that the government lawyers had made only parenthetically, just in case. And it was exactly the language that the Democratic senators had wanted to avoid. Nonetheless, with the IRS collecting money from people via their tax returns, the Court held that it was a tax and, therefore, allowed because Congress had broad constitutional authority to levy taxes even if it wanted to call them something else.

Conservative blogs and publications were furious.

"There are people in Washington—too often, Republicans—who start living in the Beltway atmosphere, and start forgetting those hundreds of millions of Americans beyond the Beltway who trusted them to do right by them, to use their wisdom instead of their cleverness," wrote columnist Thomas Sowell on Townhall.com. "How far do you bend over backwards to avoid the obvious, that ObamaCare was an unprecedented extension of federal power over the lives of 300 million Americans today and of generations yet unborn? These are the people that Chief Justice Roberts betrayed when he declared constitutional something that is nowhere authorized in the Constitution of the United States."

There were high fives all around in the White House, although President Obama and his staff were first dismayed by initial media reports that they had lost because some reporters read Roberts's Commerce Clause ruling before seeing his pivot to the tax rationale.

Another part of the ruling was a negative for the Obama team. The Court had ruled 7–2 in response to another claim that the law could not force a state—by threatening to revoke all of the Medicaid funds the state currently received—to expand Medicaid to all of their poor people, even if the federal government would pay for the expansion completely in the first three years and pay 90 percent thereafter. That was still too heavy-handed a threat, the Court ruled. However, with Washington paying so much of the tab and the states getting relieved of the cost of healthcare for their poor, the initial read at the White House was that most states, even those run by the most conservative Republicans, were likely to sign on.

KENTUCKY AT THE STARTING GATE

Carrie Banahan, the civil servant who had written the grant that got Kentucky federal funds to begin planning its Obamacare exchange, was jubilant as she left a meeting in Governor Steven Beshear's office a few days after the Supreme Court's decision. Beshear and Audrey Haynes, the governor's cabinet secretary for health and family services, had just asked Banahan to run the program, which was what she had been hoping would happen.

Beshear also had said that going ahead with the Medicaid expansion using federal money seemed like a "no-brainer" to him, though he wanted them to get some consultants to do a study verifying that the state would benefit not only in terms of the health of its people but also economically by taking Washington's money to expand Medicaid to all who needed it.

Banahan, Haynes, and Beshear were determined to make the launch a turning point that could reverse Kentucky's grim health statistics, as well as a crowning legacy achievement for Beshear, whose second and final term as governor would conclude in 2015. However, they decided to start out modestly and quietly. They wanted to hold off the political opposition as long as they could. For their headquarters, Banahan had in mind an office park just outside of town that looked more like a warehouse. Beshear liked that. No fluff. No waste. Nothing they could be attacked for.

Banahan also wanted to see if she could persuade Chris Clark, an engineer who had worked for her, to come out of retirement to help coordinate things.

Being responsible for and exposed to the dire health problems in her state had long weighed on Banahan. So much so, she later recalled, that she had tears in her eyes when she left the governor's office.

THE STALL CONTINUES IN WASHINGTON

One would have thought that the Supreme Court's decision would have generated at least as much immediate enthusiasm and activity in the White House and across the Obama administration as it had in the Kentucky statehouse. Indeed, with the Court having cleared away what looked to be the final external hurdle for the law to go forward, the insurers and the rest of the healthcare industry assumed they would start seeing the necessary regulations and other preparations flowing out from Washington with fire-hose velocity.

However, through the summer of 2012, nothing happened. There was a presidential election looming, and the Obama political team didn't want to pollute the news cycles with anything that could prompt an Obamacare story. Someone was bound to criticize anything they issued. "We literally fell a year behind," a senior CMS official told me. "We were told by the White House to do nothing, not even circulate drafts of regs, because they might leak out if lobbyists got ahold of them."

There was one exception. On June 5, Nancy-Ann DeParle, now the deputy chief of staff, announced on the White House blog that "consumers are starting to hear the good news about their health insurance costs." She was referring to rebates that were about to be issued from insurers who had run afoul of the medical loss ratio, or MLR. That was the rule that required that if insurers didn't spend a certain percentage of what they collected in premiums on customers' claims they had to refund the difference to those customers. DeParle cited three insurers who were about to send their customers about $95 million in premium rebates. About two months later, White House press secretary Jay Carney would convene reporters traveling with the president on Air Force One to remind them that "as of today, August 1, 12.8 million Americans will benefit in $1.1 billion in rebates from insurance companies that were made possible by the Affordable Care Act."

Late in June, Gary Cohen became the fourth head in as many years of CCIIO, the *center* that had been demoted from an *office*. Cohen, who had been a partner at one of San Francisco's most successful litigation firms, was serving as counsel to the state-run exchange that was starting up in California. He had previously worked at CMS, and couldn't resist the challenge of going back to run the launch of the federal exchange.

Cohen's CCIIO now had fourteen months to get the exchanges up and running. Within days of arriving, Cohen decided he had to take a fresh look at all the regulations being drafted. He was soon told by higher-ups at CMS and the White House that he should take his time.

There would be no substantive regulations having anything to do with Obamacare issued from Labor Day through Election Day, 2012. Without the regulations governing the standards for insurance to be sold on the exchange, there was no way to create the so-called business rules that the coders needed to begin building the website.

The final insurance regulations would not be issued until December 16, 2012. That was more than a year behind the already unambitious schedule that had so alarmed the White House economic team in the summer of 2010. And it was a year and a half after the White House staff meeting in July 2011, when the insurance companies were reported to be "going bananas" over not having *already* been given the rules.

A DOMINANT HOSPITAL GETS MORE DOMINANT

Yet there was regulatory activity on other fronts in the late summer of 2012. It continued a trend in healthcare that was troubling or encouraging, depending on the level of cynicism one applied to the industry.

On September 11, 2012, Yale–New Haven Hospital completed a merger with its only local competitor, the Hospital of Saint Raphael. Yale–New Haven was now a multibillion-dollar colossus. With eleven thousand employees and still growing, it was gaining fast on the thirteen-thousand-employee university that had always dominated New Haven and whose medical school is affiliated with Yale–New Haven.

The Yale New Haven Health System had already bought the hospitals further south in Connecticut, in Greenwich and Bridgeport (where school bus driver Emilia Gilbert had been forced by its lawyers to pay full chargemaster rates); and it was rapidly gobbling up doctors' practices and establishing satellite clinics throughout the region.

The takeover of Saint Raphael's had followed a long review process involving both the Federal Trade Commission and the Connecticut attorney general. Both had questioned whether what seemed to be Yale New Haven's biggest move yet in a quest for total market domination was outweighed by the fact that Saint Raphael's was already a struggling hospital in danger of closing. Despite claims from opponents of the merger that it was Yale New Haven's dominance that had hobbled Saint Raphael's, both regulators—persuaded by reams of material submitted by Yale New Haven's powerhouse international law firm—acquiesced.

"Based on the evidence developed during the investigation, and in light of the law applicable to these types of transactions—including taking into consideration St. Raphael's precarious financial condition and other expected efficiencies that will be realized through the acquisition—I have decided not to seek to block the merger under Connecticut's antitrust law," Connecticut attorney general George Jepsen announced.

Jepsen's reference to the law and precedents "applicable to these types of transactions" was his acknowledgment that when it comes to hospitals, antitrust laws are complicated.

In part, this was because healthcare is not a conventional marketplace. Sometimes maintaining competition for the sake of competition can produce inferior care. Therefore, regulators have tended to take quality care into account as much as they do pricing and choice in a way that they wouldn't in looking at the merger of two widget companies.

It was also because the way antitrust laws had been applied by regulators to hospitals was vague and arguably too gentle—which is what White House aides Zeke Emanuel and Bob Kocher had tried fruitlessly to address early on when Obamacare was being put together.

Earlier in 2012, the Federal Trade Commission had sued to block the purchase by the Saint Luke's hospital system in Idaho of the largest physicians' group practice in Nampa, Idaho. The FTC would ultimately win that suit. But these interventions in deals in which hospitals took over doctors' offices were relatively rare and almost never involved significant markets.

Sometimes, the Federal Trade Commission clamped down when it looked like a hospital merger would too egregiously eliminate competition in a region. But these cases were also uncommon, in part because the hospitals could argue that a merger would cut costs by eliminating needless duplication of services. Why have two cancer care units, or two super-expensive diagnostic labs in the same town?

Opponents of these mergers pointed out that hospitals rarely consolidated in a way that downsized their activities. On the contrary, the story of hospitals in the United States was much like the story of that other bastion of nonprofit spiraling costs: higher education. No matter how mergers were rationalized, the merged hospital chain seemed to keep building, all in the name of providing broader, more advanced care. That was certainly true—and would continue to be true—of Yale New Haven following its Bridgeport and Greenwich mergers.

Moreover, whatever efficiencies those mergers produced by way of consolidation certainly didn't produce lower prices. Three months prior to the Yale–New Haven merger, there was fresh evidence of that from a highly credible source. "Increases in hospital market concentration lead to increases in the price of hospital care," reported the Robert Wood Johnson Foundation, a respected healthcare think tank that had just finished an elaborate survey of hospital pricing. The report also stated that "at least in some procedures, hospital concentration reduces quality."

A subsequent FTC report would find that when it came to consolidation and price increases, the nonprofit hospitals' behavior was no different than that of the for-profit hospital chains.

Yale New Haven had promised that it would "blend" the lower rates currently charged by Saint Raphael's with its higher rates in a way that would result in "price neutrality." But it made no commitments that it would not raise prices as its insurance contracts came up for renewal.

Other evidence of the downside of consolidation would soon follow the Saint Raphael's takeover. Yale New Haven accelerated a strategy of buying up or starting clinics around the region and turning them into outpatient units of the hospital system. Beyond the obvious consequence of eliminating competition, this mattered because under Medicare rules, hospital outpatient units can charge more than standalone clinics. The theory is that hospitals have higher costs because they have to be open 24/7, which, of course, wasn't true of these new outpatient satellite clinics.

Two years after the merger, a study sampling medical bills across the country would pinpoint what it called "much higher prices" charged by hospital clinics, reporting that "the average hospital outpatient department price for a basic colonoscopy was $1,383 compared to $625 in community settings." In an echo of Scott S.'s $132,000 lab bills in Texas, the report found that "for a common blood test—a comprehensive metabolic panel—the average price in hospital outpatient departments was triple the price . . . in community settings."

In some cases, when Yale New Haven took over a clinic or the practice of some doctor group, there could now be two bills instead of one—a "facility charge" for the room where the patient saw the doctor, and a charge for the doctor. That meant not only higher bills, but also two co-pays for the patient instead of one, because the insurance company was now getting two bills.

Then there was the overriding question of how an insurer could negotiate discounts with Yale New Haven when it could not possibly sell insurance to area residents without including the only available hospital in its network and the increasing share of the area's doctors, whose practices were also being bought up by the hospital.

However, there was another side.

I know several people in the New Haven area who appreciate being able to go to a nearby Yale–New Haven satellite office after a hospital stay for a checkup or follow-up test. [15]

And there is a good argument that the brand and culture of the celebrated research and teaching institution with which Yale–New Haven is linked—the Yale Medical School—and the quality control that would seem to come with it helps to spread better care across the region when Yale New Haven takes over those other hospitals.

Most important, these consolidated providers seem to offer the best way out of the fee-for-service trap that Orszag had articulated so well at the Baucus summit of 2008, and that he and his staff tried, with little success, to attack when Obamacare was being written. The most practical way to implement "bundled payment" billing, instead of fee-for-service, was to have all aspects of care consolidated under the same roof in so-called Accountable Care Organizations (ACOs). That way, an insurer could offer to pay an ACO a set amount for the treatment of an illness, or, better yet, a set amount each year for each of its customers to be treated by the ACO whatever the patient might need.

Put simply, Yale New Haven was becoming either a poster child for market abuse or for real reform of the healthcare economy. One man's antitrust conspiracy was another man's trailblazing Accountable Care Organization.

A "REAL BADASS"

By the fall of 2012, Liz Fowler was ready to leave government again. As a member of the National Economic Council staff at the White House working mostly with the Treasury Department and the IRS on launching healthcare reform, she felt elbowed out by Jeanne Lambrew. With the support of Deputy Chief of Staff Nancy-Ann De-Parle, Lambrew wanted to keep control of everything. Fowler even heard complaints that Lambrew was holding up decisions on design options and other elements for the website, which was now less than a year away from its scheduled launch.

In November 2012, just after President Obama was reelected,

---

15. Disclosure: I teach a journalism seminar at Yale, and my wife and I are loyal alums.

Fowler accepted a job with Johnson & Johnson, the giant drug and medical device and supplies company. Her title would be head of global health policy. She specifically made sure that lobbying would not be part of her responsibilities.

What appealed to Fowler about the position was that it involved advising the company on how to deal with health issues around the world—from India's effort to expand healthcare in its emerging economy to how J&J should position itself amid the continuing calls by the medical device industry to repeal the Obamacare device tax. (She would advise that the company not join the call for repeal, and it didn't.)

It was, Fowler believed, an ideal job. Interesting issues. No lobbying. And a company that she thought was several rungs above her previous private employer, WellPoint, when it came to civic-mindedness.

Critics of Washington's revolving door did not see it that way, particularly a journalist writing for *The Guardian* named Glenn Greenwald—the same Glenn Greenwald who was soon to make headlines for working with National Security Agency contractor Edward Snowden to reveal the thousands of files Snowden took when he left the NSA.

Calling Fowler "the architect" of Obamacare, Greenwald noted that she had worked for WellPoint, the giant insurer, before rejoining Baucus's staff to draft the law. "The bill's mandate," he wrote, "that everyone purchase the products of the private health insurance industry, unaccompanied by any public alternative, was a huge gift to that industry." And now, Greenwald added, "the pharmaceutical giant that just hired Fowler" is a member of PhRMA—"one of the most aggressive supporters—and most lavish beneficiaries—of the health care bill drafted by Fowler." Accordingly, Greenwald concluded, "It's difficult to find someone who embodies the sleazy, anti-democratic, corporatist revolving door that greases Washington as shamelessly and purely as Liz Fowler."

Other news organizations soon piled on, though not as vituperatively, using Fowler as a hook for stories about how dozens of Baucus alumni, including many who had worked on healthcare, were now lobbyists. That was true, and it was good reason to be jaded about Washington, even if lobbying is protected by the Constitution and even if some of those lobbyists worked for clients, such as community health centers or civil rights groups, whom Greenwald would celebrate.

But Fowler was not going to be a lobbyist. More than that, given the roller-coaster ride that healthcare reform took toward passage and the fact that there were never enough votes for a public option, it was fantasy that Fowler did anything more—or less—than pull together a bill that could actually be passed by Congress.

After Greenwald became famous for helping Snowden get his leaks published, there would be debate over whether he was more an ideologue with an agenda than a journalist. That he attacked Fowler so fiercely and cluelessly—as if one Senate aide, albeit such a highly competent one, could have overcome the powers that be in Washington arrayed to protect the healthcare industry status quo—would seem to have settled that debate before it happened.

Fowler, however, let Greenwald's attack and the ones that followed get to her. She had thought of herself as one of the good guys.

Her friends tried to cheer her up. "Hey, this makes you out to be a real badass," one said. "He says you single-handedly stopped the public option. Pretty good."

CHRISTMAS IN KENTUCKY

By November 2012, only fourteen states and the District of Columbia had signed up to run their own exchanges. Hoping to get more states on board, CMS extended the deadline for that decision by a month, into December. No new states took the extra time to join. CMS would now have to build and handle the exchanges for thirty-six recalcitrant states.

Kentucky was not one of them. Governor Steven Beshear and Carrie Banahan, his choice to run their exchange, had moved quickly to find the outside help they would need following the go-ahead from the Supreme Court in late June. They immediately decided that, unlike CMS, they would hire one general contractor to pull everything together. That contractor could subcontract out pieces of the job, but it would be responsible for everything.

Working with Chris Clark, the engineer she had pulled out of retirement, and with the state's procurement officials, they had crashed a Request for Proposals that went to a half dozen contractors. By October 7, they had signed a contract with the healthcare services unit of Deloitte, the giant consulting and accounting firm, which had worked on numerous projects related to welfare, child support, and other benefits programs for states across the country.

Within days, a forty-person crew from Deloitte was on the ground in Frankfort, in the warehouse space Banahan had picked as the project's headquarters.

The Deloitte team was lead by Mohan Kumar, fifty-two, who had modernized a child support program for Kentucky a few years back. Short and soft-spoken, Kumar had studied engineering in his native India. He was a twenty-seven-year Deloitte veteran.

Kumar lived in lower Manhattan, but was about to make the inelegant Capitol Plaza Hotel in Frankfort his weekday and often weekend home. He would rarely see his wife and twin toddlers. The hotel didn't matter much; he would spend most of his waking hours in the warehouse, which everyone would soon call "the shack."

"My wife had worked in consulting, too," Kumar told me. "So she understood what the life was."

Kumar immediately presented Banahan and Clark with an agenda for the next few days. The goal was to break quickly into groups—Kumar had a Deloitte team of two hundred on the way—and make some quick decisions. By New Year's 2013, less than three months away, they wanted to have the architecture for the exchange fully sketched out, based on a complete menu of business rules. Then they could start building. In the best of circumstances, laying out a full design and getting it approved for projects less complicated than this takes six months. They had just given themselves half that time.

"They had their act together from the first hour," Banahan would later recall, remembering their first days in the shack.

"From the start, I thought the timeline was almost impossible," Kumar later told me. "Everything had to fall into place. . . . But I was stunned at how quickly Carrie and her people were willing to make decisions."

One early decision would turn out to be crucial. Would people coming onto the exchange have to put in all of their personal information first? That way their eligibility could be verified through the hookups to the federal databases. (Were they citizens or legal aliens? Did their income qualify for subsidies, and, if so, how much? Or was their income so low that they should be sent to the Medicaid enrollment process?) Or could they simply estimate their income without putting in all those personal details, get an estimate of their subsidy, and shop around for various policies with a price popping up that took into account the estimated subsidy?

That decision seemed obvious. Amazon didn't make you put in all your account information before telling you the price of a book or a toaster. Why create the hurdle of filling everything out before you were sold on buying something? Besides, Beshear's constant refrain in defending the coming exchange was that when people saw how reasonable the prices were once the subsidies were included, they would want the insurance. "Just have a look," he would say. "You'll like it. It's not about me or President Obama. It's about you."

Another obvious reason to let people browse before putting in all that complicated information was that it would lessen the load on the system by processing all of that personal data only from people who were actually buying.

Banahan and Kumar quickly decided to do that. The federal government would start out taking the opposite approach.

Having pulled a string of all-nighters through December, on the weekend of Christmas Eve, 2012, Kumar's and Banahan's teams got the big plan locked up.

Also in December 2012, another team of Banahan's people began working with a branding and marketing research firm called Reality Check, which had advised companies ranging from local favorite Jim Beam to Shell Oil. Reality Check convened a dozen focus groups across the state. With ten months to go before launch, they wanted to nail down the language and look that could sell Beshear's exchange all across Kentucky.

A January report on the results would declare that "most

respondents—even physicians and business owners—expressed little knowledge of the Affordable Care Act and its implications."

On top of that, the researchers reported that there was "suspicion" about the new law and a fear of "less choice, more control"—the government takeover that Frank Luntz had told the Republicans to shout about.

To deal with those qualms, the researchers urged that the design of the website had to "project feelings of approachability, optimism, and openness" that "respondents found comfortable, hopeful, and reassuring."

One design they showed the focus groups proclaimed "Kentucky" over the subheadline "Healthcare Marketplace," all in front of a bright yellow sun rising in the background. Some respondents described its message as "A new day in Kentucky."

"In general," the market researchers reported, this kind of look "visually positioned Healthcare Reform as a reason for hope, not fear," that offered "options and choices" and that had the aura of a farmers market.

In the final analysis, the report said, a " 'kynect' logo treatment featuring lowercase letters and a double-pointed arrow . . . conveyed a friendly, welcoming feel that helped overcome the negative emotions associated with Healthcare Reform." It was "low stress and unintimidating" while "suggesting technology."

CHAPTER 17

A GUY IN JEANS, RED LIGHTS,
AND A "TRAIN WRECK"

January–June 2013

On January 29, 2013, a man in jeans walked through the metal detectors in the lobby of the Department of Health and Human Services headquarters on Independence Avenue near the Capitol. Eric Gunderson, who was then thirty-three, had never been in the building, though it was a ten-minute cab ride from his office and it bought more of the kinds of services Gunderson sold than Gunderson's business could provide over three or four centuries.

Gunderson ran a small software shop full of twenty-something coders who specialized in doing projects for nonprofits. "Geeks for good," was how Gunderson would later describe the world they worked in. "We're not Lockheed Martin."

Nor could their headquarters be confused with Lockheed Martin's facilities, which spanned the world, capturing and fulfilling billions in military and aerospace contracts. Gunderson and his Development Seed coders worked in a converted garage hidden in an alley behind N Street in northwest Washington.

Gunderson and a deputy made their way to the sixth floor to meet in a large office with Bryan Sivak.

Sivak was the thirty-seven-year-old chief technology officer at the Department of Health and Human Services. That had been Todd

Park's job, but Park had become chief technology officer of the country, working in the White House.

Like Park, Sivak had an ideal résumé for someone running major technology projects. With a degree in computer science from the University of Chicago, he had registered his own patents, started two successful software companies, and then become the CTO for the District of Columbia, before becoming "chief innovation officer" for the state of Maryland.

He and Park had met at various industry conferences, and when Park moved to the White House he recruited Sivak to replace him at HHS.

Bearded, friendly, always smiling, and with a constant gleam in his eye, Sivak gave off an innovation vibe that seemed out of sync in a government bureaucracy. He even had a sign hung prominently on his office wall that declared, "WE HAVE A STRATEGIC PLAN. IT'S CALLED DOING THINGS."

In press interviews and on the speaking circuit he touted the "IDEA lab" that he had set up at HHS.

"Basically I'm responsible here for executing on the department's innovation agenda," he told *The Washington Post*. "That . . . includes this idea of challenging the bureaucracy to escape the status quo and think about how we can accomplish our tasks in new and innovative ways."

However, when it came to challenging the bureaucracy's control over its most ambitious project ever—the building of the Obamacare insurance exchange—Sivak, like Park before him, was on the sidelines. The innovations coming from his IDEA lab would operate along the borders of what HHS did, not intrude into the core functions controlled by all of those *offices* and *centers*. Besides, he was the chief technology officer of the Department of Health and Human Services, not its CMS unit, and no one at CMS, including its chief technology officer, reported to him. CMS, in fact, "didn't trust the sixth floor," Sivak told friends, referring to the floor at HHS headquarters where he and the others with big titles were housed.

Yet some of his projects were important. Sivak was a near-manic believer in transparency and how big data could be used to achieve it in unprecedented ways. From the day he started the job he had wanted to crunch CMS's data on hospital pricing in order to present price comparisons to the world. He ultimately persuaded CMS to do that, but, by his own account, that only came after the *Time* special report on medical prices created headlines around the issue, and his boss, Secretary Sebelius, and her advisers allowed him to push ahead.

SONYA AND THE POTEMKIN VILLAGE

Sivak had invited Gunderson to come see him because one aspect of the Obamacare website project that he had maneuvered his way into reviewing was driving him crazy. The design of the home page for the federal exchange (that would now be the gateway for the multiple insurance offerings from thirty-six states) was terrible.

It was confusing and almost impossible to navigate. It looked like a bureaucracy's website, not like Expedia or Amazon or any of the other e-commerce icons that the president liked to promise his exchange would be like.

In the same way that Todd Park had wedged his way into the bureaucracy's business when he created that comparison shopping website at HealthCare.gov in June 2010—by saying that it wasn't the real one because it wouldn't show the subsidies or allow anyone to buy anything—Sivak gently offered the CMS people his help in tinkering with the home page. He promised just to touch up the look and feel, not mess with what happened after the links brought visitors to all the information and forms to fill out that would be behind that page. What he was talking about was merely the simple public relations and marketing associated with what the world would see on the home page when they arrived at HealthCare.gov, he assured the CMS people.

So, Sivak was given the go-ahead. The CMS team had more important things to worry about.

Sivak had then contacted Gunderson through a friend of a friend because he was intrigued with the software he had heard Gunderson was using.

Gunderson, too, thought that the best strategic plan was, as the sign in Sivak's office said, "doing things."

"We got the contract as a subcontractor," recalled Gunderson. "We could never get a government contract on our own. To do that you have to have more lawyers and contracts people than coders. You have to have the suits. That's not us."

Gunderson and three colleagues from his garage, as well as four CMS people and four staffers from the CMS Office of Communications, were soon locked in a room with Sivak figuring out how to redo the home page and sending coding instructions back to the garage behind N Street.

What would emerge was what would become the famous picture (taken from a stock photo) of a young woman smiling (the team informally called her Sonya) out from a crystal-clear page. In the months that would follow the October launch of the exchange, it was the only part of the site that never broke down and never had to be fixed.

"We did it all for a bit less than a million dollars," Gunderson told me. "For us, that's a pretty big deal."

As with Park's building of the comparison shopping website, the unveiling, in late June 2013, of Sivak and Gunderson's cool-looking home page—which the president loved—created a Potemkin village. On the surface, things looked great. But behind the façade, where CGI and the other contractors were trying to build the real website—and piling up bills that would ultimately reach $840 million—there was not much to look at.

"FAST, TARGETED, LOCKED-DOWN DECISIONS ARE NEEDED"

One of the steps a worried Todd Park took from his new position as U.S. chief technology officer at the White House in the winter of 2013 was to convince HHS secretary Kathleen Sebelius that McKinsey & Company, the blue ribbon consulting firm, should be hired to look in on the implementation effort and, in consultants' jargon, "pressure test" the process.

On March 28, 2013, the McKinsey team presented a picture of that process that, for all of its effort to be polite, depicted a debacle. President Obama had come to office promising a new era of efficient, smartly managed twenty-first-century government. According to the

McKinsey report, it didn't look like those working on his most important and complicated domestic policy initiative had gotten that memo.

With less than six months to go before launch there was "indecision" about the system's requirements, the McKinsey report said. In fact, the staff was "still engaged in program design," which threatened "a materially high risk of system instability."

There was "no end to end business process view across" the many agencies involved outside CMS, such as the IRS and Homeland Security (which had to vet citizenship and legal immigration status), or even "fully within" CMS itself.

"Fast, targeted, locked-down decisions" were needed "for [the] implementation effort," but there was "no single, empowered decision making authority."

The man who many thought had that authority over building the website never saw the McKinsey report. Henry Chao—the deputy chief technology officer at CMS who had moved there from being the CTO of the *Office* of Consumer Information and Insurance Oversight when the *office* became a *center*—was not at the meeting where McKinsey presented its findings. He would later testify at a congressional hearing that he was never told about the report.

A second person whom others would later tell me had been in charge—Michelle Snyder, a career civil servant and the CMS head of the *Office* of Operations—was at the meeting.

Snyder—along with Sebelius and Marilyn Tavenner, the administrator of CMS—also sat in on meetings the following week in which the McKinsey team went through their findings with HHS officials, including Secretary Sebelius. Snyder then attended a similar McKinsey briefing with Lambrew and others in her healthcare reform policy office at the White House. Snyder, who was strong-willed and turf conscious, was not surprised by the report. She had complained to Sivak and others that she had "twelve bosses, including three or four at the White House, and no one is making decisions."

"Streamline decision making" and "name a single implementation leader," the McKinsey team recommended, while also noting, subtly, that it had worked "with a boundary condition of October 1 as the launch date," and that "extending the go-live date should not be part of the analysis."

There was nothing in the law requiring the October 1, 2013, launch. In fact, in their late 2010 deliberations the White House team had targeted enrollment to begin in July. And some of the earliest internal memos had even suggested 2012 for launch in order to have the program in place before the election, so that a new president would have to undo it instead of block it. But by now President Obama and everyone in his administration, as well as congressional Democrats, had locked onto October 1. There could be no delay. In their view the Republicans would be merciless in their attacks on the administration's competence if they let the deadline slip.

Tavenner, who was then sixty-two, is a serious, though outgoing and upbeat, leader. She had worked her way up from being a nurse to a senior executive post at HCA, the giant for-profit hospital chain, before becoming the Virginia secretary of health and human resources. "We knew there were some coordination problems, so the McKinsey report did not surprise me," Tavenner later told me. "But I was assured by Michelle [Snyder], and Henry [Chao] and others, that they were already being taken care of."

Sivak and Park, who sat in on the McKinsey meetings, had hoped the report—which was only about the management *process*, not the actual progress of the website's construction—would be a wake-up call that would allow one or both of them to take over, or at least get more involved and bring in new leadership. But Lambrew—who at the time of the McKinsey report was part of the tangled process the consultants complained about because of her habit of sitting on business rules and design sketches sent to her for review—also brushed off McKinsey's red flags. It was the typical consultants' second guessing from the sidelines, she told colleagues. To the extent the McKinsey people were right, they had only identified problems that the Obama healthcare reform team was already working on. "Sure, there may be some glitches," she told a senior White House communications staffer who had heard about the McKinsey report. "But that happens in all launches like this."

BAUCUS SEES A "TRAIN WRECK"

Max Baucus was not as sanguine. His staff, which had kept in touch with Fowler when she had been at the White House and had its own lines of communication into HHS and CMS, had been telling Baucus that he ought to hold a hearing on the progress in implementing the law he had worked for more than two years to get passed.

On April 17, 2013—about three weeks after the McKinsey report had been presented to CMS, the White House, and the Department of Health and Human Services—Baucus had Secretary Sebelius come up to Capitol Hill to testify before his Finance Committee.

Baucus and his staff had heard nothing about the McKinsey report covering the problems associated with building the exchanges, and neither Sebelius nor anyone else in the Obama administration ever told them about it.

The Finance Committee chairman was instead worried about whether people would embrace the new law by participating in the exchanges.

"As you somewhat know, Madam Secretary," he began, "I'm a bit Johnny One-Note on implementation of the law, especially with respect to signups and exchanges, et cetera, and am very concerned not enough is being done so far. . . . When I am home, small businesses have no idea what to do, what to expect. They don't know what affordability rules are; they don't know when penalties may apply. . . . People just don't know a lot about it."

Then Baucus delivered this prediction: "I just tell you, I just see a huge train wreck coming down. You and I have discussed this many times, and I don't see any results yet."

Sebelius countered that her agency was in the process of awarding hundreds of millions of dollars in grants, which Baucus's law provided for, to community organizations that would deploy thousands of "navigators," who would sit with people on the phone or in person and help them enroll.

However, she conceded to Baucus that although it was now just six months from launch—and less than that before the navigators would have to be given background checks and trained—her agency was still in the process of releasing the Request for Proposals to which the community groups wanting to deploy navigators would have to respond, detailing their capabilities and how much they would charge. Which meant that Sebelius's agency had no idea who or how many would respond, let alone what it would cost and how many they would be able to afford to deploy.

"Do you have benchmarks," the usually mild-mannered Baucus asked. "Do you have dates by which [a] certain number of people know what's going on? I mean, all these polls, for example, show that we're not making much headway," he added, referring to polls consistently reporting that Americans had little idea of how the law worked. "Do you have a goal that [in] two months—or 30 days from now when that same poll is taken that that percentage is down by X percent, and 60 days from now it's down by X—people know where to go and what to do? . . . You've never given me any data. You just give me concepts, frankly."

It got worse:

SEBELIUS: While we do not have benchmarks for how many people know what, we don't intend to do polling and testing in terms of what people know, we do have some very specific benchmarks around open enrollment and we have a campaign and a plan to lead up to open enrollment.

BAUCUS: And what is it—the campaign and the plan?

SEBELIUS: Well, Mr. Chairman, as we have discussed, there will be people on the ground starting this summer. There will be . . .

BAUCUS: How many?

SEBELIUS: I can't tell you at this point.

Baucus also said he was worried about the special exchanges being set up for small businesses to buy insurance for their employees (the provision that Olympia Snowe had insisted on). He had been told they might be delayed. Sebelius told him not to worry. "No, Sir, that is not accurate," she testified. The [small business exchanges] will be up and running in every market of the country."

THE DATA WHIZ KIDS

Sebelius did not mention one other weapon at her disposal in making Americans aware of Obamacare and getting them to enroll. Soon after the law was passed, much of the coalition that had secretly contributed to the group that funded ads supporting the law, and attacking vulnerable legislators who opposed it, had gotten together to start another organization whose donors would again remain secret.

It was called Enroll America, and its purpose was to provide the resources that the House of Representatives, now controlled by Republicans, obviously would not provide to encourage people to sign up. The major insurers had chipped in, but the funding would be dominated by healthcare reform groups, such as the liberal Families USA, and foundations with interests in healthcare reform.

Although Sebelius would later be attacked by Republicans for helping to solicit donors, including those in the healthcare industry whom she regulated, the purpose was avowedly nonpolitical—to make people aware of a new federal law and get them to participate in its benefits.

In early 2013, Anne Filipic, a star Obama campaign field organizer now working in the political shop at the White House, had become president of Enroll America. For Filipic, who was thirty-one and had met her husband canvassing for Obama during the 2008 Iowa primary, Enroll America was the start of a new campaign: fund-raising, field organizing, targeting those most likely to be persuadable, and creating the messages and media necessary to do the job. Only this time, every "vote" really counted. It was not a matter of getting to 50 percent plus one.

Going into 2013, the group had raised $5 million. In 2013, Filipic, as outwardly cheerful as she was intensely focused, would collect $27 million.

Filipic was working closely with David Simas, another campaign alumnus who had been assigned to supervise the White House's Obamacare messaging and marketing, much the way he had worked on the communications effort during the congressional deliberations.

But Filipic had another, more important day-to-day partner: a Chicago-based company called Civis Analytics.

Founded by thirty-year-old Dan Wagner, the Obama 2012 campaign's chief of data analytics, Civis was the home of the Obama campaign's "big data" techies. During the 2012 campaign, Wagner and a team of coders and data analysts had developed tools that could sift data so finely that finding and keeping track of persuadable voters to make sure they turned out to vote was brought to a new level. Their data crunching had also enabled microtargeted advertising buys through social, online, and traditional radio and TV media.

Soon after the campaign, Wagner and the group, which was now much celebrated in political and big data circles, had formed Civis to sell its services to nonprofits, governments, and companies. Its sole investor was Google chairman Eric Schmidt, who had helped organize their work as an informal Obama campaign adviser.

The Civis website described its creation this way:

> Our company was born in a large backroom of the Obama 2012 reelection headquarters. We called it the analytics cave. . . . From millions of data points, we constructed the most accurate voter targeting models ever used in a national campaign. We predicted the election outcome in every battleground state within one point. And our work guided decision-making and resource optimization across the campaign. . . .
>
> This company is our next step: we are taking our team outside The Cave to solve the world's biggest problems using Big Data.

By the time of Sebelius's testimony before Baucus's committee, Enroll America was becoming one of Civis's first and biggest clients, and the Obama White House's best hope for avoiding Baucus's train wreck.

Civis would feed data to Filipic and her team, telling them where and how to reach the uninsured with their media messages, rallies, and door-to-door canvassing.

Only this time not all votes were equal. Of particular concern were those who were called "the young invincibles"—those eighteen- to thirty-four-year-olds who didn't worry as much about health insurance because they were relatively healthy and couldn't imagine themselves being otherwise. They needed to be convinced to sign up because without them the insurance risk pools would be filled disproportionately with older, sicker people, which would cause premiums to go up, which, in turn, would cause still fewer of the young invincibles to sign up.

The challenge of luring the invincibles was particularly worrying to Karen Ignagni and the insurance companies she represented because the age band that the final version of the law had stipulated was only three to one. This meant that insurers could charge the oldest applicants no more than three times what they could charge the youngest. That was better than the two to one ratio that had been in the original drafts of the bill, but not as good as the five to one the insurers had insisted was necessary to make the premium offering to the young invincible appealing.

Yet the premium subsidies that would end up being available to most consumers would in many instances be so generous that the cost for a twenty-something to sign up would often be nearly negligible, depending on regional market factors. However, although the 2012 election was now behind them, the Obama team was still gun-shy about heralding those subsidies and the resulting low premiums, for fear of Obamacare being attacked as an income redistribution program. Instead, they pointed the press to how the reunion of the campaign's data whiz kids was going to win the day.

BULLETPROOF IN KENTUCKY

In red state Kentucky, Governor Steven Beshear had no such concerns about touting the subsidies the federal government was offering. The Supreme Court's decision the prior June had blocked Obamacare in one important respect: When it came to Medicaid expansion, the Court had ruled that, even though the federal government would pick up all of the cost for the first three years and gradually decrease its share only down to 90 percent in 2020, each state had to be able to choose whether to take the deal and expand Medicaid to all of its poor.

In line with their party's staunch opposition to anything related to Obamacare, for most Republican governors in red states, the choice was simple. They would reject the deal, despite the fact that the math seemed to dictate otherwise.

For Beshear, a red state governor who was a Democrat, the calculus was different. Kentucky had 640,000 people—17.5 percent of its population—who were uninsured. They were living in a state with some of the nation's worst health statistics. Of those 640,000 uninsured Kentuckians, 308,000 were living below poverty level and could receive the benefits of Obamacare only if Beshear expanded Medicaid.

Beshear had already waded into the thicket of Medicaid in his state, because even the limited program that Kentucky then had in place was producing a crushing burden on the state budget. The year before, he had pushed through a cost-cutting reform of the limited program over the opposition of hospitals and other providers, who, because of Beshear's changes, were now paid less per patient.

So Beshear understood not only the need the program already filled and how much expansion would mean to his state, but also what the impact of Washington picking up the enormous cost of expanding it would be. Still, as he had told Carrie Banahan, he wanted to be sure he got the numbers right and had bulletproof evidence to counter what was certain to be Republican opposition.

Soon after the Supreme Court's decision giving him a choice, Beshear had commissioned a consultants' study to do that math. The report from PricewaterhouseCoopers was unambiguous.

On May 9, 2013, three weeks after the Baucus "train wreck" hearing, Beshear used the consultants' white paper to justify his decision to expand Obamacare to reach every poor person in his state.

"The expansion," he declared at a press conference, "will help hundreds of thousands of Kentucky families, dramatically improve the state's health, create nearly 17,000 new jobs and have a $15.6 billion positive economic impact on the state between its beginning in Fiscal Year 2014 and full implementation in Fiscal Year 2021. . . . In fact, if we don't expand Medicaid, we will lose money."

"OSCAR" IS BORN

On April 30, 2013, Joshua Kushner and his partners made a set of crucial decisions that were based on math that was not nearly as clear as
the calculus presented by Governor Beshear. That was the day that the
health insurance company they were starting from scratch on a cool-
looking floor in the historic Puck Building (which his family owned)
in lower Manhattan had to file papers with the state insurance department detailing the rates they were going to charge for their proposed
bronze, silver, gold, and platinum plans.

It was, Kushner later said, "pretty much a shot in the dark."

Not quite. They had spent hundreds of thousands of dollars on
consultants who specialize in analyzing health data. They had done
elaborate market research. And they had hired a company called
MagnaCare that created networks of doctors, hospitals, and other
providers for unions that ran their own insurance programs, and then
negotiated the prices to be paid to those in the network.

Kushner's partner, Mario Schlosser—who had modeled trading
strategies for a hedge fund and then worked at McKinsey—had
crunched data he had bought related to fifteen million claims in the
New York area spanning four years. Schlosser had programmed the
data to weed out the doctors who billed too much for average results
or engaged in excessive lab testing. So, they had kept all of Magna-
Care's network of hospitals—which was pretty much every hospital
in the New York area—but not all of its doctors. And they planned to
have their online concierge service encourage patients to use the most
cost-effective half of the doctors that they did keep in the network.

The data would constantly be updated and analyzed to do everything from evaluating physicians to predicting what kinds of preventive services or other interventions individual patients might need and
then encouraging them to get it.

By now, Kushner, Schlosser, and Kevin Nazemi (the third cofounder, who was overseeing the creation of the overall product and
its branding and marketing) were beginning to have what looked like
a real company. About six months before, in one of their brainstorm-
ing sessions they were struggling to figure out a name for the venture.

They wanted something that would "humanize" health insurance. Kushner's answer: "Oscar," the name of his late great-grandfather.

They had also hired a slew of suits—seasoned insurance executives who knew the landscape and were excited, rather than put off, by how Kushner and his partners disdained their industry as a bunch of knuckle draggers about to be shown up by the guys in the Puck Building.

In January 2013, they had completed a license application with the state containing thousands of pages of details about their financial plans, their networks, and their suppliers.

Then the guys from Oscar had begun to do what start-ups usually do first: seek outside investors.

Kushner later told me that he had originally planned to have his own successful venture fund, Thrive, put in all the money. However, as he talked about Oscar with venture capital friends, some had asked about investing with him. Whether it was that or a desire to spread some of the risk, or both, by the beginning of 2013, Kushner and his partners had prepared a PowerPoint deck for potential investors that presented their vision for a health insurance company that was not really a health insurance company as the industry knew it.

Oscar intended to outsource pretty much everything that conventional insurance companies did. MagnaCare would handle the network of doctors, hospitals, and clinics. A pharmacy benefit manager, Caremark, would handle prescription drug claims and the network of pharmacies to fulfill them.

Another vendor, based in Ohio, would handle all claims processing, billing, and the issuing of Oscar's stylized ID cards. It had agreed to charge $8.25 per member per month, plus a $150,000 setup fee. That meant that Oscar didn't have to invest in the costly infrastructure that other insurers had, and that its costs would go up only as its number of customers went up.

Separate visiting nurse and behavioral health (for illnesses such as drug abuse) services had been signed up, too.

"Oscar's assembly and orchestration of best-in-class vendors creates a uniquely asset-light and nimble insurer which is able to service members in novel ways," the investor presentation declared.

The data related to all of those outside services would be integrated so that the customer, and Oscar, had a complete, up-to-date dashboard of everything going on healthwise in the consumer's life. Customers would get emails reminding them to fill prescriptions (and that if they used a generic they would pay nothing at all). Oscar's medical staff would get an alert if a patient had called into the telemedicine service (which was also free) an abnormal number of times. Maybe something more serious was wrong, and the person should be encouraged to see a doctor rather than end up in the (more expensive) emergency room.

Customers could log in and search for doctors in their network and see who was closest to their home or workplace. They could see who had what quality ratings (based mostly on a database of patient surveys Oscar had bought), and what the cost and their co-insurance payment would be. Other insurers had started trying to provide this kind of online information, but their efforts were clumsy, often incomplete, and hard to navigate. Oscar's would be different.

There was "huge leverage in data-driven optimization across the healthcare system," the investor deck promised.

And with Oscar having completed an expensive licensing process that presented "extremely high barriers to entry" for any other like-minded start-up, it was "now in a unique position to dominate a previously non-existent market."

That referred to the market in which individuals, rather than employers, bought health insurance. It was a market that had all but vanished in New York when the state passed a law that required that insurance companies not exclude people with preexisting conditions or charge them more, but that did not include a mandate that everyone had to buy insurance. That meant that people not provided insurance on the job would be inclined to buy it only if they had medical problems. As a result, premiums in the individual market had skyrocketed, precluding most New Yorkers from being able to buy insurance on their own.

Now, with Obamacare, that mandate was in place. Better yet, Kushner's investor deck noted, Oscar expected that 80 percent of its customers would be buying that insurance with Obamacare's federal subsidies.

Oscar would be competing for those customers, the investment presentation said, with "legacy" insurers who had "hard-to-read mailers, poor communication, no consumer-centric organizations, incompatible technology layers, and hundreds of confusing products." Or, as Kushner told me, "We'll be competing with companies who spend all of their time getting customers and then avoiding them once they get them."

With "one million uninsured" in New York City, it was a "$6B+ opportunity in New York City alone," the opening page of the deck declared.

However, the pages at the end—the ones that came after all the advantages of Oscar were celebrated—presented a less cheerful picture. Insurance, even Oscar-style, is not a Silicon Valley– or Silicon Alley–like home run (or strikeout) business. In the best of all worlds, with that medical loss ratio now in place, it still has to pay out 85 percent of the premiums it collects to healthcare suppliers, and then has to use the remaining 15 percent for all of its administrative costs before there is any profit.

And unlike Kushner's investment in start-ups such as Instagram, this one needed lots of money from the first day. Someone or something named Oscar can't just collect premiums from people and promise to pay their medical bills if they get sick. State regulators don't allow that. As condition of getting a license, an insurance company has to put sufficient funds on reserve to assure that those bills can be paid.

When the state insurance department looked at Oscar's initial plans it decided that it needed to deposit $30 million, based on a formula of one dollar in reserve for every four dollars of premiums Oscar projected it was going to get in 2014.

Beyond that, the state required that all of Kushner's budgeted $15 million in losses before Oscar was projected to break even had to be sitting in a bank.

So that meant $45 million up front and in reserve, *plus* another $15 million for what would be spent in actual start-up costs for investments in people and infrastructure.

Yet, a page at the end of the investor deck showed that in the group's "conservative" projection, after depositing or spending that

$60 million, Oscar would have just $100,000 in positive cash flow in 2016. The column showing the "achievable" projection said $10 million, and the one for the "imaginable" projection listed $45 million.

A follow-on page showed much bigger numbers if Oscar could eventually roll out nationally. But most investors usually focused on the conservative projections—unless, like Kushner, they were as enthused about the idea of disrupting an industry they despised as they were about making a surefire bet.

Ultimately, Kushner would get investments from several other venture firms, but his Thrive Capital would still be the dominant funder in the first year.

Although the rates that Oscar filed on April 30, 2013, were based on reams of data analyzed by Schlosser and the actuaries Oscar had hired, and, therefore, hardly the "shot in the dark" that Kushner described, there was still a huge amount of guesswork involved, about which even the actuaries had little to go on.

One example: Would the cost of Oscar's unique, free telemedicine service, for which it would pay doctors to respond to callers within minutes on a per-call basis, actually result in no net cost because the telephone chats would head off so many expensive emergency room and doctors' office visits? Their projection was that one in eight phone calls would avoid an "average health care visit" with the cost of the visit averaged between high fees for an emergency room and lower costs for a doctor's office. But maybe it would be one in four. Or one in ten. No one really knew. There was no precedent, no historical data to rely on. But unlike the Congressional Budget Office's projections for Obamacare, Kushner and his team had to try to score it.

A second example: Oscar's advertising and general ethos was intended to target New York's younger professional set. If it succeeded, Oscar would be capturing the young invincibles, whose healthcare costs would be lower than an average mix of young and older customers. However, Obamacare had a provision that required insurers who paid out less than was paid out by insurers with an average risk pool to pay into a fund to compensate insurers whose risk pool was above average. How was that going to work? The rules had not been set. Would that completely nullify Oscar's advantage?

Finally, there was the question of how anyone coming to the exchange would know how "cool" Oscar was. Could its logo be displayed? More important, it seemed as if the only information displayed on the New York State exchange's opening comparison shopping page would be the premium and maybe the amount of the deductible. How would people know that Oscar customers got generic drugs, telemedicine, and other benefits for free?

Yet Kushner, Schlosser, and Nazemi pressed on. Like all entrepreneurs they were sure they would think of ways to solve all that. Their basic idea, they thought, was just too good—too disruptive—not to succeed.

CHAPTER 18

TWO MONTHS TO GO

July–August 2013

In June 2013, I came up with what I thought was a great idea for another special report for *Time*. As with that earlier story, this one was born of simple curiosity.

I had gotten the idea for the first article when I became curious because so much of the debate over Obamacare seemed about how we could insure millions of Americans against the stupendously high cost of healthcare in the United States, rather than why the cost was so high to begin with. What and who was behind all of those high prices? Where was all that money going? To find out, I would trace the money and profits behind every line item in hundreds of pages of bills given to seven patients.

Now, I told my editors, I was curious about something else: Launching Obamacare, with its e-commerce insurance exchanges and thousands of other complexities, seemed like the most ambitious domestic government project since Medicare. In fact, it was going to be far more difficult, I pointed out, to pull off than Medicare. Medicare was about getting an identifiable subset of the population to sign up to get something for free. With Obamacare, people had to be sold on buying a confusing product and given exactly the correct subsidy to do so. Even those that didn't buy—all adult Americans—would somehow have to prove that they had insurance, and employers would have to prove that they were providing it to their workers.

How were they going to do all of that?

So we had agreed that through the summer I would make multiple trips to Washington to look in on how this massive program and its core e-commerce website was being built. I even told my editors that based on the efficient, dedicated people I had seen at the CMS campus in Baltimore while reporting on the vetting and processing of Alan A.'s Medicare bills for the first article, this was likely to be an uplifting saga of unsung heroes. Whatever the political dysfunction in Washington, Obama's managers and these civil servants were going to prove that big government could work.

The story would come out in late October, after what I thought would be a triumphant launch.

WHO'S IN CHARGE HERE?

As I was returning from my first round of interviews that plotline started to blur. On the train back to New York, I flipped through the notes I had taken while talking with eight people who were working on the project at the Department of Health and Human Services, CMS, and the White House. I saw that almost as an afterthought or conversation starter I had asked each who was the person in charge of the launch of the federal exchange. I hadn't paid much attention to the answer, until I sat on the train reviewing the notes.

There were seven different answers:

Jeanne Lambrew at the White House;
Michelle Snyder, who ran CMS operations;
Gary Cohen, who ran CCIIO—the *Center* for Consumer
    Information and Insurance Oversight that had been
    demoted from being an *office;* he got two votes;
Marilyn Tavenner, the head of CMS;
Kathleen Sebelius, the HHS secretary;
Henry Chao, the deputy director of the CMS technology
    office;

And David Simas, who was overseeing the marketing and messaging of the launch from the White House communications office.

I also noticed that I had asked a spokesman for CMS, who was taking me around for interviews, who was in charge. Now I saw that he
had said, "It's kind of complicated." Whereupon he had taken my
notebook and drawn a diagram with four diagonal lines crossing one
another and forming a kind of lopsided triangle. It was incomprehensible.

Finally, my notes reminded me that when I had asked one person
at CMS if I could watch the October 1 launch from their control room
or command center or whatever they were going to call it, she had
responded, "Which one?" There were actually going to be four or five
command or operations centers, she had explained: one for each of
three CMS offices, another at HHS, and maybe another at the White
House.

When I got home that night I told my wife that I was not so sure I
was going to be able to write the launch saga I had sold the *Time* editors on. The launch looked like it had problems.

"THOUGHTFUL" IMPLEMENTATION

By then I also knew that on the evening of July 2, 2013, the Treasury
Department had released a statement on its website headlined "Continuing to Implement the ACA in a Careful, Thoughtful Manner."

The notice began by observing that the country's private businesses
were concerned about "the complexity of the requirements" related
to the forms they would have to fill out to prove that they were providing adequate health insurance to their workers in order to avoid
paying the penalty for not doing so.

That was an understatement. Everyone involved—employers,
White House staffers, and people at the Treasury Department, the
IRS, and the Labor Department—had been tied in knots trying to
figure out how the names, Social Security numbers, hours worked,

and details of insurance coverage for every American worker could be assembled and made to flow efficiently.

Therefore, according to the second paragraph of the website posting, Treasury was giving up, at least for now. "The Administration is announcing that it will provide an additional year before the ACA [Obamacare] mandatory employer and insurer reporting requirements begin," the Treasury notice declared.

Despite having had three years and three months since the law was signed in that East Room ceremony, the Treasury Department had been unable to complete the paperwork to implement the widely attacked and hotly defended employer mandate. It was just too complicated to be put in place for the launch.

At the time, I had chuckled over the way Treasury had tried to spin the news with that "Careful, Thoughtful" headline.

But what I didn't know was that this decision, too, was part of a larger story of turf fighting and a breakdown in coordination. I would later find out that Gary Cohen, the head of CMS's CCIIO, who was one of the people I was told was "in charge," did not know about the decision until about two hours before the Treasury Department website announcement.

That week, *Bloomberg Businessweek* had begun preparing a profile of Cohen, to be published in August, with the title "Hidden Hand: The Insurance Expert Behind Obamacare." His job, the magazine would report, was "to make sure Obamacare doesn't flop."

Cohen certainly had enough people to help him. When he had taken the job little more than a year before, in June 2012, there were 30 people working at CCIIO. Now there were 370, many of whom were trying to iron out the details of the employer mandate—until they found out on the evening of July 2 that for now there would be no mandate.

Cohen's boss, CMS chief Tavenner, was not told until two days before about the employer mandate being jettisoned, and only after the decision had been made by Lambrew at the White House, at the urging of the Treasury Department and with the unenthusiastic approval of the White House communications office.

When the Congressional Budget Office got news that the mandate had been dropped, it "scored" the loss of the penalties expected from enforcing it as costing the government $12 billion. It was not a game changer for a trillion-dollar program. However, it was real money, even in Washington—amounting, for example, to 150 percent of the annual FBI budget.

"WAY OFF TRACK AND GETTING WORSE"

Six days following the announcement that the employer mandate was being put aside, a series of panicked emails about a broader problem circulated through CMS.

Gary Cohen's *Center* for Consumer Information and Insurance Oversight—the unit that had been demoted from an *office* but was still supposedly responsible for the coordination of everything on the website—had finally realized that the CMS technology group (the *Office* of Information Services) was not anywhere close to on schedule in building the website.

The July 8, 2013, email chain started with Jeffrey Grant, a staffer at Cohen's CCIIO, emailing his immediate bosses. "We just got off an extended set of development planning meetings with OIS," Grant wrote, referring to the CMS Office of Information Services, where deputy director Henry Chao was supposedly in charge of the website. "The upshot," he continued,

> is that the FM [the federal insurance exchange] build appears to be way off track and getting worse. We also were finally told that there are only 10 developers total working on the build for all functionality. Only one of these developers is at a high enough skill level to handle complex issue resolution, which now appears to be required for all aspects of our build. . . . We are one week out from production deployment, and we are being told already that it doesn't work. . . . Due to coordination issues between CGI [the main contractor] and [another contractor] there has been no independent testing and CGI still cannot support user acceptance [consumer] testing, originally scheduled for early June.

It was now July 8—less than three months before launch. Any commercial website of this complexity—certainly sites like Orbitz or Amazon, to which Obama and his team compared the coming exchange—would have long since locked down everything and begun rounds of user testing.

The email continued with a list of other woes. It concluded with this indictment of lead contractor CGI: "So, while OIS [the CMS information services office] has always said we had an independent team for [the exchange] development, they have never revealed the seriously substandard level of staffing that this team has. We believe that our entire build is in jeopardy."

What was as revealing as the problems Grant's email outlined was how, for all of its explosive meaning, it didn't fly around the Internet the way juicy emails often do. More to the point, it didn't even fly around the government, or for that matter within CMS, itself. It stayed in its Washington silo.

Grant sent the email to only two midlevel bosses in CCIIO, not even to Gary Cohen, the CCIIO head. (I'm pounding away on the acronym here to help you get the feel for the culture that produces these kinds of bureaucratic meltdowns.) The email was not sent to Henry Chao or anyone else at the division that the author was complaining about—Chao's Office of Information Services. It was only after the email had been forwarded up the chain, at about 6 p.m., to two more levels of CCIIO people—but still never to CCIIO boss Cohen—that it was sent to Henry Chao for comment.

Chao's response was immediate. He didn't use it to raise questions about what was going on. Instead, he forwarded it to two of his deputies and to two people at CGI with only this request: "Can you get me a response on this to refute what Jeff [Grant, the original email's author] is saying?"

To Chao, this was an opening salvo for a debate about the quality of his work, not an effort to identify and solve a problem. The Grant email needed to be refuted, not considered and acted upon to help ensure a successful launch of the country's health insurance exchange.

By 10:15 the next morning, a CGI executive had responded to Chao and others in Chao's office (but with no copies to anyone at

CCIIO) that "I met with the FM [insurance exchange] team. . . . While I understand some of Jeff's [Grant's] concerns, there is a bigger picture around where we stand with FM and our plans to get the work done." The CGI executive then outlined plans to add staff, though he said that the current staffing levels were "per the budget." In Beltway contractor language that meant CGI was going to ask for more money than was in its original contract.

The CGI executive continued his rebuttal, writing that any "defects" were "being addressed," while hinting that some of the features planned for the launch might have to be delayed: "We are working through program-wide priorities" was the code for that.

The CGI executive also wrote that "we still don't have all the requirements" spelled out, meaning some of the business rules had still not been decided, and, he added, "we are facing some challenges where prior decisions are being re-opened." In other words, any delays won't be our fault.

The highest ranking official who saw that email chain was Chao. He never passed it up to his superiors at CMS. He never sent a reply back to Jeffrey Grant or anyone at CCIIO, which they could circulate to higher-ups. Instead, he called Grant and said that his team had looked into the issues he had raised and that this was all a matter of how, in the course of managing priorities, sometimes some aspects of a project would look like they were being neglected when they weren't. Everything was under control.

The email chain was not shared with anyone at the White House— where Jeanne Lambrew and David Simas in the messaging shop had been "re-opening decisions" about some of the rules and about the look and feel of the planned e-commerce site.

ARE THEY GOING TO "CRASH THE PLANE"?

For all the assurances Chao gave the people in CMS outside his shop, he was hardly sanguine. On July 16, 2013, a week after he had received and seemingly accepted CGI's rebuttal to Grant's warning, Chao emailed key members of his staff about CGI, directing them to "convey just how low the confidence level" in CGI was at CMS. Chao told his staff to make clear to CGI how angry he was that the company had just made a "request for more money . . . when we constantly struggle to get a release done."

But for Chao it was not really about the money. "I just need to feel more confident they are not going to crash the plane at take-off, regardless of price," he concluded. "Just get that message conveyed."

One of Chao's staff members thought their usually calm boss was, he later told me, "starting to lose it. He was talking about a plane crash."

Yet the next morning, when Chao and his boss, Marilyn Tavenner, testified on Capitol Hill before a House subcommittee about how the build was progressing, he didn't seem worried about the plane crashing.

"As of this month, all the infrastructure and the required, you know, hardware, software capacity, all of that is available and up and running," Chao calmly assured the subcommittee, though he added this qualifier: "The specific application software, such as . . . the enrollment and eligibility pieces, the loading of the [insurance plan] information to process an enrollment and a payment to an issuer, that is an ongoing process. All that code and those databases are still being built throughout the summer."

"So both of you are testifying today that these shortfalls . . . are going to be 100 percent complete on October 1st," one congressman asked.

"Correct," said Chao.

"Yes, sir," replied Tavenner. "We will start October 1, and we will certainly have hiccups along the way, and we are prepared to deal with this."

"HIGH RISKS" AND "DEFECTS"

As Chao and Tavenner were testifying on July 17, a consulting firm called TurningPoint was delivering a brutally pessimistic report to CMS about the progress of the project. TurningPoint had been hired to issue a series of what is called "independent verification and validation reports," which monitor whether the contractors working on a project are on schedule and on budget.

TurningPoint's July 17 presentation delineated so many "high risks" and "defects" that the McKinsey consultants' April report looked cheery by comparison. This was not just a critique, as McKinsey's was, of disjointed management and foot dragging. TurningPoint also delved into all the technical specifics, such as whether the website was being built with enough capacity to handle anything close to the traffic and complex transactions it might generate. "The existing capacity planning is not adequate," the auditors said. "The system's capacity to support future growth cannot be verified."

There were pages of red flags, in the form of reddened areas on grids, detailing all varieties of small and large technical shortcomings.

But Chao cannot be criticized for not telling Congress about TurningPoint's warning. He didn't know about it, he later testified at another congressional hearing.

TurningPoint's reports were kept in a silo at CMS separate from Chao's silo. The firm had been hired by Gary Cohen's *Center* for Consumer Information and Insurance Oversight, not by Chao's *Office* of Information Services. And by the time someone at CCIIO shared it with relatively low-level people at the Office of Information Services, those Office of Information Services staffers thought it was incorrect, dated, or otherwise not worth bumping up to Chao.

Nonetheless, on July 20, Chao was apparently worried about the assurances he had given Congress three days before. So he sent an email to his staff and to the team at CGI, to which he attached a C-SPAN video of his testimony. "I would like you [to] put yourself in my shoes standing before Congress," he wrote, "which in essence is standing before the American public, and know that you speak the tongue of not necessarily just past truths but the truth that you will make happen, the truth that is a promise to the public that millions of people depend on for us to make happen."

Although demonstrating that, as his colleagues had told me, he was not a good communicator, it seems as if Chao was trying to rally his staff to make his testimony turn out to be true even if it was "not necessarily" true when he gave it.

Six days later, another flurry of internal emails at CMS warned that the small business exchanges were not going to be able to be launched in October. Like the employer mandate, they had to be thrown overboard. Those were the exchanges, meant to allow small business owners to buy insurance online for their employees, that HHS Secretary Sebelius in April had told a concerned Max Baucus would be up and running on schedule "in every market in the country."

Meanwhile, at the White House, the only Obamacare news was good news. On July 18, 2013—the same day that a Treasury Department official was quoted, despite the looming trouble with the small business exchanges, promising that no other provisions of the law would be delayed the way the employer mandate had—President Obama was back in the East Room delivering a speech hailing the billions of dollars in insurance premiums that had been refunded to consumers because of the medical loss ratio rule. There was no particular news hook for the event; the 2012 rebates under the rule had been distributed months before. The president simply invited some of the families that had gotten rebates to a speech reminding America of what David Simas had long since identified as the most politically winning aspect of the law.

A CAMPAIGN REUNION

Through the summer of 2013, the press became captivated not by the struggle to build the website that all of those panicked internal emails and consultant reports reflected, but by what everyone thought was the real drama—the Obama 2012 campaign reunion story. The campaign whiz kids were back, and they were gearing up to use big data, new media, and all of their other tricks to win one more campaign for Obama, a campaign to get everyone to sign up for health insurance.

Put simply, the political debate and punditry around the launch was mostly about whether the old Hope and Change team could get people to come to the website exchanges, not what would happen once they got there.

Simas, who now had the title of White House deputy senior adviser for communications, made the rounds of major news outlets, providing colorful details of how, under his direction, big data was being fed by the campaign whiz kids at Civis to the field troops being organized by former campaign colleague Anne Filipic at Enroll America. They were going to target specific precincts, say, in Miami or Houston, to identify the uninsured and convince them to enroll.

"We want multiple touches," Simas told me when I interviewed him in his tiny White House basement office, where he sketched out those "touches" on a whiteboard: social messaging, door-to-door canvassing, community rallies, targeted radio ads. "The idea is to take the abstraction of Obamacare, and make it into an actionable reality."

On July 17, *The Washington Post*'s Ezra Klein and Sarah Kliff published a long feature on the progress of the rollout. Unlike most of their competitors, they devoted a lot of space to detailing the technical and regulatory challenges involved in launching a complicated program still bitterly opposed by Republicans and barely understood by the public.

Nonetheless, their headline was "Obama's Last Campaign: Inside the White House Plan to Sell Obamacare," under which there was a large picture of Simas gazing out from in front of the White House.

Klein and Kliff set up the coming drama this way:

> Deep inside the White House, in a bare room that the chief of staff uses for meetings, David Simas is still thinking about turnout.
>
> Turnout has been Simas's job for years now. As director of public-opinion research and polling for President Obama's re-election campaign, Simas was at the center of the effort to find and persuade young and minority voters to go to the polls like they did in 2008. . . .
>
> Now Simas, a sad-eyed Massachusetts native with a facility for PowerPoints, needs to reach those same groups again—with a much harder ask. This time, he doesn't just need them to vote. He needs them to buy health insurance, and, in some cases, spend hundreds of dollars a month for it. If they don't, the new insurance marketplaces—the absolute core of Obamacare—will be filled with older, sicker people, and premiums will skyrocket. And if that happens, the law will fail. . . .

Simas is focusing his formidable analytical resources on understanding this group. He begins clicking through a PowerPoint that holds reams of data on these young adults. . . .

A couple more clicks and Simas is showing which television channels they like to watch (Spike TV, among others), which social-media platforms they use (Twitter, Facebook) and who they listen to ("No surprise. It's mom."). "We can figure out the message that works best for this group," Simas says.

The focus on young, minority voters. The heavy reliance on microtargeting. The enthusiasm about nontraditional communications channels. The analytics-rich modeling. It sounds like the Obama campaign. And administration officials don't shy away from the comparison.

Even Jeanne Lambrew—who was supposed to be the White House official overseeing the website build—agreed that Simas's work was what the launch was all about: "When I hear the conventional wisdom about Obamacare," she told the *Post,* "this is the difference between the Karl Roves who put their fingers to the wind and the Nate Silvers of the world who looked at the numbers."

Implementing President Obama's most important domestic policy seemed to be all about campaigning, not about governing.

The officials at CMS and HHS whom I interviewed during the summer of 2013 were similarly focused. I was regaled with stories about the demographic targeting being done. In fact, the CMS staff claimed that its data, more than that supplied by Civis, was fueling the campaign.

My questions about the technology were brushed aside so briskly and confidently that my initial impression that not having one person in charge spelled disaster was beginning to feel like an overreaction.[16]

When I talked to Simas, he, too, assured me that "everything has been tested and is working perfectly. . . . Our challenge is getting the right people to show up."

---

16. It was only months later, after I began working on this book, that I became aware of the panicked internal emails, infighting, and lack of leadership that preceded the launch.

THE BLANK CALENDAR

What got me suspicious again had to do with what became the much-publicized "official White House" Obamacare calendar.

A July 23, 2013, report in *The New York Times*—another one focusing on Simas, his spreadsheets, and his "war rooms"—described it this way: "Royal blue and emblazoned with the White House seal, the 'Official Affordable Care Act Enrollment Countdown' is a paper calendar that keeps track of the time before uninsured Americans can begin signing up for coverage under the president's signature health care law. On Tuesday, the top page said simply: '70 Days Left.'"

Ah, I figured, when I read that story. That must be the shorthand version of their detailed battle plan. On the back of each numbered day must be the list of things that have to have been completed on such and such date for everything to come together. In management circles, the long version of this project playbook is sometimes called a Gantt chart.

That had to be why, I assumed, the *Times* had noted that "when Denis R. McDonough, the White House chief of staff, first saw the document in a meeting in the [White House] Roosevelt Room, he immediately dispatched his aides to the West Wing basement to get copies for all of President Obama's top advisers." McDonough—who was telling reporters he was personally spending an hour or two a day on Obamacare—obviously wanted everyone focused on getting everything done that needed to be done, task by task.

So, I asked the White House press office to send me a copy of the "Official Affordable Care Act Enrollment Countdown." That way I could see their real launch plan and, by reviewing all the checked-off milestones, understand why they were all so confident that everything was going to be ready.

Seven weeks later, what I got was twenty pages, each with a descending number. There was nothing else on either side of the pages. It was all blank.

IN LATE JANUARY 2013, deputy chief of staff Nancy-Ann DeParle had gone back into the private sector to help lead a private equity firm.

DeParle had told Obama in 2010 she wanted to do that, but she had stayed on when he promoted her to deputy chief of staff. Her decision to leave before the launch—when all the key decisions still had to be made and implemented—surprised many of her colleagues, and had left Lambrew as the key point person supervising CMS and other agencies building the website.

Throughout the summer, Obama had regular meetings about the rollout with Lambrew, chief of staff McDonough, Valerie Jarrett, David Simas, and other members of his communications staff. Except for Lambrew routinely reporting that the build was on track, the meetings were about the political effort. Which celebrity had Jarrett or Simas lured into making pitches for people to sign up? Should the president make some calls of his own to recruit them? Which states looked especially promising? What presidential speeches or other events to boost enrollment were on the calendar? Could retailers such as Walgreens be recruited to help by distributing literature?

According to McDonough, Obama always ended every meeting by saying something to the effect of, "This is all good, but remember it won't matter if we don't get the technology right." The president had the right instinct, but was talking to the wrong people. No one in the room had any idea how or if the technology worked. Along with mock-ups of computer screens showing that everything was looking good, they had only gotten reports that there might be some of the normal glitches affecting every start-up, but that as a general matter everything was a go.

"You've got to have a culture in place where people aren't afraid to admit there's a problem," was all Obama would volunteer when I asked him about those meetings and whether his simple admonition about the technology at the end of each session might not have been enough.

"YOUR PROBLEMS ARE ALL HYPOTHETICAL"

On July 29, 2013, a stock analyst writing on the Seeking Alpha website recommended insurance company stocks, which he said were undervalued given the likely positive impact of the launch of Obamacare.

Indeed, the stocks of the major insurers had all jumped dramatically since President Obama had signed the law in March 2010, outpacing the overall post-recession Wall Street recovery.

Karen Ignagni, who ran the insurance lobby, wasn't feeling as good about Obamacare. Her companies had frontline exposure to the problems with the build of the e-commerce site, because it was their products that had to be linked into the website for the e-commerce to happen. She had rounds of meetings with the CMS people in Baltimore, telling them that every report she got was that the exchange was not going to be ready. "Why not let October be a month where people can browse the various offerings, but not buy?" she suggested. "Or perhaps you could just delay everything a month? What are your contingency plans," she kept asking. There were no contingency plans, she was told. "Your problems are all hypothetical," the CMS officials told her. "We're not seeing anything like what you are describing."

STILL A "BILL," NOT A LAW

All of this behind-closed-doors angst was playing out through a summer in which the politics of Obamacare seemed to have become even more bitter than they had been during the Tea Party summer four years before. Despite the president's reelection, and despite the Supreme Court's ruling, the Republicans acted as if Obamacare were still a pending bill to be debated, rather than the law of the land to be implemented.

The closest historical precedent might have been resistance to the Supreme Court's *Brown v. Board of Education* decision desegregating public schools. Yet that at least could be attacked as the decision of nine men in robes, not the duly elected House, Senate, and president.

When Senate minority leader Mitch McConnell got wind of an effort by the Obama administration to enlist the National Football League and other professional sports organizations to get their players to do public service commercials to encourage Americans to sign up for coverage (much the way Mitt Romney had enlisted the Boston Red Sox to promote Romneycare), he and Senator John Cornyn of Texas successfully urged the league to steer clear. "Given the divisiveness and persistent unpopularity of the health care law, it is difficult to understand why an organization like yours would risk damaging its inclusive and apolitical brand by lending its name to its promotion," McConnell and Cornyn wrote to the NFL.

At the same time, a group of conservative twenty-somethings, called Generation Opportunity, sprang up to urge the young invincibles to ignore the law's mandate. They should not be lured into paying high premiums for insurance they don't need, Generation Opportunity argued, just to support older people, who would pay lower premiums if the invincibles bought into the scheme and, thereby, lowered the overall risk profile of those in the insurance pool. Paying the penalty for ignoring the mandate was a better deal—and the right way to protest the new law and help torpedo it.

Generation Opportunity, which was funded largely by conservative billionaires David and Charles Koch, soon started showing up at some of Anne Filipic's Enroll America rallies and even staging rallies of their own on college campuses perceived to have more conservative students. The group had a creative—or, their critics would say, perverse—sense of humor that yielded a soon-to-be-viral series of Web videos. The most popular showed Uncle Sam crawling out from between the legs of a woman being examined in a doctor's office. The message was classic Frank Luntz: Reject government interference in the doctor-patient relationship.

THE "DEFUND" CAUCUS

In August 2013, a cadre of the most conservative Republicans, led by freshman Texas senator Ted Cruz, began staging a series of "defund" rallies, aimed at encouraging conservatives to demand that Congress stop funding Obamacare. They had the leverage to do it, Cruz argued. Republicans could simply threaten to block any new budget, due October 1, or block any increase in the debt ceiling due soon thereafter, if Obamacare wasn't defunded as part of a new budget and debt ceiling deal.

"We have, I believe . . . the last good opportunity we will have to defund Obamacare," Cruz declared at a July 30 meeting of the Heritage Foundation, whose political action committee was organizing the rallies. "If we do not pursue this strategy, we are saying we surrender. Obamacare will be a permanent feature of the American economy."

KENTUCKY GOES ALL IN

But in one of the reddest of red states, Obamacare was picking up steam.

Through the spring and summer, Kentucky Health and Family Services cabinet secretary Audrey Haynes, her kynect executive director, Carrie Banahan, and Deloitte's Mohan Kumar had pushed their team on all fronts. Attractive shopping bags and literature had been designed with the "kynect" logo and the pastel colors and rising sun that the focus group researchers had suggested. A plan was put together for how the material would be distributed to the "kynectors" or "navigators," that Sebelius had promised Senator Baucus were going to be hired, and to community groups that Haynes, a seasoned political operative, was helping to recruit. A calendar was created full of fall events where the marketing materials and troops would be deployed—such as the annual Bourbon Festival in Bardstown and the Apple Festival in Paintsville, near the poorest, reddest part of the state.

In Kentucky, unlike Washington, the technology part of the work was being given equal if not more attention at the top. Banahan and Deloitte's Kumar regularly briefed Secretary Haynes and occasionally Governor Beshear, not only about their progress but also about problems they were encountering along the way.

Banahan and Kumar rode themselves and the contractors mercilessly, often working through the night and weekends so they would not miss any deadline on the elaborate milestone chart that was their bible.

They had farmed out discrete portions of the work to multiple subcontractors. Even CGI, which was having so much trouble as the main federal contractor, worked on a piece of the Kentucky project.

By April 2013, Kumar—who would take no vacation during the fifty-one weeks preceding the launch and worked through multiple weekends—had finished a first version of the site for Carrie Banahan to take on the road to test with focus groups and in community meetings. She had come back with design and flow changes that Kumar's team incorporated into new versions.

By June, the Deloitte people began "pressure testing" their site, giving it the kind of end-to-end run-throughs that the people at CMS would be worried still had not been done on the federal website in August. They found multiple problems and sometimes had to tell Haynes or even the governor that one or more of the issues might force a delay. But they fixed them, one by one.

Now, on August 22, the feds from CMS arrived to see if Kentucky had its act together. In this case, the feds were from CCIIO, not the CMS Office of Information Services that was building the federal exchange. CCIIO had its own technology team, working completely apart from the CMS Office of Information Services, because it was CCIIO that was in charge of vetting and regulating the fifteen state-run exchanges.

Chris Clark, the soft-spoken engineer Banahan had pulled out of retirement to supervise Deloitte's engineers, was happy to have the feds kick his tires. He had thrown himself into the project, thrilled that even his six-year-old son understood that he was, as Clark later told me, "working on something important."

"Did you do good work for kynect today, Daddy?" his son would ask on the nights Clark got home before his son went to bed. "He'd seen the kynect commercials and had the [shopping] bag," Clark later told me. "He was excited about it."

Clark had already hosted another group of federal inspectors who had tested his site for security vulnerabilities and found everything in order. Now it was time for the big end-to-end test. Clark wasn't worried about it, because he and the Deloitte team had done all that themselves first.

The inspectors made Clark put his exchange through six hundred different consumer scenarios—a single person who qualified for Medicaid, a family who had a twenty-five-year-old who already had employer-paid insurance, or someone who wanted a gold plan but would receive a subsidy to help pay for it based on the price of the second lowest priced silver plan (because that was the way the law worked).

The testing lasted three days.

"We were the first state to say we were ready for testing," Clark recalled. "And those CCIIO guys put us through the ringer. But it was all fine."

IN WASHINGTON, 38 PERCENT STILL UNDONE

The CMS feds from CCIIO were pleased when Clark showed data demonstrating that Kentucky's site could handle at least ten thousand users at the same time. Yet the CMS feds from Chao's Office of Information Services were hoping their *federal* exchange site covering thirty-six states would be able to handle only fifty thousand users (though it was actually being built to handle only ten thousand, if that).

Kentucky has about 4.3 million people. The federal exchange site's thirty-six states have a population of more than 200 million. In other words, at headquarters CMS was planning to handle fifty times Kentucky's population with, at best, five times the computing capacity its people had seen in Kentucky.

The same day, August 22, 2013, that one arm of CMS was pressure testing a fully built version of the Kentucky exchange, the Henry Chao arm of CMS was meeting in Baltimore with their CGI contractor team going over fifteen pages of spreadsheets spelling out items for the federal exchange that still had not been completed. As *The Washington Post* would report three months later, for each item CGI had listed its level of confidence—high, medium, or low—that it could be completed by the October 1 deadline. Most were labeled high or medium, though some were rated low. But even many of those not rated medium or even high were deemed by CGI to be dependent on the performance of other contractors.

Two days later, on Saturday, August 24, a CGI email to CMS reported that 62 percent of the exchange was now built.

CHAPTER 19

THIRTY DAYS TO GO

September 2013

On September 6, 2013, CGI executives warned Chao in an email that "due to the compressed schedule there is not enough time built in for adequate performance testing."

Yet ten days after that CGI senior vice president Cheryl Campbell told a House of Representatives subcommittee that "at this time, CGI Federal is confident that it will deliver the functionality that CMS has directed to enable qualified individuals to begin enrolling in coverage when the initial enrollment period begins on October 1, 2013."

Make believe you're a lawyer and reread that statement looking for the escape clauses. Campbell was saying CGI would *deliver the functionality that CMS had directed to enable qualified individuals to begin enrolling in coverage*. What if they could "begin" enrolling but not complete the process? What if the other contractors hadn't delivered on their pieces of the puzzle, such as the mechanism vetting the identity of consumers *after* they began enrollment? How many "qualified individuals" would be able to enroll? What if CMS had directed the wrong functionality? And what if it all hadn't been tested to check for all of that?

By now, Bryan Sivak—the chief technology officer at CMS parent HHS, who had built the exchange's consumer-facing home page and was supposed to be his agency's chief innovation officer—was whispering to friends that there was "no way" the launch was going to succeed. He had created and launched dozens of software projects, he told anyone who would listen, and there were always bugs that you could never anticipate no matter how good the coders were—"and these guys probably weren't very good," he feared. "You can't do something like this without months of testing," he confided.

Sivak talked to Sebelius and others at the Department of Health and Human Services about his qualms. But he was told that he didn't have the information they had—which was true because Chao and the others had shut him out. The staff working on the build had assured her, Sebelius told him, that while there might be some glitches, everything was proceeding on course.

As for Todd Park, who was now the chief technology officer at the White House, he had tried to go to Lambrew's meetings, but was shut out of most of them and not given the information he requested about the status of the build. He occasionally called or emailed Chao, but Chao assured him that they were going to fix whatever problems still loomed. "Todd is just too nice a guy to have dumped on these people or gone to higher-ups to blow the whistle," recalled one of his close colleagues. "So, he just accepted it when they told him everything was okay, and passed that up the chain, saying the CMS team was working really hard and that they were good people."

CMS head Tavenner was "nervous but confident," she would later tell me. "We knew it was a big project with lots of moving parts, and I knew Henry [Chao] was nervous. But tech people are always nervous at launch. . . . He never said that we needed to delay it. And, frankly, we were much more focused on the marketing and whether we could get the message out so people would come to the exchange."

"OBAMACARE WILL QUESTION YOUR SEX LIFE"

Tavenner and the rest of the Obama team couldn't be blamed for worrying about getting their message out. There was all kinds of noise that they had to shout over. As the October 1, 2013, launch approached, a barrage of Republican attacks increasingly picked up traction in the press.

The Republicans made headlines with a charge that the economic recovery was lagging because 8.2 million part-time workers couldn't find full-time work because the employer mandate requiring full-timers to be given health insurance made it too expensive for them to be hired. Yet the CBO had said the mandate's effect on employment would be minimal. Besides, the mandate had now been delayed for at least a year.

The *New York Post* ran a column—which was then circulated widely online—headlined "Obamacare Will Question Your Sex Life." The article tried to twist the law's incentives to expand the use of electronic medical records into a mandate that people had to tell the government whether they were "sexually active." The author was Betsy McCaughey, a conservative healthcare activist and former New York State lieutenant governor, who had launched the "death panel" charges in 2009 that Sarah Palin had trumpeted.

There were multiple stories, including a front-page article in *The Wall Street Journal,* describing how the young invincibles were unlikely to sign up because the Obamacare premiums they would have to pay would be so much higher than the insurance they could buy now. Although that was often true, it was not the full story. First, the insurance they could buy under Obamacare had far more complete coverage, including for preventive care, than the policies many had been buying, some of which had such severe limits that the coverage was nearly worthless. (Remember how Sean Recchi's and Steven D.'s insurance coverage evaporated when they got cancer?)

Second, and most important, the premiums the press usually described didn't take into account the subsidies most Americans would get from the government to help pay for them. That gap in most of the articles describing the high premiums was, in large part, the Obama administration's fault. The political team was still gun-shy about touting how much of a welfare program Obamacare actually was.

As October 1 neared, the press came up with their own negative stories largely based on ammunition supplied by the stumbling launch effort.

When the administration finally announced that the small business exchanges that Sebelius had promised to Baucus would be "ready in every market" would not be ready, *Politico*'s headline was "Another Obamacare Delay." The article reported that a planned Spanish language version of the website was also being put off, and mentioned that a link allowing the federal exchange to transfer Medicaid applications to the states electronically had been delayed earlier that week.

Republican senator Orrin Hatch of Utah, who had been a booster of Baucus's reform ideas at the June 2008 summit, gave *Politico* a killer quote to end the story: "This law will never be ready for prime time. It's what happens when government takes over healthcare."

Another *Politico* article—"Obamacare: One Blow After Another"— tied the dropped or delayed exchange features with the Republican governors' refusal to launch their own exchanges or to expand Medicaid, along with the overall "unrelenting Republican opposition," to paint a picture of a program that was just plain jinxed.

All of the incoming fire directed at Obamacare seemed to come together on the home page of Matt Drudge's *Drudge Report* on September 23. Featuring a picture of President Obama in a surgeon's gown staring out at readers and holding a stethoscope pointed at them, *Drudge*'s headline, in red, was "T Minus 7 Days." Surrounding that were these subheadlines linking to other stories:

- "Doctors Brace for Health Law's Surge of Ailing Patients." This was a *Bloomberg Businessweek* article that was, in fact, a balanced story speculating that hospitals might be overwhelmed with newly insured patients (which never happened, in part because there is an oversupply of hospital beds in the United States), but pointing out the obviously positive impact of people getting access to healthcare for the first time.
- "*Forbes*: Obamacare Will Increase Healthcare Spending by $7,450 for Family of Four." This linked to an opinion piece in *Forbes,* written by someone who had a grant from a conservative foundation to study healthcare economics. More important than the writer was his math, which confused overall national expenditures for healthcare, which obviously would go up under Obamacare as more people got care, with a *family's* expense. And a close read revealed that

the $7,450 in the headline was the supposed total increase in cost over eight years.

• "Movement Grows to Repeal Obamacare Exemption for Congress." This was an issue that opponents had cooked up, by distorting a provision inserted into the law by Republican Charles Grassley. When Grassley was still negotiating with Baucus, he would later tell me, he mentioned to Baucus that at a town hall meeting someone had asked why, if these exchanges were going to be so great, members of Congress shouldn't have to use them. Grassley thought it was a good idea, and so did Baucus.

So Grassley's staff had written a provision requiring members of Congress and their staffs to use the exchanges to buy insurance. The provision, as proposed by Grassley, also made clear that the government would still pay for the insurance for the members and their staffs just the way it now did. They would just have to use the exchanges to buy it and get reimbursed by the government for the same share the government already was paying. After all, why should congressional staff be the only employees thrown off their employers' insurance under Obamacare?

However, when the final bill was drafted, the language had somehow become less clear, and there was a plausible, though tenuous, way to read it as not providing for the same employer reimbursement that had always been in place. For staffers making $80,000 a year with families, that could mean a sudden $10,000 or $15,000 drop in income.

To fix the problem, members of Congress from both parties, including Grassley, had suggested that the federal Office of Personnel Management should issue a clarification that made sure Grassley's intention would prevail. But now this had been exploited by the Obamacare opponents. Across the blogosphere and cable news echo chamber there were outraged complaints that Congress and the administration were secretly seeking to exempt Congress and its staff from the horrors of Obamacare.

Some of the negative press had to do with the fact that anything bad about healthcare now had a new law, or person, to blame it on. One of the most courageous aspects of Obama having persevered and insisted on getting broad reform passed was, as his communications director Jennifer Palmieri later told me, that "we knew that from now on we owned everything about healthcare, good and bad."

Employers had been cutting back on their insurance benefits for years. Now, when they announced higher deductibles or co-insurance obligations, they could blame it on Obamacare. Most did, which often resulted in news stories about the new burdens being put on workers. It was true that the more generous coverage of preventive care that was now required for all insurance packages added extra costs. But that was not nearly as much of a factor in raising premiums as were the continuing upward trends in medical costs. Besides, that more complete coverage made the workers' insurance more valuable.

Similarly, when firms dropped coverage of workers altogether, which was another long-term trend, most of the press coverage linked the move to Obamacare, although Obamacare would force those same firms to add coverage once the employer mandate kicked in.

Even the coming Obamacare changes meant to contain costs got a negative spin. Now, whenever hospitals announced job cuts or other cost-cutting measures, which was not often, it was blamed on the new law's tightening of Medicare payments to hospitals—which had been negotiated with the hospitals' lobby in return for hospitals getting all of those newly insured customers.

Besides, if healthcare costs as a percent of the economy were going to be cut, that had to mean that the abnormally high percentage of American workers employed in the healthcare industry—about 16 percent versus less than 10 percent in France, which had better health-care outcomes—had to come down. So, yes, jobs would be lost.

Of course, hospitals talked about the cuts not only as costing jobs and hurting the economy but, more poignantly, as endangering patients. That piece of the blame game had started in December 2012 when *The New York Times* ran a story about how threatened cuts in hospital payments might affect patient care. Steven Safyer, chief executive of Montefiore Medical Center, a large ostensibly nonprofit hospital system in the Bronx, complained to the *Times,* "There is no such thing as a cut to a provider that isn't a cut to a beneficiary. . . . This is not crying wolf."

Actually, Safyer seemed to be crying wolf to the tune of about $196.8 million, according to his hospital's IRS filing for the year closest to when he talked to the *Times* reporter. That was his hospital's operating profit. With $2.586 billion in revenue, Safyer's business was more than five times as large as that of the Bronx's most famous enterprise, the New York Yankees. Surely, without cutting services to patients, Safyer could have cut what had to have been some of the Bronx's better non-Yankee salaries: his own, which was $4.065 million or those of his chief financial officer ($3.243 million), his executive vice president ($2.22 million), or the head of his dental department ($1.798 million).

PTSD?

Polls taken throughout September 2013 showed the cost of all the bad press. CNN reported that support for Obamacare had slipped from 51 percent in January to 39 percent. Fox News reported that "68 percent of Americans are concerned about their personal healthcare" under the new law. A poll by the Kaiser Family Foundation (which specializes in healthcare issues) found that 64 percent of all Americans and 74 percent of uninsured Americans did not know the exchanges were opening on October 1, and "slightly over half of those polled said they do not have enough information about the law to understand it." An *Atlanta Journal Constitution* survey echoed the same lack of awareness, but noted that a higher number disapproved of it than said they understood it.

These and other polls generated their own headlines and still more bad-news stories.

About ten days before the launch, I asked one of the press people at CMS whether anyone was considering a delay in the launch in order to make sure everything would work smoothly.

"Are you kidding?" he shot back. "Do you have any idea what they would do to us?"

He then described the mood there as "all of us walking around with PTSD"—post-traumatic stress disorder. "We are all just in a defensive crouch, afraid to do anything or say anything. We just want to launch and prove everyone wrong." Two of his colleagues used the same PTSD analogy that day.

Public relations people and government administrators comparing their stress to that of soldiers stopping bullets or stepping on improvised explosive devices was more than an over-the-top expression of self-importance and self-pity. It was emblematic of their amazing ability to be indignant—to assume the role of the victims—when it was their own failure to govern that had fortified and emboldened the opposition. From the president and Valerie Jarrett on down, they had sloughed off the details of governing when it came to their most important and difficult domestic initiative. It was as if they either believed that they were big policy thinkers who were above worrying about the details of making the law work, or that they didn't understand that effective government does not happen automatically. Or both.

All of which had produced the ammunition for the fierce, multi-front attacks that had, indeed, shocked them. Many of the people working on Obamacare at CMS and HHS, even the press spokesmen, were veterans of congressional staffs or advocacy groups that had been in the healthcare reform fight for years. They believed in the cause, so much so that they had gone along, though not always happily, with the strategy of accommodating the Republicans by adopting the Republican Romneycare plan. To the extent that the new law was so complicated that there were all of these hiccups in implementing it, that was only because those accommodations to the conservatives involved strapping reform onto the old patchwork system instead of scrapping it and going with the single-payer, Medicare-for-all alternative that most of them favored. In their indignant view, Republicans should be the last ones to attack them for that.

In 1936, Social Security enrollment had been delayed because no one in the pre-digital age could figure out how to create a system that would produce twenty-six million uniquely identifiable account numbers for America's workers. But although Republicans had relentlessly attacked Social Security, once the law was passed the blowback over the launch problems had been relatively minimal. That was a management dilemma, not a political issue.

With little political fallout, Lyndon Johnson got Congress to delay the deadline for signing up for Medicare by two months in 1966 because he wanted more people to have a chance to enroll. (Ninety percent of those eligible had already signed up, which apparently was not enough for LBJ.)

Times had changed. Congressional districts had been gerrymandered to make legislators more worried about primary challenges from their right or left than about pleasing the middle. Big money had come to dominate campaigns, issue advocacy, and lobbying in a way that similarly encouraged fighting until the bitter end, rather than compromise.

So, the CMS people launching Obamacare were right. Almost anything anyone did or said threatened to spark another firefight in today's Washington. In September 2013, they didn't dare look up from their foxholes and tell the White House that October 1 wasn't going to happen.

LIKE APPEASING THE NAZIS

The Republicans, of course, wanted more than a delay. They wanted to block the law for good. And, as with Senator Cruz of Texas and his defund rallies, some were willing to go further than others to make that happen.

On the afternoon of September 24, 2013, Cruz began what would be a twenty-one-hour-plus mock filibuster[17] calling for his fellow Americans, and especially fellow Republicans in the House and Senate, to resist funding Obamacare. There should be no budget in time for the October 1 start of the new budget year if there was any funding for Obamacare in it, Cruz declared. If the administration didn't agree, the Republicans, using their House majority, should shut the government down. They should even refuse to extend the debt ceiling when that deadline came in mid-October.

---

17. Under Senate rules, it was not actually a filibuster because the speech was required to end at 1 P.M. the next day.

In a talkathon that later devolved into the senator reading bedtime stories from the podium to his children at home in Texas, Cruz began by comparing the need to resist Obamacare to the British failure to resist the Nazis. "Look, we saw in Britain," he said, "Neville Chamberlain, who told the British people, 'Accept the Nazis. Yes, they'll dominate the continent of Europe, but that's not our problem. Let's appease them. Why? Because it can't be done. We can't possibly stand against them.' "

Cruz railed against his fellow senators for not appreciating the risk that Obamacare would destroy healthcare for America's families. Like Chamberlain, they, too, were not rising to the occasion. "If you're concerned about the health care of you and your family and if you're concerned about losing your health insurance and you ask what is the United States Senate doing, the answer is an empty chair," he said, gesturing around the near-empty Senate chamber.

Cruz then lodged a more general complaint against his Senate colleagues who, he said, seemed more concerned with "cocktail parties in Washington, D.C." than with their constituents. Referring to calls that he said were pouring in from around the country, begging legislators to resist and defund, Cruz noted, "It is apparently an imposition on some members of this body for their constituents to pick up the phone and ask for assistance."

As I heard him say that, I picked up the phone and called Cruz's local constituent service office in Houston. Could someone there give me information about how to enroll in Obamacare?" I asked, when I was put on the phone with one of the senator's case workers. "No. We don't support the bill, and think it's a bad idea," I was told. "You should call the federal government's or HHS's 1-800 number or something like that."

I wondered if they would have helped me get a passport if Cruz didn't believe in the laws allowing foreign travel.

HIDING THE SUBSIDIES

Just as Cruz was picking up steam on the near-empty Senate floor, HHS secretary Kathleen Sebelius—along with Gary Cohen, the head of

CCIIO, who was apparently the day's choice to be the person in charge—was holding a telephone press conference to provide an overview of the insurance offerings that would be available the following week on the federal and state exchanges. They had good news to report.

The overall premiums were lower than the Congressional Budget Office had projected. And in most places, though with notable exceptions, there was likely to be a competitive market because multiple insurers had decided to participate.

Not mentioned, and, in fact, deflected by Cohen when a reporter asked about it, was whether the lower-than-anticipated premiums might be because the insurance companies were offering severely narrowed networks that would limit patients' choices of doctors and hospitals.

What was also not mentioned was the best news: The way the federal subsidies worked in conjunction with these premiums made the actual cost to most consumers surprisingly low—because the taxpayers were picking up most of the tab. For example, in the Dallas–Fort Worth market, a twenty-seven-year-old with an income of $25,000 could get the second lowest priced silver plan for $145 a month and the lowest priced bronze plan for $74. For a family of four earning $50,000, the lowest priced bronze plan would cost $26 a month. In Mississippi, the same twenty-seven-year-old could get the lowest priced bronze plan for $8. Even in high-cost New York, a family of four earning $50,000 would pay just $282 for the second lowest priced silver plan and $131 for the bronze plan.

That was because the subsidies for these people were so costly—$661 a month for that New York family. But the Obama administration was still reluctant to emphasize that.

"THESE ARE OUR FRIENDS, OUR NEIGHBORS, OUR FAMILIES"

In Kentucky, Governor Beshear had no such worries. He was barnstorming his state, telling people that even if they didn't like him or Obama, they would like what they saw when they went to kynect and found how little their insurance was going to cost because of the subsidies. "Just take a look on October 1. You'll be surprised," he said.

Steven Beshear was relishing the launch. Everything was locked down and ready to go. "We were ready to make history, to take a giant stride for the health of our people," he later told me.

On September 10, 2013, the governor, his cabinet secretary Audrey Haynes, and exchange director Carrie Banahan sat at a table in the capitol and gave the press a detailed briefing about kynect. Every chart Banahan mounted on the easels was polished and compelling—the home page mock-up, a sample of the marketing literature, charts projecting the numbers of uninsured likely to get subsidies on the exchanges, and the larger numbers likely to be covered by the state's Medicaid expansion. The most convincing displays were the ones showing how the federal subsidies would reduce costs for those above the poverty line who did not qualify for Medicaid. One sketch of a self-employed farming family earning $34,000 said they would pay $47 a month.

Beshear's rationale for the whole enterprise was equally compelling, especially because he seemed so confident about it. In the reddest of red states, he and his team had anything but PTSD. He was pushing Obamacare because he knew, he said, that so many of his fellow Kentuckians "roll the dice every day. . . . They live knowing that bankruptcy is just one bad diagnosis away. . . . These are our friends, our neighbors, our families. . . . You sit in the bleachers with them at high school games."

"HEALTH INSURANCE SHOULDN'T BE BRAIN SURGERY"

When I went to the Puck Building in lower Manhattan in late September to see how the Oscar people were doing with just days to go before launch, I found the same informal loft-like floor, except that, instead of the twenty or so early recruits I had seen earlier in the summer, it was now filled with thirty-seven people.

About a third looked like insurance and healthcare types. The rest were in jeans and T-shirts (plus the requisite hoodie or two), sitting at a long table tapping on keyboards.

There was a Ping-Pong table and a section where free soft drinks were dispensed.

The walls were lined with screens showing dashboards of website visits and incoming phone traffic, most likely coming from the ads Oscar had launched.

Oscar's marketing firm had produced both online messages and outdoor billboards, which were concentrated in the trendy neighborhoods where the marketers assumed they would be seen by the young professionals—freelancers, coders, actors—whom they had targeted.

"Health insurance shouldn't be brain surgery . . . unless you need brain surgery," proclaimed one of my favorite pitches.

The website had been completed and was now taking inquiries from people who had seen the ads or gotten social media messages suggesting they have a look at this strange insurance company website. They would be contacted after the October 1 launch.

True to Kushner's original idea, the look and language of the Oscar website—hioscar.com—was jarringly informal, almost as if taunting the Cignas and Aetnas of the world.

In alternating blue and pale green type (which echoed Kentucky's friendly look, though with a hipster gloss) the home page announced: "Hello, New York, We're Oscar, a new kind of health insurance company that is making insurance simple, intuitive and human. In other words, the kind of healthcare we want for ourselves.

"Your 24/7 doctor. Talk with our doctors for free," the next page urged, explaining the telemedicine feature using a sketch of a doctor connected to a patient via a phone.

"Stay healthy with our free perks" topped the next page, above cartoon sketches of "free generic drugs" and a blond cartoon character in a doctor's gown depicting "free doctor visits." (A "few free primary care visits" were provided each year "so you don't need to think twice about visiting your doctor.")

As I spoke with Kushner and his partners, Kevin Nazemi and Mario Schlosser, a small white dog patrolled the floor. "That's the Tumblr dog," Nazemi said, explaining that the pet belonged to their CTO, who had worked at Tumblr, the micro-blogging and social networking website.

Looming on the far wall was the Oscar mission statement, also on an electronic screen: "Our way of life: We want to introduce people to the idea of great health insurance. . . . In a world where health insurance experiences can be inhuman, we've created one that isn't."

Everything was cool about the whole setup, except perhaps for the body odor that seemed to permeate the open space.

What was not so cool was that nobody who visited the New York State insurance exchange website to shop around would be aware of Oscar's free telemedicine, generic drugs, or primary care visits. Under the rules, only the name of the company, the premium for each plan (bronze, silver, gold, platinum), and the deductible would be visible on the state exchange page summarizing all of the competing offerings. Only when a shopper clicked through to the Oscar pages would those features be displayed.

The state's summary page would also display an overall quality rating for the providers in each insurer's network. For most insurers it was a meaningless measure, based on surveys of hospitals and doctors. It almost always yielded the same "+" for every company. However, because Oscar was a new insurance company, it would get an "NA" for not available, even though all the providers in its network had been in business for a long time and were essentially the same providers that were in the competitors' networks.

Fortunately for the Oscar team, Oscar's premiums had ended up being at least the third or fourth lowest in every category, which meant Oscar would be visible at or near the middle of the front page, where the companies were arranged in ascending order of their premium charges.[18] According to consumer surveys, premiums were typically the most decisive factor for shoppers, even if deductibles and other dynamics might be more indicative of what was actually the best bargain.

On the other hand, unlike most of its eight competitors, Oscar would enter the competition with a name that no one knew, and with that NA for quality.

Kushner's business plan had projected that 7,500 people would sign

18. Under the rules for the New York State exchange, as well as other exchanges, insurers set their rates without knowing the rates of their competitors and could not change them for a year once they were set.

up by the time the October 1 launch enrollment period ended on March 31, 2014. Oscar would need a lot of word of mouth, propelled by those ads and the distribution of its literature in targeted neighborhoods, to get that many people to click through and buy.

Still, as a crew of new customer service call center people were being tested with mock questions ("I'm thirty-two. Why do I need this?") in a glass-enclosed room off to the side, Kushner and his partners were pumped.

They thought they had cracked the code. That they understood the numbers. That their outsourced telemedicine doctors would not create a budget hole. That they would kill the competition with what they could save by crunching the data and avoiding their competitors' last-century paperwork and infrastructure. And that they had created the look and feel and messaging that could break through. For them, this really might be another "disruptive" high-tech home run.

They couldn't wait for next week's launch.

"WE'RE GONNA KNOCK YOUR SOCKS OFF"

At 10:51 A.M. on Thursday, September 26, 2013, Henry Chao sent a memo to colleagues around CMS reporting that "it looks like the bar" for traffic—the maximum traffic the exchange could handle—"is set at 10k concurrent users." That was the amount that another unit of CMS had found that Kentucky could handle.

Worse, it was not clear why Chao thought the bar was set even that high. About an hour earlier he had received an email from one of his deputies stating that the only testing done so far had been for five hundred concurrent users.

On the morning of Sunday, September 29, a worried Todd Park emailed Chao, with a copy to CMS operations chief Michelle Snyder, asking if "the team" had run various kinds of performance and capacity tests. He got no answer before the launch.

Meanwhile, President Obama and his White House aides had begun to lower expectations. However, they were still focused on how many people would enroll, not whether they would be able to. So in background briefings they emphasized that October 1 was simply the beginning of a six-month enrollment window and that in Massachusetts most people had waited until near the end of that state's sign-up period before enrolling.

October 1 was not Election Day; it was the beginning of a campaign, they explained, without dwelling on whether the voting machines were going to work.

On Monday, September 30, Obama told NPR, "I would suspect that there will be glitches. . . . When Massachusetts, just one state, set this up, it took quite a long time. It took several months before everything was smoothed out."

The president was not trying to underplay what he suspected would be a disaster. He was clueless, not deceptive. He really thought there might be glitches, but that they would be minor. That is what his senior staff told him. There would be some hiccups, but this was really going to work. People would come to the site, sign up, and all the bitter politics would be in the past. Just like Social Security and Medicare.

White House chief of staff Denis McDonough had a friend who had been pestering him with calls in September. The friend warned the chief of staff that his insurance industry contacts thought the exchange wasn't even close to being ready. One had even told McDonough's friend that his company was thinking of pulling out to avoid being involved in what was going to be a fiasco. "My people say he's overreacting to some last-minute problems," McDonough had assured his friend.

Now, on the evening of September 30, just hours before the launch, McDonough called the same friend. "Based on the reports I'm getting I think we're gonna knock your socks off tomorrow," he promised.

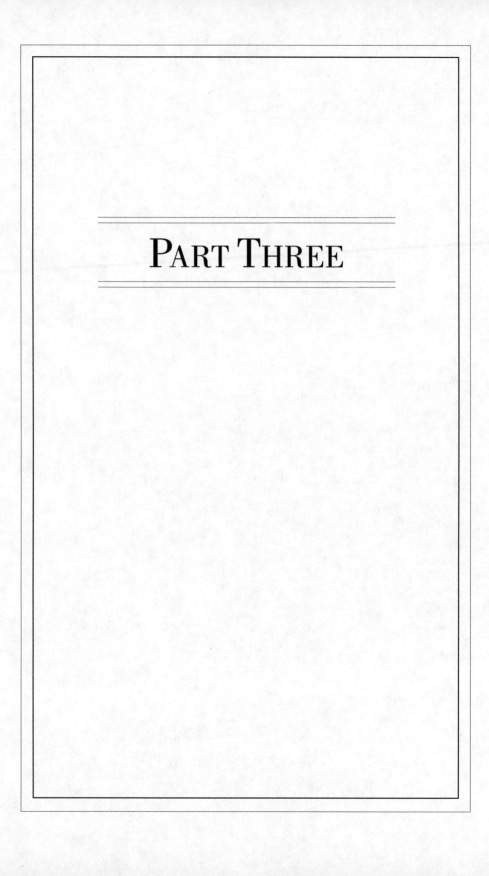

PART THREE

CHAPTER 20

THE CRASH

October 1–3, 2013

A FEW MINUTES AFTER MIDNIGHT ON THE MORNING OF OCTOBER 1, 2013, CMS administrator Marilyn Tavenner was sitting by the phone in her apartment watching television. She was nervous. She had told her staff to call her as soon as the website was up so she could check it out.

Now she called into the office to find out what the problem was. Why hadn't anyone called her?

"No problems," one of her deputies said. "We just wanted to watch it for a while before we called you. It's fine." Tavenner smiled, then went to sleep.

At the shack in Frankfort, Kentucky, Carrie Banahan had organized a full-staff celebration to mark the launch. She and her fellow Kentuckians were used to the fireworks show, called Thunder Over Louisville, that the Kentucky Derby puts on to kick off the week of celebrations around the big race. Fireworks were too dangerous for the low-ceilinged shack, so Banahan had arranged for a room full of Bubble Wrap—the kind used to protect fragile goods when they are shipped.

At 12:01 she popped the first bottle of champagne, and flipped the

switch on kynect.ky.gov. Everyone stomped on the Bubble Wrap.
Thunder Over Kynect.

A "BITTERSWEET" MORNING

The first challenge at the Department of Health and Human Services
and its CMS unit later that morning had to do only indirectly with
Obamacare. True to Ted Cruz's promise, Republicans had refused to
pass a budget unless Obamacare was defunded. They were also threatening not to pass an increase in the debt ceiling.

Opposition to Obamacare had shut down the government, and
seemed on its way to causing a more calamitous default on the national
debt.

More immediately, this meant that the first job for the senior staff
at HHS and CMS wasn't to worry about traffic or enrollment at their
new website, but to figure out which "nonessential" employees they
had to send home because they could not be paid.

Beyond the most senior people, the definition of who was "essential" depended largely on what budget bucket they were in. That
meant hundreds of people who had worked on Obamacare had to
leave the building as it was launched.

"It was so bittersweet," recalled Chiquita Brooks-LaSure, a veteran
healthcare reform advocate who was one of Gary Cohen's deputies at
CCIIO. "We were finally giving people coverage in this country. But
now we were sending our colleagues home who had helped make it
happen." Even Mandy Cohen, a highly regarded physician who was
overseeing policy and communications with the non-insurance healthcare community, had to be furloughed.

At his Bethesda, Maryland, office, Gary Cohen had planned a
morning celebration for his 370 CCIIO staff members. The festivities
were scrapped. Instead Cohen had to furlough about 40 percent of his
people, before driving into Washington to join Tavenner.

At about 8 A.M., Tavenner met with senior staffers, including
Brooks-LaSure and Julie Bataille, who ran the CMS press relations
shop. Bataille reported that there was no news of any import yet from
Gary Cohen's CCIIO command center in Bethesda, Maryland, the

command center run by CMS Office of Operations head Michelle Snyder in Baltimore, or the tech command center overseen by Henry Chao and housed at an office rented by contractor CGI in Herndon, Virginia. Everything seemed to be working, but they had no enrollment numbers.

As for actual traffic online, the CMS people had access only to the same data point that any website operator has—how many visitors had come. They had never installed a dashboard that would give them up-to-the-minute traffic numbers for individual pages, let alone the number of people who had actually enrolled. All that would have to be tabulated at the end of each day. But they did know that visits to the home page were high. Amazingly high: over a million visits by 7 A.M.

There were smiles all around. "Chiquita [Brooks-LaSure] had tears in her eyes," Bataille would later recall. "We were finally doing this. We were all just so proud."

At about 8:15, Bataille began hearing from some of the CMS people who had offices in the HHS building and had not been furloughed that they were seeing Twitter chatter about the website not working. Soon, the Twitter messages were multiplying, almost by the second.

The operations centers still said they had nothing to report, no real signs of trouble. One reported in at about 8:30 that the only problem was traffic on the phone lines, which had become jammed.

The traffic was now so high, one senior person reported to one of the CMS press people, that he was beginning to think they had been "hacked by some right wingers. But so far so good."

"HAVE A GREAT DAY"

By now Bataille was picking up reports from call center supervisors that people were complaining about something having to do with the identity verification process for registering an account. Either it was broken or the instructions about how to use it were unclear.

I already knew that. At 8 A.M. I had gone online pretending to be from Indiana (one of the thirty-six states on the federal exchange) and was told, first, that, unlike in Kentucky, I had to establish an account before I could browse around. To establish an account I had to provide my name and Social Security number. Then I had to answer some "security" questions in order to prove I was who I said I was.

The process is used by many security-conscious websites. A big data company—in this case Experian, the giant credit rating and background checking service—would assemble questions that presumably only I, and Experian, would know how to answer. What brand was the first car I owned? Where was the first house I had ever bought using a mortgage? If I answered the questions correctly, I was me.

The instructions about how to proceed to the quiz were, indeed, unclear. And when I figured them out, it did seem that something was broken. None of the questions appeared, yet I was told I had failed.

It looked like one of the risks of having multiple contractors with no one in charge of the whole package was playing out. Experian routinely connected this software into hundreds of website deployments. Either lead contractor CGI or Experian, or both, seemed to have failed to complete the link for HealthCare.gov.

I tried again. This time I got three questions, but before I could check the multiple-choice boxes, the screen went blank. On the third try, I got no questions. Instead, I was taken back to the home page Bryan Sivak had built, and to "Sonya," the smiling young woman whose face dominating the screen was about to become the ubiquitous image accompanying every news story about the website. By now Sonya seemed like she was laughing at me.

I tried one more time. Same result, except that this time I couldn't even get back to Sonya. Instead, I got a message that would become the staple of the news coverage of the launch: "We have a lot of visitors to our site right now and we're working to make the experience here better. Please wait here until we send you to the login page."

While I kept that screen opened hoping to get back to the log-in page, I tried the handy option allowing me to do a live chat with one of the customer service people whose scripts Mandy Cohen and Julie Bataille had slaved over. This service had been put up live in the weeks prior to the launch, and when I had tested it then with various questions, the answers I got were so quick and so smart that I had begun to think maybe they really were going to pull this off.

Now, I typed in my question about the identity verification glitch. This answer repeated itself eight times over fifteen minutes:

"Please be patient while we're helping other people."

Then I got a ninth message: "Your chat session is over. Thanks for contacting us, and we hope we've answered your questions. Have a great day."

I emailed a press spokesman—the first one who had talked to me about his colleagues' post-traumatic stress disorder ten days before—to ask about the glitch, and about the fact that by now I had been waiting nearly forty-five minutes to get back to the log-in page.

Here's what I got back:

> This is what we're telling reporters right now:
> "We have built a dynamic system and are prepared to make adjustments as needed and improve the consumer experience. This new system will allow millions of Americans to access quality, affordable health care coverage. . . . Consumers who need help can also contact the call center, use the live chat function, or go to localhelp.healthcare.gov to find an in-person assistor in their community."

It was a parodylike attempt to glide over reality with the kind of happy talk—"dynamic"!—that Washington reporters roll their eyes at.

My own reaction to that statement and to the "Have a great day" live chat sign-off was more jaundiced. I remembered all the speeches Barack Obama had made about the arrogance, lack of accountability, and overall incompetence and consumer unfriendliness of insurance companies.

Then again, the press statement was the product of honest ignorance. No one at HHS and CMS, including the press office, had any idea of what the problems really were. Even if the staff at any of the command centers had been inclined to level with their bosses or the press flacks, they, themselves, didn't know much, either. They had no idea of how many people were getting through and enrolling. By now, 8:45, they had heard something from Bataille about the identity verification problem, but throughout the day they would not know what the rates of error were for the identity check, or even what the wait times were for the home page.

AT LAST: "KATHY IN ILLINOIS"

However, by 10 A.M. there were cheers in Tavenner's conference room, including a "woo-hoo" from Tavenner herself. They had just gotten word—through a Twitter message—that a woman in Illinois had successfully enrolled her family. "It was such a great moment," Chiquita Brooks-LaSure later told me.

The CMS spokesman called me with the good news—though on background, not to be attributed to him, because at CMS everything was always on background, never to be attributed to anyone (even the people whose job it was to talk to the press). "This means the system works, even the identity part," he said excitedly. "We did it! Now, it's only about capacity, and we can fix that in a few hours or maybe by tomorrow."

It soon turned out that they could not confirm that the Illinois woman had actually enrolled, because the system couldn't provide the information. It was only several hours later—during which Tavenner and Bataille repeatedly had to delay a press conference so that they could give reporters the information—that the first enrollment was verified.

For the rest of the first week in October, CMS's Web page apologizing for delays would tell visitors, "We appreciate your patience and look forward to helping you get quality, affordable coverage just like Kathy did"—which was followed by a link to a newspaper article describing the triumphant experience of Kathy in Illinois.

"THE SAME WAY YOU'D SHOP ON AMAZON"

By midmorning, everyone in the outside world who cared was aware of the identity verification problem. It was all over social media. Twitter had become the dashboard for real-time monitoring of the government's most expensive, ambitious website ever.

As word about the identity problem came in to the command center run by Chao and hosted at CGI, the CGI people were already grousing that they had warned that the system needed to be tested end to end and that Experian had done a lousy job.

At CCIIO's command post, the toldya-so's were all about CGI and Chao.

At the White House, there was also frenzied activity amid charges and countercharges. But it was all about the government shutdown, not the Obamacare website. What functions and people had to be suspended? How should the president's schedule be changed? What was the exact deadline, based on available Treasury funds, for getting the debt ceiling raised before the government would be in default? And what would be today's plan of attack to force the House Republicans to relent?

As for Obamacare, they knew there were some problems, but Sebelius had assured chief of staff Denis McDonough that it was all about the traffic, which was so huge that it had busted one of the pipes—the identity verification process—that would soon be fixed. The system worked. We know this because we spoke to the lady in Illinois (who was soon besieged by all the reporters Tavenner's people had sent her way, with her permission).

True, the site was now not even allowing people onto the home page to encounter the identity verification hurdle. But that, too, was all about traffic, the White House team was told. Despite the worried internal emails at CMS just days before about insufficient capacity, the White House staff were all told that they could fix that quickly, too.

In a noon Rose Garden statement, with a dozen citizens whom the White House press office said were about to benefit from buying insurance on the new exchanges standing behind him, President Obama lashed out at the Republicans: "One faction of one party in one house of Congress in one branch of government shut down major parts of the government. All because they didn't like one law. This Republican shutdown did not have to happen."

Obama then turned to the program the Republicans were holding hostage, explaining how the rollout of the exchanges that morning would help the people standing behind him.

"Sky-high premiums once forced Nancy Beigel to choose between paying her rent or paying for health insurance," Obama said. "She's been uninsured ever since. So she pays all of her medical bills out of pocket, puts some on her credit card, making them even harder to pay. . . . Well, starting today, Nancy can get covered just like everybody else."[19]

"So if these stories of hardworking Americans sound familiar to you," the president continued, "well, starting today, you and your friends and your family and your coworkers can get covered, too. Just visit HealthCare.gov, and there you can compare insurance plans, side by side, the same way you'd shop for a plane ticket on Kayak or a TV on Amazon."

However, Obama warned, the website wasn't going to be like Amazon on day one. "Now, like every new law, every new product rollout, there are going to be some glitches in the sign-up process along the way that we will fix," he said. "I've been saying this from the start. For example, we found out that there have been times this morning where the site has been running more slowly than it normally will. The reason is because more than one million people visited HealthCare.gov before seven o'clock in the morning. To put that in context, there were five times more users in the marketplace this morning than have ever been on Medicare.gov at one time."

Obama didn't point out that it was CMS—whose experience with websites only extended to the little-used Medicare site he had just mentioned—that was running HealthCare.gov.

"A HIGH-CLASS PROBLEM"

Presidential press secretary Jay Carney's 2 P.M. press briefing illustrated how the Obamacare launch and its attendant problems had been eclipsed by the shutdown. Only four questions were about Obama-

---

19. When I later talked with Beigel, I found that because of problems with the state-run website in Maryland, where she lived, she was not able to enroll until November, and only then with the help of a navigator. But when she was able to see a doctor, on January 3, 2014, he discovered a life-threatening infection, requiring urgent surgery. Obamacare, she told me, "literally, truly was a lifesaver for me."

care. The first was with whether the president was willing to make any changes to the law, including postponing the mandate, as part of a deal to end the shutdown and debt ceiling standoff. The second was about how confident the administration was that the young invincibles really would enroll.

Only the third question, from Major Garrett of CBS News, asked about "the consumer experience on the websites—some have had glitches, some have been slow. . . . Is that entirely a product of over-expected use, or are there some internal mechanistic things you have to fix because they're not quite ready?"

"Well, I'm not an expert on Web design," Carney replied, "so, I can't guarantee that there aren't glitches that are just technical in nature. And I'm sure there are, as we said there would be, as with any large-scale rollout of a policy like this. It was true of Social Security. . . . But what is unquestionably the case is that there has been an enormous amount of interest, as we've seen by the number of people who have visited the website.

"And it's kind of like people trying to get tickets to the first Pirates home play-off game," Carney added, warming to the theme. "I mean, you know when you go on the site and it's hard to load the page that it's because a lot of people like you want to find out if tickets are available, and the great news about this is it's not one game, it's not one night; the seats are unlimited and the availability will be there for every American family that wants affordable health insurance. So we take this, as Bill Clinton used to say, as a high-class problem."

Through the afternoon, the Twitter noise continued. Brooks-LaSure and Julie Bataille, who was in charge of press communications, called the operations people supervising the outsourced customer call-in phone banks. Yes, there was that woman in Illinois, but they were hearing about all kinds of problems, she was told. Bataille and her colleagues were now trying to log on themselves, and failing continually. They tried calling the customer service hotline and got a strange-sounding busy signal.

Still, all of that seemed to be consistent with Bill Clinton's "high-class problem." It was all a matter of that rush of first day traffic built around a successful launch.

THE TIGER TEAMS IN ACTION

At 8 A.M., there had been a gathering of the people from CCIIO who would be participating twice a day in meetings of the CCIIO "war room"—which should not be confused with the CCIIO "command center," which was where designated CCIIO operations people would spend the day.

This first war room meeting at 8 A.M. had been convened to spell out how the subsequent meetings would work. It seemed like they had their act together, according to minutes of the meeting compiled by a staff person. A "CIRT Team" would "report cross-cutting issues to raise to Michelle [Snyder, the CMS chief of operations] and Marilyn [Tavenner]." Not mentioned was Henry Chao, who was supposed to be in charge of the website's technology.

"CIRT is a Tiger Team; it stands for Critical Incident Response Team," the minutes explained.

By the time of the war room's second meeting, on the afternoon of October 1, 2013, there had been a lot of "critical incidents," and things seemed considerably less buttoned up.

Everything seemed to be going wrong, not just the identity proofing.

Some of the problems that had surfaced were near comic: A majority of people who managed to get far into the application process were answering "yes" to a routine question about whether they were currently in prison and, therefore, ineligible for federal help in paying their premiums. Apparently, the website had worded the question with some kind of double negative and "most people would answer it in a way that mistakenly indicates they are incarcerated when they are not," the minutes of the meeting reported. Testing would have caught that.

A report that an offering of a dental insurer in South Carolina had been "suppressed" was discussed in the same conversation in which someone else reported, "We heard that the capacity was 100,000 people, and there are 150,000 people on." Capacity, of course, was nowhere near 100,000, or even 10,000.

The connection to the IRS's data for income verification—which everyone had feared would be the toughest link to build—was working. But it didn't matter. No one could get that far because "identity proofing" was "an ongoing issue."

Insurance brokers, who under the law could help people sign up and get a commission from the insurance company, had been given a special connection to log on. That was not working, either.

Worse, the CMS caseworkers who had been assigned to handle insurance company questions or complaints had all been furloughed because of the shutdown, as had the two people who were supposed to run a conference call for insurance company technical people.

As for the headline news, one member of the Tiger Team reported to the others in the war room that there were "5,800 applications in the world right now—unsure if they are completed at this point."

SIX ENROLLMENTS, FLICKERING LIGHTS

By the next morning, the war room would be told that as of 8 A.M. October 2, 2013, "6 enrollments have occurred so far." No one knew where that 5,800 number had come from.

In the Henry Chao/CGI command center, there was just a rolling all-day meeting that first day, where no one took notes. "It was chaos," recalled someone who was there. "No one seemed to be in charge. The only decision made was to order more servers" to increase capacity. But that was complicated by government procurement rules and by the fact that they had not reserved any servers to provide backup.

At the Department of Health and Human Services building, where CMS's top officials and press and congressional liaison staffs were housed, the people who had not been furloughed—a minority—stayed until nearly midnight, talking to congressional staffers and the press about the woman in Illinois, about how capacity was being added, and about all the traffic.

The only number they provided had to do with all the visitors. One million had visited before 7 A.M., as the president had happily reported. There were 2.8 million visits through the day. "On background," they emailed reporters, "the system is functioning, with in-

dividuals being able to start and finish enrollment on-line. We expect
to continue improving the time it takes to enroll in the coming hours."

"At least that's what they're telling us," one of the press relations
people told me, referring to the information the operations staff was
providing. "At this point, who knows? We'll see in the morning."

As Tavenner, Bataille, Brooks-LaSure, and others walked the halls
in the building that night, lights flickered on and off in a way that conveyed how surreal the day that they had been anticipating for years
had become. The office lights were set to be off unless motion was
detected, and with so many people having been furloughed, almost all
the lights were off unless one of the survivors walked by an empty office, whereupon they would flash on, then shut back off. Enough, perhaps, to trigger a bureaucratic version of PTSD.

FURY IN THE FIELD

Anne Filipic, the president of Enroll America, told the press and her
staff she was frustrated by the crash of the website, but that she was
sure things would be fixed soon. Actually, she was furious. In the
Obama campaign, the technology had been like plumbing, an afterthought. Of course, it worked. Now, the sign-up rallies she had
planned around the country, run by all those field troops she had recruited, and backed by all the social media advertising she had placed,
had become the equivalent of a postponed election.

Enroll America's campaign machine hit a wall. Her people—
hundreds of whom were paid and thousands more who were
volunteers—were turning over the prospective customers they had attracted to the navigators, who were supposed to help them enroll. But
the navigators couldn't get online, either, nor could they get through
on the phone lines. "We had to take down names and hope to contact
them when the website was fixed," Filipic later told me.

Filipic's Ohio director had been a legal aid lawyer whose cases had
included defending patients being hounded by hospital debt collectors. He was excited to be doing something proactive instead to head
off that problem. Only now he and his volunteers could only take
names.

A QUICK FIX IN KENTUCKY

From midnight through 10 A.M. on October 1, 2013, in Frankfort, Kentucky, everything worked as planned.

Health and family services secretary Audrey Haynes did some early morning TV and radio shows. Her boss, Governor Beshear, continued a series of "fly-arounds" across the state urging people to try out kynect. Banahan stayed in the shack.

They were all tired, not only from the celebration the night before, but also because in the weeks leading up to the launch they had criss-crossed Kentucky with town halls and community group meetings, and with those "fly-around" appearances by the governor.

"It doesn't cost you a dime to go online and check it out," Beshear had told dozens of audiences. "You owe it to yourself and your family. . . . If you want your ideology to stand in the way, fine."

There was predictable hostility, especially in the poorest parts of Kentucky, where the Obama administration's perceived anti-coal policies made most people more than a little cynical about any Democrat, especially those selling an Obama healthcare reform scheme.

"Some people showed up at meetings, showing guns on their holsters," Banahan would later recall. "But that's okay. You have to meet people where they are and take them for who they are. We told them we didn't want to talk about politics. We wanted to talk about their healthcare, about why they should talk to one of our 'kynectors' "—Kentucky's version of navigators—"in their community and check this out for themselves."

By 9:30 A.M. on October 1, "the trends were incredible," recalled Mohan Kumar, who led the Deloitte contractors building kynect. Twenty-four thousand people had visited the kynect.ky.gov website, and 858 had completed applications. Everyone in the shack knew that because they had a dashboard set up to monitor everything in real time. In fact, within a few days, anyone logging on to the Kentucky.gov website could have known the numbers because they would be posted online in daily updates.

Then at 10:45, just as the governor was about to do another television appearance, part of the website crashed. "I told them to get busy fixing it," Beshear later recalled. "I actually wasn't worried. If we've got a down hour or a down day, it wouldn't matter. This is a lifetime event. To me it was the most important project I would ever do in terms of people's lives."

The problem was one they had anticipated and, in fact, rehearsed, and it had nothing to do with kynect.ky.gov. Rather, it involved the state's overall consumer website, the place people log on to for transactions involving driver's or hunting licenses. The team had decided early on that it would be easier and faster to use the current system for people to establish an account with the state rather than build a new system just for health exchange accounts. The drawback was that visitors to kynect would have to go through a registration system that had not been built to accommodate all of this new traffic. They thought they had accounted for that by adding servers to the state system. However, despite repeated tests to simulate the traffic, they were uneasy about it.

That was the pipe that broke at 10:45. But because the kynect team had decided not to require people to register their information before browsing, it did not affect anyone's ability to browse, get prices and estimates of their subsidies, and even save their tentative choices. It was fixed by about 3 P.M. because Deloitte had arranged to have extra servers standing by just in case.

"I was rattled, sure. You always are in a situation like this," Kumar later told me. "But not outwardly so," he added with a chuckle. "And not that much. I knew we had all that extra capacity we could plug in."

"If Mohan was worried, he didn't show it," Banahan later told me. "He is just not the type."

By 7:30 the next morning, October 2, kynect had had 88,119 unique visitors.

One thousand eight hundred and thirty-three people had been enrolled—compared to six on the federal exchange covering thirty-six states.

Kentucky's website data demonstrated this was not anything like buying an airplane ticket or a book online—how infinitely more complex the challenges are when a country insists that healthcare can be sold as a consumer product in a conventional marketplace. Those 88,000 visitors viewed an astounding 1,168,000 pages, or thirteen pages per visit. And they spent an average of twenty-eight minutes. Visitors spend an average of nine minutes on Amazon.

More important, unlike the Amazon experience, nearly 95 percent of visitors did not even complete a transaction when they visited kynect. In fact, the Kentucky team's research had told Banahan and Kumar that people would have to visit seven to ten times before they would think they had enough information to make a purchase.

No one buys a book or an airplane ticket that way.

And in Kentucky, relatively few insurance companies had decided to participate in the first year of the exchanges, which meant that the options consumers had to choose from were more limited than in other states.

Everyone working on all the exchanges—the federal version and the fifteen built by the individual states and the District of Columbia— had done research telling them how long an online process this would be. But the ratios of visitors to page views or time spent still surprised everyone that first day—if, unlike the people in Washington, they had the dashboards to see it happening.

AT OSCAR, NO NEWS IS NO NEWS

Oscar's launch day was all about waiting. It was as if Joshua Kushner and his team should have had T-shirts made with "shooting in the dark" as their start-up's business plan.

The night before, most of the team had stayed in the office until after dinner listening to (and, in some cases, fielding themselves) the several dozen calls that came in from people who had seen their online ads and wanted more information. Many seemed especially enthused about the telemedicine feature. At their hioscar.com website there had been over a thousand visits in the last week, and a video they had posted on YouTube had had two thousand views.

Small numbers, but it seemed like people were interested. Still, throughout the launch day, they had no idea whether anyone was buying from their weird new insurance company.

Nor would they know the next day, or the day after that, or even the week after that. No insurance company would. The way the New York State exchange had been set up—and the way the federal exchange also worked—insurance companies would not get enrollments as they happened. Rather, they would be sent in batches if and when that piece of the technology hook-up worked. New York State officials had told Oscar that it might not be until November 1, 2013, before they would get their first batch, though they were shooting for mid-October.

Potential customers could go to hioscar.com for information, and 5,177 did on October 1, which Kushner and his team were able to track by the second. But if they wanted to enroll they were sent to the state exchange, where, of course, they would see the options offered by all eight competing insurers, six with established names.

The only news the morning of October 1 was that New York, like Kentucky, had gone down by midmorning. However, as in Kentucky, New York had arranged for standby servers and was back up within a few hours, although, unlike Kentucky, the site would suffer other glitches and outages through the first month.

Other than that, all that Kushner and his team were sure of by the morning of October 2 was that they had close to forty enrollees, because most of the now-forty-person staff had enrolled that morning. They also knew from a tweet that someone had been so impressed with their website that "I almost signed up—then realized I don't live in new york."

THE OBAMA TEAM FUMBLES THE EASY STUFF, TOO

The next day, October 3, 2013, a process server near New Haven, Connecticut, proved that the Obama administration hadn't just stumbled in building the complicated website. It was failing at the easy stuff, too.

Jeremy Kopylec, a warehouse worker who lived in Northford, Connecticut, was sued by Yale–New Haven Hospital for $6,129. The suit was the result of a bill Kopylec incurred four years earlier, when he was taken to the emergency room after what he later told me was a "minor motorcycle accident."

At the time of the accident, Kopylec said, he had just gotten a job following a period of unemployment, but that his "insurance hadn't kicked in yet. So they came after me for the whole bill. . . . I told them I could not afford it."

"I spent about two and a half hours in the ER, and all they really did was clean up some road rash," Kopylec, twenty-seven, recalled, adding that "since the marshal came with the summons, I've worked out a plan to pay all of it off in monthly payments" of $100, extending over the next five years.

But what about those provisions that Iowa senator Chuck Grassley had inserted into Obamacare prohibiting exactly that kind of collection suit by purportedly nonprofit hospitals unless and until the hospital made aggressive efforts to determine if the person needed financial aid? And what about the related provision prohibiting chargemaster rates to be charged to such people? Under the law, those provisions could have taken effect the day the president signed the law in 2010.

That Kopylec did not get the protection that Obamacare now required was not a matter of Yale–New Haven violating the law. It was not about a website not working. Nor was it about Republican efforts to sabotage the law or some judge blocking it. It was because the simple rules still hadn't been written by the Obama administration to enforce the law.

It was surprising enough that such an obviously appealing and important consumer protection rule had not been written in time to protect California cancer patient Steven D. in early 2011—ten months after the law had gone into effect—leaving his widow to fight off bill collectors. But the suit against Kopylec was filed more than three and a half years after Obama's East Room signing celebration.

A first draft of the rules had not been published for initial comment in the *Federal Register* until June 26, 2012—more than two years after Obamacare was passed. That was just an initial draft, called "Proposed Regulations." The American Hospital Association had then complained—no surprise—that the drafted rules were too prescriptive. Nothing had happened since. No final rules had been issued. There were still no restraints on hospital bill collection practices or chargemaster charges for the neediest patients.

About a month after Kopylec was sued, I tried to find out from the Obama administration what had happened to the regulations. Assistant Treasury secretary Mark Mazur, who oversaw the IRS and was the administration's point man for tax issues related to Obamacare, told me: "These things take time. It's something we're actively working on."[20]

---

20. Soon after I wrote about the delayed regulations and the Yale–New Haven suit in *Time* in December 2013, the IRS promulgated them. On February 1, 2014, Yale–New Haven changed its billing policies and now charges all uninsured patients the average it charges to all insurance companies, not chargemaster rates, according to the hospital system's spokesman.

CHAPTER 21

MELTDOWN IN D.C., DANCING ON EIGHT TOES IN KENTUCKY, AND FRUSTRATION IN OHIO

October 4–17, 2013

"HERE'S WHAT WE KNOW AFTER SEVENTY-TWO HOURS. WE'VE HAD over seven million unique visitors . . . come through. It is a volume that no one anticipated."

So began a breezy, banter-filled live conversation between White House healthcare communications czar David Simas and the crew at *Morning Joe* at 7:44 A.M. on Friday, October 4, 2013. "Just for perspective," Simas added, talking to the New York studio from the White House lawn, "Southwest Airlines in an entire month has 6.4 million unique visitors. NBC in an entire month has 12 million unique visitors. We had 7 million. And so the overwhelming volume has really caused us to add more servers, more engineers, to tackle the problem, identify the issues, fix them. So today is going to be better than yesterday was. . . . We've got another 178 days left to go. So I feel pretty good about where we are.

"Where the holdup has been has been at the initial stage, when people try to create the account," Simas continued, sidestepping a question about enrollment numbers. "Once you create the account, as you saw, you go into the application and the plan compare, and it's easy and it's intuitive and it makes a lot of sense. . . . And we believe that within a couple of days the wait time is going to be significantly, significantly reduced, as we saw from yesterday and the day before."

He had no way of knowing it, but nothing in Simas's statement was accurate. In fact, by now, as the identity verification layer that Simas blamed as the gating problem was being fixed, more problems were exposed. And wait times, while barely improved, were irrelevant because people were hitting errors on almost every page that were throwing them off the website completely once they got past the wait on the home page.

The various war rooms knew that, even if they hadn't told Simas or White House healthcare reform boss Jeanne Lambrew. About thirty-six hours before, at the late afternoon October 2 CCIIO war room meeting, someone reported that there were now forty thousand people waiting interminably in the "waiting room"—staring at the website page carrying the "please wait" message that had flashed at me on October 1.

By then, the end of the second day, "approximately 100 enrollments" had happened, according to minutes of the war room meeting, although no one in the war room had an exact number. And the target for any significant changes to be made to fix the site had been extended from October 15 to November 22, implying that real fixes were going to take that long.

By October 4, the morning Simas took the microphone on the White House lawn, the same war room group reported that the identity verification process was broken again. When they had added capacity to handle traffic going through that pipe, the system had quickly failed. "It may not have been a capacity issue," the meeting minutes reported. "Now they are looking at changing the software."

As Simas spun the *Morning Joe* crew from the White House lawn on the morning of October 4, enrollments totaled just 248 people.

A DANCE IN KENTUCKY

Kentucky had 4,739 by that morning, and by midafternoon would have nearly 2,000 more.

Among them were Tommy and Viola Brown, who were sixty-three and sixty-two years old respectively and two weeks away from celebrating their forty-sixth anniversary.

As he got up from a card table at a community center in Shelbyville, Kentucky, at about 2 P.M. on October 4, 2013, where one of Carrie Banahan's "kynectors" had been huddled with him and his wife, Tommy Brown was all smiles.

"Everything go okay?" I asked.

"Perfect," he said.

Pointing to a poster just outside the entrance advising people of counseling sessions available at the center for those with heart disease, arthritis, or diabetes, he said, "See that? Between us, Viola and I have all of that and a lot more."

Brown explained that in 2007, while hauling merchandise at the auto parts wholesaler where he worked, he had tripped and broken his neck and crushed five vertebrae in his back. The vertebrae had been fused together in an operation, but the fact that his neck was broken, he told me, wasn't discovered for several years. As a result he continued to suffer painful nerve damage, and had not been able to work for the last three years. Before that, he had fought off two bouts of cancer.

Once Brown was unable to work, he had been unable to get insurance. Every insurance company, he said, "turned me down because of my condition, or wanted to charge me a price that was way out of my league." He had not seen a doctor in so long, he told me, that "I have no idea who my doctor is."

Because he was sixty-three, Brown had been able to receive about $1,100 a month by opting for early Social Security benefits.

Viola Brown, who was sixty-two, had heart disease and severe diabetes, which she was only occasionally able to get checked up on at a free clinic.

Neither of the Browns was able to afford any of the medicines—for pain relief, heart disease, or diabetes—that a doctor would have prescribed for them or that the clinic doctors had told Viola Brown to use. "When we had money, we would buy the drugs," Viola said. "When we didn't, we would go without."

On the day we met she, too, had not seen a doctor of any kind, even one at a clinic, in more than two years.

The Browns had heard about kynect from television ads Banahan had purchased. "We thought it was too good to be true," Viola Brown told me. "It seemed like the answer to our prayers."

A week before, at the center where they pick up their food stamps, they had been told that they could get help enrolling in kynect at the community center. Which is where they had just found out that it was not too good to be true. The Browns had qualified for Medicaid (called Passport in Kentucky), which meant, they were told, that all of their care would be free and generic versions of any drugs they needed would cost a dollar each.

"I just did a little dance in there, when they told me we had been enrolled," Viola told me. She was near tears, but all smiles. "Now we can go to the doctor—and get our medications for a dollar. And you know it's hard for me to dance," she added.

Why was that?

"I only have eight toes left because of the diabetes."

Four of the five families I spoke with at the Shelbyville enrollment center that day had been put into the Medicaid program that Beshear had expanded, a plurality that would ultimately mirror all Kentucky Obamacare enrollments. (Eighty percent would qualify for Medicaid.)

The fifth family lived about 100 percent above the poverty line of $24,000 for a family of four. They had bought a silver plan with a premium of $1,039 a month. A $541 subsidy brought the cost down to $498. However, with a deductible of $4,900, the total cost of the insurance and the deductible still meant that the family might pay about $11,000 a year (in premiums plus deductible outlays) before their insurance kicked in if they suffered illnesses requiring extensive medical bills.

That potentially high demand on available income was one of the weaknesses of Obamacare—a result of the compromises made in Washington during 2009 and 2010 to balance the cost to the government with coverage that would be affordable to families like this one. Yet it was still quite an improvement. The family, which included someone with severe preexisting conditions, had been paying more than $1,500 a month, which had forced them to go deeply in debt. And that plan had had a $6,000 deductible.

Shelbyville is in Shelby County, which had voted 67–33 percent for Mitt Romney over Barack Obama. The Browns are white as is 90 percent of Shelby County. Of the four people among those who were enrolling that afternoon who said they had voted and were willing to share their choice with me, all four had voted for Romney. Yet Beshear's message—or perhaps simply the lure of "answered prayers" that Viola Brown had expressed—seemed to have gotten through. What they were doing at those card tables with the kynectors was not about Barack Obama. In fact, none mentioned Obamacare, except for the one enrollee who said that kynect was "a lot better than Obamacare."

"KENTUCKIANS NOT BUYING OBAMACARE"

Nonetheless, for Kentucky's two leading Republicans, kynect was all about Obamacare and Obama. Perhaps oblivious to what their constituents on the ground were experiencing, Senators Mitch McConnell and Rand Paul went on the attack with an op-ed column in the Louisville *Courier-Journal* the morning the Browns enrolled.

Their piece, entitled "Kentuckians Not Buying Obamacare," said the new law would lead to layoffs, higher taxes, and people losing their current health plans.

"The governor likes to tout his so-called discounts for health insurance. . . . What he won't tell you is that most Kentuckians won't receive them," they wrote. "As so often happens when our friends on the left set out to fix a problem, their ideas, however well-intentioned, end up hurting the very people they sought to help. That's just what we're seeing with Obamacare."

BOMBING IN OHIO

Sean and Stephanie Recchi, who are Republicans, agreed that Obamacare didn't offer them much help.

Sean Recchi is the small businessman from Ohio who had been diagnosed with cancer in 2012. He and his wife then found out that their insurance policy covered only $2,000 a day in the hospital. The hospital of their choice—Houston's MD Anderson Cancer Center—had refused even to give Sean a treatment plan and an initial dose of a drug that could block the spread of his cancer until it received $83,900 in advance.

"I don't think Obamacare will help us; I don't want anything to do with it," Stephanie Recchi told me when I checked in with her on October 3, 2013, to ask if she had tried to get some much-needed insurance on the new website, which in Ohio was part of the federal exchange.

Yet the key provisions of Obamacare seemed as if they were drafted by someone sitting next to Sean Recchi in that MD Anderson holding room that day in 2012 when he had had to wait for his check to clear before a doctor would see him. The Recchis were a family facing the ultimate preexisting condition—cancer. Although by October 2013, Sean was in remission, he was regularly seeing doctors in Ohio and taking drugs costing hundreds of dollars a month, for which he now had no insurance.

Stephanie, Sean, and their two children were also a perfect match for the demographic that Obamacare was designed to serve: a working-class family of four earning, they estimated, $40,000 a year and unable to get insurance from an employer because the Recchis had just started their own two-person business. They would now be able to get significant subsidies to buy coverage on the exchange.

Nonetheless, on October 3, Stephanie Recchi, like Mitch McConnell and Rand Paul's imagined Kentuckians, wasn't buying Obamacare.

"I hear a lot of bad things about it—that it doesn't cover preexisting conditions, and it's too expensive," Stephanie Recchi told me the morning two days after the launch.

Where had she heard that? "Television ads and some politicians talking on the news—just a lot of talk that this is a bad law."

Journalists should cover stories, not steer them. Nonetheless, hearing myself sound like Governor Beshear, I urged her to try to find out more about it because it seemed geared to people in her situation. So, on October 4, Stephanie Recchi began pounding away at her laptop to have a look at what was offered on the Ohio version of the federal exchange. But every time she tried she was either put into the "waiting room" or sent to a page that froze up and crashed.

WHITE HOUSE PANIC

On Saturday, October 5, 2013, a *USA Today* story quoted U.S. chief technology officer Todd Park saying that they had expected 50,000 to 60,000 users, but had been overwhelmed by 250,000 concurrent users. Actually, as the internal emails leading up to the launch noted, they were prepared for only 10,000 users at launch and hadn't even met that target.

The same day, President Obama, in an interview with the Associated Press, urged Americans to be patient. Fixes to the website were on the way, he promised.

But in the White House that weekend, everyone was losing patience, including the president. The communications team was especially distraught. They had been sending press secretary Jay Carney out every day to talk about what a good problem this was—how the interest was so overwhelming that all they needed to do was make some fixes to catch up with demand.

"By the first weekend," one senior Obama adviser would later tell me, "we were sitting there saying, 'For the fourth day in a row we've been saying it's volume and it'll get better in a day or two. That's not going to work next week.'"

It certainly wasn't going to work if and when the government shutdown drama ended and the crashed website became the country's top story. Indeed, the great irony was that the Republicans had shut down the government to attack Obamacare, but the government shutdown was now shielding Obamacare from the wall-to-wall negative coverage it otherwise would have gotten during its first days.

The meeting that Saturday, October 5, like those during the three days before, was enormously frustrating to Obama and chief of staff McDonough. No one on the launch team—Lambrew from the White House, Tavenner from CMS, and Sebelius from HHS—seemed to know anything. Their aides were equally without answers.

Often, someone would take out a laptop to see if the website was even up at all, or to check the latest Twitter chatter. There were no numbers, just vague estimates of when fixes would be made based on an ever-changing, just-as-vague list of the fixes. It was the domestic crisis equivalent of using the Internet and Twitter to see how the raid on Osama bin Laden's hideout was going.

The Saturday meeting ended like the others. The president urged everyone to keep at it, keep McDonough posted, and report back tomorrow with what they all hoped would be better news. Meantime, Obama and his team had a government shutdown and debt ceiling to contend with.

Monday, October 7, began with White House Obamacare communications guru David Simas initiating a series of tweets alternating between attacking Republicans for the shutdown and retweeting good news stories about someone having successfully enrolled in Obamacare.

That same morning Bryan Sivak replied to an email from an executive at Amazon's Web services division. It had been sent to him because the Amazon executive assumed that someone with the title of chief technology officer of the Department of Health and Human Services must be the guy in charge of the website. Amazon wanted to know if there was anything it could do to help. "I wish there was," Sivak replied. "Actually, I wish there was something I could do to help."

But by that afternoon, Obama and McDonough had decided that they did, indeed, need help.

First, they told Todd Park—who had been trying to work on HealthCare.gov since he had been at HHS—that he was finally going to be put in the game. The president and his chief of staff wanted Park involved in HealthCare.gov as his highest and only priority. "I went from White House chief technology officer to full-time HealthCare .gov fixer," is how Park breezily described his new portfolio to me months later, with no hint of what a told-you-so moment this was.

Second, McDonough reached out to Jeffrey Zients, a highly regarded manager who had won high marks as a deputy director of the Office of Management and Budget. Among other projects, Zients—who in looks and résumé was the epitome of the buttoned-up business executive—had overseen the successful Cash for Clunkers economic stimulus program in 2009 that encouraged people to turn in their old cars and buy new ones. He was slated to become director of the president's National Economic Council in January 2014.

Zients, who is not an engineer, would be teamed with Park, the chief technology officer.

Their first job, Zients later told me, was "finding fresh eyes who could decide whether the thing was salvageable." In other words, as with the decades-old debate over the American healthcare system itself, the question on the table was whether HealthCare.gov could be fixed or whether they would have to scrap the whole thing and start over.

Jon Stewart's *Daily Show* the next evening with guest Kathleen Sebelius seemed to point to the more dire answer.

Stewart, who was sympathetic to the healthcare reform cause and whose viewers are overwhelmingly the "young invincibles" Sebelius needed to sign up, was merciless, and Sebelius came off as someone for whom mercy was the only hope. The prior week Stewart had been attacking Republicans for the shutdown. Now, he took the chance to attack the other side. He whipped out a laptop, turned to Sebelius, and said, "I'm gonna try and download every movie ever made and you're gonna try and sign up for Obamacare, and we'll see which happens first." The audience roared. Sebelius laughed, weakly.

How many people have signed up? Stewart asked. "I can't tell you because I don't know," Sebelius replied. The audience laughed a bit more. Stewart frowned. "The Democrats are as good as the Republicans at doing a shutdown," Stewart said.

"It was like watching one of those fights where the ref takes too long to step in and the guy gets carried out on a stretcher," recalled one member of the White House political team.

OBAMA REFUSES TO NEGOTIATE

The shutdown fight continued. Obama, sensing the Republicans were in political quicksand, refused to negotiate until the Republicans in the House voted to approve a budget and extend the debt ceiling. The Republicans, meanwhile, were beginning to look for a face-saving way out by getting something, anything, in the way of an Obamacare compromise.

One idea that the press speculated might work was repeal of the 2.3 percent Obamacare tax on medical devices. It was something that might attract some Democratic votes in the Senate because some Democrats, such as Al Franken of Minnesota, had already been pushing for repeal. The idea drove many of the reformers crazy, because the device makers' profit margins were so high and, in fact, their business had improved dramatically since the Obamacare tax had gone into effect. For example, Medtronic, which was based in Franken's home state, showed no sign of the carnage predicted by the industry's lobbyists and congressional sympathizers. Net earnings for the company's fiscal quarter ending on October 25, 2013, would be up 40 percent over the prior year.

Obama refused to negotiate on that or anything else.

LOOKING FOR "ACTIONABLE INTEL"

Through the second week of the launch, things only got worse. A CCIIO war room meeting on October 8, 2013, reported that "every single individual who needs to go to DHS [the Department of Homeland Security for a citizenship or legal alien status check] is essentially failing."

The October 10 meeting reported that "75% of traffic to the VA [the Department of Veterans Affairs, to check to make sure an applicant didn't already have veterans' healthcare benefits] is matching to deceased individuals."

On October 15, the group was told that these "Tiger Team" war room meetings were being canceled altogether.

By October 17, Denis McDonough had had enough of White House meetings where nobody knew anything. McDonough, whose background had been in national security before becoming Obama's chief of staff, decided he needed to go to the field and get what he later told me would be his own "actionable intel." He had a driver take him to CMS headquarters in Baltimore, where he could question the troops himself.

McDonough came back from Baltimore rattled by what he had learned about how and why the website was failing in front of a national audience of stunned supporters, delirious Republican opponents, and ravenous reporters.

What he was able to pry out from the beleaguered crew in Baltimore was that even on October 17—by which time traffic to the site had collapsed because its failure was now the subject of daily headlines across the country—only three in ten people coming to HealthCare.gov were able to get on at all. And, of the lucky third that did, most were likely to be tossed off because there were so many other bugs.

McDonough returned and briefed the president and Jeffrey Zients, who had by now come to the White House to work with Todd Park. None of them knew if there was any alternative but to scrap the site and start over. The president wanted their take on that within days.

As McDonough and Zients were digesting what the chief of staff had learned in Baltimore, presidential press secretary Jay Carney was going through what White House messaging adviser David Simas would later tell me was "probably the most painful press briefing we've ever seen. . . . It was like one of those scenes out of *The West Wing,* where everyone's yelling at him."

Thursday, October 17, was the day the government shutdown finally ended. Now, the Obamacare disaster was center stage.

Carney gamely tried to fend off the vultures. He had little to work with. Pressed repeatedly on when the site would be fixed, the best he could say was that "they are making improvements every day."

As the president and his chief of staff now knew, "they" were, in fact, not making improvements, except by chance, much as you or I might reboot or otherwise play with a laptop to see if some shot in the dark could somehow fix a snafu.

BAD NEWS AT OSCAR

Also on October 17, 2013, Oscar's Joshua Kushner, Mario Schlosser, and Kevin Nazemi finally got some real numbers, when the first batch of Oscar enrollment files arrived from the state.

Until now, the vibes from Web traffic and social media had seemed good, but they had no idea how many paying customers they had attracted.

The news was terrible. New York State reported that there had been 107 transactions for enrollments in their insurance policies. And those were not necessarily all enrollments. If someone had enrolled and canceled, as Schlosser had done a few times to test the system, that would have been two transactions but no net enrollments.

One hundred and seven (or fewer) customers for the first half month was lousy. Still, they remained optimistic. "We always believed that we have the right combination of naïveté about how the industry had always worked and the confidence and ability to try to do something different and better," Kushner told me.

CHAPTER 22

THE RESCUE

E ARLY ON THE MORNING OF FRIDAY, OCTOBER 18, 2013, GABRIEL Burt, whose résumé actually includes work as a rocket scientist, woke up in a room at a Doubletree Inn in Columbia, Maryland, about twenty-five miles outside of Washington. Burt, thirty at the time, had flown there from Chicago the night before, toting an overnight bag for what he thought might be a two- or three-day trip. By the following weekend his wife would be flying in to resupply him. He wouldn't get home until December 6.

Burt was the chief technology officer at Civis Analytics in Chicago. That's the company, funded by Google's Eric Schmidt, whose data analysts and technologists had achieved rock star status in the Obama 2012 campaign, and whose data Enroll America's Anne Filipic was already using to target the uninsured young invincibles.

Park, the White House CTO, had connected to Civis via the White House political office. Only now, the White House was interested in the other side of the house at Civis—its technology whiz kids, not its analysts who had been crunching demographic targeting data to feed potential enrollees to Filipic's now-frustrated field-workers.

On October 11, when Park had called from the White House, Mikey Dickerson—who worked at Google as a "site reliability manager"—had been in town visiting Burt and Civis CEO Dan Wagner. They were friends and Obama 2012 campaign alums. Dickerson, who was thirty-four at the time and favored cartoon-decorated T-shirts over suits and ties, had taken a leave from Google in 2012 to help with scaling the Obama campaign website and to create its Election Day turnout-reporting software.

"I consider Mikey a mentor," Burt would later tell me. "We were picking his brain about our company when Dan got a call about the healthcare site. . . . We all wanted to do something." Dickerson agreed that weekend to join Burt in a rescue squad.

GEEKS IN A VAN

By the afternoon of October 18, 2013, Burt had left his room at the Doubletree and was at the Maryland headquarters of QSSI, one of the contractors that had been hired by CMS to build and run the website that was now eighteen days into becoming a national debacle. Of the many contractors that had worked on HealthCare.gov, QSSI—which was responsible for, among other things, the successful connection of the website to the IRS database—was thought to have performed the least badly, and certainly better than CGI.

That same afternoon, Mikey Dickerson, the Google engineer, who was in California preparing to fly east the following Monday to join Burt, jumped on what he later described as a "really bizarre conference call."

The call was led by the now-energized Todd Park. Park was riding in a White House van around D.C., Maryland, and Virginia with the beginnings of a hastily assembled team trying to assess the damage.

Also in the van was Paul Smith, another Chicago-based techie whom Burt had recruited. Smith, thirty-six, had been deputy director of the Democratic National Committee's tech operation. He immediately put fund-raising for a start-up he was planning on hold to join the group.

Another passenger was Ryan Panchadsaram, twenty-eight, whose title was senior adviser to Park. He had come to the White House as part of a program called Presidential Innovation Fellows, which was launched by Park to bring high-tech achievers into government to work on specific projects that they design. (The program was already responsible for a series of innovations in making government data and healthcare records more available electronically.)

"I decided we should all go introduce ourselves to the people we were going to help," Park later recalled, explaining the van ride.

The team started by driving from the White House to meet Marilyn Tavenner, the CMS administrator, at her Washington office. She was thrilled to see them.

They then drove off to Baltimore to meet other senior CMS officials. It was during that drive that Park decided to loop Dickerson and some others into a rolling conference call. "We were passing around an iPhone with a speaker so we could all talk," Park said. "I wanted us to get to know each other."

"I had no idea who this guy leading the call was, and couldn't hear a lot of it," recalled Dickerson. "Finally, I jumped in and asked, 'Who am I talking to? Who is leading this call?' And the guy says, 'I'm Todd Park.' So I Googled him and saw he's the chief technology officer of the country and had founded two healthcare technology companies. Oh, I figured. Not bad."

Park's van continued on from Baltimore, stopping at the two main contractors working on the website. It turned out that the engineers at both QSSI and even CGI were not as defensive or hostile as Park and the others had feared.

"These guys want to fix things. They're engineers, and they were embarrassed," recalled one of the members of Park's gathering band. "Their bosses might have been turf conscious, but by then the guys in the suits really didn't want to have anything to do with the site, so they were glad to let us take over."

When the meetings with the contractors ended at a CMS outpost in Herndon, Virginia, at about 7 P.M., the rescue squad already on the scene decided they had more work to do. One of the things that had shocked Burt and Park's team most—"among many jaw-dropping aspects of what we found" is how one rescue squad member later put it—was that the people running HealthCare.gov had no "dashboard," no quick way for engineers to measure what was going on on the website, such as how many people were using it, what the response times were for various click-throughs, or where traffic was getting tied up.

So late into the night of October 18, Burt and the others spent about five hours coding and putting up a dashboard.

What they saw, recalled Park, was a site with wild gyrations. "It looked awfully spikey," Ryan Panchadsaram, the White House innovation fellow, remembered. "The question was whether we could ride that bull. Could we fix it?"

The team went home at about 2:30 A.M. on Saturday, October 19.

CALLING SILICON VALLEY

At the White House, the decision had still not been made whether to save or scrap HealthCare.gov. Jeffrey Zients wanted still more eyes from Silicon Valley on the problem. At about six in the morning on Saturday, October 19, 2013, he emailed John Doerr, a senior partner at Kleiner, Perkins, Caufield & Byers, the Menlo Park–based venture capital powerhouse whose investments include Amazon, Google, Sun, Intuit, and Twitter. Could Doerr call him when he awoke to talk about the healthcare website? Zients asked.

When Doerr quickly called back, Zients said, "We're pulling together this surge of people to do this assessment to see if the site's fixable or not. We've got to do it incredibly quickly. Do you know anyone?" Doerr recommended a relatively new Kleiner, Perkins partner named Mike Abbott, the former chief technology officer at Twitter.

"Mike saved Twitter's technology when it was failing," Doerr told me later, referring to the days when the Twitter "fail whale" error message icon was ubiquitous. "His being there gave me the confidence to make the largest investment we had ever made—over $100 million. . . . He had also worked at Microsoft and led the team at Palm that rebuilt their system. . . . Yet he's really low-key and well-liked."

Abbott, who was forty-one at the time, spoke to Zients the next day, Sunday, October 20. He flew to Washington on October 21.

That day, Obama offered what *The New York Times* called "an impassioned defense of the Affordable Care Act" in a Rose Garden statement, "acknowledging the technical failures of the HealthCare.gov website, but providing little new information about the problems with the online portal or the efforts by government contractors to fix it."

However, Obama did mention, without elaborating, that "we've had some of the best IT talent in the entire country join the team. And we're well into a 'tech surge' to fix the problem."

The president did not volunteer that his new team's first job was to decide whether to kill the website altogether and start over.

"The first red flag you look for," explained Abbott, the former Twitter CTO, "is whether there is a willingness by the people there to have outside help. If not, then I'd say it's simpler to write it new than to understand the code base as it is if the people who wrote it are not cooperating. But they were eager to cooperate.

"The second thing, of course, was, what were the tech problems," Abbott continued. "Were they beyond repair? Nothing I saw was beyond repair. Yes, it was messed up. Software wasn't built to talk to other software, stuff like that. . . . A lot of that was because they had made the most basic mistake you can ever make. The government is not used to shipping products to consumers. You never open a service like this to everyone at once. You open it in small concentric circles and expand"—such as one state first, then a few more—"so you can watch it, fix it and scale it."

What Abbott could not find, however, was leadership. He was never able to figure out who was supposed to have been running the HealthCare.gov launch. Instead he saw multiple contractors bickering and no one taking ownership for anything. Someone would have to be put in charge, he told Zients. Beyond that, Abbott recalled, "there was a lack of urgency" despite the fact that the website was becoming a national joke and crippling the Obama presidency.

By then, Mikey Dickerson—the Google reliability guru and Burt mentor—had arrived. "I knew Mikey by reputation," Abbott recalled. "He was a natural fit to lead this team."

Looking over the dashboard that Park, Burt, and the others had rigged up the prior Friday night, Abbott and the group discovered what they thought was the lowest hanging fruit—a quick fix to an obvious mistake that could improve things immediately. HealthCare.gov had been constructed so that every time a user had to get information from the website's vast database, the website had to make what was called a query into that database. Well-constructed, high-volume sites, especially e-commerce sites, will instead assemble the most frequently accessed information, such as the summaries of the insurance plans, a layer above the entire database, in what is called a cache. That way, the query can be faster and not tie up the connections to the overall database. Not doing that created a huge, unnecessary bottleneck. It was like slowing down traffic on an entry ramp to an otherwise empty highway.

The team began almost immediately to cache the data. The result was encouraging: The site's overall response time—the time it takes a page to load—dropped on the evening of October 22 from eight seconds to two. That was still terrible, but it represented so much of an improvement that it cheered the engineers. They could see that HealthCare.gov could be saved instead of scrapped.

Also weighing in by this time on the phone and through chat lines was another Silicon Valley legend recruited by Zients, who also happened to be named Abbott. Marty Abbott had been the CTO of eBay and now ran a consulting business that offered high-tech crisis management and evaluation. Venture funds paid him "tens of thousands of dollars a day," said Zients, to kick the tires, hard, of potential companies seeking their money. The companies themselves hired him when their websites or other technology crashed.

"It was pretty obvious from the first look that the system hadn't been designed to work right," Marty Abbott later told me. "It was not really managed at all, and wasn't architected to scale."

Marty Abbott volunteered his time, which would be limited to participation in multiple conference calls in the first few weeks of the salvage effort. Mike Abbott was also a volunteer; he ended up staying in the D.C. area until October 23, then would participate through December on conference calls, sometimes doing two or three a day.

Mikey Dickerson, Gabriel Burt, and the others—who had arrived for what they thought would be a few days, but would end up staying eight to eleven weeks—were told that government regulations did not allow them, even though they offered, to be volunteers if they worked for any sustained period. So they were put on the payroll of contractor QSSI as hourly workers, making what Dickerson said was "a fraction" of his Google pay.

On Wednesday, October 23, the day after their first breakthrough with the caching, Abbott, Dickerson, and the rest of the team gave Zients and Park their verdict: They could fix the site by the end of November, six weeks away, so that "the vast majority" of visitors could go on and enroll.

"I was, like, never worried," Dickerson later explained. "It's just a website. We're not going to the moon."

A few hours later on the afternoon of October 23, Zients and chief of staff McDonough told the president the news.

There was one additional, ironic piece of the plan: The general contractor Zients and Park had chosen to coordinate things, they told the president, was QSSI, which had handled some of the more successful functions of the ailing website. QSSI's parent company was UnitedHealth Group, the giant insurer. Which meant that the largest player in an industry that had opposed Obamacare in 2010 was now about to take a lead role in saving it. And profiting from it.

That same day, another insurer, WellPoint, told stock analysts during a conference call that it was raising its earnings estimates for the year and that interest in the Obamacare exchanges appeared "robust."

STAND-UPS AND HICCUPS

It was above a "Smile Center" dental clinic in a nondescript office building in Columbia, Maryland, in a four-thousand-square-foot room rented by QSSI—its walls lined with Samsung TV monitors showing various dashboard readings—that the rescue of Barack Obama's healthcare reform law would be attempted.

All the years of Ted Kennedy's crusading, all of Liz Fowler's drafting, all of the days wrangling votes on Capitol Hill in 2009 and 2010, all of the backroom deals and furious lobbying by all of those industry players, all of the frantic efforts to game the CBO scoring process, all of the millions of hours and billions of dollars spent writing regula-

tions and building the almost junked website—the fate of all of it—
now depended on Mikey Dickerson's stand-ups.

Stand-ups, which became a standard part of Mike Abbott's playbook at Twitter, are Silicon Valley–style meetings where everyone
usually stands, rather than sits, and works through a problem, or a set
of problems, fast. The group then disperses, acts, and reports back at
the end of the day, during a second stand-up.

Put differently, they were not like any of the meetings held in the
CMS war rooms.

Dickerson held the first of his stand-ups on October 24, 2013. Until
the end of November he would convene them every day, including
weekends, at 10 in the morning and 6:30 in the evening.

Each typically ran about forty-five minutes ("causing some of us to
sit down," Dickerson conceded). An open phone line connected people working on the website at other locations; in fact, the open line
remained live twenty-four hours a day so that everyone could instantly talk to the others if an issue suddenly came up.

Dickerson immediately established the rules, which he posted on a
wall just outside the control center.

Rule 1: "The war room and the meetings are for solving problems.
There are plenty of other venues where people devote their creative
energies to shifting blame."

Rule 2: "The ones who should be doing the talking are the people
who know the most about an issue, not the ones with the highest rank.
If anyone finds themselves sitting passively while managers and executives talk over them with less accurate information, we have gone off
the rails, and I would like to know about it." Explained Dickerson
later, "If you can get the managers out of the way, the engineers will
want to solve things."

Rule 3 was equally blunt: "We need to stay focused on the most
urgent issues, like those that will hurt us in the next 24–48 hours."

A CONGRESSIONAL INQUISITION

As Mikey Dickerson convened that first stand-up, Congressman Fred
Upton, the Republican chairman of the House Energy and Com-

merce Committee, began what would become a series of brutal congressional hearings on what to everyone (except those in the room with Dickerson, above the Smile Center) had become the hopeless website debacle.

With Democratic committee members, including healthcare reform champion Henry Waxman, left with little more to say than that the law was already helping millions of Americans because of provisions unrelated to the website, Upton and his Republican colleagues were unsparing.

"Over the past several months leading up to the October first launch, top administration officials and lead contractors appeared before this committee, looked us in the eye, and assured us repeatedly that everything was on track," Upton began. "Except that it wasn't, as we now know too well. So, why did they assure us that the website would work? Did they not know, or did they not disclose?"

Upton's witnesses were representatives of four of the contractors, including CGI as well as QSSI, the UnitedHealthcare subsidiary that Zients and Park had just chosen, unbeknownst to the committee, to coordinate the rebuild being done by Dickerson and his crew.

Each witness testified that the decision to launch the site on October 1, 2013, had been made by their client, CMS, not by them.

"Prior to October first," Upton asked the group, "did you not know that the HealthCare.gov website was going to have crippling problems, or did you know about these problems and choose not to disclose them to the administration?"

Cheryl Campbell, CGI's leader on the website project, offered the first answer: "So, Chairman, from a CGI perspective, our portion of the application worked as designed. People have been able to enroll. Not at the pace—not at the experience we would have liked, but the end-to-end testing was the responsibility of CMS. . . . Our portion of the system . . . was ready to go live, but it was not our decision to go live."

The three others provided much the same answer.

At the same October 24 hearing, Upton alluded to another problem that he said his constituents had begun contacting his office about: They were getting notices from their health insurance companies that their policies had to be canceled beginning January 1 because the new law no longer allowed them to be sold.

Readers of the *Federal Register* on June 17, 2010, would have known that, because of Jeanne Lambrew's tough grandfathering rules, millions were going to have their policies canceled. The *Federal Register* notice had said so. But neither Upton nor his constituents were devotees of the *Federal Register*.

"The president promised Americans that they could keep their health plan if they liked them, no matter what," Upton noted. "Yet, here we are, twenty-four days into open enrollment, and more people are receiving cancellation notices in just two states than the . . . Americans that the administration boasts have . . . begun applying in the entire country. This is a troubling fact, but we still don't know the real picture, as the administration appears allergic to transparency, and continues to withhold enrollment figures."

No one else mentioned the cancellation issue during this hearing. Its turn in the headlines would come a week later.

PROGRESS . . . THEN A CRASH

The next day, October 25, 2013, the White House press office announced that its new "tech surge" team had a rebuild plan that would see the website functioning well enough so that the "vast majority" of visitors would be able to enroll with no glitches by December 1.

By now, Mikey Dickerson's stand-up culture—identify the problem, solve the problem, or try again—was taking hold. The team began working stretches of two, three, or four days, during which each of them might have had five or ten hours of sleep cumulatively. They often changed clothes only when they had time for a shopping trip to the nearby mall.

They and the dozens of willing, even eager, engineers they were leading, who worked for the contractors who had failed so badly when they were leaderless in the run-up to October 1, pounded away on the bugs that Dickerson had demanded they identify every morning, focus on, and clear up in time for the evening stand-up. They began to sweep across increasingly big swathes of a punch list that detailed fixes needed across almost every feature and link on the e-commerce site, ranging from the major bugs (such as people not being able to save the information they entered in order to complete the process in a later visit) to relatively easy repairs (such as links that didn't take visitors to the right page).

Well, actually they hummed along happily until the whole site crashed at 1:20 A.M. on Sunday, October 27, two days after Zients had announced that all would be well by December 1. A switch had failed during maintenance work at a data center. The outage lasted thirty-seven hours, during which Dickerson and his team could do little because they had no website to look at.

Two days later, at 4 P.M. on October 29, it went down again. This outage lasted forty hours, including the afternoon of October 30, when Health and Human Services secretary Kathleen Sebelius testified about the website's troubles before another House of Representatives subcommittee. The indignant Republican members flashed images on their tablets and iPhones of the website being down as they questioned her.

"In her testimony, Ms. Sebelius came across as a hapless official," *The New York Times* reported.

"Those outages were totally demoralizing," recalled Gabriel Burt, the Obama campaign alumnus and CTO of Civis. "We thought we were on our way. We had gotten some momentum, but lost it."

"We just kept saying, 'Let's pick ourselves up and fight,'" recalled Todd Park, who was now pretty much living at the Maryland control center. "And when the site came back we pushed ahead nonstop. . . . We went from doing three or four releases"—upgrades or changes to the website—"in October to twenty-five in November."

"The team," Zients recalled, "ran two-minute drills to perfection. We had the best players on the field. Some plays didn't work. We talked about those. But there was never any finger-pointing. People just hustled right back to the line, and we ran the next play."

"THE PRESIDENT WAS TRULY FURIOUS"

While the site was down on October 29, 2013, NBC News delivered another blow—a lead story on its evening newscast and on its website headlined "Obama Administration Knew Millions Could Not Keep Their Health Insurance." Senior investigative correspondent Lisa Myers reported:

President Obama repeatedly assured Americans that after the Affordable Care Act became law, people who liked their health insurance would be able to keep it. But millions of Americans are getting or are about to get cancellation letters for their health insurance under Obamacare, say experts, and the Obama administration has known that for at least three years.

Four sources deeply involved in the Affordable Care Act tell NBC News that 50 to 75 percent of the 14 million consumers who buy their insurance individually can expect to receive a "cancellation" letter or the equivalent over the next year because their existing policies don't meet the standards mandated by the new health care law. One expert predicts that number could reach as high as 80 percent. And all say that many of those forced to buy pricier new policies will experience "sticker shock."

Then NBC delivered this knockout punch:

None of this should come as a shock to the Obama administration. The law states that policies in effect as of March 23, 2010, will be "grandfathered," meaning consumers can keep those policies even though they don't meet requirements of the new health care law. But the Department of Health and Human Services then wrote regulations that narrowed that provision, by saying that if any part of a policy was significantly changed since that date—the deductible, co-pay, or benefits, for example—the policy would not be grandfathered.

The story of the cancellations was exploding everywhere by the time the NBC report aired. Obama had broken his "keep your insurance" pledge. Now, according to the NBC report, it appeared he had known all along he was breaking his promise. The information had been published by his own people in the *Federal Register* years before.

The president was blindsided. He had never been briefed on the grandfathering issue. True, insurance industry lobbyist Ignagni and some insurance executives had mentioned the problem to Valerie Jarrett. But healthcare reform policy chief Lambrew had assured Jarrett that it was not a real issue—that the insurance people always complained about consumer-friendly regulations.

Obama had not known that Larry Summers's and Peter Orszag's staffs had been rebuffed as early as 2009 by the communications team, when they warned that the president should qualify his "keep your insurance promise" with language about how some plans would have to be canceled because they weren't good enough. It complicated the message, they were told.

When McDonough and the current communications team first asked Lambrew about the cancellations a day or two before the NBC report, she had told them it was not a big deal, that people would understand. When they pressed her for numbers, she said, accurately, that no one really knew how many individual plans were out there in the market, let alone how many would have expired anyway and not be subject to any kind of grandfathering. That was true, but in the political firestorm that ensued any canceled or expired policy would now become a policy that Obamacare had canceled.

It was only when McDonough and the communications team pressed her and Sebelius that they found out that their administration had published the estimates of millions of cancellations in the *Federal Register* more than three years before.

"Remember, those regulations were written when the Obama people were riding high," one insurance executive later explained. "They had all been having fun bashing the insurance companies, especially Lambrew. She thought those regs were a compromise. If it was up to her, she'd have killed all those plans in 2010, not 2014."

"The health reform people—Jeanne [Lambrew], and the others who worked for her, had tin ears," a senior White House communications adviser later told me. "Maybe they were just so used to all the fights over reform in the industry that they weren't sensitive to the larger political arena where this was going to be played out. Whatever the reason," this adviser added, "it was unforgivably bad, horribly stupid, that we walked into this right after the website failure. The president was truly furious. 'This was a problem we brought on ourselves,' he told us. 'We should have known this was coming.'"

Yet he was still no-drama Obama. There was no yelling. Just a calm series of questions to Lambrew and the rest of the staff. How did this happen? How many people were really affected? How do we know that? What can we do about it?

"It was worse than yelling," recalled one shell-shocked staffer who attended one of the first meetings with the president following the explosion of the cancellation grenade. "It was a calm, piece-by-piece dissection of everything, peeling it back, layer by layer."

"I ALWAYS THOUGHT SOMETHING MIGHT BRING ME DOWN"

The first victim thrown into the ring to fight off the new firestorm was Marilyn Tavenner, the head of CMS, who testified on October 29, 2013, before another House committee. She now had to explain a catch-22: People were getting their current policies canceled. However, they couldn't buy new ones that, even with the subsidies, might cost more—because they were much higher quality insurance policies—because the website didn't work. Yet they were facing a penalty under the individual mandate if they didn't have insurance by January 1.

"What's become abundantly clear," said Kevin Brady, a Republican from Texas, "is that the flaw is not the website; the flaw is the law itself. This is what happens when you inject 159 new federal agencies, bureaucracies, and commissions between you and your health care.

"Why should the American people believe you now?" he asked Tavenner. "You've had nearly four years to get it ready. Now you're saying in four weeks more, it'll be great. So what's different? Why should anyone believe these claims?

"My constituents are frightened," Brady concluded. "They are being forced out of health care plans they like. The clock is ticking. The federal website is broken. Their health care isn't a glitch."

The best Tavenner could do was apologize "that the website is not working as well as it should," and repeat the vague promise that it would work for the "vast majority" of visitors by December 1. She refused to give enrollment numbers, saying the totals for October would not be available until mid-November.

Tavenner is a sharp, self-assured, and commanding presence in most rooms. Here, she looked wilted, in shock. She seemed to sink deeper into the chair the more the inquisition dragged on. "I had had an ideal career," she later told me, referring to a résumé that had begun with a college degree in nursing and had culminated in the government's top healthcare operating job. "But I always thought something might bring me down. I guess this was it."

Nonetheless, when she got back to the office, Tavenner "was as solid as a rock," recalled one of her deputies. "She kept telling us we can't worry about blame. We can't look back. We just have to let the new tech team help us fix this." That meant that she had had to push aside Henry Chao and Michelle Snyder. Tavenner especially felt bad about Snyder. The career civil servant had wanted to retire the year before, but Tavenner had persuaded her to stay to work on the launch.

The night of Tavenner's hapless turn in the congressional barrel, the Republican National Committee began airing a series of hilarious Web videos, entitled "I'm Obamacare." They depicted a disheveled obese person, "Mr. Obamacare," commiserating with a fit, good-looking young man, "Mr. Private Sector," about how baffled he was handling challenges like technology or customer service.

It added up to a stunning reversal of political fortunes, all having to do with the nuts and bolts of governing competently. On October 17, the day the government shutdown had ended, the Republicans were thought to be grievously wounded for having closed the government over Obamacare. Now, in just twelve days, the Obama administration had managed to overturn the political landscape. The Republicans were riding high because of Obamacare.

Anne Filipic, the former Obama campaign field organizer now running Enroll America, knew that. By the end of October, her troops had gathered more than forty-three thousand commit cards from the uninsured, mostly the cherished young invincibles, who wanted more information or even help signing up. But she couldn't sign them up. In the precincts she had targeted in Houston her people had generated a ton of interest, but had only been able to get about fifty people enrolled.

Meantime, Filipic's opposite numbers at Generation Opportunity— the group organized and funded by the Koch brothers and other opponents of Obamacare to discourage the young from enrolling— applied their brand of humor to the opportunity Filipic's former White House colleagues had handed them. They gave contractor CGI their "Youth Defender Award" for "doing more than anyone to date to save young people from the increased costs and privacy invasions of Obamacare." Secretary Sebelius was named runner-up.

THE DRUG COMPANIES WIN ANOTHER ONE

On November 3, 2013, CMS's Tavenner handed a victory to the pharmaceutical companies. She issued a regulation allowing them to pay a patient's out-of-pocket expenses for brand-name prescription drugs.

This allowed the drugmakers to proceed with a clever, seemingly pro-consumer strategy to undercut the aggressive deals the insurance companies on the exchanges were offering to patients who opted for less expensive generics.

The insurers were willing to cut or even eliminate their customers' co-insurance obligations if they chose generics. For example, a brand-name prescription might cost $100, and the generic might cost $20. The insurance company might say that the co-insurance for the brand-name version was 30 percent, but that the co-insurance for the generic was only 10 percent. That would make the patient's out-of-pocket cost $30 for the brand name (30 percent of $100) but only $2.00 (10 percent of $20) for the generic. In fact, Oscar's deal was that the generic would be completely free for the patient.

To trump that, the drug companies wanted to pay patients for all of their out-of-pocket costs for brand-name drugs.

Tavenner's ruling meant that patients would not worry about the cost difference between generics and brand names and, in fact, pay less for the brand names—because the drug company would pay that entire $30 out-of-pocket cost to the patient for its branded drug. This gift to the patients was well worth it to the drug company, because its cost to produce the brand-name drug, for which it would now still get $70 from the insurance company, might have been a dollar or even less.

The insurers had argued that because the exchanges received government funds to pay for the premium subsidies, a rule in effect that did not allow drug companies to offer the same deal to Medicare patients (because they, too, had their bills paid with government funds) should apply. Tavenner turned them down. With all the political fights raging over Obamacare, why tell patients they could not get their favorite drugs for free, courtesy of the drug companies?

"AS MUCH AS WE CAN, AS FAST AS WE CAN"

Google's Mikey Dickerson was so adamant about the need to forgo finger-pointing and move on to the next play that during one stand-up in mid-November he demanded a round of applause for an engineer who had called out from the back of the room that a brief outage had probably been the result of a mistake he had made.

The team's progress was steady, but their punch list was enormous. Jeffrey Zients, though not a techie himself, had assembled a terrific team that had gelled perfectly. However, his engineers could move only so fast. Zients had carte blanche to add resources, but putting ten people on a fix that would take one coder ten days didn't turn it into a one-day project. Coding didn't work that way.

"Jeff was a great leader, but there were limits," Dickerson told me. "He would ask us every day if we were going to make the deadline. . . . He'd say he had to report on how we were doing to the president. And I'd say till I was blue in the face, 'We're doing as much as we can, as fast as we can, and we're going to do that no matter what the deadline is.'"

THE QUEEN OF ERRORS REIGNS

As Dickerson marched his troops through the punch list in November, he added to the team, mostly with recruits he had worked with at

Google. Jini Kim, a thirty-three-year-old who looked ten years younger, had been a Google superstar before leaving to start her own healthcare data analytics service. She put that aside, arriving on November 21, 2013, to become the team's "queen of errors."

Kim's job was to work with a group at a separate office near Dulles International Airport in Virginia devoted to dealing with longer term issues the site would face following the November 30 deadline. That meant she regularly had to drive the forty-plus miles between the Virginia office and the Maryland command center. One afternoon, it provided the native Californian with a terrifying experience maneuvering through her first blizzard.

The most important longer term issue Kim worked on was scale: Would HealthCare.gov be able to handle the traffic that a revived and working site would generate?

One of the hurdles to increasing capacity was the error rate—the rate at which any clicks on the site generated a result that it was not supposed to, such as a time-out or the popping up of the wrong page. In October the error rate had been an astoundingly high 6 percent. That meant that even the lucky few who got onto the site invariably had something go wrong, because at 6 percent, just fifteen or sixteen clicks on the site would, on average, produce a problem.

THANKSGIVING 2013 FELL ON November 28, and what for most of the country was a long holiday weekend became three days of two-minute drills for Mikey Dickerson and his crew, all aimed at keeping the president's promise of a website working for the "vast majority" of visitors by Sunday, December 1. Dozens of items remained on the punch list. For example, people still couldn't go back a page on the website.

The fixes began being pumped out even faster. At the same time, the engineers executed a major upgrade in the hardware powering the system, giving it more capacity and reliability. "You normally don't do hardware and software changes at the same time," Zients told me. "Because if something breaks you don't know what the cause is. But we . . . had to take chances."

"CAN OBAMACARE SURVIVE?"

The rest of the world remained skeptical. The brutal congressional hearings continued. Even the Democratic-controlled Senate felt compelled to get into the act, although its hearings were milder, despite Max Baucus's growing anger over how his law had stumbled so badly out of the gate and how much he and his staff had been kept in the dark about all of the problems.

Bad news dominated the headlines, many of which were based on emails and other documents the congressional committees had subpoenaed revealing all of the internal worrying and bickering at CMS prior to the launch.

"We knew we really had something as we began getting these documents," one Republican staffer recalled. "One was better than the next, showing how panicked these guys were and how they had lied to us when they testified that summer that everything was on track. Every page was a smoking gun."

As they sifted through the emails and memos, however, the investigators struggled to find evidence to prove that the people at the Obama White House were not simply as clueless as everyone else about what had really been going on during the summer. Except for the McKinsey consultants' report and briefings—which were in late March and April—there was nothing indicating that Obama or any of his staff people had seen any of those CMS documents.

When it came to Obama and his direct reports, this seemed to be more about aloof, incompetent management than a cover-up, though the Republicans would try to make the latter charge stick.

ON NOVEMBER 13, 2013, CMS issued its first report on monthly enrollments, covering the disastrous October rollout. The press was invited to a conference call, which started nearly a half hour late while Muzak on the phone line repeated the song "Just Because I Love You."

"To date, 106,185 persons have enrolled and selected a Marketplace plan," the accompanying white paper began.

It was not until the third paragraph down that what should have been the headline number was provided: 80,000 of those 106,185 enrollees had come from the state-run exchanges, such as Kentucky's, New York's, and California's. That meant that just 26,794 people had enrolled over the entire month through the federal exchange covering thirty-six states—less than 5 percent of what the administration had been counting on for the first month. It averaged out to twenty-four enrollments per day in each state on the federal website.

The same day, *The Washington Post* ran a front-page story headlined "Troubled HealthCare.gov Unlikely to Work Fully by End of November." Citing "an official with knowledge of the project," the *Post* reported that "government workers and technical contractors racing to repair the Web site have concluded . . . that the only way for large numbers of Americans to enroll in the health-care plans soon is by using other means so that the online system isn't overburdened."

Mickey Dickerson and his people were too busy to read newspapers.

The next day, November 14, Wolf Blitzer opened his CNN *Situation Room* show by calling Obamacare a "snowballing debacle." The rolling headline under Blitzer flashed "Can Obamacare Survive?"

WINNING OVER THE RECCHIS

For Sean and Stephanie Recchi, Obamacare became good news on the day Blitzer's show aired. Confused by what they could figure out from the sputtering website, yet curious about what I had told them about how the law didn't allow insurers to discriminate against those with preexisting conditions, the Ohio couple—who had struggled to pay for Sean's cancer treatments—had gone to a local insurance agent for advice.

"When they came to my office, Stephanie [Recchi] told me right up front, 'I don't want any part of Obamacare,'" recalled Lancaster, Ohio, insurance agent Barry Cohen. "These were clearly people who don't like the president. So I kind of let that slide and just asked them for basic information and told them we could go on the Ohio exchange"—which was actually the Ohio section of the federal Obamacare exchange—"and show them what's available."

What Stephanie soon discovered, she told me, "was a godsend." The business that she and her husband had launched—which sold a product that enabled consumers to store their DNA or that of family members for future genetic testing—had recently received investor interest after being featured on an episode of the television series *CSI*. She estimated to Cohen that their income would be about $90,000 in 2014. Even at that level, her family of four would qualify for a subsidy under Obamacare.

The Recchis and their agent soon zeroed in on a plan with a $793 monthly premium that provided full coverage, although with a deductible of $12,000 for the entire family, meaning the Recchis would pay the first $12,000 in expenses. After the deductible was reached, there would be no co-payments for anything, including all drugs.

The Obamacare subsidy, assuming the $90,000 income that the Recchis had estimated, brought their monthly premium cost down to $566 from $793. If their income was the same $40,000 Stephanie had estimated for 2013, the subsidy would increase and their premium would be just $17 a month.

"They had budgeted insurance at $1,200 for each of them plus two new employees, for their new business," says Cohen. "That's $2,400 a month for the two of them, compared to $566, so they were thrilled. . . . They had seen all those stories on television, and because of their views about Obama, they believed what they wanted to believe—until they saw these policies and these numbers."

"Here I get full protection for $566, compared to no protection for almost $500," Stephanie says, referring to her old plan that had cost $469 and that the MD Anderson Cancer Center had scoffed at. "This is wonderful."

Actually, it ended up better than that. Because Cohen could enter only the Recchis' *actual* reported 2013 income onto the website, not their anticipated income if and when the investment deal is completed, and because that income turned out to be less than the $40,000 Stephanie had estimated, the website moved them automatically into Medicaid—meaning their coverage, for now, was free.

That was because Ohio governor John Kasich had decided to buck many of his fellow Republican governors and accept Obamacare's subsidies so that he could expand Medicaid coverage.

Kasich's decision, however, illustrated one of three aspects of the Recchis' story that threw cold water on an otherwise fairy-tale ending.

First, if Kasich had followed the lead of Obamacare resisters such as Texas governor Rick Perry, the Recchis would have been in a through-the-looking-glass situation. If, as it turned out, their income was below the poverty level, in Texas they would have had to pay the full $793 for their insurance. However, if their income actually *was* $90,000, rather than below the poverty level, they would pay only $566.

That's because the law as written had required all states to accept the government's subsidy for Medicaid to be extended to everyone with incomes below the poverty level (and, in fact up to 33 percent above the poverty level). As a result, no premium subsidies in the exchange plans were provided for people below the poverty level, because they would presumably go into Medicaid. But then the Supreme Court had ruled in its otherwise pro-Obamacare decision in June 2012 that the states' expansion of Medicaid had to be voluntary. That left the poor in states such as Texas or Florida that did not expand Medicaid faced with having to pay more than those who are *not* poor but who got subsidies if their incomes were below 400 percent of the poverty level. Unlike those middle-class families, the poor families could only buy health insurance without subsidies because they were supposed to have been sent into Medicaid. The move by most Republican governors to block them was, President Obama later asserted to me, a "completely unnecessary and mean spirited decision to continue to deny coverage to those who need it most because of politics."

Fortunately for the Recchis, Kasich and Ohio had opted to expand Medicaid.

The second asterisk to the Recchis' happy ending was that even once the website was fixed by the surge team so that visitors could use it, Sean and Stephanie still needed help from Cohen, their insurance agent, to make sense of it all. There were all of those "bronze," "silver," "gold," and "platinum" levels of coverage to figure out, each featuring multiple variations of premiums, co-pays, co-insurance, and deductibles. Worse were the hard-to-find and harder-to-understand lists of which hospitals and doctors were in each insurance company's network. And those lists were models of clarity compared to the lists of drugs that were covered by each plan.

"There is no way the Recchis or anyone else can figure out what they're buying without someone who has been trained sitting with them," said Cohen. Sure, that was a self-serving assessment. Yet in interviews across the country with people who had already signed up for Obamacare, I found no one who fully understood the benefits, the costs, and, most important, the limits of what they were buying unless they were helped by agents or by "navigators"—the enrollment assistants trained and licensed by officials operating the exchanges. Indeed, I needed Cohen's help to understand it, and I have a law degree and have been writing about all of this for two years.

Understanding those details, including the limits, related to what consumers are buying put another damper on the Recchis' story: Their insurance—whether Medicaid for now, or the private plan they are likely to transition to later—was not going to cover them at MD Anderson in Houston. No Ohio plan would. In fact, only two of seventy-nine plans offered in Texas on its federally run Obamacare exchange included coverage at MD Anderson.

MD Anderson is extravagantly expensive and, with its well-deserved international brand name, has more than enough business without letting insurance companies beat them down for discounts in return for being included in the new, relatively narrow networks set up for many of the policies sold on the exchanges.

More generally, one of the ways insurance companies had tried to limit their costs and the premiums they were charging on the Obamacare exchanges was to use these narrow networks that are limited to the hospitals, doctors, and other providers who offer them relatively cost-effective prices. Because there was often little or no relationship between cost and quality in the dysfunctional world of healthcare economics, this did not necessarily mean patients would receive inferior care, though it might. But it did mean that, contrary to the other promise President Obama had made in promoting Obamacare, patients would often not be able to "keep their doctor" or be treated at the hospital of their choice.

In other words, expanding coverage to people like the Recchis while trying to control premium costs was going to mean that not everyone got the platinum care they wanted and that others would get. When it came to healthcare, as opposed to buying a car, that might be difficult to accept.

"No, we don't get MD Anderson, but we do get the Cleveland Clinic and lots of other good care," Stephanie told me. "We understand that."

ZEKE ON DEFENSE

The crash of the president's signature domestic initiative dominated the Sunday talk shows through the end of November. Even the president's defenders added to the fallout. On a December 1, 2013, *Fox News Sunday* appearance, Zeke Emanuel, now ensconced as a deputy provost at the University of Pennsylvania and a fellow at the Center for American Progress, brushed aside criticism of the narrow networks. Fox host Chris Wallace said the narrow networks seemed to break that Obama promise that you could "keep your doctor." People who wanted to keep their doctor, "could pay more," Emanuel replied.

Ten days before that, I had appeared with Emanuel on a panel at the Council on Foreign Relations in Manhattan to discuss the American healthcare system. When I casually mentioned that Obamacare had neglected tort reform, Emanuel angrily declared that "President Obama has done more for medical tort reform than any president in history." As he continued—citing the pilot projects to be carried out by CMS that were written into the law but that he had criticized in White House meetings as meaningless—the audience began hissing.

The Council on Foreign Relations is a polite, mostly upper-crust group. I had never seen an audience there hiss, even when leaders of the most hostile, anti-American countries had come to speak.

The hissing continued.

Out of the corner of my eye I noticed a man get up and storm out, as if someone from Hamas had just decreed death to Israel.

That afternoon, Joseph Cari, the angry man in the Council on Foreign Relations audience, called me to explain why he had walked out. Cari, a wealthy financier from Chicago, explained that he had been a national finance chairman for Al Gore's 2000 presidential campaign and had been active in Democratic Party fund-raising on and off since. He was incensed at what he believed to be Emanuel's dodging. And, as a businessman, he harbored a longtime resentment of his party's willingness to let trial lawyers dictate the Democrats' position on sensible tort reform. "Whatever city the Democrats go to for a fund-raiser," he said, "it is always the top trial lawyers who help organize it. And they won't let any Democrat touch tort reform. How could he [Emanuel] have said that?"

Ten months later, when I checked with CMS about those pilot projects Emanuel had extolled, I was told by a spokesman, on background, that the program had never been funded at CMS.

TURKEY DAY, DEADLINE DAY

After a slew of fixes on November 27, 2013, the day before Thanksgiving, and more on Thanksgiving morning, the tech surge team went to Todd Park's house for turkey. Later that night, they returned to the office to execute still more fixes, where they shared pies brought in by Jeffrey Zients.

On Sunday, December 1, Zients issued a public report, impressively detailing the website's rescue. A series of hardware upgrades had dramatically increased capacity. The system was now able to handle at least fifty thousand simultaneous users and probably more. There had been more than four hundred bug fixes. The percentage of the time the website was up and running had gone from an abysmal 43 percent at the beginning of November to 95 percent (still bad compared to any good e-commerce site). And Jini Kim and her team had knocked the error rate from 6 percent down to .5 percent. (By the end of January it would be well below .5 percent and still dropping.)

The press generally accepted the new numbers, but questioned whether the site would be able to handle the traffic surge expected ahead of the December 23 deadline for people who wanted coverage effective on January 1, which was when the mandate requiring coverage kicked in.

Zients, Park, and the rescue crew were worried about that, too. Yet throughout December, their numbers kept improving, helped by Jini Kim's falling error rate and by a group of new Dickerson recruits who parachuted in for stays of a few weeks or, in some cases, vowed to stay until the close of enrollment at the end of March.

Andrew Slavitt, the executive overseeing the work of QSSI, which Zients had installed as the general contractor to work with the surge team, was mightily impressed. Slavitt's title was executive vice president of Optum, of which QSSI was a subsidiary. Optum itself was the analytics and consulting unit of UnitedHealthcare, the giant insurer. Beginning in December, Slavitt started taking various members of the Silicon Valley surge team aside and attempted to recruit them. UnitedHealthcare knew that the basic insurance business was not the key to its future, he told them. But Optum—its fast-growing data cruncher—*was* the future. In fact, he told Mikey Dickerson, "Optum was going to be the Google of healthcare. You should join us."

Dickerson told him that he already worked for the Google of Google.

MORE RETREATS ON THE RULES

On December 19, 2013, the Obama administration threw in the towel on insurance cancellations, announcing that anyone who faced a hardship because their plan had been canceled would be exempt from the requirement of the individual mandate throughout 2014. The hard line on grandfathering that Lambrew and the other Obama people had taken had now completely backfired. Now, hundreds of thousands of people, maybe millions, already with insurance in the individual market—the same market that the exchanges were meant to serve—would not have to buy new, better insurance on those exchanges.

"LIKE A ROCKET SHIP"

Early on Monday, December 23, 2013, Dickerson and the team gathered at the command center early to see if what they had rebuilt could handle the expected last-minute stampede of people who wanted to be covered beginning January 1.

"I'll never forget that day," Todd Park told me. "We'd been experiencing extraordinary traffic in December, but this was a whole new level of extraordinary. . . . By nine o'clock traffic was the same as the peak traffic we'd seen in the middle of a busy December day. Then from nine to eleven, the traffic astoundingly doubled. If you looked at the graphs it looked like a rocket ship."

Traffic rose to 65,000 simultaneous users, then to 83,000, the day's high point.

Everything held together.

The result: 129,000 enrollments on December 23, about five times more in a single day than what the site had handled in all of October. Because the sign-up deadline for getting insurance that would take effect on January 1 had just been extended by another day, until Christmas Eve, Park and the team slept a few hours at the Doubletree and came back at dawn. Traffic was again at levels never seen until the day before—and produced 93,000 more enrollments.

As it got later on the afternoon of Christmas Eve, the band was starting to break up. Paul Smith, the former Democratic National Committee techie who had put aside fund-raising for a start-up to join the team, left early to spend the holiday with his wife and young daughter, whom he had not seen in weeks. Although he was living only about thirty miles away in Baltimore, the commute had become an impossible luxury in the frantic weeks in the run-up to the deadline.

Before Smith left, he gave an impassioned speech about what a privilege it had been to work on the project and to work with this crew. Then, recalled Park, "We all had a hug."

Later that night, Park talked by video chat to Mikey Dickerson's parents in Connecticut. He thanked them for lending their son to the team and to the country.

Just after midnight, Park went home, and Dickerson went back to his room at the Doubletree. He would not return to Google until January 5. He spent the days after Christmas helping to organize a new crew of pit bosses who would cycle in and out of the operations center—which would look calm and whose video dashboards would all display a remarkably stable system when I visited there in mid-February 2014. (By then, one screen would report that the current average response time—once a ridiculous eight seconds per page—was down to .343 seconds.)

"Jeff was good at pumping us up, and so was Todd," recalled one of the team members, referring to Zients and Park. "We even got to meet McDonough, the chief of staff, and that was good. But we really didn't need to be pumped up much. This is what we do. And this job had special meaning."

That may be why none of the group—even those, like Dickerson, who had worked for President Obama during one or both of the campaigns and had gotten to meet him multiple times at campaign headquarters—would express surprise or regret that the group that had rescued the president's signature policy initiative did not get to meet Obama (who spent Thanksgiving 2013 at the White House) or even get a thank-you phone call. "I'm sure he's got a lot of other things to do," said Jini Kim, chuckling.

On December 29, the Obama administration announced the last-minute surge of enrollments. There were now 1.1 million people enrolled through the federal exchange, 975,000 of whom had enrolled in December alone, following the tech team's rescue.

They still had a long way to go to meet the target of seven million enrollees by March 31 that the CBO had set and that the press was fixated on. Yet getting close now looked possible.

In Kentucky, Carrie Banahan and her team closed out the year with 175,000 enrollees, nearly 30 percent of the state's 630,000 uninsured. Of those, 140,000 were enrolled in Medicaid for free.

A BARGAIN IN BROOKLYN

One of those who waited to sign up until almost the last minute before the December 24, 2013, deadline was Gretchen Barton, thirty-two, who ran a small film production company with her husband in Brooklyn.

Barton enrolled in Oscar on the New York exchange just before Christmas.

She had first bought health insurance about nine years before after she cut her foot on a piece of glass and had to pay all the bills herself. "I realized, I was twenty-three, and it's time," Barton told me.

But the insurance premiums for Barton and then for her and her husband had climbed steadily from an initial $121 a month. In early December Blue Cross Blue Shield notified her that the monthly premium for 2014 would be $913. She need not do anything, the notice said, and her policy would be continued at the new rate.

Barton and her husband had decided instead that they should look for alternatives. Barton had gone onto the New York State website in November, but she was unable to make a decision—except that she didn't think she was interested in this company called Oscar, because she had never heard of it. However, after a second visit to the exchange, where none of the other options appealed to her (though most were cheaper than $913), she got curious about Oscar and Googled the company.

"It seemed different," she later recalled. "It seemed like a bunch of smart young guys who were doing something new and different. It resonated with me. . . . Then my husband and I called their customer service line, and within a minute we were on the phone with this smart, amiable guy—an actual person—on the phone. . . . It was so nice. . . . I loved the idea of the telemedicine. . . . And he was able to answer all of our other questions."

The next day Barton and her husband signed up for an Oscar silver plan at $766 a month. However, it cost them $500 because they were entitled to a $266 subsidy.

Within days, Barton would get a call from another of Oscar's "real" people confirming her order. About a week later, in early January, she would use the telemedicine hotline to have a doctor call in a prescription for a generic drug that cost her nothing. Soon, she was talking up Oscar at a Brooklyn beauty salon (which is how I found her, because one of the people who heard her extolling Oscar worked at Oscar).

The only trouble Barton would still have with insurance companies was the seven calls she would have to make before Blue Cross Blue Shield stopped pulling $913 a month out of her checking account and refunded it.

CHAPTER 23

THE FINISH LINE

January 1–April 15, 2014

Although the Obamacare website had now obviously recovered there was still no smoothly functioning electronic link connecting the exchange to the insurance companies so that someone signing up would actually be enrolled automatically by the insurer. Instead, CMS had to send the forms over to each insurer through a separate process that often required the insurance companies to enroll their new customers manually. Worse, in many cases the information contained in the sign-ups was getting garbled.

Barack Obama had learned his lesson. In conversations with his staff about this in December, Obama, wanting to make sure he was not burned by another exchange-related crisis, repeatedly asked about this. How could they be sure that when people showed up at a local drugstore on New Year's Day to fill prescriptions with the insurance that they thought they had bought on the exchange, they would actually have a verified insurance card or, failing that, would at least have a valid policy on file that the druggist could check?

Everyone on the Obama staff now had visions of news cameras and tweets recording the newest fiasco—hordes of angry customers being stopped from getting their drugs or turned away from being treated at some clinic. Obama drilled down, wanting more this time than bland assurances. The staff brought him the details from HHS and CMS about exactly what was being done. "We failed at . . . launch," President Obama later told me. "We learned from that and worked hard to pull ourselves out of the hole we put ourselves in before the end of open enrollment."

On January 1 and through the first week of 2014, there were sporadic reports of problems, but no new crises. The CMS policy and technical people, aided by the remaining tech surge team, had worked through the holidays with the insurance companies to make the jerry-rigged manual process mostly work.

BACK TO BUSINESS: A $7 BILLION STOCK DEAL

Through the first half of January, Obamacare seemed to be settling into the rest of the healthcare landscape as something that was here to stay, for better or worse. While David Simas and his White House messaging group plugged away at boosting sign-ups ahead of March 31, 2014, when the enrollment period would be over until the fall, healthcare news coverage returned to more of the conventional fare.

On January 2, IMS Health Holdings, a company you've never heard of, caused a buzz in the industry when it began an initial public offering of its stock. The company collected and sold, according to its prospectus, "one of the largest and most comprehensive collections of healthcare information in the world, spanning sales, prescription and promotional data, medical claims, electronic medical records and social media."

When the IMS stock went on sale in April, the price paid resulted in a valuation of the company of nearly $7 billion.

EMERGENCY ROOM INCENTIVES

On January 13, 2014, the Department of Justice announced that it was joining in litigation brought by eight whistle-blowers alleging that Health Management Associates, a chain of seventy-one for-profit hospitals, billed Medicare and Medicaid "for medically unnecessary inpatient admissions from the emergency departments at HMA hospitals and paid remuneration to physicians in exchange for patient referrals."

The government alleged that a scorecard was kept to track emergency room admission rates. Doctors who hit a target of admitting 50 percent or more of patients sixty-five years old or over to the hospital would get a color code of green.[21]

The charges came as HMA was about to be bought by another hospital chain, Community Health Associates, which would create the nation's second largest collection of for-profit hospitals. The merger would be completed by the end of the month.

The company's slide presentation for investors the following month would say that the newly merged chain was "well-positioned to participate as a network provider on various health insurance exchanges," with "hospitals located in 26 of the top 30 highest uninsured states."

Seven weeks later, another giant hospital chain, Tenet Healthcare, would announce that it expected Obamacare to boost its cash flow in 2014 by $50 million to $100 million.

A "VIRAL" HEALTH INSURANCE COMPANY?

The same day that the Justice Department announced the suit against the hospital chain, the giant annual show-and-tell for everyone who is anyone when it comes to the money side of healthcare convened in San Francisco—the J. P. Morgan Healthcare Conference 2014.

Dozens of pharmaceutical, insurance, biotech, data analytics, insurance, and other companies in fast-developing healthcare fields presented slide shows to investors. Some, such as WellPoint and Walgreens, were established names. Others were start-ups in genomic analysis or "digital medicine." All reported in one way or another that Obamacare was going to advance their fortunes.

---

21. On August 4, 2014, the Department of Justice announced that the hospital chain had agreed to pay $98 million and sign a Corporate Integrity Agreement to settle all of the suits.

And then there was Joshua Kushner from Oscar, who told the investor crowd that Obamacare had enabled his company to exist. Kushner presented a thirteen-slide deck that depicted his ads—"Health insurance that won't make your head explode. And if it does, you're covered"—and that emphasized Oscar's "Our World vs. Old World" look and feel. There were no cost, enrollment, or revenue projections. No numbers at all.

The J. P. Morgan audience was silent.

"It was depressing. We were like aliens there," Kushner told me when I caught up with him about two weeks later. "Someone asked what our exit strategy was, and I said we were trying to change the industry, not sell the company." Someone else asked how Oscar could protect itself from being mimicked by bigger competitors. "I told them that I hope the industry copies us."

Kushner could have presented some good numbers had he wanted to. By the time we talked on January 29, Oscar already had 5,413 members. Given what everyone expected to be a flood of last-minute sign-ups, it now seemed that the team would easily exceed its target of 7,500 by the time enrollments ended on March 31.

The key was word of mouth. "We are creating the first viral health insurance company, how weird is that," the partners began to joke, according to cofounder Mario Schlosser.

In October, 80 percent of Oscar's modest number of enrollees had come directly from the state insurance exchange website (though they, too, might have heard of Oscar because of the company's cool-looking ads and social media buzz). However, by January only 20 percent of the much larger number of enrollees had started on the state exchange website. The other 80 percent had been directed there after going to the hioscar.com website or contacting Oscar by phone or email.

Schlosser said that the first week following January 1 when coverage went into effect had been "a little scary." Several seriously ill patients had immediately sought treatment. Although Schlosser and his partners had expected some pent-up demand from those previously uninsured, seeing people, mostly with cancer, actually start racking up five- and six-figure bills was still head turning. "But," said Schlosser, "we're not sitting there saying, 'Oh, shit, she's got cancer.' That's the business we chose to be in. People here are excited to take care of someone. And," he added, "we want her to go to Sloan Kettering because it may be more expensive in the short run, but she'll get better care, which will be better for her and probably for us in the long run."

Beyond that, Kushner and his partners and their now forty-two employees seemed as exhilarated as they had been the week before their launch—in fact, more so because the dashboards lighting the wall were reporting real numbers in real time that continued to be encouraging.

Their customers were already heavily engaged with Oscar. Ninety-eight percent had created online accounts, and 57 percent had already searched for doctors and other providers on Oscar's easy-to-use website.

Perhaps most encouraging was that 65 percent had entered their health profiles, which would now be supplemented every time they went to a doctor, used the telemedicine service, or were prescribed a drug. These real-time profiles would enable Oscar, for example, to send emails reminding them when a prescription had to be refilled, and, of course, to feed Schlosser's data analytics machine.

Kushner and his partners could tell how many patients were using the telemedicine service or taking advantage of the free generics. They liked what they saw when comparing the cost of all that to what the data said they had saved in more expensive care and gained in the goodwill their patient feedback reports said they were accumulating. Which in turn was fueling the data on where their new business was coming from: word of mouth and social media referrals to their website.

Another dashboard tracked member calls to the customer service center or to the telemedicine doctors (ten to fifteen calls a day). Three or more calls from the same patient to either service in a seven-day period created an alert, which someone higher up at Oscar had to investigate.

That system had given them a heads-up on their first screwup, a woman who had been mistakenly denied a mammogram because the outsourced service that vetted radiology procedures had mislabeled her request.

OBAMA ON THE ATTACK

On January 28, 2014, Obamacare was back in the headlines. The president devoted a portion of his State of the Union address to it, attacking House Republicans for now having voted repeatedly and fruitlessly to repeal it. "Now, I don't expect to convince my Republican friends on the merits of this law," he said. "But let's not have another forty-something votes to repeal a law that's already helping millions of Americans. . . . The first forty were plenty. . . . We all owe it to the American people to say what we're for, not just what we're against."

Then Obama introduced a guest in the House of Representatives gallery: "If you want to know the real impact this law is having, just talk to Governor Steve Beshear of Kentucky, who's here tonight. Kentucky's not the most liberal part of the country, but he's like a man possessed when it comes to covering his commonwealth's families. 'They are our friends and neighbors,' he said. 'They are people we shop and go to church with . . . farmers out on the tractors . . . grocery clerks . . . they are people who go to work every morning praying they don't get sick. No one deserves to live that way.' Steve's right. That's why, tonight, I ask every American who knows someone without health insurance to help them get covered by March thirty-first."

In the Republican response that night, Congresswoman Cathy McMorris Rodgers of Washington State cited a constituent whose policy had been canceled and was about to be forced to pay $700 a month more in order to comply with the mandate. *The Spokesman-Review* newspaper in Spokane, Washington, quickly reported that the policy the woman could buy to replace her canceled insurance might cost $400 or $500 more, not $700, and would provide much more complete coverage.

However, the congresswoman was right, in the sense that Obamacare had its share of winners—like the cancer-afflicted Sean Recchi, or the Brown family in Beshear's Kentucky—and losers. That was inevitable. "No gay couple is going to want to pay for insurance that has maternity coverage," PhRMA's Billy Tauzin complained to me. Maybe, but for years, women have had to buy insurance that included treatment for prostate cancer.

OBAMACARE'S CLEAREST WINNERS

Throughout the first weeks of 2014 there did seem to be one clear group of winners—the healthcare industry. The day Obama delivered his State of the Union speech, Amgen chief executive Robert Bradway hosted a conference call with stock analysts to discuss his year-end results. Amgen is the pharmaceutical company with the master lobbyist who had been so concerned about how biologics would be protected. And CEO Bradway had been part of Tauzin's PhRMA executive committee that oversaw PhRMA's negotiations with Baucus's staff.

On the conference call, Bradway reported that his company's operating income had grown by 24 percent, and that the dividend was being increased 30 percent, after having been increased 31 percent in 2013.

As for the first year when the Obamacare mandate would be in place and the exchanges up and running—"we expect solid growth in revenues and adjusted earning per share during 2014," Bradway said.

An Amgen executive vice president provided a window on how pharmaceutical companies like his have used television and print advertising—allowed in the United States but not in Canada or Europe—to generate rapid growth and defend the company from other brands, including less expensive generics. Referring to Enbrel, an Amgen arthritis and psoriasis drug, he noted, "Our investment in direct-to-consumer advertising with [pro golfer] Phil Mickelson continues to drive brand awareness, which is important as physicians continue to honor over 90 percent of Enbrel patient requests. We remain the value share leader in both rheumatology and the dermatology segments and we're confident in Enbrel's potential growth. . . . In the U.S., our direct-to-consumer campaign has been very successful."

He noted that another Amgen brand, Prolia, "is now the most requested brand by new postmenopausal osteoporosis patients. We are launching a new campaign with [actress] Blythe Danner in the next few weeks to continue raising patient awareness."

In 2013, Amgen spent $5.18 billion on what its annual report called "selling, general and administrative" expenses, much of which would have been advertising and marketing. The same year it spent $4.01 billion on "research and development" and $3.35 billion to produce its products. It reported operating income of $5.87 billion.

INEFFECTIVE COMPARATIVE EFFECTIVENESS

One aspect of Obamacare that did not seem to be bothering Amgen's Bradway or any other drug company CEO was the new law's provision for an independent panel that would vet the comparative effectiveness of different drugs, devices, and treatment protocols. This was the rule that the drug and device industries had fought so hard to water down, in part by requiring a large board that included industry members, and in larger part by requiring that Medicare could not make any decisions about whether to pay for various treatments or drugs based on the panel's findings.

Comparative effectiveness had been one of Peter Orszag's pet issues when he was Obama's budget director. On January 28, 2014, the same day that Bradway held his conference call and Obama delivered his State of the Union address, Orszag, who now worked for Citigroup, weighed in with an op-ed article at Bloomberg News in which he criticized what the comparative effectiveness panel had done in the nearly four years since Obamacare had become law—which was not much.

Entitled "The Vital Medical Research Obama Isn't Pushing," Orszag outlined the intended purpose of the panel this way: "So-called comparative effectiveness research is needed to find out, for example, whether spinal fusion surgery works better than the alternatives in relieving back pain, or whether proton beam therapy is worth the extra cost to treat prostate cancer."

However, he wrote, citing a recently released Center for American Progress study, in the nearly four years since Obamacare had become law, "So far, only 37 percent of [the comparative effectiveness panel's] research funding has gone to comparing two or more treatments. . . . A full 25 percent of the budget has been dedicated to 'communications tools and education initiatives.' Communication and education are important, but right now the crucial objective should be generating the raw information to be communicated."

Worse, Orszag wrote, "out of the 284 studies the [panel] has funded to date, only 34 (or 12 percent) address" any of the subject areas that the Institute of Medicine had identified as the highest priorities for such research. In fact, according to the Center for American Progress report that Orszag cited, there had been no studies done of the effectiveness of expensive medical devices such as neurostimulators for back pain and artificial knees, and only 3 percent of the comparative effectiveness panel's funded studies were directed at drugs. The president needs to put the panel "back on track," Obama's former budget director wrote.

OBAMA GOES *BETWEEN TWO FERNS*

With the rebuilt website improving steadily, the Obama team could now turn to what they were good it—campaigning, in this case for sign-ups.

Anne Filipic was ramping up for the final push, targeting her "Get Covered, America" campaign to eleven states, including Ohio, Texas, and Florida, where the numbers of uninsured were highest and the likelihood that the Republican-controlled state government would run its own campaigns was lowest.

Filipic had arranged "partnerships," she told me, with 2,300 civic, religious, union, and healthcare organizations across the country. Using the demographic targeting data from Civis, the Chicago-based company founded by the Obama campaign whiz kids, her people would end up having conversations with 670,000 consumers, reach 2.5 million by email, draw 1.85 million unique visitors to its website, and stage 22,000 rallies, meetings, and other outreach events.

And then there were the White House–run efforts. They culminated in a promotional coup that began, according to *Politico,* with a plea that Valerie Jarrett, communications director Jennifer Palmieri, and press secretary Jay Carney made to Obama on February 12, 2014. Jarrett had met the day before with actor Bradley Cooper, who suggested that Obama should go on *Between Two Ferns,* the online mock interview show hosted by comedian Zach Galifianakis, to push Obamacare to Galifianakis's mass audience of young invincibles.

Obama was game. The gig was planned for the following month, in the run-up to the March 31 deadline.

"THE BEST DAY IN THE HISTORY OF
THE AFFORDABLE CARE ACT"

On February 12, 2014, the same day Obama was recruited for *Between Two Ferns,* HHS secretary Kathleen Sebelius announced startling enrollment figures for the prior month. As of the end of January, more than 3.3 million people had signed up on the state or federal exchanges, with 1.1 million having signed up in January alone. Rather than the pace dropping off after the December 24 deadline (for insurance coverage starting January 1, 2014), it had actually picked up, and was likely to accelerate more as the overall enrollment deadline of March 31 approached.

"Yesterday, politically, was the best day in the history of the Affordable Care Act," journalist Mark Halperin said the next morning on MSNBC's *Morning Joe.* "They are now in a stronger position to get this implemented than they ever have been."

That February 12 surprise overshadowed the bad news from the day before—when the Obama administration announced that most of the employers who would have been subject to the mandate requiring them to provide health insurance to their workers would be granted yet another delay. In July 2013 they had been given a free pass for 2014. Now the mandate was lifted for most employers for 2015, too. That would knock a total of $19 billion (in expected employer penalties) off the revenue CBO had projected for Obamacare.

The deadline was changed not by Congress, which had ostensibly been guided by the CBO's scoring in voting for the law, but by a unilateral Obama administration decision.[22]

With that change, and others, I now counted nearly $100 billion in negative changes by executive fiat since the CBO had scored the law as being deficit neutral. And that didn't include the $200 billion in costs

---

22. Republicans in the House of Representatives would vote in July to sue the president for allegedly overstepping his authority in making this decision.

put aside when the Democrats had scrapped the doc fix, but promised to put it into another law.

Two months later, the CBO would announce that it was no longer going to score changes in the rules and schedules related to Obamacare because there were so many and they were so interrelated with other revenue and expense drivers.

STILL A FLAWED MARKET

On February 13, 2014, *The Wall Street Journal* published a long feature under the headline "For Many, Few Health Plan Choices, High Premiums on Online Exchanges." The article provided a different kind of reminder of the healthcare market's continuing problems.

A "study shows that hundreds of thousands of Americans in poorer counties have few choices of health insurers and face high premiums," the paper reported. "Consumers in 515 counties, spread across 15 states, have only one insurer selling coverage through the online marketplaces, the *Journal* found. In more than 80 percent of those counties, the sole insurer is a local Blue Cross & Blue Shield plan. Residents of wealthier, more populated counties in the U.S. receive lower-priced choices than those living in counties with a single insurer."

In some wealthier areas, such as near the Colorado ski resorts, prices were also unusually high. But the real message of the *Journal* story was plain to anyone drilling down into the offerings of insurance companies on the exchanges across the country. For many people, even with generous subsidies, insurance coverage was going to be unaffordable, or at least a major burden. Millions of families would be victims of the compromise that the Democrats had forged. To keep the law's overall cost down, they could not make the subsidies more generous—a compromise forced by the reality of the larger compromise they were making: creating a law that extended coverage by buying it in a market where the underlying prices for medical care were by far the highest in the world.

For example, suppose a couple we'll call the Johnsons, each sixty-three years old, lived in Florida, and their kids were out of the house. Suppose, too, that they ran a small boat-chartering business that made them $62,000—just below 400 percent of the poverty line for a family of two adults. That meant that they would qualify for a subsidy of $9,024 to pay for their insurance.

But even with that $9,024 subsidy, they would pay about $5,000 a year in premiums (depending on the plan they chose). On top of that, they would still have a deductible of about $12,000. That meant the Johnsons' total medical costs (premium and amounts paid to meet the deductible) could take $17,000 ($5,000 in premiums, plus $12,000 in deductibles), or 27 percent, out of their $62,000 in pre-tax income. To be sure, that would happen only if the Johnsons suffered enough medical mishaps to reach their deductible limit, and it does not account for the fact that Obamacare offered them a lot of preventive care for free, with no deductible. But if they did reach that deductible limit, it seemed a stretch to call a law requiring them to pay 27 percent of their income to comply with the mandate the "Affordable Care Act."

Yet the news would get even worse if the Johnsons made even $50 more than what we just postulated was their $62,000 income. That's because of a little-noticed quirk in the law that industry insiders called "the cliff."

An income at 400 percent of the poverty line was $62,040 for a family of two like the Johnsons. Up to that amount, they would get a subsidy. But if they earned any more than that, even a dollar more, they would get no subsidy. In other words, earning an extra $50 would cost them their entire $9,024 subsidy. They would be "taxed" $9,024 on an extra $50 of income.

That meant that insurance and out-of-pocket costs (again, assuming they had enough in medical bills to hit their deductible) would cost this family, now making $62,050, an unaffordable $26,000. After taxes, that would probably be half of their disposable income. And even if they enjoyed perfect health and never had to pay a penny toward their deductible, their premiums would still be $14,000 a year—a huge expense (22 percent of their income) for a family earning just over $62,040 before taxes.

Only a small percentage of people signing up for the exchanges were likely to fall over that steep a cliff, though many would likely face the crunch—27 percent of income—that the Johnsons would face even with a subsidy. Those going over the cliff would mostly be older people, like the Johnsons, in expensive healthcare states whose income was just over 400 percent of the poverty level. Younger people, to whom insurance companies were charging lower rates, or people in lower healthcare cost states, where all premiums are likely to be lower, were less likely to qualify for substantial subsidies if they had incomes approaching the 400 percent of poverty line, and, therefore, would not lose much if they went over the line.

Yet in a program that was hoping to sign up seven million people in just the first year, this could leave tens of thousands on the exchanges who would come close to or fall over a steep cliff. That would be a lot of families, and a lot of anecdotes for the president's opponents when those people realized what had happened to them later in 2014 or in 2015, when the government would complete a check of how their incomes matched up to their subsidies.

That, too, presented a looming problem. Even with all the progress that had been made, the Obamacare website's system for verifying the incomes that people list in order to get subsidies was gummed up, much the way Larry Summers had predicted it would be in those White House meetings during 2009. It was likely to take months or years for the government to notify those receiving subsidies that they seemed to have understated their incomes, either innocently or deliberately, and must submit additional documentation or face demands for the subsidies to be returned to the IRS.

"I'm already advising some clients who may be at or near the cliff to watch their incomes toward the end of the year," said Barry Cohen, who was Sean and Stephanie Recchi's insurance agent, when I asked him about this in February 2014. "Maybe they can stop working overtime or take a month off. If not, they could get hammered with huge tax bills that they never expected."

MORE FRIDAY NIGHT REGULATIONS AND
MORE PULLBACKS FROM THE LAW

On Friday night, March 14, 2014, CMS issued 335 pages of new Obamacare regulations, documenting a further retreat from the original law.

Grandfathering restrictions on insurance plans that did not meet the law's coverage requirements were loosened yet again. Now people with those plans had until 2016 before they had to get new insurance or be in violation of the mandate. Also, insurance companies were allowed not to count the additional costs of having to do the extra work related to the website's problems in calculating administrative costs under the medical loss ratio, meaning they would not be penalized for spending whatever extra money for administration versus paying claims that they could claim resulted from the government's technology failures.

Perhaps most important over the long term, CMS also announced in the Friday night filing that it was going to clamp down on insurance companies whose networks were too narrow.

This meant that two key components of the law now faced additional risk. The individual mandate would be weakened by the exemption given people holding those old, insufficient policies. And the cost savings that could come from narrow networks might be undermined. Both were political necessities given the hostility to the law that the polls continued to report. But each tampered with the law's financial equilibrium.

All of these changes fed a new question that was now competing with the drama of how many enrollments the Obama team would end up with on March 31: Would all of these retreats, plus the current enrollment numbers that still showed a disproportionately low number of younger enrollees, force insurers to raise their premiums drastically when they had to start filing their rates for the 2015 year?

"O-Care Premiums to Skyrocket," reported *The Hill,* a newspaper distributed on Capitol Hill. The article quoted unnamed insurance industry officials, one of whom said he expected his rates to triple. That story was widely picked up online and circulated in industry circles.

The speculation about the premiums was just that. No one really knew what the insurance companies were going to do. Besides, whatever the insurance companies did would have little to do with how they calculated premiums over the longer term. That was because by May 2014—when they would have to start filing their rates for 2015—they would have only four or five months of data about their actual customer base and the claims they had made and were, therefore, likely to make in the future. In subsequent years, they would have lots more data.

More important, most of the press covering the drama of how high premiums would go routinely linked that question to whether customers, especially the younger, healthier ones, would get sticker shock and decide not to buy. Yet that ignored the core reality of Obamacare and its premium subsidy provision. Under the law, the amount of a premium subsidy was geared to a limit that people with incomes below four times the poverty line could be asked to pay for the second lowest priced "silver" plan available to them.

So, if the most I could pay for that silver plan was, say, 7.5 percent of my income, and the cost of that plan went up by $100, but my income stayed the same, my subsidy—the government's cost, not my cost—would go up by that $100. Higher premium rates—assuming the second lowest priced silver plan went up as much as the other plans—were mostly a problem for taxpayers in general, not for these consumers.

THE FINAL BLITZ

While guesses about premium increases for year two persisted, team Obama began its final campaign push for year one. A press announcement on March 11, 2014, promised that two thousand phone operators were being added to the crew of twelve thousand to handle the expected end-of-March surge, and that the administration's "aggressive outreach is helping to make a difference." How much of a difference? No one would offer a prediction.

Also on March 11, the edgiest gambit in that outreach effort—Obama's appearance with Galifianakis on *Between Two Ferns*—went live. It became a viral sensation, snaring eleven million YouTube views and spiking traffic on HealthCare.gov 40 percent higher than it had ever been.

Better yet, the site handled the traffic.

Between Two Ferns was the culmination of a two-month blitz that featured more than three hundred radio appearances by Obama and his team, including Jarrett, and thousands of events organized by his political operation and by Filipic's Enroll America. This was team Obama's sweet spot, something they knew how to do.

On March 11, the Obama administration was suddenly able to get the up-to-the-minute numbers that Sebelius and Tavenner had told Congress and the press in the fall were not available. On a conference call with Enroll America and other volunteers that day, Obama announced that there were now 4.2 million enrollees, with the number going up by the minute. They had added 900,000 in just the last eleven days, and the surge ahead of the deadline was still to come.

At about one o'clock on Saturday afternoon, March 15, Obama made a surprise call into the speakerphone at the command center to thank Todd Park, Mikey Dickerson, and their team, and to urge them on for the final push. Using examples of newly insured families, he told them how meaningful their work was. Some of the coders had tears in their eyes.

By now Park was back in the Maryland control room, all day, every day. Dickerson, too, had come back from Google for the final push. Jini Kim, the Google star who had been working on her own health-care data analytics start-up, had never left.

By the beginning of the last week in March, they were nearing 6 million sign-ups for the combined state and federal exchanges. The 7 million target suddenly seemed possible.

Then the real surge began. By March 24, they were enrolling well over 100,000 a day just on the federal exchange, the same or more than they had done on the December 23 deadline day. Sometimes the phone lines were overloaded, and some people had to wait for a few minutes online. But everything held together.

On March 31, the last day, 209,000 people enrolled on the federal exchange, nearly double the number that had signed up in all of October and November. By midnight, the total was 4.8 million on the federal exchange.

The state exchanges, with notable exceptions (Maryland, Minnesota, Oregon) hummed along, too. By midnight they had 2.3 million.

The grand total was 7.1 million, 100,000 above the original target. That night, QSSI, the UnitedHealthcare subsidiary that was the general contractor working with the surge team and whose office housed the command center, invited everyone down to the building lobby to celebrate. They toasted themselves with champagne outside the Smile Center.

ANOTHER CAPITOL HILL "EMERGENCY"

Another milestone, little noticed outside Capitol Hill and in the medical community, was also reached on March 31, 2014. It was a reminder that the website might have been fixed, but Washington wasn't.

Congress passed an eleventh-hour emergency doc fix to put off the unrealistic, formula-driven reductions in Medicare's payments to doctors that had been passed in 1997 and suspended at the last minute sixteen times since.

It had to be done that way because of the Obama team's broken promise to the American Medical Association (see page 154) that, in return for its support of Obamacare, a permanent fix would be included in the healthcare reform law. That provision had then been thrown overboard as the law was coming up for a vote, because keeping it out of the bill would produce a much more favorable Congressional Budget Office score. The doctors had then been promised, however, that once Obamacare was passed, the Democrats would get a permanent fix voted on separately. Now that, too, had not happened; thus emergency fix number seventeen.

GOING OVER EIGHT MILLION

The next day, April 1, 2014, Obama trumpeted the enrollment numbers in a Rose Garden ceremony. Sebelius, Jarrett, and McDonough, all smiling, sat together in the front row. Park and his team, however, took little time to celebrate. Yet another set of rule changes issued by CMS allowed anyone who had started an application to continue to complete it up until April 15. So the rescue squad had to keep the website humming.

By April 15, the federal and state exchanges together passed eight million sign-ups, a million more than the rosiest projection before the launch. And 28 percent were eighteen-to-thirty-four-year-olds—the coveted young invincibles. That was below the original target of 30 to 40 percent but close enough to avert the disastrous demographic "death spiral" that would have come if few young people had signed up, forcing insurers to raise premiums to cover the riskier older customers, which, in turn, would have discouraged still more younger customers.

And because younger people were less likely to be early buyers, it seemed likely that more would be attracted after the first year, especially if the subsidies that made their actual premiums so low were emphasized in the second year. In fact, soon after the enrollment period ended, Enroll America's Anne Filipic issued a report analyzing her organization's efforts, in which she concluded that her messaging in 2015 should put much more emphasis on the generous federal subsidies.

In addition to the eight-million-plus exchange enrollees, approximately six million more Americans had been enrolled in Medicaid as a result of Obamacare's expansion of the program to those states that decided to allow it.

That meant a total of fourteen million enrollees.

Almost thirteen million of those fourteen million were getting subsidies or getting their coverage for free—all six million Medicaid recipients, plus 87 percent of the eight million people in the exchanges.

"This thing is working," said Obama, taking another victory lap in the White House press room on April 17.

In May, Obama invited the tech surge team, including Mikey Dickerson, to an East Room celebration honoring them and Anne Filipic's Enroll America troops. (Todd Park told me Dickerson actually dressed up for the occasion in "a jacket over the T-shirt.") When Obama called out Dickerson and his crew, the room spontaneously erupted in a chant, "Tech team, tech team."

A few weeks later, White House CTO Todd Park described to me how a new version of the website—"Marketplace 2.0"—was being staffed by alumni of the tech team and some of their Silicon Valley colleagues. It was, he said, being built in modules "according to Silicon Valley best practices," and designed for any and all mobile screens. And it was going to be tested on 1 percent of the population and then broader test groups before being rolled out for the 2015 enrollment year that would begin November 15.

That radical change in approach was not the only lesson learned from the October 2013 debacle. The Obama administration also decided that the HealthCare.gov website should get—guess what?—someone in charge.

Kathleen Sebelius had left as secretary of health and human services in April, once the initial enrollment period was over. She had been replaced by Office of Management and Budget director Sylvia Burwell, a seasoned manager. One of Burwell's first announcements was that she was going to hire an exchange CEO.[23] And that CEO, she said, was going to report to Burwell's new chief operating officer—Andrew Slavitt. Slavitt is the executive from the UnitedHealthcare subsidiary who had overseen the tech surge team, including Mikey Dickerson—and had tried to recruit them to join his UnitedHealthcare unit because it was, he promised, going to become the Google of healthcare.

To top that, in August, the Obama administration announced that Mikey Dickerson, who had been pursued by Todd Park, had been hired to run a new "U.S. Digital Service," which a White House press release described as "a small team of the country's best digital experts that will work in collaboration with other government agencies to make websites more customer friendly, to identify and fix problems, and to help upgrade the government's technology infrastructure."

Meanwhile, lawsuits were flying around pitting states whose own exchanges had crashed, such as Oregon, Minnesota, and Maryland, against their contractors. It was a reminder that the federal government didn't have a monopoly on public works mismanagement.

OVER THE TOP AT OSCAR

In Manhattan, Joshua Kushner, Mario Schlosser, and Kevin Nazemi didn't get their final enrollment files from the state until the third week in April 2014.

---

23. In August, Kevin Counihan, who had run the successful Connecticut exchange, was appointed CEO of the federal exchange.

The numbers were terrific.

The tally was 15,800—more than double the projections Oscar had given prospective investors. In the final weeks, Oscar got an impressive 10 percent share of everyone who enrolled in the New York counties where Oscar competed. If it matched that market share next year, it would reach in two years the 40,000 customers Kushner and his partners had projected for the end of the third year.

Their start-up expenses had run according to plan, but the medical claims Oscar had to pay out were running higher. They had hoped to get to a medical loss ratio—the amount of claims they paid out as a percentage of the premiums they received—of 87 percent by year-end. It now looked like it would be about 90 percent. However, they were confident that they could get the ratio under control by digging into the data to discover more ways their customers could cut bills while getting as good or better care, and by expanding the risk pool with customers beyond those who had enrolled in the first year and spreading the resulting larger premium revenue across stable costs for administration and infrastructure.

By April, Kushner and his partners had raised more than $150 million. They were going to use it to expand into New Jersey in 2015 and into parts of Texas and California the following year. A majority of the money was from third parties, not Kushner or his own investment firm.

Oscar—which by April had seventy employees, up from forty-two in January—was hot. On paper, its value, based on the percentage of the company that the last investors got for the amount they invested, was $700 million.

They had tried, Kushner and his partners told me after the March enrollment tallies came in, to learn from their early mistakes. Now all customer calls were routed to their office in the Puck Building first, before the routine ones—a customer asking about an ID card or a provider asking about an unpaid invoice—were sent to their outsourced call center in Ohio. Any caller there who asked for a supervisor was routed back to them in New York.

"By us being here next to the [twenty people] getting calls," Kushner explained, "we can see problems in the system and keep improving the system quickly."

The biggest immediate challenge following the end of the enrollment period was preparing their 2015 rates for New York and, now, for New Jersey. "Last year, when we started, everyone was working from the same data sold by the same consultants," explained Schlosser. "Now we had our own data from our own customers and our own costs from our own providers. But it was only four or five months' worth, and we had no idea what the other guys would do with their data. . . . Once you file the prices you can't change them for the whole year," Schlosser added. "We also now knew that premium prices really counted. Would someone go crazy and undercut everyone?"

By September, with ninety staff members and three dozen more due by the end of the year, Oscar was deep into staffing up for its New Jersey launch and recruiting for its 2016 forays into Texas and California.

KENTUCKY WINS THE DERBY, MRS. BROWN SEES A DOCTOR, AND MCCONNELL TREADS LIGHTLY

March 31, 2014, was "crazy busy," Carrie Banahan told me in early April. Her call center was inundated, even with 150 extra operators having been added. The website had a record number of visitors and concurrent users. But it never went down.

By midnight on March 31, Kentucky had enrolled an astounding 370,829 people out of 630,000 uninsured Kentuckians, or 58 percent.

The federal government had by now spent $840 million just to build its website—more than triple its original budget. Carrie Banahan and her team had spent less than $154 million of the $254 million Washington had made available to Kentucky for building the kynect site and for marketing it.[24]

---

24. The total federal budget for the technology, plus all the support staff and marketing, was $3.52 billion, which included the support paid to the fourteen states, including Kentucky, and to the District of Columbia, which built their own systems.

By April, Viola Brown—who had signed up on October 4 and been covered as of January 1—had been able to see three separate doctors who were "helping her with all kinds of problems," her husband, Tom, reported. She was getting the medication she needed to control her diabetes. More important, one of her new doctors had discovered a cardiac problem that had required urgent treatment.

In late May, Senate minority leader Mitch McConnell of Kentucky told a reporter for Louisville newspaper *LEO Weekly* that he favored repealing Obamacare—but wanted to keep his home state's now-popular kynect.

Kynect was, of course, Obamacare—enabled by Obamacare's Medicaid expansion, the individual mandate, and the premium subsidies. While still showing himself completely devoted to manning the partisan barricades, McConnell, who was facing what looked like a tough reelection campaign, was now apparently realizing that in Kentucky, at least, the program had been such a resounding success that he had to tiptoe around it.

In fact, by the end of July, so many more people in Kentucky had signed up for Medicaid, which was not limited by the April 15 enrollment deadline, or had had a changed life circumstance that allowed them to enroll on the exchange after the deadline (such as losing a job that had provided insurance), that 521,000 Kentuckians—12 percent of the state's population—were now covered under Obamacare. Everyone in Kentucky probably had benefited from, or knew someone who had benefited from, the law that McConnell had fought from the beginning.

In June, Viola Brown was told she might have to have open-heart surgery. But by August her doctor had decided that the medication she was taking seemed to be taking hold. She needed to be closely monitored—with regular visits to her cardiologist—but "for now," she told me, "I don't need the surgery.

"I'm probably alive because of kynect," she added.

PART FOUR

CHAPTER 24

STUCK IN THE JALOPY

THIS IS THE PART WHERE I AM SUPPOSED TO TELL YOU WHAT I MAKE of all this—what the Obamacare saga really means, what it portends, and what we might do about it.

First, the easy stuff that I was thinking about as the enrollment returns came in on March 31, 2014.

Do I wish that the National War Labor Board had ruled in 1943 that health insurance benefits did, in fact, count as wages and, therefore, that adding them would not be allowed under the wartime wage control regulations?

Sure. Along with the follow-on decision by the IRS that insurance benefits could be tax free, that was the fork in the road that set the United States off in the wrong direction—putting employers on track to be the primary providers of health insurance. That is a different path from that taken by every other developed country, all of which produce the same or better healthcare results than we do at a far lower cost. Without employers offering insurance to workers, the pressure on politicians to provide a public program would have been unstoppable.

America's dysfunctional healthcare house, with the bad plumbing and electricity, leaky roof, broken windows, and rotting floors, would never have been built and become so entrenched in its special interest foundations that it could not be torn down. We would have never been stuck with the broken-down jalopy that we could only repair piecemeal. Pick your favorite metaphor for the hurdles faced by reformers for the past seven decades.

Was the way that the bipartisan spirit of Max Baucus's June 2008 healthcare summit—when Senator Kent Conrad exclaimed, "This is what I thought the U.S. Senate would be like"—degenerated into a bitterly partisan fight and a government shutdown a national embarrassment?

Of course. The question is whether that summit is an artifact of a better time that is not coming back, or whether America will somehow overcome the way special interest money has forced so many Republicans and Democrats into their respective corners, avoiding compromise because they are more worried about challenges from the less moderate wings of their parties than they are about getting anything done.

Should we be amazed at how Barack Obama, who seemed not to care much about healthcare at that Las Vegas forum in 2007, became the president who refused to lose the fight for broad reform?

Yes. And we should admire him for it.

Should we also be amazed, and disappointed, at how Obama treated the nitty-gritty details of implementing the law as if actually governing was below the pay grade of Ivy League visionaries?

Absolutely. This failure to govern will stand as one of the great unforced disappointments of the Obama years.

Should we be embarrassed and maybe even enraged that the only way our country's leaders in Washington could reform healthcare was by making backroom deals with all the interests who wanted to make sure that reform didn't interfere with their profiteering?

Of course. We'll be paying the bill for that forever.

But should we blame Obama and Baucus for making those deals?

I don't think so. The Browns of Kentucky got healthcare because of those deals. They and six million others got Medicaid because of those deals. Eight million more got insurance on the exchanges, of whom 87 percent got government subsidies to buy it.

That's 14 million people with new insurance. Subtracting those whose policies were canceled even under the watered-down cancellation rules and who bought new coverage on the exchanges or went without insurance, that is still about 10.3 million newly insured Americans, according to an estimate in an August 28, 2014, report by *The New England Journal of Medicine*. As a result, in one year, the percentage of nineteen-to-sixty-four-year-old Americans who are uninsured dropped to 15 percent from 20 percent.

"Millions of Americans have gained access to affordable coverage, and some of the worst insurance company abuses are now things of the past," is how President Obama described the bottom line to me. He's right.

So, yes, given the choice, all those deals seem to have been worth it, because all of the realistic alternatives were worse.

At the same time, we should recognize that the quality of medical care is going to continue to be jeopardized by the broken economics of the marketplace, which provides rich incentives to everyone except those actually treating all of these newly covered patients. As doctors remain bogged down in paperwork and face mounting business pressures, the portion of our best and brightest who want to care for the sick instead of cashing in on the business of healthcare is likely to drop.

From 2011 to 2013, the median physicians' and surgeons' income in the United States rose 1.4 percent, to $187,200. In just one year, from 2011 to 2012 (the last year for which complete figures are available), total cash compensation for the CEOs of nonprofit hospitals surveyed by the trade publication *Modern Healthcare* grew an average (a median was not provided) of 24.2 percent, to $2.2 million. And from 2011 to 2013, total compensation paid to the CEO of drugmaker Amgen rose 92.3 percent, to $13.6 million.

Is Obamacare going to take its place alongside Medicare and Social Security as a broadly popular program that strengthens the legacy of the Democratic Party?

Probably not anytime soon, and maybe never. It's more likely that polls will continue to find that a majority of Americans disapprove of the new law. Beyond the lingering reputational stain of the bungled launch, there's the reality that unlike Social Security and Medicare, Obamacare was directed at a minority—the roughly 20 percent of people who were uninsured and another 5 to 10 percent (depending on your definition) who, like the Recchis, were underinsured. The rest of us were essentially unaffected, except that when our employers raised our deductibles or co-pays—because healthcare costs kept going up— they now had something and someone to blame it on. They could, and usually did, say that their cutbacks were because of Obamacare. President Obama took on all the baggage of our healthcare system when he took on healthcare reform. And Republicans aren't likely to help him or any other Democrat any time soon improve on the law by agreeing to even the most obvious fixes.

Is it depressing to see that Washington, surrounded with all those edifices re-minding everyone of our glorious history—the Capitol dome, the Supreme Court Building, the Jefferson and Lincoln memorials, the White House, the Washington Monument—has become so mired in cynicism and red tape that many of the best and brightest refuse to run the gauntlet of working there, or re-fuse to seek contracts to help the government do its work?

Yes, especially because that repellent climate creates a talent vacuum that allows people with less talent and little sense of mission to hang on to those jobs.

Was it painful to see one of the best and brightest who did serve, Liz Fowler, dragged down by Glenn Greenwald and other journalists, who assumed the worst, or knew readers would assume the worst, because in Washington that's not a bad assumption?

Definitely. And it's something we should think about every time we assume that everyone in public life is in it for himself or herself.

Should we be disgusted with the government procurement and technology management system that produced the October 1, 2013, version of HealthCare.gov?

What other reaction could there be to a system that rewards an insular group of Beltway contractors who have never met a botched product, cost overrun, or missed deadline they can't pin on someone else?

Does the relentless, magical work of the tech team led by Todd Park, Jeffrey Zients, and Mikey Dickerson—who cared nothing about gaining glory or money for what they did—suggest that America's troubles have more to do with what Washington has become than what the American people have become?

Obviously, yes. And their work should stand as a reminder of what Washington could be like if, even without an emergency like the one this team swooped in to fix, we could attract more talented, motivated people to work there.

Despite Todd Park and company's work on the website and the new appointment of experienced managers to run the exchange, will government contracting by well-connected incompetents really change now that the crisis has passed? Will someone like the newly recruited Mikey Dickerson really be able to change such an embedded Washington culture, or will the contracting establishment inside and outside the government reject this T-shirted transplant?

I'm skeptical. But maybe government really can be moved to fix itself when a crisis like the website launch debacle shines a spotlight on the need for change. "Mikey Dickerson now works at the White House (frequently without a jacket or tie)," the president told me. "And he is leading an effort to simplify and improve digital services to help make sure America's government can be innovative, flexible, and help bring in the talent we need. . . . I have sent a very clear mandate throughout this administration that it is time to shake things up, change the pace of business."

Perhaps, but on July 8, 2014, CGI won another federal contract qualifying the company to do multiple projects for the General Services Administration.

Should we admire Oscar and its founders and be glad that Obamacare gave birth to their different kind of insurance company?

Sure. However, the harder question is whether Oscar's consumer-centric ethos, cool technology, and commonsense use of telemedicine and free generics can overcome the reality that insuring against the cost of hospital bills, MRIs, and miracle drugs is not a terribly good business.

Are we fooling ourselves by assuming that with even the best website, health insurance can be bought with the ease of choosing an airplane ticket?

Of course.

"What you saw towards the end of the last open enrollment, when the Marketplaces were working," Obama told me, "was that for the first time, people could compare plans, side by side, and see exactly what they were going to pay for coverage that met their families' needs."

Not really. According to consumer research firm J. D. Power, users of the exchanges found significantly more ease and satisfaction with the enrollment experience when they enrolled in person or by phone with the help of a navigator or agent. Other surveys found that people typically paid attention only to the monthly premium, not the deductible, the co-insurance, or the maximum out-of-pocket provisions, which could end up being more important than a $30 or $50 difference in the monthly premium. In fact, many consumers did not even know what those other terms meant. Nor was it easy to tell what hospitals or doctors were in an insurer's network, much less whether that insurer had negotiated a better deal with a hospital than another insurer (which would mean that even the same co-insurance percentage could produce a lower out-of-pocket cost).

So, yes, Obamacare provided more coverage, but its exchanges aren't doing for healthcare what travel websites did for buying airplane tickets. In fact, while travel agents have been largely pushed aside by travel websites, the Obamacare exchanges create more need for insurance agents.

Beyond all that, does the Affordable Care Act really provide affordable care?

Yes, for millions of Americans. But not for everyone. Millions of others, particularly in the middle class, will continue to struggle to pay for healthcare.

The huge premium increases that some in the industry and the press speculated would come when the 2015 rates were filed mostly did not materialize. But increases still seem to have averaged about 8 percent, well above inflation.[25] And even with some of the large insurers, such as UnitedHealthcare, creating more competition by entering the exchange market more aggressively in 2015, premiums are destined to continue to increase as healthcare costs continue to rise. Insurance profit margins are so thin that premiums have to go up when claim costs go up.

Thus, insurance on the exchanges may not be affordable for the portions of the middle class whose subsidies to pay for it decline rapidly as incomes approach or exceed 300 percent of the poverty level—about $72,000 a year for a family of four—and zero out at 400 percent. More important, premiums in the much larger portion of the

---

25. There were lots of variations across the country, but generally premiums seem to have been raised 6 to 12 percent from the 2014 to the 2015 coverage year, with deductibles also increasing. A study by the PricewaterhouseCoopers consulting firm put the average increase at 8.2 percent. However, in some states, such as Florida, the increases were much higher. When Oscar filed its rates for 2015 on June 13, 2014, its average price increase was 5.3 percent.

market—employer-based insurance—are continuing to increase at the same or greater pace that they did in the years leading up to Obamacare.

Which only raises the other half of the same question.

Is Obamacare affordable for the country? Can we continue to let the healthcare industrial complex that negotiated those deals prosper at our expense when we have now given them so many millions of new customers whose bills taxpayers are paying through Medicaid or those exchange subsidy premiums?

It is hard to see how the country's budget or the budgets of American businesses and families can continue to shoulder that burden—a burden that continues to be a huge competitive disadvantage in a global economy.

"Frankly what we've seen in progress on costs has surpassed almost anybody's most optimistic expectations," the president insisted to me.

But there is actually little evidence of that.

True, some of the reforms that the Obama economic team were able to get into the law have worked incrementally. The new penalty that hospitals pay for Medicare patients who have to be readmitted within thirty days of being treated seems to have focused many hospitals on providing the care and follow-up that prevents these readmissions—despite the fact that the hospital lobby fought to make the penalty formula so low as to be almost negligible compared to the hospitals' overall revenue. And while the Medicare experiments in bundled care have produced mixed results in terms of actual savings, they, too, have focused providers on looking for alternatives to the conventional fee-for-service model.

However, these improvements have been marginal at best. The battles and closed-door deals of 2009 and 2010 emasculated the efforts by the White House economic team to use reform to "bend the cost curve." Like its Romneycare predecessor, Obamacare was the product of a choice—most would say a choice forced by political reality—to increase coverage first and deal with costs later, if ever. As a result, although there may be short-term lulls in cost increases related to the general economy or quirks such as the expiration of expensive drug patents, we seem destined to continue to spend 16 to 20 percent, and maybe more, of our gross domestic product on healthcare. Other countries will spend half to two-thirds of that with the same or better results.

When it comes to individuals and families, the bill will be the same 16 to 20 percent or more of their incomes, paid by a combination of money from the families' own wallets, employer contributions (paying for their workers' premiums, which results in lower wages), and, increasingly, the government, through Medicaid, Medicare, and the exchange premiums, which becomes part of a family's tax bill.

In fact, it will only get worse as employers continue to increase deductibles and blame it on Obamacare.

At the same time, less visible changes in the insurance rules governing who pays what—such as raises in co-payments and co-insurance rates for prescription drugs—continue to increase the burden on consumers.

With Obamacare, the government's share for protecting those who do not have employer-based coverage is destined to keep rising, too—because of the law's expanded Medicaid coverage and expensive premium subsidies, which will be only partially offset by the taxes, fees, and Medicare savings extracted in those deals with the industry.

WHEN YOU'RE LYING THERE "NAKED"

These questions seemed to have clear enough answers as I waited for the final enrollment numbers to arrive on March 31, 2014. Put simply: Obamacare gave millions of Americans access to affordable healthcare, or at least protection against not being able to pay for a catastrophic illness or being bankrupted by the bills. Now everyone has access to insurance and subsidies to help pay for it. That is a milestone toward erasing a national disgrace. But the new law hasn't come close to making health insurance premiums and out-of-pocket costs low enough so that healthcare is truly affordable to everyone, let alone affordable to the degree that it is in every other developed country.

More important, it hasn't done much to fix the healthcare system. It is just stuffing more people into the jalopy, which is only going to make the jalopy more expensive to keep running.

HAVING NOW SEEN THAT problem from so many sides, could I think of any practical, realistic ways to fix it?

That's the puzzle I was struggling with as the enrollment deadline neared on March 31. That is, that's what I was thinking about until about five o'clock that afternoon, when I sat with my wife in my doctor's office staring at his plastic mock-up of a heart. He showed us where the bubble was perched on my aorta. The aneurysm had grown so big that there was now a 15 to 17 percent chance every year that it would suddenly burst, he explained. When that happened, I would likely bleed to death before getting to the emergency room.

Three nights later, I was in the hospital, where I had that dream about the CEO of New York–Presbyterian Hospital stopping me as the gurney took me into the operating room

I later heard that New York–Presbyterian chief executive Steven Corwin, himself a heart surgeon, often reminded his employees that "when you're lying there in our hospital, you're naked in every way. Physically and emotionally. It's everyone's job here to understand that."

The people treating me understood that. And for a while it threw me. Was a journalist who questioned hospital administrators about the line items on their bills missing the forest for the trees?

It was hard not to think that amid the Mother Teresa care I got when I was terrified about coughing and blacking out, or when I woke up in a sweat with a nurse standing over me after I had relived my surgery in a dream.

However, over the next few days, I came around to a middle ground about how this experience balanced but did not crowd out my chargemaster view of the healthcare world.

It even helped me begin to frame an unusual idea for how we could go beyond Obamacare and fix American healthcare.

BEYOND OBAMACARE

The idea developed gradually during my weeks of recovery.

At first, pieces of it came in the form of seemingly random thoughts that popped up during the extra time I had to read and watch television. But they soon began to come together.

When I read that Republicans were making what was quickly proved to be the false charge that a large portion of the eight million people who had signed up on the exchanges were not paying their premiums, while also continuing to pursue a series of court challenges to the law, it was another reminder that the opposition, like the Japanese soldiers who hid out in the Philippines for years after World War II ended, was not about to give up anytime soon. By now, President Obama was clearly resigned to the continuing battle. "Keep in mind," he told me, "not only did the ACA become law, it was upheld by the Supreme Court in 2012, and, in the same year, voters rejected the candidate who promised to repeal it. Despite all that, you've seen a sustained effort to sabotage the law at every turn—from fifty-something repeal votes to efforts aimed at defunding its implementation, to lawsuits. This from a party that's typically opposed to frivolous lawsuits."

So, although Obamacare would generally fade as a Republican piñata in the November 2014 midterm elections, legislative fixes to Obamacare were not likely.

I began watching the networks' six-thirty evening news shows more regularly and homed in on something I had only casually noticed before: the predominance of drug ads. That provided a new window on the profit margins that motivate not only extravagant lobbying, but what I now saw was over-the-top media spending. One night, out of fourteen commercials on one broadcast, I counted nine for drugs. Five of them ran a full minute, instead of the usual thirty seconds, because the announcer had to fast-talk his way through an encyclopedia of dire warnings about side effects. I then began to notice the same thing in magazines. Again, the ads were typically extra long—two or three pages to cover all the warnings. It seemed like the drug industry was single-handedly propping up two declining media businesses—television's nightly newscasts and consumer magazines.

One of the ads I kept seeing was for Celebrex, which is used to treat arthritis and other muscle and joint pains. Along with eleven other prescriptions I had left the hospital with, I was taking two Celebrex pills a day.

I loved those white, blue-striped pills, though my surgeon had warned I should not stay on them too long because of possible side effects. The tagline for Celebrex on its website and ads was "For a body in motion." It rang true to me, and I admit I felt even better about taking it after seeing the ads, even with all the warnings.

I did some research after watching one of the TV spots and found out that Celebrex was pharmaceutical giant Pfizer's fourth largest selling drug in 2013 (ahead of Lipitor and Viagra), with sales of $2.9 billion.

I paid, or rather my insurance company paid, $50 for each pill. My neighborhood druggist paid a wholesaler about $49.50 for it. That's right; it's not the drugstores that thrive on the country's nearly $300 billion a year in prescription sales, although my local druggist no doubt paid more than one of the drugstore chains.

Based on what the usual industry profit chain looks like, Pfizer probably sold my pill to the wholesaler for about $48.

In 2013, Pfizer's actual incremental cost of producing and shipping its products, before counting expenses for marketing, overheard, or research and development, was 18.6 percent, yielding a gross profit margin of 81.4 percent. To keep the math simple, let's call it 80 percent.

If Celebrex fell within the range of that profit for all Pfizer products, it would mean that Pfizer's incremental profit on each of my $50 pills was $38.40 (80 percent of the $48 that Pfizer sold the pill to a wholesaler for). During my recovery, my insurance company was giving Pfizer $76.80 a day in profit for my two pills.

I also found that Pfizer had been involved in litigation over a deal it had tried to make with a generic drugmaker to extend its Celebrex patent, which was set to expire the month after I had started taking it, and thereby delay the generic company's entry into the market. These deals with generic companies were becoming increasingly controversial. But by then I had no reason to care about saving money on a generic rather than paying $50 for the real thing. I had long since exhausted the limits on my UnitedHealthcare policy of both my deductible and on my maximum out-of-pocket payout, so my cost for the drug was zero either way. Why not get the brand name I saw on television?

My newfound devotion to Celebrex and understanding of the profits it yielded was a reminder of how badly broken the healthcare marketplace is.

Which brings us to my insurance policy and my bills.[26]

MY CHARGEMASTER

Within two weeks of being discharged from the hospital, I had received thirty-six different first-class envelopes from UnitedHealthcare. Each had an Explanation of Benefits for a separate treatment related to my surgery—one for each prescription drug, one for each lab test done outside the hospital, one for each doctor, such as my anesthesiologist or my surgeon, and one covering my main hospital bill.

This was all the paperwork that the Oscar people had told me they were determined to eliminate by sending or emailing one explanation containing all the charges. However, when I checked, I found that UnitedHealthcare had an option I could have chosen to get these online. I also learned that Oscar was still sending these same notices, one by one, too. Unlike UnitedHealthcare, they had not yet found a way to get around regulations requiring them to use snail mail, and they had not found an outsourced vendor who could consolidate the notices. "We're hoping to get that done in the next few months," Oscar's Mario Schlosser told me. "We're building our own system, and because we're a start-up we've been super paranoid about all the regulations."

26. At the time, because the company I had started had been purchased by RR Donnelley, Donnelley was the provider of my UnitedHealthcare policy. Donnelley self-insured, meaning UnitedHealthcare processed the claims, but Donnelley reimbursed United for them.

By now, I was supposed to be able to understand medical bills and insurance notices, I thought. And I was so bored hanging around my house that I was even looking forward to diving in and translating them.

But several of the "explanations" were incomprehensible. One said the amount billed for one prescription was zero, but that I owed $152.84.

"I have no idea what that means; I would have no idea how to decode that," said Stephen Hemsley, the president and CEO of United-Health Group, when I handed that document to him across a conference table in his Minnetonka, Minnesota, office a few weeks later. "It should never be sent that way, but state regulations dictate how we have to communicate."

Hemsley promised to have his staff, one of whom was sitting next to him taking notes, send me the regulations that dictated that the explanation I got had to be worded that way. What I got instead were citations to general New York state and federal regulations that required that the explanations be sent but in no way required the incomprehensible wording I had received. In fact, one provision in the regulations seemed to require the opposite: "The notification shall set forth, in a manner calculated to be understood by the claimant . . ."[27]

What did it say about the competence and purpose of an industry, I thought, when the chief executive of its largest, most successful company can't explain the most basic communication he sends to his customers?

The most voluminous Explanation of Benefits had to do with the hospital bill, which was actually in two documents because the anesthesiology, $5,071, was separate from the rest of the bill: $149,872.50 for my surgery and eight-day stay. (My surgeon's $19,400 was also separate, as was a $23,000 bill for a cardiac catheterization.)

---

27. I was later told by someone on Hemsley's staff that because a pharmacy benefit manager handled prescription payments for UnitedHealthcare, United, for some reason, did not record it as an amount billed to the insurer and, therefore, with no further explanation, put zero in as the "amount billed" in those situations. This explanation also didn't shed light on why an amount billed was listed on the Explanations of Benefits United sent me related to many of the other drugs.

The $150,000 bill was a chargemaster aficionado's dream, all twenty-two single-spaced pages of it. Blood and urine tests and intra-venous supplies of various fluids—which Medicare would pay $10 to $15 dollars for—were billed at $19.84 to $308.97 each. There were 124 of these charges on the first six pages of the bill.

In all, according to an estimate provided to me by New York–Presbyterian's finance office, which I checked against the Medicare bill coding database, Medicare would have paid a total of $60,000 to $70,000 to cover this $150,000 bill.

Every aspirin I got was $0.13, which is lower than the charge on other hospital chargemasters I had seen, yet still a markup of 400 to 500 percent for an item you can buy in a drugstore for two or three cents a pill.

"Patient education"—whatever that was, which apparently had happened on the day of my surgery, according to the bill—was $82.69.

Every time a cheerful guy had wheeled in the portable x-ray ma-chine to check my battered chest, which was once or twice a day, that was $451.59.

Three days after the surgery, someone spent what I remembered was fifteen or twenty minutes explaining that I should begin trying to walk the halls, which I had already started to do on my own. On the bill that had become "Physical Therapy Initial Eval," for $351.79. Under that was "PT Therapeutic Exercises," presumably for when he walked me down the hall, for $186.54.

One item was missing from the New York–Presbyterian charge-master that I had often seen on other hospital bills listed as a "cough suppressant" for $50 or $100: the heart-shaped, firm red pillow with the logo of the hospital's cardiac service that a nurse had given me to clutch to my chest whenever I felt a cough coming. Yet pretty much everything else in the chargemaster playbook was there.

All of those hundreds of miscellaneous items were on top of room and board, which was $63,000, plus a $3,750 charge because I chose a private room once I got out of the cardiac intensive care unit.

But the biggest surprise was at the bottom of the bill.

UnitedHealthcare's discount for the total of all of these crazy charges was just 12 percent!

New York–Presbyterian was keeping 88 percent of that $351.79 chargemaster charge for a few minutes of "Physical Therapy Initial Eval," not to mention the $63,000 for eight days of room and board and the inflated prices for lab tests and fluids.

How could that be? The hospitals that had churned out the charge-master bills I had examined for the *Time* article typically discounted 30 to 60 percent off these fantasy prices when billing insurers, even as they stuck hapless patients without insurance with the full charge. Why would a heavyweight like UnitedHealthcare, the country's larg-est health insurer, tolerate only a 12 percent reduction? United had even knocked down the separate bill from my surgeon—who was considered a master of aortic aneurysms—by 65 percent, from $19,400 to $6,697. (The surgeon was an employee of the doctors' practice unit of the hospital's affiliated Weill Cornell Medical College, from whom I got that bill.)

I asked insurance industry contacts if there was something bizarre about my bill and the 12 percent discount. There wasn't. "If you want to sell insurance in New York, you have to have New York–Presbyterian in your network—and they know it," one told me.

"That's right," Hemsley, the CEO of United, agreed when I showed him the bill. "Some hospitals can drive a hard bargain because people want to be treated there and employers want to provide that to them, even if we can supply data that says there may be places to get the same or better treatment for less money."

Part of the reason for the hospital's leverage was size. New York–Presbyterian was the product of the 1998 merger between what were probably the city's two most prestigious hospitals and medical teaching institutions: Columbia Presbyterian, which included the Columbia University College of Physicians and Surgeons; and New York Hospi-tal, which included the Cornell University Medical College (now called Weill Cornell Medical College). The combined hospital system now had nearly 22,000 employees and 2,500 hospital beds, more than 125,000 annual patients, and nearly 2 million outpatient visits.

The hospital owned or was allied with more than a dozen other hospitals and clinics around New York. The latest financial report it had filed with the IRS, covering the 2012 calendar year, reported that

New York–Presbyterian had revenue that year of $3.9 billion and operating profit of $504 million, a robust 12.8 percent of its revenue.[28]

With that kind of footprint and resources it seemed obvious that an employer would have to gulp hard before signing on with an insurance company that didn't have these merged providers in its network, even an employer like mine that was self-insured and cared about costs.

However, New York–Presbyterian's leverage was about more than size. Like many New Yorkers, even before my surgery I regarded New York Hospital and Columbia Presbyterian—and now its merged colossus—as the city's leading medical centers. My children had been born at New York Hospital and received great care there. A large portion of what seemed to be the best doctors had practicing privileges there and taught at one of its two medical schools. New York–Presbyterian was always in the news, it seemed, as the hospital of choice for people who could go anywhere—such as former president Bill Clinton, who had had heart surgery there. There were also, I admit it, the ubiquitous ads promising that "Amazing Things Are Happening Here."

But that vaguely good vibe had now been replaced by something more tangible: eight days in which they had stopped my heart, fixed it, and brought it back. Would I ever let some insurance company steer me to another hospital after all of that?

As I thought about the powerlessness (not to mention cluelessness) of the UnitedHealthcare CEO when it came to my bills and Explanations of Benefits, juxtaposed against the strong hand that New York–Presbyterian seemed to be playing, my idea began to take shape.

MY $40,000 BED

When I was able to move around, I went back to the hospital to ask its top executives about that paltry 12 percent discount on its chargemaster prices.

---

28. I am defining operating profit as the excess of revenue over expenses (in this case, $269.6 million), plus the amount listed as a depreciation expense (in this case, $234.8 million) because depreciation is an accounting charge, not an actual cash expense.

But before arriving in their suite on the first floor, I want upstairs to look around the cardiac recovery unit where, in hospital CEO Steven Corwin's words, I had been "naked in every way." Dressed now in a suit and feeling fine, I had a more clear-eyed view than I had had the last time I was there of the work Corwin and his people did. It was no less impressive.

Walking past the elegant, sunny atrium (funded by, and named for, corporate mogul Ronald Perelman) where my wife and children had waited for news from my surgeon, I was retroactively scared for them, and glad they had been able to wait in a place that was trying so hard not to be scary.

Near the swinging doors through which they had wheeled me into the hall outside the operating room, a man covered from head to toe in hospital patient garb was waiting on a gurney. He was holding the hand of a woman whom I guessed was his wife. One attendant spread the doors open so another could push him through.

He probably didn't know that when he got through the doors into the hall outside the operating room the super-solicitous attendants were going to ask him if he wanted to stand up and walk in and get on the table himself. I had accepted the invitation, thinking—only half-facetiously—that I might as well take a few last steps.

On a wall down the hall I noticed a banner I had not seen before, celebrating one of the floor's units for its safety record. Another poster called out a non-doctor for some other achievement.

I saw someone being wheeled carefully into a room, presumably having graduated to this side of the floor from the intensive care unit where patients like me started to come back from the dead. Had I looked that helpless?

I walked past my friend—a Jamaican, I think, with two kids in college and some investment property in North Carolina—who had wheeled a movable scale into my room every day, always eager to strike up a conversation while also checking to make sure someone had cleaned my bathroom. He smiled, but he was focused not on the guy in the suit, but on the patient in the room at the left waiting for him. "Looking good," he told him.

I saw the small, quiet woman who had taken my blood twice a

day—taken it so skillfully that I swear I never felt even a pinprick. I had told her she was the best phlebotomist in the world once she had told me how to pronounce her profession. She, too, wasn't focused on the guy wearing a suit.

Then I reached for my notebook to write something down. It wasn't there. I had taken it out in the lobby, and must have dropped it. When I got down to the lobby, the security guard was waiting for me. "You left this," he said, cheerfully. Which reminded me of how courteous my wife and kids had said the guards had been when they had come to visit at all hours of the day and night.

"I GO AROUND ALL the time to meet new employees during orientation," New York–Presbyterian chief executive Steven Corwin told me when we sat down in his conference room with Robert Kelly, an anesthesiologist, who is the hospital's president. "And I ask them, 'Okay, how many of you are going to be taking care of patients?' About half the hands go up. So, I tell them, 'That's wrong. Guess what? All of us take care of patients. That's what we do.' That includes the security guard you just told me about," Corwin added.

When our discussion shifted from culture and patient care to finances, Corwin and Kelly talked about the investments New York–Presbyterian had made that, they said, put their high prices in context. They were constantly trying to recruit the best doctors from around the world to teach and lead practice areas, or sometimes to establish new practice areas they had targeted. They had spent $30 million to automate lab testing and speed up test results when they were needed immediately. They were running a multimillion-dollar program directed at poor families in upper Manhattan, aimed at monitoring their health and coordinating their care before they got seriously ill.

When they mentioned the cost of stocking their hospital with the high-end equipment used to treat patients like me, I asked for details and later got this tally:

The night before my surgery I underwent what is called a biplane catheterization to provide the doctors with a video image of what was going on in my heart. The equipment in the combination lab and operating room where that was done cost $2.7 million. (I got separate bills for this procedure totaling $23,000.)

The equipment used by my surgeon, my anesthesiologist, and their teams in the operating room cost $522,000. (My big bill had included $20,992 for use of the operating room during my six-and-a-half-hour operation.)

The equipment used just for me in the cardiac intensive care unit and then in the "step-down" room I graduated to cost $105,000. That included $40,000 for the "critical care" bed in the ICU, and $15,000 for the step-down bed.

Other than making me wonder whether I had missed a story in not looking at how medical economics had gone so wild that even people selling hospital beds had figured out that the sky was the limit, I got Corwin's and Kelly's point about how they were on the receiving as well as the giving end when it came to big bills.

Then I handed Corwin a copy of my twenty-two-page chargemaster bill and asked him to explain it.

Had UnitedHealthcare really only been given a 12 percent discount off all those high lab test bills and $451 portable chest x-rays?

"That's right," Corwin said, without hesitation, although he noted that for some services more common than my heart surgery New York–Presbyterian's discounts off the chargemaster were higher. More generally, Corwin offered the standard explanation that the hospital loses money not only on the Medicaid recipients, who are 30 percent of its patients, but also on the 30 percent of the beds filled with Medicare patients. Therefore, Corwin said, he has to make it up on charges for his privately insured patients.

Medicare claims that its fees cover what should be the actual costs plus overhead for every treatment, with regional cost factors included. If a hospital's actual costs are higher it must be operating inefficiently, Medicare officials argue.

"We lose 20 percent on Medicare patients," Corwin insisted. "And we operate as efficiently as possible but without affecting the high-touch care that happens at the bedside."

Why do hospitals take Medicare patients if they lose money on them, I asked, adding that all along the highways in Florida—which obviously has a high percentage of Medicare patients—hospitals have billboards, like the ones he has in New York, trying to attract patients. "Well, it's better to have a bed filled at a discount rate than have it go empty," he replied. "So incrementally, it is profitable. But not when you count the overhead."

"When you add back into overhead all the subsidies a place like New York–Presbyterian gets for teaching [medical students], research, and other things, I guarantee Medicare is profitable for them," one former senior Medicare official directly involved in setting rates told me. He did concede that the hospital probably loses "something" on Medicaid patients. Yet, as we can now tell from the rosy earnings reports from publicly held hospital chains since Obamacare launched, even the expansion of Medicaid boosts hospital profits because these patients now have insurance and, therefore, do not become charity cases or debt-collection problems.

Besides, whatever New York–Presbyterian makes or loses caring for Medicaid and Medicare patients, and even with all those "high touch" expenses (which I had certainly appreciated), the hospital is accumulating hundreds of millions of dollars in operating surpluses every year. "Yes," Corwin acknowledged. "But that kind of financial strength preserves this institution and makes us able to do more."

"THE OTHER HOSPITALS DO IT, TOO"

Even the $22.8 million (according to its 2012 IRS filing) that New York–Presbyterian spent on marketing and advertising, including a sponsorship as the "official hospital of the New York Yankees," made sense when Corwin and Kelly put it in the context of helping recruit the best doctors and boosting employee pride and morale.

The marketing budget included funds for a prominent "Amazing Things Are Happening Here" billboard on Manhattan's West Side Highway and, in 2013 and 2014, for unusual cooperation with and promotion of an ABC prime time show called *NY Med* that allowed cameras to chronicle the challenges and triumphs of the hospital's staff.

Didn't all that also drive their ability to negotiate hard with

UnitedHealthcare? "Of course," Corwin acknowledged. "But," he reiterated, "that allows us to have the resources to continue to do more research and expand care."

"The other hospitals do it, too," Kelly, the president and chief operating officer, added, noting that "we just lost the billboard to NYU"—the NYU Langone Medical Center.

NYU, along with hospitals and clinics run by Mount Sinai Hospital and the North Shore–LIJ Health System, were three fast-growing hospital conglomerates that were Corwin and Kelly's main competitors. In each case, they gave bigger discounts to insurers, because New York–Presbyterian was perceived to be the more indispensable brand. Yet because of their own good reputations and their takeover of other hospitals and doctors' practices, each was indispensable enough that they, too, were included in most insurers' networks without having to extend deep discounts.

Didn't New York–Presbyterian's leverage to bargain hard for high prices not only allow for better care but also for higher salaries for themselves and everyone else, I asked Corwin and Kelly. After all, even when all that research and "high touch" care was paid for, they still had hundreds of millions of dollars in profits and were able to pay themselves (according to the 2012 IRS filing) $3.58 million and $2.6 million respectively. In all, eleven New York–Presbyterian executives were paid over $1 million. The hospital had even paid Corwin's semi-retired predecessor $5.6 million in 2012 for his work as a vice chairman helping with fund-raising and lobbying on behalf of the hospital's academic centers. I got the usual answer about how complicated the business they managed was and about how compensation consultants reviewed their salaries with the board to make sure they were on a par with industry standards.

But I also got more. New York–Presbyterian has a board of financial, business, and civic luminaries, and Corwin provided a detailed explanation of how the board sets bonuses, which typically account for about half of each executive's overall income.

The bonuses were awarded according to a meticulous set of metrics. Importantly, only 35 percent of these benchmarks had to do with the financial results of the hospital, a portion that was unusually low compared to other ostensibly nonprofit, high-revenue hospitals whose bonus criteria I had looked at. Most nonprofit boards talked a lot about quality and patient satisfaction in explaining their compensation practices on their annual IRS filings, but rewarded the bosses based mostly on the dollars.

At New York–Presbyterian, another 40 percent was based on the results of an elaborate satisfaction survey given to all patients. And 25 percent was based on a menu of quality metrics, such as rates of infection, mortality, or readmission of discharged patients.

"This is not a board that sets easy goals," one board member later told me. "We set them so they never hit 100 percent." The same board member added that a quality control committee of the board met every month to review any untoward incidents, to go over all the quality metrics for the month, and to hear presentations from different practice units of the hospital.

It seemed that these people hadn't saved my life casually. The people on the top, the ones with the million-dollar incomes, were incented, at least according to the board's documented criteria, to worry as much about patients like me as the phlebotomist or my surgeon did.

In fact, Corwin and Kelly—who had each continued to practice part-time while they worked their way up through management—insisted that that was the point. They told me that they thought it essential that people running a hospital be doctors first and, to some degree, keep being doctors so that they didn't lose that grounding.

LET THE FOXES RUN THE HENHOUSE—WITH CONDITIONS

As I was leaving Corwin's office, my idea for how to fix Obamacare and American healthcare gelled: Let these guys loose. Give the most ambitious, expansion-minded foxes responsible for the chargemaster even more free rein to run the henhouse—but with lots of conditions.

Several months before, when I had spoken on a panel with two other impressive doctor-CEOs running two other prestigious medical organizations, I had begun toying with the same thought.

One of the panelists was Glenn Steele, Jr., a former cancer surgeon and professor at Harvard Medical School who runs the multi-facility

Geisinger Health System in central and northeastern Pennsylvania. Geisinger is famous for charging a flat price for various categories of diseases. Its doctors are all employed by the hospital. With the flat-rate system, Steele explained, they have no incentive to pile on unnecessary care or tests. They got paid based on quality metrics, not the number of times they see a patient or read an x-ray.

Most important, while allowing itself to be in the network of several insurers, Geisinger also had its own insurance plans. Pay Geisinger for insurance and you get Geisinger care for whatever you need.

As with the few healthcare providers that are similarly organized around the country, Geisinger was thought to be an outlier that succeeded because its base was in a relatively remote area with less than the usual competition.

The other panelist I met that day was Gary Gottlieb. He had no such geographic cushion. Gottlieb runs Partners HealthCare in Boston and Cambridge. Like New York–Presbyterian, Partners had been formed by the merger of the area's two most highly reputed hospital brands, both of which were affiliated with Harvard Medical School: Brigham and Women's Hospital and Massachusetts General.

When I had coffee with Gottlieb the morning before the panel, he described experimental contracts he had signed with Blue Cross Blue Shield in Boston. For a portion of the insurance company's population, Partners would take the risk that it could cut costs while maintaining quality.

Under a complicated formula, a certain amount would be designated to cover that patient population. If Partners' hospitals, labs, and doctors provided the care for less, it would share in the savings—but only if it also met a specified set of quality metrics. If the baseline quality metrics were exceeded, Partners' share of the savings would be increased. If Partners ended up spending more, it would eat the excess, though less so if the quality benchmarks were exceeded.

That seemed like a significant step forward, one that Gottlieb attributed in part to the fact that these kinds of experiments covering private insurance patients had been inspired by Obamacare's own similarly structured pilot programs involving Medicare patients. "There are a lot of problems with Obamacare," Gottlieb told me.

"But the attention it focused, at least in the industry, on costs with those pilots, has made a lot of us realize that we have to change how we operate."

Gottlieb, who was paid $3.5 million in 2012, ran a system with more than $10 billion in revenues that, to the dismay of some consumer advocates, had kept swallowing up other hospitals, doctors' practices, and outpatient clinics. Yet Gottlieb seemed, like Steele of Geisinger, to be potentially more a part of the solution than the problem. He, too, had started as a doctor. In fact, his practice specialty had been psychiatry for geriatrics. How coldhearted could someone be who went to medical school to provide that kind of care?

However, when it came to consumer protection, Gottlieb's view of the world was complicated by more than the consumer advocates' suspicion that he was trying to gobble up the market. Unlike conventional healthcare reformers, Gottlieb saw price transparency—the apple pie of healthcare reform—as having a downside. He explained to me that if, as was the transparency movement's basic goal, a patient could readily see that his charge for a colonoscopy, an x-ray, or even an outpatient surgical procedure would be much less at the clinic across the street than at Gottlieb's hospital, the patient would likely decide to go there, or his insurance company would make him go there. Gottlieb would then lose those profits, which, he said, supported the other, unprofitable types of care, such as mental health treatment, that he had to provide.

"I'll compete with anyone on cost and quality, if you give me the whole patient," he told me. "But if the patient can pick and choose what he buys from me, à la carte, my business collapses.

"People with hip replacements also have dementia," he added. "Someone with heart disease not taking his medication might also be depressed. We want to compete on how well we treat that whole patient."

The CEO of a giant hospital system was claiming he would be happy to compete on how well he treated the "whole patient." That had a nice ring to it.

At another event, I had been intrigued by a third doctor/hospital leader: Delos "Toby" Cosgrove, the CEO of the Cleveland Clinic, the hospital system that dominated Ohio and had such a good reputation that patients traveled there from all over the world.

Cosgrove had been a celebrated heart surgeon; in fact, he was a trailblazer in perfecting the operation I had just undergone. He had performed more than twenty-two thousand cardiac surgeries, and had built the Cleveland Clinic's heart program into one of the world's best. Along the way he had patented thirty products used in thoracic surgery.

When Cosgrove was, he told me, "plucked from the operating room" to become CEO of Cleveland Clinic in 2004 because of his success running the cardiac program, "I knew nothing about business." By now, he was regarded as one of the savviest hospital executives in the world, widely admired for the way he ran what he had propelled into a $6 billion, seventy-five-facility enterprise.

I had watched Cosgrove at a program about healthcare reform blanch when another panelist implied that he dominated his market too much. "Not possible," he had said. "If we expand too much the FTC will be all over us."

Should the Federal Trade Commission really want to stop a guy like Cosgrove from dominating healthcare in Cleveland, I wondered.

But then I remembered Jeffrey Romoff, the CEO of the University of Pittsburgh Medical Center (UPMC), who had been enmeshed in all of that litigation over whether he had conspired to control his market. Romoff truly did dominate healthcare in Pittsburgh and, he had told me, saw any attempts to hold him back as "impediments" he needed to overcome.

By now, UPMC had settled its litigation with, and was about to complete its divorce from, Highmark Insurance—the Blue Cross Blue Shield company it had been accused of conspiring with to control the provider and insurance markets respectively in western Pennsylvania.

Through 2014, UPMC was filling the Pittsburgh area airwaves and every billboard not already taken by Highmark touting its own insurance company as the one that patients could use to get full access to its facilities—because, beginning in 2015, UPMC would no longer recognize Highmark Insurance.

Romoff was playing hardball and winning.

At the same time, UPMC was fighting a lawsuit from the city of Pittsburgh that might have embarrassed other hospital executives. The city charged that the hospital system's prices and profits were so high and its salaries, including Romoff's (which by now was more than $5 million), were so exorbitant that it did not deserve nonprofit tax-exempt status and should, therefore, be subject to the city's payroll tax. That would mean a lot to Pittsburgh because UPMC was Pennsylvania's biggest non-government employer.

UPMC's first defense was that it didn't actually have any employees; only its subsidiaries did. By the summer of 2014, a state judge would agree. He dismissed the case, though the city would be allowed to file the same action against the various subsidiary hospitals. Nonetheless, the suit had highlighted UPMC's status as perhaps the world's most tough-minded, profit-oriented nonprofit.

So, to put it charitably, Romoff didn't seem to be the kind of hospital leader that Drs. Corwin, Steele, Gottlieb, and Cosgrove were.

Yet it was when I went to see Romoff (once I was able to travel) that the idea I had begun playing with after those talks with Corwin and the other doctor-executives became fully formed.

Sitting in front of a window in his suite atop the U.S. Steel Tower, overlooking his city's football and baseball stadiums, Romoff laid out a vision for healthcare that put it all together for me. I began to see how the patient-centered culture and aggressive marketing of "amazing things" at Corwin's hospital, how Steele's flat-rate, no-bill-padding regime at Geisinger, how Gottlieb's wish to compete for the full menu of a patient's health needs, and how Cosgrove's having brought world-class care to Cleveland—how all of that—could be combined and taken to a whole new level, based, oddly enough, on Romoff's plan for world dominance, or at least dominance in western Pennsylvania.

I spent much of my time with Romoff talking about his insurance company, which was run by Diane Holder, an elegantly dressed, long-time UPMC administrator sitting to my right. A hospital with its own health insurance company, they explained, was called an "integrated delivery and finance system." UPMC aimed to produce a model of that for the country. In fact, it had started another business to sell consulting and data analytics services to other hospital systems that wanted to do the same thing in their regions.

By now Highmark's insurance market share in the Pittsburgh region had shrunk from 65 to 45 percent. Romoff calculated that with all the business he was taking away with his own insurance company, plus the inroads made by other insurers with whom he had now signed network deals, Highmark's share would be at 25 percent by the end of 2014 and still sinking. He expected that his own insurance company would end up the leader in the market—and he was going to do everything he could to get to 100 percent.

Would he be worried about being so successful that he drove out all the other insurance companies, I asked. "Of the things that keep me up at night, that is not one of them," he answered, with a smile.

Romoff was unabashedly trying to become the dominant insurer. And, of course, he was already by far the dominant provider through his twenty hospitals and hundreds of clinics, labs, and doctors' practices.

In other words, like Geisinger, only on a larger scale and with little competition in the market, Romoff could sell me health insurance, which would cover me when I used Romoff's hospitals, clinics, doctors, and labs.

There would be no middleman. No third-party insurance company. Other hospital systems, such as California-based Kaiser Permanente, had tried the same thing. But Kaiser was not perceived as having the network of best-brand hospitals and doctors that dominated their markets the way UPMC did.

To me this was a hugely appealing idea, despite UPMC's record of high prices and its take-no-prisoners approach to competition. Why? Because it was the structure that made sense, not the particulars of Romoff and UPMC.

The insurance company would not only have every incentive to control the doctors' and hospitals' costs, but also the means to do so. It would be under the same roof, controlled by Romoff. Conversely, the hospitals and doctors would have no incentive to inflate costs or overtreat, because their ultimate boss, Romoff, would be getting the bill when those extra costs hit his insurance company. Steele had already proved this on a smaller scale at Geisinger.

As Romoff put it, "All the incentives are aligned the right way. It's the beauty of being the payer and provider at the same time. The alignments of interest are just so pure."

"When the incentives are not aligned," he added, supplying a quote that could easily be read the wrong way, "it's why seniors dying of cancer get chemo when they should just get hospice care."

To illustrate their point, Romoff and Holder, the head of his insurance unit, along with chief medical officer Steven Shapiro, described their "Low Back Pain Quality Initiative."

Experts have long considered the treatment of back pain as exhibit A in any discussion of medical waste. We spend more than $85 billion a year on it. Yet doctors who have studied the problem believe that 30 to 50 percent of the expense is wasted on needless operations and other treatments when rest or physical therapy would work better.

In 2012, Romoff and his two executives explained, UPMC had initiated the back-pain initiative for patients with its insurance who used its facilities. It involved a new treatment protocol that, according to a UPMC white paper, "emphasized increased use of physical therapy and discouraged the use of high tech imaging studies or other radiologic procedures during this period, unless significant neurologic findings were present."

"Patients were happier, and we saved a ton of money," Romoff told me.

Maybe, but how can we know that the patients were happier or better off? And how could we know that those aging cancer patients Romoff had mentioned—who would have no place to go in and around Pittsburgh except to UPMC if Romoff has anything to say about it—wouldn't be denied chemotherapy that they actually needed if Romoff-employed doctors were the ones holding the prescription pads?

The cabbie who drove me in from the airport to see Romoff swore by UPMC and how its surgeons had repaired his large intestine. But do we want Romoff to have all that power? Isn't his interest the one that was most "purely aligned" of all?

That's where doctor-leaders like Corwin, Steele, Gottlieb, and Cosgrove come in—along with strong oversight and regulation.

Hospitals are already consolidating. We saw that in New Haven, and can see it in Corwin's New York, Gottlieb's Boston, and Cosgrove's Cleveland.

Let's let them continue. More important, as they continue, let's encourage them to become their own insurance companies, à la Romoff, so they can cut out the middleman and align those incentives.

Let's harness their ambition to expand, rather than try to figure how and when to contain their ambition.

Why shouldn't I be able to buy Toby Cosgrove's Cleveland Clinic Health Insurance? What a great brand! I would know that I can use all of his facilities and doctors, and he would know that his incentive now—which, he says, has always been his incentive—is to provide good care, not expensive care full of unnecessary and overpriced CT scans and blood tests. I would know that determining the nature of that care was going to be done not by insurance companies but by doctors whom I could hold accountable.

But let's ensure that accountability by insisting on tight regulation, mostly through the smarter use of federal antitrust law and state regulatory authority, in return for giving doctor-leaders such as Cosgrove, Corwin, Steele, or Gottlieb the freedom to expand and also to become their patients' insurance companies.

The first regulation would require that any market have at least two of these big, fully integrated provider–insurance company players. There could be no monopolies, only oligopolies, as antitrust lawyers would call them. The larger markets, such as New York, Los Angeles, and Chicago, might have to have four or five or even more players to make the competition real and to make sure, with accompanying regulatory requirements, that their footprints were big enough and their marketing plans robust enough to serve patients throughout their regions, not just in the wealthier areas.

If Yale New Haven Health System has become too big for its market to allow for that real competition, it would have to spin off facilities to a new player that could compete on price and quality with its own credible brand. Maybe Gottlieb, Corwin, or Cosgrove would want to expand there.

If that proved impossible, or if one of the integrated healthcare oligopolists competed so effectively that it forced the others out of business, then it would be regulated still more—the way a public utility is—with still tighter controls on profits.

That would mean that the hospital and all the doctors it controlled would be subject to pricing and service delivery standards that reformers have sought since the mid-twentieth century. Healthcare in the United States would finally be treated as a public good, not a free market product. However, the change would have come, jujitsu style, not by a government takeover but because the private players had driven it to that state.

This new structure would also acknowledge that most doctors have lost the independence the American Medical Association said it was protecting for them throughout the twentieth century, when, beginning with Harry Truman's push for universal government health insurance, it opposed reform. But that loss of independence came through privately consummated mergers of doctors' practices and buyouts by hospitals, not by government fiat. Those doctors would now be incented to provide quality care, not pile on the bills for extra treatment, because they would be working for the entity paying the bills—because the hospital system would also be the insurance company.

These fully integrated brands could also pursue recent innovations offering less expensive, more consumer-friendly healthcare, such as storefront urgent care centers that are smart alternatives to expensive, time-wasting hospital emergency rooms. These urgent care centers are now being opened piecemeal by for-profit and often lightly regulated companies. Why not put them under the banner and branded accountability of the big hospital systems? In fact, Cosgrove's Cleveland Clinic has already opened a dozen "urgent care" and "express care" (for more routine needs) centers. I'd rather pay him to care for me than pay a walk-in center owned by a private equity fund.

The second regulation would cap the operating profits of what would be these now-allowed dominant market players, or oligopolies, at, say, 8 percent a year, compared to the current average of about 12 percent. This could be done in the form of consent decrees, in which the regulators allow the oligopolies to exist under a specific set of conditions, such as this profit cap. That would force prices down—except at Geisinger, which already charges only enough to record operating profit margins of 4 to 5 percent a year. Better yet, an excess profits pool would be created. Those making higher profits would have to contribute the difference to struggling hospitals in small markets, such as rural areas.

A third regulation—which, again, the hospital systems would have to agree to in return for them being allowed to achieve oligopoly or even monopoly status—would prevent hospital finance people from playing games with that profit limit by raising salaries and bonuses for themselves and their colleagues (thereby raising costs and lowering profits). There would be a cap on the total salary and bonus paid to any hospital employee who does not practice medicine full-time of sixty times the amount paid to the lowest salaried full-time doctor, typically a first-year resident.

For example, the lowest-salaried doctor in the University of Pittsburgh Medical Center system makes $52,000. Thus, Romoff's salary and bonus would be capped at $3.12 million, significantly lower than his current draw of more than $5 million. The Cleveland Clinic's Cosgrove, on the other hand, who made $3 million in 2012, according to the Cleveland Clinic's latest filing with the IRS, would not be affected much, if at all. Nor would Glenn Steele at Geisinger or Gary Gottlieb at Partners. With his starting residents now making about $58,000, Corwin would only have to take a cut of about $100,000.

A salary of $3 million, along with the satisfaction of doing on a grand scale what they hoped to do when they became doctors in the first place, ought to be enough to keep these doctor/hospital leaders engaged. If it also incents them to pay residents more, so much the better.

A fourth regulation would require a streamlined appeals process, staffed by advocates and ombudsmen, for patients who believe adequate care has been denied them, or for doctors who claim they are being unduly pressured to skimp on care. In fact, an ombudsman's office would be embedded at each oligopoly company.

A fifth regulation would require that any government-sanctioned, oligopoly-designated integrated system had to have as its actual chief executive (not just in title) a licensed physician who had practiced medicine for a minimum number of years. Sorry, Mr. Romoff. The culture of these organizations needs to be ensured, even if that means choosing leaders based on something in addition to their business acumen and stated good intentions.

Sixth, any sanctioned integrated oligopoly provider would be required to insure a certain percentage of Medicaid patients at a stipulated discount.

"Wait a minute," I can hear my readers thinking. "All of these guys [except Steele at Geisinger] generate thousands of those obscene chargemaster bills a year. Now you're going to put them in charge?"

Which brings me to my final regulation: These regulated oligopolies would be required to charge any uninsured patients no more than they charge any competing insurance companies whose insurance they accept, or a price based on their regulated profit margin if they don't accept other insurance. In other words, no more chargemaster. All four of these doctor/hospital leaders had told me they thought the chargemaster was a ridiculous, embarrassing relic that they would dispense with if other hospitals did. Now they would have to.

All of this may seem complicated, but the rules required to set up this structure would be a drop in the bucket compared to the thousands of pages of laws and millions of pages of rules and regulations now on the books. And it is certainly more realistic than pining for a public single-payer system that is never going to happen. This kind of consolidation is already happening. We just need to seize onto that momentum, control it, and push it in the right direction.

CUTTING OUT THE MIDDLEMAN

Combining the work that the Corwins, Gottliebs, Steeles, and Cosgroves of the world do with Romoff's plan boils down to this: Allow doctor-leaders to create great brands that both insure consumers for their medical costs and provide medical care.

Fully integrating this way incorporates the core goals of the public-payer plans that the reformers have long championed—control the incentive to run up costs and eliminate the for-profit insurance company middleman that has an incentive to skimp on care. Yet it is done in combination with private sector competition and innovation, as exemplified by these doctor-leaders.

Let them act on their ambitions. Let them compete with other legitimate players in their markets, or even with one another if they want to expand.

That kind of competition is already happening, as the fight over the billboard between New York–Presbyterian and NYU Langone illustrates. Only it is blurred by the insurance companies in the middle, which makes it competition by proxy, at best. As things stand now, an employer who wants to get healthcare for his workers, or an individual who is shopping on the Obamacare exchanges, has to figure out which insurance company has which hospitals and doctors in its network and what discounts it has negotiated. This change would create a new, clearer competitive process.

Put differently, I'd rather give my money to Steven Corwin based on the promise that all of his doctors and facilities are available to me than hope for the best with UnitedHealthcare.

The narrow networks that began being offered on the Obamacare exchanges in October 2013 as a way of lowering premium costs are an embryonic version of this idea, at least in theory. In the narrow network version, insurance companies bargained with the providers in return for including them in their networks. If the insurer's narrow network seemed to have good hospitals and doctors and the premium price was right, that network could become a brand the consumer bought.

In practice, it had not worked out that way. In the best of circumstances, finding out which hospitals or doctors were in a network often involved difficult online journeys through multiple website pages and look-up tools. In the worst of circumstances, the information either wasn't there or was inaccurate, which, in fact, spurred pending suits against Blue Cross Blue Shield in California soon after Obamacare launched. The result has been competition only on the price of monthly premiums, with consumers often disappointed when they later realized they could not go to the doctor or hospital of their choice.

But even if everything about those networks was clear, they could never be as clearly defined and consumer friendly as these sanctioned and regulated hospital system–centered oligopolies would be. Now, I could just go on the exchange and pay Corwin for keeping me healthy. Period. Full stop. There would be total clarity about which facilities and doctors are in my network.

Or my employer could pay him after negotiating the price.

If Corwin and his integrated system charged too much or didn't do a good job, my employer or I (if I was in the individual market) could switch to another competitive New York brand like Mount Sinai or NYU Langone. And all of that competition would be fortified by advances in data transparency that would make each competitor's quality ratings for various types of care readily available.

Corwin's high price for my open-heart surgery would truly be tested in the market, because he would be competing with other high-quality health systems, like Mount Sinai or NYU Langone, to capture all of my business or my employer's business. He and his network of hospitals, clinics, and doctors would be insuring me not only against heart surgery, but for routine treatment and x-rays if I twist my ankle or get the flu.

I BET THAT WITH this plan we could cut 20 percent off of the two thirds of our overall healthcare bill not paid by Medicare or Medcaid.

The savings would come from each of the two sides of current healthcare commerce—the payer (or insurance) side and the provider side. Here's a sketch of how the math could work:

First, administrative costs for insurance—including vetting claims, paying bills, paying managers and executives, and distributing profits to shareholders—now account for 15 to 20 percent of private healthcare costs. Couldn't half or more of that be saved by cutting out the middleman insurance companies? Corwin or Cosgrove would still have to employ managers, actuaries, accountants, and sales people on the "insurance" side of their now-integrated operation, but surely not to the same extent that an insurance company responsible for paying bills from multiple third-party hospitals and other providers would. Nor would they have to deliver profits to shareholders.

So, let's say we could save 10 percent by eliminating the middleman.

Second, on the provider side of the equation, the dynamic that Peter Orszag rightly identified as the main culprit in driving costs so high—the incentive for overtreating and overtesting that comes with fee-for-service billing—would have been eliminated. And the overall incentive to maximize revenue would be tamped down by the new regulation capping operating profit at 8 percent.

That could likely save another 10 percent (although economists like Orszag might posit a higher estimate).

The total, then, could be 20 percent of nongovernment healthcare costs—or $400 billion a year, and maybe a hundred billion more to be saved by allowing Medicare and Medicaid to pay those integrated providers this way—which would be the ultimate in bundled pricing.

That would go a long way toward bringing American healthcare costs as a percent of our gross domestic product closer to those of the countries we compete with.

"I COULD LIVE WITH SOMETHING LIKE THAT"

"Insurance and healthcare are two fundamentally different businesses, and I'd rather be in the healthcare business, where my job is to worry only about the patient," said Corwin, when I bounced the idea off him. "The incentives are totally different. Mine is to care for the patient. The insurance company's is to spend as little as possible on that care."

But aren't hospital systems like his, Gottlieb's, and Cosgrove's already making deals with insurance companies or with Medicare and Medicaid, under which they take the risk—and enjoy part of the savings—of treating patients at a set price rather than on a fee-for-service basis? So aren't they already dealing with those conflicting incentives? Why not go all the way? "That's a fair point," Corwin said.

Besides, I asked, as a patient, wouldn't I rather you make the decisions about my care than have them have to be approved by an insurance company? Wouldn't I feel better if you were the ones accountable for that, with the right regulations in place?

"I see your point," he said, adding that one of his competitors—the North Shore–LIJ hospital system, which was fast expanding throughout the metropolitan area—had recently begun offering its own insurance plan. "At this point I would be reluctant," Corwin continued, "but maybe we would look at it if we got larger . . . and if we could be sure we could integrate everything we added with our culture and standards."

What about capping his salary and bonus at a multiple of the money earned by his lowest paid resident? "I could live with something like that," Corwin said.

The Cleveland Clinic's Toby Cosgrove was further down the road toward embracing the integration idea when I asked him about it in August 2014. "The first thing we can agree on about the healthcare system in the United States," Cosgrove said, "is that it is not a system at all. It's just a collection of disparate providers. We have to consolidate to treat the whole patient," he explained, echoing Gary Gottlieb's skepticism about "à la carte" medicine.

"So, yes, we are consolidating," Cosgrove continued, noting that although the number of hospital beds in the United States has declined in recent years from one million to eight hundred thousand, "there is still only 65 percent occupancy. . . . The hospital on Nantucket," he explained, referring to the Massachusetts summer resort where he has a house, "dates from a time when there was little specialized care and poor transportation. Now it should be an emergency room and a helicopter connected to a hospital in Boston. That's what I learned in Vietnam," he added, referring to his time as an air force surgeon. "We stabilized them and got them to where they could get the best care."

Doctors, said Cosgrove, have consolidated their practices, often under the umbrella of hospital systems like his, "because medical knowledge doubles every two years. So you continually need to specialize still more to keep up. And the more you consolidate, the more you can specialize. The more you specialize and do a lot of just one or two things, the better you are at them, and the more cost-effective you are. That's why they call it 'practicing' medicine."

Would integrating insurance into that system be the next logical step beyond consolidation? "That seems right," Cosgrove said. In fact, he added, "We recently applied for an insurance license."

"AETNA IS BLOCKBUSTER"

Major laws like Obamacare usually get tinkered with and improved in the years following their initial passage. However, in today's Washington that is not a likely prospect anytime soon.

But this system of branded, integrated, and regulated oligopolies could be put in place by changes in federal or even state regulatory policies. No new law has to be passed in dysfunctional Washington to allow hospital systems to become insurance companies. Some, such as Geisinger, Kaiser Permanente, and UPMC, already are, with more, such as the Cleveland Clinic, moving in that direction. And the Federal Trade Commission or state regulatory authorities, not Congress, could put the regulations I have in mind in place.

The insurance companies, of course, wouldn't like it. But except for the reprieve in the individual market that the Obamacare exchanges gave them, they are rapidly exiting the real insurance business anyway. Large employers now mostly self-insure; the insurance companies just set up the networks for them and process the payments, which come out of the employers' funds—two functions, and costs, that this change would eliminate.

Similarly, the insurers' actuaries have much less to do when it comes to calculating risk, because they are not allowed to take preexisting conditions into account. Their gauging of the right age bands (how much they can charge an older person versus a younger one) has now also been set by the new law. Besides, as Oscar is in the process of proving, that kind of actuarial work can be outsourced, meaning Corwin of New York–Presbyterian could buy it as easily as Joshua Kushner did.

"Aetna is Blockbuster," Zeke Emanuel told me when I started

thinking about this idea. What he meant was that just as the video rental giant got overtaken by upheavals in how media is delivered, large insurers such as Aetna are going to be overtaken by changes in the structure and delivery of healthcare.

Maybe, but the largest insurer, UnitedHealth Group, intends to be part of that change, not its victim. Its Optum subsidiary (whose QSSI unit helped rescue the Obamacare website) has become a giant player in healthcare system consulting and data analytics, with earnings in 2013 of $2.3 billion, a 61 percent increase over 2012. Although United's insurance business is still much larger, Optum is growing far faster and enjoys far higher profit margins.

Moreover, Optum has started going into the business of providing care by buying doctors' practice groups and opening urgent care centers.

Might United reverse the process I have suggested, in which hospital systems become insurance companies, by being an insurance company that buys up hospital systems? "We've already done that in Brazil," UnitedHealth Group chief executive Stephen Hemsley told me. "We operate the largest hospital system there. . . . So, yes, I could see that."

United's advantage, Hemsley added, would be that "we have the data analytics skills, the financial resources, and financing and regulatory experience that hospitals going into insurance might not have."

As for Oscar, Kushner and crew are nimble enough to switch to a better business model, too. Cosgrove, Corwin, and the others could hire them to burnish their brands and provide a much clearer, friendlier consumer entry point into their services. Oscar could become their provider of its un-insurance-like products: its customer service process, its friendly website, its data crunching, and its customer dashboard innovations, with all those alerts and other helpful messages for patients. Oscar could also be used to set up a system coordinating coverage across these brands when patients need medical care outside of the region where they live.

After I learned of my heart problem, I had gone onto Cosgrove's Cleveland Clinic website to get information from his famed cardiac care center. The emails and promotions I have gotten since (which I requested) have been helpful, but Joshua Kushner and his team could do wonders for Cleveland Clinic's brand and what it delivers.

I was surprised that when I asked Kushner about that he did not push back. Oscar's goal, he said, had always been "to be the front door for consumers to navigate a system that is unfriendly and has all kinds of obstacles." That was why he was encouraging his team to perfect Oscar's concierge service. The goal is for customers to contact an Oscar concierge first—and get a real person—to discuss an encounter they might be planning with an otherwise difficult system. "We can help them and save money, if we can direct them to the right care and explain costs and our network to them in advance," he explained. "We want to be that entryway. And then we want to be their guide, by reminding them to fill prescriptions or go for their annual checkup."

And, he added, "We have already talked to a few hospital systems about helping them do that."

BUT WHAT ABOUT THE THOUSAND-DOLLAR PILL?

As I began to frame the Corwin, Steele, Gottlieb, Cosgrove regulated oligopoly idea, a drug called Sovaldi burst onto the scene. It was an in-your-face reminder that America's healthcare cost crisis was not just about getting hospitals and doctors off the fee-for-service treadmill and aligning their interests with those who pay for healthcare. There was also the problem of costs that have nothing to do with the services hospitals or doctors provide.

Of the big issues that Obamacare did not address, chief among them was the uncontrollable cost of drugs. Pharmaceutical companies have been steadily boosting profit margins by taking a tougher stance on pricing in the United States—so much so that *Bloomberg Businessweek* reported in the spring of 2014 that "since 2007, the cost of brand name medicines has soared, with prices doubling for dozens of established drugs that target everything from multiple sclerosis to cancer, blood pressure and even erectile dysfunction."

Beginning in the spring of 2014, Sovaldi, sold by a relatively obscure company, took the issue up several levels in visibility.

In March, Henry Waxman, the California Democratic congress-man and pharmaceutical company nemesis, had begun to attack the pricing set for Sovaldi, sold by a pharmaceutical company called Gil-ead Sciences. Gilead was considered something of a lone wolf in the industry. It was not even a member of PhRMA, the pharmaceutical lobbying group, but its conduct put all pharmaceutical companies on the defensive.

Sovaldi, it seemed, was a miracle cure for the potentially deadly hepatitis C liver virus. When it began marketing the drug in early 2014, Gilead priced it at $1,000 a pill. It took eighty-four pills, or $84,000 over the twelve-week, pill-a-day treatment period, to rid the patient of hepatitis C.

Millions of Americans have chronic hepatitis C, which often be-comes debilitating or life threatening.

The press took the story and ran with it. Sarah Kliff, the former star *Washington Post Wonkblog* healthcare reporter who had moved on to *Vox,* calculated that "California . . . might have to spend more on buying Sovaldi for its Medicaid beneficiaries than it currently does on all K–12 and higher education."

Or as the Kaiser Health News service pointed out, if every hepati-tis C patient took the drug, the country would spend $300 billion on it—doubling the country's current bill for all prescription drugs.

Karen Ignagni, the head of America's Health Insurance Plans, the insurance lobby, began issuing almost daily press releases and studies, using Gilead's Sovaldi as the poster child for drug prices run amok.

Meantime, Wall Street analysts touted Gilead's soaring stock price and pointed out that its CEO's holdings had made him an overnight billionaire.

The exact price Gilead chose for Sovaldi said something in and of itself about the nonexistent regulatory environment drug companies knew they faced in the United States. Rather than set the price at, say, $989, or $1,021—at least to create the impression that it was based on some calculation other than "Let's charge whatever we want"—the company had chosen a simple round number, $1,000. At the same time, it was charging far less in countries outside the United States that regulated drug prices.

Yet Sovaldi, itself, wasn't the problem. The thousand-dollar pill was just an attention-getting example—fueled by the company's brazenness in selecting that fat round number—of what was to come. Why couldn't another company charge $2,000 for another lifesaving drug next year?

"This is the tip of the iceberg," Steven Pearson, president of the nonprofit Institute for Clinical and Economic Review, which tracks the effectiveness of new treatments, told the Kaiser Health News service. "We have about a year or two as a country to sort this out before more specialty drugs hit the market."

Patents for drugs, as well as expensive medical devices, are government grants of monopoly. The need to control how these monopoly products are priced is clear. Drug and medical device price controls belong on any list of necessary reforms that Obamacare missed and that have to be put in place if healthcare bills aren't going to continue to cripple the rest of the economy.

TRAGIC CHOICES

There is something about healthcare that I came to understand better during my hospital stay—something that overlays all of these considerations of costs and savings. It's what makes dealing with these issues so politically difficult.

When it comes to our health, we don't care about cost-benefit analyses; we care only about maximizing the benefit.

Suppose you're shopping for a car, and *Consumer Reports* convinces you that in terms of reliability, safety, and everything else, the Chrysler model you are considering is 90 percent as good as the Ford you are also looking at. Suppose also that the Chrysler cost only 60 percent as much as the Ford. You would likely buy the Chrysler.

But what if your surgeon told you that one type of patch he was going to use on your aorta was 90 percent as good as another, but costs only 60 percent as much? Which one would you choose? Obviously, the costlier model. No amount of savings is worth a 10 percent discount on your life.

And that analogy assumes that you have as much information about the comparative effectiveness of medical treatments and devices as you do about cars, which you don't. It also assumes that you will believe that the cheaper product is almost as good or just as good—which, when it comes to medical care, you either won't believe, or you'll be scared enough not to take the chance.

A law professor of mine, Guido Calabresi, co-authored a profound book in 1978 called *Tragic Choices,* which analyzed how societies fumble around when allocating scarce resources, ranging from who should be drafted to fight a war to who should receive a kidney transplant. The basic message of the book is that even in societies that try hard to be fair or to appear to be fair, the combination of politics, emotion, and unequal distribution of power rarely makes these decisions rational or satisfying to many on the receiving end of them.

Medical care, especially as it has evolved in the United States since Professor Calabresi pinpointed these issues, involves the ultimate allocation of scarce resources. When I started reporting this book, a congressman mentioned to me, cynically, that "every body part, every disease has a lobby of victims, often funded by the industry." Each of those body part or disease lobbies, he explained, roams the halls of the Capitol looking for more research money, or for a dispensation so that Medicare will pay for this experimental drug meant to cure skin cancer or that new medical device meant to alleviate back pain. It is no surprise, then, that groups of hepatitis C sufferers have been contesting any attempts by insurers or Medicare to limit the distribution of Sovaldi to those whose condition the insurers decide has reached the most urgent stage.

I was reminded of that primer on medical lobbying when I saw my surgeon for a follow-up visit. He casually mentioned that if everyone got an MRI, as I had, no one would die from aortic aneurysms because they would all be caught like mine was.

I checked later that day and found that, according to the federal Centers for Disease Control and Prevention, 10,431 people died from aortic aneurysms in 2011, the latest year for which the data had been tabulated.

The chargemaster bill for my MRI had been $1,950, which my insurance company knocked down to $294.

My doctor had sent me for the test because he became suspicious when he took my pulse during a routine checkup. However, most doctors aren't skillful enough or cautious enough to weed out possible victims that way, nor is taking a pulse anything close to a foolproof way to find an aneurysm. So let's suppose we spent $300, through private insurance coverage or Medicare and Medicaid, to test all 240 million American adults to see if they had aortic aneurysms growing in their chests. That would cost $72 billion.

Suppose we economized and tested everyone only every four years. That would average out to $18 billion a year. Yet it would potentially save more than three times as many Americans as were lost in the September 11, 2001, attacks, which we have spent hundreds of billions to prevent from happening again, even trillions if you count foreign wars. So, would an aortic aneurysm lobby, consisting perhaps (if I had not been saved) of my widow or children (and backed by the MRI lobby), be so unreasonable in demanding that the country spend the $18 billion?

Then again, wouldn't it be crazy to spend all that money to find the fraction of a fraction of a percent of people—10,000 out of 240 million—who are susceptible to that, rather than spend it on general preventive care or on cancer research?

Put simply, money is a scarce healthcare resource. We have left it to Washington to allocate it based too often on who has the best lobby or the hottest fund-raising campaign. And anyone who tries to rationalize those tragic choices faces a firestorm of political opposition. Which was why Obamacare's thousands of pages of law and follow-on regulations were filled with all kinds of goodies—or necessities, depending on your view—pushed by the most effective body part and disease lobbies. It's also why figuring out how to deal with Sovaldi is impossible absent price controls.

Skill is also a scarce resource. That was driven home to me when I checked in with Tom and Viola Brown in Kentucky in July 2014 and Viola told me that one of her doctors had discovered a severe heart problem. For the next several months the doctor was going to monitor her to see if medication would suffice. However, Mrs. Brown told me, open-heart surgery was likely going to be necessary at some point.

Before cardiothoracic surgeon Leonard Girardi operated on me I was able to check him out, because the New York State Department of Health posts data online tallying the outcome of all cardiac surgeries by all of the state's heart surgeons.

The stats for Girardi, a soft-spoken, fifty-one-year-old graduate of Harvard College and Cornell Medical School, were as good as the word of mouth about him. In 2011, the last year for which records were available, Girardi had performed 238 operations of the type he was going to perform on me. He had lost no one, earning him the highest rank in the state, which factored in the condition of the patient being operated on and the complexity of the procedure. Girardi had averaged between 500 and 600 heart surgeries of any kind (including my type) a year over the past fifteen years. He had rarely lost a patient, and the few he lost were far advanced in years or had arrived near death in the emergency room. You wouldn't know it from his modest, friendly bedside manner, which exuded the opposite of surgeon-as-God arrogance, but in New York cardiology circles Girardi was considered among the best of the best.

There are no analogous publicly available statistics kept in Kentucky. In the more general national and state quality ratings that CMS and Kentucky publish related to cardiac surgery, Louisville's Jewish Hospital and St. Mary's HealthCare—where Viola Brown told me she would have her surgery if it became necessary—ranks as "average." However, the data is limited, and the hospital is reputed to have one of the best cardiac care centers in the region. That Viola Brown, thanks to Barack Obama and Steven Beshear, had had her condition discovered and could now be treated for it there, was, of course, a great benefit for her.

But the hospital doesn't rank as high or have the same reputation as New York–Presbyterian.

The actual skill of the people treating Mrs. Brown is not the point. The point is that skills will vary—and that the data transparency movement is now likely to make those variations clearer than ever, as data like New York's becomes more complete and consumer friendly, and as other states offer the same information. So those at the top of the rankings will increasingly present yet another scarce resource forcing another type of tragic choice.

Let's suppose we could get an exact—or what would purport to be an exact—quality rating for Viola Brown's doctor to compare to Leonard Girardi's. Let's further suppose he or she ranked in the 60th or 75th or even 85th percentile, while Girardi was up at 99-plus.

Who wants number 85 instead of number 99?

What's the fair way to allocate the scarce resource called Girardi once the transparency movement makes his and everyone else's comparative status clear? Who will make that tragic choice?

All of these issues related to scarce resources are only going to intensify. That's true here and around the world, because of a catch-22 about advances in medical care. These advances will generally mean that everyone lives longer. With older populations everywhere, every country's healthcare needs and expenses as a percent of their overall economy are destined to rise.

Compared to the rest of the world, the United States is staring into that future from a ditch. We already spend 50 to 100 percent more as a portion of our gross domestic product on healthcare than our competitors do. Obamacare is not likely to change that. Indeed, by making the deals he made—by making the right tragic choice and giving healthcare to people like Viola Brown—Barack Obama likely dug us deeper into the ditch.

The best prospect for digging out is that now that we have paid the ransom the industry demanded in Washington to get coverage for Viola Brown in Kentucky, perhaps the resulting sticker shock, exacerbated by renegades like the makers of Sovaldi, will cause us to demand real change on the cost side, too.

Maybe all the new customers created by the Obamacare exchanges will set off a fiscal crisis that will force us to rethink how we pay for healthcare.

Maybe it will make us throw aside the lobbyists and allow drug companies to reap healthy profits but not Sovaldi-sized, screw-you profits.

Maybe it will force Democrats to defy the trial lawyers and allow sensible tort reform.

And maybe it will force us to allow doctors like Corwin, Steele, Gottlieb, and Cosgrove, helped by industry disrupters like the Oscar team, to have a toughly regulated shot at revolutionizing the system by aligning the interests of those who provide care with those who pay for it, while cutting out the middleman insurance companies.

Maybe putting them in the driver's seat on a well-policed highway will allow us to junk the old jalopy and stop rewarding those who want to keep pumping gas into it.

ACKNOWLEDGMENTS

A s I explain in the text, I got interested in the economics and politics of healthcare as a novice in mid-2012. That was when I became curious about why healthcare costs so much more in the United States than anywhere else and decided to use the bills of actual patients to find out. The result was a twenty-four-thousand-word article that no conventional magazine editor would publish.

Richard Stengel, who was then editing *Time,* defied convention and published "Bitter Pill" as an unprecedented Special Report. His gutsy decision to dispense with *Time*'s usual editorial package—as well as the matching enthusiasm and editing skill of his then-deputies, Nancy Gibbs and Michael Duffy—are the reason this book happened. The popular reaction to *Time*'s Special Report spurred me to write more on a subject that I now realized deeply touched most Americans but often left them frustrated and mystified.

The fight over Obamacare, the struggle to implement it, and its impact, or lack thereof, on our broken healthcare system then became the obvious subjects that would enable me to tell the larger story of healthcare in America.

Although this book is about Obamacare and that larger story, it is a story best told in the context of how the American healthcare system works or doesn't work, both for patients needing care and for those who profit in the marketplace where that care is provided. Therefore, portions of that original *Time* article have made their way into this book, usually paraphrased and in expanded or updated form, but sometimes word for word. The same is true of four subsequent articles

I wrote for *Time,* including a cover story chronicling the rescue of the HealthCare.gov website. I estimate that in all about 15 percent of this text is derived in some way from material previously published in *Time.*

In using the Obamacare saga to tell the broader story of American healthcare politics and economics, I benefited from the work of reporters who had been on that beat long before I parachuted in. *The New York Times, The Wall Street Journal, The Washington Post, Politico,* and *ProPublica* were especially helpful. Indeed, Charles Ornstein's reporting at *ProPublica* guided me on several issues and assured me that I wasn't off base on others. I'm sure his work has done the same for many other journalists.

Several industry publications, such as *Modern Healthcare,* were also helpful. As soon as it was launched and *The Washington Post*'s Sarah Kliff started writing there, *Vox* became another great source of guidance.

A half dozen books about the history and politics of American healthcare provided the basics of the education I needed and, as cited in the Source Notes that follow, the basis for some of what I reported.

The book of books for anyone interested in the subject is Princeton professor Paul Starr's Pulitzer Prize–winning *The Social Transformation of American Medicine* (Basic Books, 1982). Professor Starr followed that sweeping history of American healthcare with a book that was even more useful for my recounting of the recent years of the American healthcare battle: *Remedy and Reaction: The Peculiar American Struggle Over Healthcare Reform* (Yale University Press, 2011). It was my guide to the struggle of twentieth-century American presidents to reform the system, and to the obstacles and accidents of history that befell them along the way.

Inside National Health Reform (University of California Press, 2011), written by a true insider—former Ted Kennedy healthcare aide John McDonough—provided a road map of the ins and outs of the Obamacare legislative process, allowing me to start from a base of knowing the chronology, the players, and many of the issues. My interviewing was much smarter because of McDonough.

David Blumenthal and James Morone's *The Heart of Power* (University of California Press, 2010) provided a similar history of past political battles, as did *Power, Politics, and Universal Health Care,* by Stuart Altman and David Shactman (Prometheus Books, 2011).

Landmark, a book published by *The Washington Post*'s reporting staff, who exhaustively covered the passage of Obamacare as it happened, also provided important grounding as I began my reporting.

I also want to thank Professor Uwe Reinhardt, the renowned Princeton healthcare economist, whose writings and conversations provided great insight.

Although I conducted all of the interviews and did most of the research, two of my former Yale students, Elaina Plott and Tessa Berenson, helped gather materials related to some of the Yale–New Haven Hospital court cases and the 1943 War Labor Board decision on health insurance benefits. Additionally, the *Time* research staff, particularly Andrea Sachs, helped nail down some of the factual material in the portions first published in *Time.*

At Random House, Executive Editor Will Murphy provided great guidance, mixing encouragement with sharp line editing and questioning, as well as a perfect pitch for talking me out of including material that complicated the narrative while encouraging me to add information that explained it more clearly. Will did a terrific job with a difficult subject and author.

Publisher Susan Kamil and Deputy Publisher Tom Perry were enthused about this project from the start and oversaw the work that their colleagues at Random House did in making everything come together. In that regard, Benjamin Dreyer, Evan Camfield, and Richard Elman were attentive to every detail required to transform my typing into a finished book worthy of Random House's standards. Editorial assistant Mika Kasuga tirelessly coordinated all aspects of my work with this editing and publishing team, after which London King, Leigh Marchant, and their respective publicity and marketing teams kept coming up with creative ways to give this book the largest audience possible. Finally, I want to extend a special appreciation to copy editor Michelle Daniel, who did much more than the usual polishing, including catching a bunch of careless errors and making several suggestions to improve the reader experience.

I owe great thanks to David Kuhn. I always knew he was a good friend and great editor, because we had worked together on one of my magazine ventures. Now I know he's a great agent. He is still willing to edit manuscripts, and he retains his knack for making writers keep the narrative moving. But now he also helps mightily to turn all that into a winning publishing plan.

Three longtime journalist-friends—Jill Abramson, Jim Warren, and Bob Woodward—were dragooned into reading drafts and providing detailed advice and criticism. So, too, was another former Yale student, Louise Story, who is now a star *New York Times* reporter.

I am also grateful to physicians Peter Bach and Jennifer Brokaw, as well as to two physicians who asked not to be named. All helped me through the world of medicine and medical terminology.

And, of course, I owe a huge debt to the sources listed on the pages that follow, who gave me so much time and tolerated even the most rookie (and, on occasion, hostile) questions. I am equally grateful to the many more sources who are not listed because they asked not to be, or because their input, while helpful to my overall education, was not directly a source for an event in the narrative.

I interviewed 243 people—many of them multiple times—over twenty-seven months in the reporting that made its way into *America's Bitter Pill*. That means I took up a lot of people's time, for which I thank them. I asked even more of several of those sources—the families who opened their medical records to me—and I owe them a special debt.

Finally, there's my family. Yes, I'm grateful for how Emily, Sophie, and Sam and their mother, Cynthia, tolerated me when I was absorbed in researching, organizing, and writing all of this. But that was easy compared to how I pestered them to read various parts of even the earliest drafts.

Beyond that, I can never forget the support of a different kind that they provided during the days described in the first chapter, staying with me at all hours in the hospital and helping me recover at home (once I convinced them that my surgery was not an over-the-top act of undercover journalism). For all of that—and for Cynthia's loving and wise partnership in this as in everything else—I am forever thankful.

APPENDIX

Q&A WITH PRESIDENT OBAMA

Author's Note

As the text and Source Notes indicate, most officials of the Obama administration cooperated in the reporting of this book.

President Obama agreed to answer questions put to him in writing because, assistant press secretary Eric Schultz explained, "He wants to his voice to be in this book, but wants to offer more thoughtful answers than a brief in-person interview" would provide. I would have preferred an in-person interview, as should my readers, because written answers run the risk of being filtered by the president's communications apparatus, and because, as demonstrated below, many of the president's answers deserved the kind of follow-up that only a conversation can facilitate. However, I was assured that the president had read all of my questions and personally signed off on the answers.

Below is the full text of the questions submitted to the president, and his answers, we well as those questions that he specifically declined to answer.

Dear Mr. President:

I have been informed that you have agreed to answer, in writing, a limited number of questions for the book that I am writing about the saga of healthcare reform. The questions will be based on the letter I wrote to you on May 19 outlining my areas of inquiry.

I much appreciate your willingness to engage in this discussion.

As discussed with your press office, I will quote your answers in the book as having been prepared and authorized by you personally.

I am limiting the questions below to a subset of what I outlined in the May 19 letter, although if you want to comment on other issues I raised in the letter, that would, of course, be that much better.

Here are the questions:

QUESTION 1

With regard to point #1 in the letter (healthcare policy in the context of Professor Guido Calabresi's *Tragic Choices*), how much did you worry about "owning" all of American healthcare as you pushed ahead? Do you think Americans who believe themselves to be on the short end of decisions about the allocation of scarce healthcare resources will ever accept those decisions? (Narrow networks that are provided in lower-cost insurance plans would be a good current example.) Do you think democracies—and ours in particular, in today's Washington—can handle these "tragic choices" well without resorting to expert, independent panels akin to the base-closing panels?

THE PRESIDENT'S ANSWER

Declined to answer.

QUESTION 2

Is it fair to say that the more you dug into the issue of healthcare during the 2008 campaign—and the more you met people like Mrs. Amy Chicos (in Iowa) on the campaign trail, who were besieged by medical bills—the more you became determined to take this on? Relatedly, I know that many on your staff urged at the start of the Administration that you put healthcare aside in favor of worrying about the stimulus package and the economic recovery. Why didn't you?

THE PRESIDENT'S ANSWER

Well, we didn't have the luxury of working on just one big issue—the times demanded more. Within a month of my inauguration, we passed the Recovery Act. By virtually every independent economist's estimation, that set of policies helped stave off another Great Depression. And combined with a lot of other actions we've taken since then, helped put us on the longest stretch of uninterrupted private sector job creation in our history. We had to take action and we did.

But America can do more than one thing at a time. And I believed that reforming our health care system wasn't a side project, but a vital part of rebuilding our economy. My top priority has always been to restore the notion that America is a place where if you work hard, you can get ahead. And even before the crisis, few things were doing more to expose working families to economic insecurity than a broken health care system. It was clear that we couldn't address the problem of the middle class falling behind in the long term, without taking on health care in the short term. And we had a once in a generation chance to do it.

Everywhere I went on that first campaign, I heard directly from Americans about what a broken health care system meant to them— the bankruptcies, putting off care until it was too late, not being able to get coverage because of a pre-existing condition. I didn't just learn about this through the stories of others, I had my own, watching my mom struggle with health insurers to get the care she needed when she was sick. The more people I met, the more it seemed that those kinds of experiences were happening to far too many people. And when the going got tough, thinking of those Americans and what they were going through is what kept me going.

QUESTION 3

With regard to #7 in the letter (the anecdote about what others thought was your flat performance at the your first candidates' forum, focusing on healthcare, in Las Vegas in 2007), how would you characterize your performance? Someone on your staff said you said it was "not my best night." True? Also, do you recall Hillary Clinton's performance? (I know this was a long time ago and seems unimportant in the scheme of things, but I consider your evolution from this point an interesting aspect of the narrative. Any memory you have of it would be helpful.)

THE PRESIDENT'S ANSWER

Declined to answer.

QUESTION 4

Do you recall a memo that Peter Orszag wrote to you just after the law was passed urging you to put in charge someone with experience launching and running ventures as complicated as healthcare.gov? What were your reasons for not doing so? If you do not recall the memo, do you recall Peter and Larry Summers advising you to do this? Would you tell a president succeeding you that he or she should heed advice like that when it comes to challenges of this nature?

THE PRESIDENT'S ANSWER

At this point, I am not so interested in Monday Morning quarterbacking the past. We failed at its launch. We learned from that and worked hard to pull ourselves out of the hole we put ourselves in before the end of open enrollment. I can tell you this. We learned a lot of lessons. And we've taken steps to apply those lessons across the government.

[Health and Human Services] Secretary [Sylvia] Burwell has hit the ground running at HHS. She has made significant changes to ensure accountability and transparency as we head into the second open enrollment period. There is a new Marketplace CEO and CTO position, for example.

We've also created a digital service corps to rapidly and effectively prevent, diagnose, and fix technology problems across the federal government. A lot of the HealthCare.gov challenges came from government trying to adapt to technology that is constantly changing and evolving. The digital service corps will create the culture required to help government change along with it. That's going to make a difference in the long run.

Ultimately, technology has the opportunity to dramatically improve the way people can interact with their government, to make it easier to get answers and services. What you saw towards the end of the last open enrollment, when the Marketplaces were working, was that for the first time, people could compare plans, side by side, and see exactly what they were going to pay for coverage that met their families' needs. That is revolutionary in the individual market, where before the ACA, you often had to pass a medical screening just to find out what a plan cost.

But on the lessons I have taken from the HealthCare.gov experience, it is fair to say we are embedding those lessons in much bigger work my administration does today. If you believe in making government work for people, you have to operationalize that—and we have work to do in these final years and plenty of room to improve.

QUESTION 5

What do you think the odds are that Todd Park and the alumni of the tech surge team that you have now brought into the Administration can truly change how the government manages technology and technology procurement? How will they be empowered to make changes if (or inevitably, when) they run into red tape and resistance within agencies? Put differently, how can the procurement establishment be prevented from rejecting a guy like the tee-shirted Mikey Dickerson?

THE PRESIDENT'S ANSWER

Well, it wouldn't be the first time we beat the odds. That is in some way the history of the American experience—us beating the odds through sheer will and dedication to improve things for people. Mikey Dickerson now works at the White House (frequently without a jacket or tie). And he is leading an effort to simplify and improve digital services to help make sure America's government can be innovative, flexible, and help bring in the talent we need, empowering the great people who already work across the government to take on some of our biggest challenges. I have sent a very clear mandate throughout this administration that it is time to shake things up, change the pace of business. And I hope and expect that future presidents will maintain that attitude.

QUESTION 6

Denis McDonough told me that you always ended the pre-launch meetings with the admonition that none of the plans to attract enrollment would matter unless the technology worked. What would you tell a future President about how perhaps that admonition was not enough?

THE PRESIDENT'S ANSWER

The first week I was on the job, I sought out advice from my first Defense Secretary, Bob Gates, who had been around longer than I had. He said, "One thing you should know, Mr. President, is that at any given moment, on any given day, somebody in the federal government is screwing up." Which is true, because there are two million employees, and they do remarkable work every day. But, even if you're firing at a 99.9% success rate that still leaves a lot of opportunity for things not to go as planned.

So you've got to have a culture in place where people aren't afraid to admit there's a problem. And you've got to have a team in place that's coordinated and flexible enough to tackle the problems that arise. If you don't have either of these, small problems become big problems quickly.

QUESTION 7

With regard to #4 in the letter (the political climate), how would you explain the difference in what has happened with Obamacare following its passage compared to the mostly-bipartisan acceptance of Social Security and Medicare once the political fights over passing that legislation were over? (I refer to, and document in the book, the willingness of most on both sides of the aisle in those prior instances to focus on the best ways to implement and improve those laws.)

THE PRESIDENT'S ANSWER

Keep in mind, not only did the ACA become law, it was upheld by the Supreme Court in 2012, and, in the same year, voters rejected the candidate who promised to repeal it. Despite all that, you've seen a sustained effort to sabotage the law at every turn—from fifty-something repeal votes to efforts aimed at defunding its implementation, to lawsuits. This from a party that's typically opposed to frivolous lawsuits.

In contrast, consider what happened when the prescription drug program Medicare Part D was enacted. It had some early challenges. There were technical implementation problems impacting millions of people. Democrats weren't happy with many aspects of the law. It even added hundreds of billions of dollars to the deficit, unlike the ACA, which will help lower the deficit. But once it was the law, everyone pitched in to try and make it work. Democrats weren't about to punish millions of seniors just to make a point or settle a score, they held town halls to get seniors signed up. And a decade later, the program is wildly popular.

But even as more and more data rolls in on the ACA, even with a historic slowdown in health care cost growth, and millions of people gaining coverage, Republicans are still staking their platform on repealing this progress. This is painfully clear in the decision by some Republican Governors to not expand Medicaid. Now, you've seen some Republican Governors do the right thing, and expand coverage to their residents, and I'm hopeful that more will. But it is a completely unnecessary and mean spirited decision to continue to deny coverage to those who need it most because of politics.

But it should be pretty clear by now that I didn't do this because it was good politics. I did it because I believed it was good for the country. I did it because I believed it was good for the American people.

QUESTION 8

Two questions about Valerie Jarrett:

a. I am told by five people who have served in senior capacities in the Administration that Ms. Jarrett often told them that "the President wants you to bring us your solutions, not your problems," and that this may have been why you were unaware of troubles associated with the healthcare.gov launch. These same people also said that on matters in which she was involved she was "the real chief of staff." I feel compelled to ask you to comment on that.

b. I am also told by three senior officials that Ms. Jarrett agreed with you that Nancy-Ann DeParle should be the person in charge of the implementation of the health reform law, including the website. Is this true?

THE PRESIDENT'S ANSWER

Declined to answer.

QUESTION 9

With regard to #3 in the May letter ("Can Anyone Fix The Jalopy"), do you think there will be a time ten or twenty years from now when the political climate will have changed and we can more thoroughly "fix the jalopy" that is our nation's healthcare system? For example, do you think it will ever be possible to pass legislation that does more to control costs (such as price controls on prescription drugs, or authorization for Medicare to negotiate prescription drug prices)?

THE PRESIDENT'S ANSWER

There's always going to be more that can be done to improve public policy, whether it's strengthening the economy, or increasing energy independence, or making health care affordable—but now, for the first time, we have addressed some of the worst problems of our health care system, and we have a foundation to build on and improve. Millions of Americans have gained access to affordable coverage, and some of the worst insurance company abuses are now things of the past.

And on health care affordability, there was a lot of pundit chatter that dismissed the ACA's initiatives to promote value, improve efficiency, and reduce waste, and a lot of those people are having to rethink things now. Frankly what we've seen in progress on costs has surpassed almost anybody's most optimistic expectations. I remember some prominent reporter saying that Congress would be popping the champagne if they passed a deficit reduction bill with that big of an impact today. And the lesson that all of us should take away from that is that there are a lot of ways to address our deficits and our health care costs that don't rely on just cutting benefits, or turning Medicare into a voucher program. What the ACA has already shown is that we *can* make a dent in that, and that it can pay huge dividends for families and the federal government's balance sheets. We can do more, and my budget includes a number of policy changes to build on this progress. Congress also needs to keep pursuing that kind of change, and prioritize reforms that reduce inefficiency and waste before telling older Americans who worked their whole lives that Medicare isn't going to be there as it was promised to them.

QUESTION 10

Your reputation as "No-Drama Obama"—that is, as someone who has little tolerance for egos, turf battles, shouting matches, and so forth—has been borne out in my reporting. Notwithstanding the obvious benefits of this leadership style, do you think it might also have had the consequence of letting conflicts within the White House and the Administration (such as disputes related to the planning and launch of healthcare.gov) simmer beneath the surface, outside your view?

THE PRESIDENT'S ANSWER

You need to create a culture where people feel free to admit there's a problem, but you also need a structure where those problems make it to the right people so actions can be taken.

In hindsight, there should have been one central person in charge, a CEO of the Marketplace. Now we have that in Kevin Counihan, who successfully launched the Marketplace in Connecticut, and Secretary Burwell has made many other significant changes to ensure accountability and transparency moving forward.

I mentioned the work Mikey Dickerson and others are doing to simply and improve digital services across the government, and I expect that those efforts will help us bring in new talent, and work more effectively with the great talent we already have to improve the experiences that Americans have with the government.

QUESTION 11

How would you explain to a sixth or seventh grade class the process that led to the passage of Obamacare—the negotiations with the various industry sectors, the lack of bipartisanship, the sheer complexity and length of the statute?

THE PRESIDENT'S ANSWER

Declined to answer.

METHODOLOGY AND
SOURCE NOTES

R EADERS DESERVE TO KNOW AS MUCH AS POSSIBLE ABOUT WHY AN
author thinks he knows what he says he knows.

Although I have tried to make it clear throughout the text who or
what my sources are, these notes are intended to supplement the text
by providing information about sources where I decided that something in the text required an explanation or elaboration that would
interrupt the narrative.

In some cases where I thought an additional explanation or note
was especially important and I did not want to count on readers finding it in this section, I included a brief footnote in the text.

GENERAL METHODOLOGY

In no case is a thought attributed to someone directly unless that person told me about that thought.

In no case is a conversation or a discussion in a meeting quoted unless at least one participant in that conversation or discussion was my
source.

In several chapters, particularly those covering the deliberations by
the Obama administration and Congress as the healthcare reform legislation was being conceived and then implemented, I quote from
notes taken during meetings or a journal kept contemporaneously by
one of the participants in those meetings. In those instances, I had access to the notes or the journal and then followed up to confirm their
meaning with the author and with at least one other participant in the
discussion or meeting.

If I described a source in the text generally but without a name it was because the source had set ground rules prohibiting his or her name from being used. Where I can shed more light than I did in the text, I do so in these notes.

Where I had multiple sources, they are listed in order of the importance of the information they provided. For example, if two sources are listed, the first source may have offered the information, which the second source confirmed. Titles used for the sources are the ones they held at the time of the events in question.

I always have firsthand knowledge of emails, internal memos, focus group reports (such as those done in Kentucky), or stock analysts' reports that are quoted in the text because I have read them.

Source references, such as books or newspaper articles, are listed below only where it is not clear in the text that I relied on the reporting of others.

References are not listed for general statements (about developments in some aspect of the healthcare industry, for example) if they are widely known and uncontroversial. Similarly, references are not provided for widely reported news events, or for unambiguous statements of fact, such as the date of a public event. Nor are they listed if the material is obviously taken from a public record such as a budget, a campaign debate or presidential speech, or the transcript of a congressional hearing.

If the text quotes from a newspaper article or television program, the reference is not cited here if the text makes the source and the date clear. However, I have provided links in these notes to videos or documents when I think a reader might want to see them.

References to any company's revenue or profits are based on its publicly filed financial reports for the period in question.

I always use the latest information that I can find when citing data such as the amount spent nationally on a certain type of medical care or treatment, unless I am using it to relate to an event taking place at that time in the narrative.

In cases where estimates are inexact or vary—such as data on healthcare spending—I veer toward the lower estimates in order not to overstate a point.

All revenue, profit, and salary data for nonprofit hospitals referred to in the text is taken from the nonprofit hospitals' IRS Form 990 filings, which are available at http://www.guidestar.org/.

SOURCE NOTES

CHAPTER 1: LOOKING UP FROM THE GURNEY

4 **We spend $17 billion a year on artificial knees and hips, which is 55 percent more than Hollywood takes in at the box office:** These are 2009 revenues for artificial knees and hips and 2013 revenues ($10.9 billion) for Hollywood, derived respectively from this healthcare industry website: http://www.60obn.com/?tag=orthopedic-implants, and this movie industry data site: http://boxofficemojo.com/yearly/chart/?yr=2013. Therefore, the actual difference is likely to be significantly more than 55 percent, because spending on knees and hips surely increased between 2009 and 2013.

4 **America's total healthcare bill for 2014 is $3 trillion:** Actually, it is $3.093 trillion, according to this report from the federal government: http://www.cms.gov/Research-Statistics-Data-and-Systems/Statistics-Trends-and-Reports/NationalHealthExpendData/downloads/proj2012.pdf. However, this was a forecast done in 2013. The real number is not likely to be known until late in 2015 or early in 2016. I think it is likely to end up higher. This report by the Deloitte consulting firm used a different calculating method and estimated spending in 2010 to be $3.2 trillion, which means it would be significantly higher than that in 2014: http://www.deloitte.com/assets/Dcom-UnitedStates/Local%20Assets/Documents/us_dchs_2012_hidden_costs112712.pdf.

4 **We spend more on healthcare than the next ten biggest spenders combined:** This comes from an industry report compiled in 2011 by McKinsey & Company's McKinsey Global Institute.

4 **There are 31.5 MRI machines per million people:** See table 2 of this report from the Commonwealth Fund: http://www.commonwealthfund.org/~/media/files/publications/fund-report/2013/nov/1717_thomson_intl_profiles_hlt_care_sys_2013_v2.pdf.

4 **We spend $85.9 billion trying to treat back pain:** "Expenditures and Health Status Among Adults with Back and Neck Problems," *Journal of the American Medical Association,* February 13, 2008. Note: This number is for the year 2005; it has obviously increased significantly since then.

5 **as much as we spend on all of the country's state, city, county, and town police forces:** "Sourcebook of Criminal Justice Statistics," http://www.albany.edu/sourcebook/pdf/t142006.pdf. Note: This is for the year 2006.

5 **We've created a system with 1.5 million people working in the health insurance industry but with barely half as many doctors:** "The Anatomy of Healthcare in the United States," *Journal of the American Medical Association,* January 5, 2014. The actual numbers are 1,509,000 health insurance workers and 831,000 physicians (both for the year 2011).

5 **Medtronic . . . enjoys nearly double the gross profit margin of Apple:** The actual gross profit margins were 39.3 percent for Apple (for the quarter ending June 30, 2014) and 74.1 percent for Medtronic (for the quarter ending July 31, 2014).

5 **nine of the ten largest pharmaceutical companies in the world have signed settlement agreements:** Website of the Office of the Inspector General, U.S. Department of Health and Human Services: https://oig.hhs.gov/compliance/corporate-integrity-agreements/cia-documents.asp#cia_list.

5 **the outsized salary of the guy who ran the supposedly nonprofit hospital:** Salaries of hospi-

tal presidents are taken from the latest publicly available Form 990 financial report that the hospitals in question have filed with the Internal Revenue Service.

7 **Healthcare is America's largest industry by far, employing a sixth of the country's workforce:** U.S. Bureau of Labor Statistics, compiled by taking employment data from all health-related categories.

8 **the healthcare industry spends four times as much on lobbying as the number two Beltway spender:** Data compiled from the Center for Responsive Politics' OpenSecrets.org website.

10 **60 percent of the nearly one million personal bankruptcies filed in the United States last year resulted from medical bills:** This is a widely reported statistic. See, for example, http://www.cnn.com/2009/HEALTH/06/05/bankruptcy.medical.bills/.

11 **Montana's Max Baucus . . . had a picture on his desk of a constituent he had befriended:** David Schwartz and Liz Fowler, who were senior healthcare counsel on Senator Baucus's Finance Committee staff, with Schwartz assuming that title after Fowler left to work in the private sector.

11 **a mother who . . . had to take an $8.50 an hour job as a nightshift gate agent at the Las Vegas airport:** Liz Fowler, and Mary Fowler—her mother.

11 **Ted Kennedy's firsthand experience with healthcare issues:** His autobiography *True Compass* (Twelve, 2009); his wife Vicki Kennedy; and his former senior healthcare adviser John McDonough.

CHAPTER 2: CENTER STAGE

13 **Democratic presidential candidates' forum:** The event is available at the C-SPAN Video Library at http://www.c-span.org/video/?197322-1/campaign-2008-health-care-forum; a transcript is available at http://2008election.procon.org/pdf/Dem20070324.pdf.

16 **The Scooter Store, based in New Braunfels, Texas, was allegedly using millions of dollars in television ads:** Details of the charges and settlement of the case are taken from a press release detailing the charges and settlement from the U.S. Department of Justice, May 11, 2007: http://www.justice.gov/opa/pr/2007/May/07_civ_344.html.

17 **another team of federal prosecutors was pursuing a far bigger target—the Aventis unit of Sanofi:** Details are taken from a press release detailing the charges and settlement from the U.S. Department of Justice, September 10, 2007: http://www.justice.gov/opa/pr/2007/September/07_civ_694.html.

17 **"CIA" had become a favorite acronym having to do with renegade drug companies:** In every conversation I had with officials of the U.S. Justice Department or the inspector general's office at the U.S. Department of Health and Human Services, they were routinely referred to that way.

19 **the entrenched, sorry state of the American healthcare system (history of healthcare proposals put forward by Theodore Roosevelt, Franklin Roosevelt, Harry Truman, and Richard Nixon, and general history of healthcare reform):** I used multiple sources, including archives from *The New York Times*. However, the best books about the history of American healthcare and efforts to reform it are the Pulitzer Prize–winning classic *The Social Transformation of American Medicine* by Paul Starr (Basic Books, 1982) and Starr's terrific follow-on book, *Remedy and Reaction: The Peculiar American Struggle Over Healthcare Reform* (Yale University Press, 2011). Two other extremely valuable books were *The Heart of Power: Health and Politics in the Oval Office,* by David Blumenthal and James A. Morone (University of California Press, 2010), and *Power, Politics, and Universal Health Care,* by Stuart Altman and David Shactman (Prometheus Books, 2011). The work of these authors informed much of what I wrote about the history of healthcare reform, from the development of medicine into a sophisticated, expensive profession, to the decision of the War Labor Board not to count health insurance benefits as compensation, to the Wilbur Mills scandal.

19 **The plan was called Blue Cross (history of Blue Cross and Blue Shield):** Thomas C. Buchmueller and Alan C. Monheit, "Employer-Sponsored Health Insurance and the Promise of Health Insurance Reform," National Bureau of Economic Research Working Paper No. 14839, April 2009, http://www.nber.org/papers/w14839.

20 **the forerunner to New York–Presbyterian:** From the hospital's website: http://nyp.org/about/history.html.

20 **in 1929, Americans spent about 1 percent of the country's gross domestic product on anything related to healthcare:** This data was compiled from government archives by http://www.usgovernmentspending.com/healthcare_spending. However, Harvard healthcare economist David Cutler estimated in an email to me that it might have been as much as 3.5 percent.

20 **By 1966, it was 6 percent:** "Health Care Cost Tripled Since '50; Federal Data Show Rise to $36.8-Billion in Nation," *The New York Times,* January 16, 1966.

20 **Theodore Roosevelt had proposed a national health insurance plan:** The history of the healthcare proposals put forward by Theodore Roosevelt, Franklin Roosevelt, Harry Truman, and Richard Nixon relies on multiple newspaper archives, plus the books cited above by Starr, Blumenthal and Morone, and Altman and Shactman.

22 **Harry Truman—influenced, historians say, by the number of recruits he had met during the war who showed up for duty too sick to fight:** Blumenthal and Morone, *The Heart of Power.*

22 **Union opposition:** Again, this is from several of the books mentioned, but particularly from "Remedy and Reaction."

23 **The AMA spent what in 1949 was an astounding $1.5 million to campaign against the plan, labeling it as socialized medicine that would be "the key to the arch of a socialist state," which would destroy doctors' independent relationships with their patients and lead to doctors becoming government employees:** Starr, *Social Transformation of American Medicine,* 285.

23 **In 1940, fewer than ten million Americans had private healthcare. By 1950, 76.6 million enjoyed that protection:** This comes directly from Altman and Shactman, *Power, Politics, and Universal Health Care.*

23 **By the time the candidates appeared that night in Las Vegas in 2007, 162 million nonelderly Americans:** Buchmueller and Monheit, "Employer-Sponsored Health Insurance and the Promise of Health Insurance Reform." National Bureau of Economic Research Working Paper No. 14839, April 2009: http://www.nber.org/papers/w14839.

24 **In 1965, Medicare had been projected by a House of Representatives committee to cost $12 billion by 1990:** The projections of the House Ways and Means Committee can be found at http://ssa.gov/history/pdf/Downey%20PDFs/Social%20Security%20Amendments%20of%201967%20Vol%205.pdf.

24 **Its actual cost by then was $110 billion:** This can be found at http://medicare.commission.gov/medicare/history.htm.

26 **Emilia Gilbert—a school bus driver earning about $1,800 a month, whom I wrote about in the** *Time* **article—fell victim to these coverage gaps:** This is one of the cases included in my *Time* special report. I interviewed Ms. Gilbert and had full access to all of Ms. Gilbert's bills.

27 **Medicare, which pays hospitals based on their costs, plus overhead and a small profit margin, for providing each service, would have paid about $825 for all three tests:** Determining how much Medicare will pay for a given treatment or test is a frustrating, complicated process. First, it requires determining what is called the "HCPCS code" that Medicare assigns to the procedure being billed. If it is a hospital treatment, the hospital's charges are tied to a code called a DRG. Figuring out the correct code often takes help from a doctor or other medical professional in order to translate the acronyms and abbreviations on the bill into a precise identification of the procedure. Then, one must consult a difficult-to-navigate Centers for Medicare and Medicaid Services website—http://www.cms.gov/apps/physician-fee-schedule/search/search-criteria.aspx—and add in factors such as the location where the

treatment took place (because Medicare payments take regional cost factors into account), and whether it took place in a hospital or at an outpatient facility (which gets paid less). When that information is entered, the result is the price that Medicare will pay that hospital or clinic for the treatment or test in question.

28 **In describing the forces that impelled the push for healthcare reform,** *Harvard Business Review* **would later cite a 2007 study:** Brad Evans, "Obamacare Website," *Harvard Business Review,* March 18, 2013.

28 **Yale New Haven, which has a tax exemption as a nonprofit institution, was on its way to recording operating income of more than $125 million:** As noted above, all hospital and salary data in the text is taken from the nonprofit hospitals' IRS Form 990 filings, which are available at http://www.guidestar.org/.

28 **President Bill Clinton had appointed his wife to come up with a plan for a massive overhaul of the country's healthcare system:** For the history of Hillarycare I reviewed multiple archives of various publications, particularly *The New York Times,* but the source I relied on most was the classic history of Hillarycare by master journalists Haynes Johnson and David Broder: *The System: The American Way of Politics at the Breaking Point* (Little, Brown, 1996). In addition, I drew from Blumenthal and Morone, *The Heart of Power,* cited above.

29 **The answer was Mitt Romney and a young economics professor named Jonathan Gruber (Gruber bio and history with Romneycare):** Gruber; former White House National Economic Council director Larry Summers; and David Cutler, the Otto Eckstein Professor of Applied Economics at Harvard, who was the senior healthcare adviser to the Obama 2008 primary campaign.

30 **an idea first floated in 1989 by economist Stuart Butler:** Stuart Butler, "Assuring Affordable Healthcare for All Americans," an October 2, 1989, lecture that was subsequently published by the Heritage Foundation and can be found at http://healthcarereform.procon .org/sourcefiles/1989_assuring_affordable_health_care_for_all_americans.pdf.

32 **Nixon announced a plan that would force employers to buy insurance for all of their workers:** Details of the Nixon plan are from White House press office archives and from Starr, *Remedy and Reaction,* and Blumenthal and Morone, *The Heart of Power.*

33 **Romney, citing the original Heritage Foundation article, would deride the "free riders" who refuse to buy insurance and call the mandate "the ultimate conservative idea":** I found this because the Web publication *Business Insider* discovered it in Michael Kranish and Scott Helman's biography of Romney, *The Real Romney.* See http://www.businessinsider.com/guess-what-mitt-romney-once-called-the-ultimate-conservative-idea-2012-8#ixzz23kadtNvH.

34 **On the stage with Romney, celebrating the governor's signing of what would come to be called Romneycare (Romneycare celebration at Faneuil Hall):** The event was videotaped and is available on YouTube: https://www.youtube.com/watch?v=-GL6Sw_U1gk. I also interviewed four people who were there, including Gruber.

36 **Obama had promised a union rally that he would fight for the single-payer system:** The pro-reform group Physicians for a National Health Program found a video of then state senator Obama's speech to a union rally and posted it on YouTube: http://www.pnhp.org/ news/2008/june/barack_obama_on_sing.php.

36 **Obama's team was less enthusiastic about the idea that the issue would fire up the troops:** According to a senior Obama campaign political aide, a mid-level policy adviser, and a junior person in the polling operation.

37 **was not how Mary Fowler, then sixty-two, had planned to spend her retirement:** Information about Liz Fowler and her family is from Liz Fowler, her mother, Mary, and— briefly—her father, Robert. Fowler's account of her history working for Max Baucus was corroborated by three colleagues who served on Baucus's Senate staff; the academic degrees and honors listed in the text were independently checked.

39 **WellPoint, the insurer that rejected Mary, traced its roots:** The history of WellPoint is taken from its website: http://www.wellpoint.com/AboutWellPoint/CompanyHistory/.

42 **Healthcare spending as a percent of England's gross domestic product is lower, but outcomes are better in England, compared to the United States:** There are several agencies that report on these comparisons, including the Organization for Economic Cooperation and Development (OECD). The OECD studies can be found at http://www.oecd.org/els/health-systems/health-data.htm. A vivid comparison of healthcare expenditures and results for the United States and England (as well as many other countries) can be found at table 2 in this report from the Commonwealth Fund: http://www.commonwealthfund.org/~/media/files/publications/fund-report/2013/nov/1717_thomson_intl_profiles_hlt_care_sys_2013_v2.pdf. The relevant numbers, as reported in table 2, are that in 2011 England spent 9.4 percent of its gross domestic product on healthcare, while the United States spent 17.7 percent. Among other healthcare quality measurements, the rate of "avoidable deaths"—defined as deaths that would have been "amenable to health care"—was 13 percent lower in England. The British system, which citizens can supplement by paying for private care, attracts regular public complaints, particularly over long waits for elective surgery. But another measurement in the same table shows that in polls taken in 2010, the system's overall approval rating was 62 percent compared to 29 percent in the United States.

CHAPTER 3: MAX, BARACK, HILLARY, BILLY, AND THE GATHERING CONSENSUS

43 **Baucus told Fowler and the rest of his staff that he was determined to set the stage for systemic healthcare reform in 2008:** Fowler.

43 **When Baucus, then sixty-six, met with his staff to discuss healthcare, he often talked about Lester Skramsted:** David Schwartz and Fowler, who were senior aides to Baucus.

45 **Hillary Clinton was furious about the Kennedy endorsement:** Senior Clinton policy adviser Neera Tanden.

47 **Kennedy and Baucus formed an alliance to lay the groundwork for healthcare reform:** Although supplemented with interviews of many of the key players—such as Fowler, senior Kennedy healthcare aide John McDonough, and two senior aides to Republican senators— much of this material is derived from the excellent account provided by John McDonough in his book *Inside National Health Reform* (University of California Press, 2011), which chronicles the journey of Obamacare through Congress from the perspective of a top Kennedy aide.

49 **The Obama campaign called the ad "Billy":** The ad can be viewed on YouTube: https://www.youtube.com/watch?v=NCROog9CfAw.

51 **Karen Ignagni was thinking the same thing in the summer of 2008:** Ignagni and then-AHIP vice president for communications Robert Zirkelbach.

51 **The individual market was in deeper trouble. In fact, it was in danger of drying up completely:** Special Report from the United Hospital Fund, published by the New York State Health Foundation, 2012, http://nyshealthfoundation.org/uploads/resources/BP4-20120820-B.pdf.

CHAPTER 4: "THIS IS WHAT I THOUGHT THE SENATE WOULD BE LIKE"

54 **the June 16, 2008, healthcare summit that Baucus and Fowler had organized:** I obtained a transcript of the Baucus healthcare summit proceedings. It does not seem to be available online.

CHAPTER 5: A NEW PRESIDENT COMMITS, AND HIS CAMP DIVIDES

60 **Neera Tanden had been the Clinton campaign's chief domestic policy adviser (Neera Tanden's background and decision to join Obama campaign):** Tanden, two close associates, publicly available biographical material, and the Jason Horowitz *Washington Post* profile cited in the text.

61 **Tanden attended her first meeting with the new boss and his senior staff:** Tanden, two Obama political aides, one of whom was there.

61 **"You know," Obama said, "I think maybe Hillary was right about the mandate":** Tanden.

64 **Most of the Obama people, including newly appointed chief of staff Rahm Emanuel, didn't want to bother with healthcare in the early days of the administration:** Rahm Emanuel, Zeke Emanuel, Peter Orszag, Neera Tanden, former Senator Tom Daschle, and White House healthcare adviser Bob Kocher, among others.

64 **some of the people being asked to frame Obama's economic package disagreed (early debates during the transition about the substance of reform):** The same sources as listed immediately above, as well as Jonathan Gruber and David Cutler.

65 **Daschle had a better idea. He would do both:** Rahm Emanuel, Zeke Emanuel, and Daschle.

69 **Lambrew treated Emanuel as if she thought he was a know-it-all:** DeParle, Zeke Emanuel, two Obama policy aides, and one congressional staffer who frequently witnessed the interaction between the two. (Lambrew declined repeated requests to be interviewed, so I never could ask her what she thought.)

69 **To Emanuel, Lambrew was the naïve, left-wing policy wonk:** Zeke Emanuel, Nancy-Ann DeParle, and a close colleague of Zeke Emanuel.

70 **Jarrett thought that extending coverage should, indeed, win out over fights about cost control:** Summers, Orszag, Zeke Emanuel, Rahm Emanuel, DeParle, and Kocher.

71 **Summers, Orszag, Kocher, Zeke Emanual, and the rest of the economic team, however, saw reform in terms of their turf:** Summers, Orszag, Zeke Emanuel, Kocher, Gruber, and Cutler.

71 **Lambrew was fine with that prescription. Expanding coverage was the priority:** Zeke Emanuel, DeParle, Gruber, and Orszag.

72 **He, too, was confident the new Obama team could go further than Gruber thought:** Daschle.

CHAPTER 6: EVERY LOBBYIST'S FAVORITE DATE

74 **Baucus's staff sent their white paper to the Obama transition team as a courtesy, and incorporated minimal suggestions:** Kocher, Fowler, and Zeke Emanuel.

74 **Baucus had wanted to draft actual legislation. Fowler convinced him not to:** Fowler.

75 **However, Baucus was sure of one thing:** Fowler and a senior member of Ted Kennedy's staff who was privy to a conversation Kennedy had with Baucus.

76 **An initiative that Grassley had pressed Baucus to include was also something Zeke Emanuel was obsessed with:** Senator Charles Grassley, Zeke Emanuel, and two senior aides to Grassley.

79 **In fact, Baucus and his team had wanted to go further:** Fowler, Kocher.

79 **The white paper—Baucus's "Call to Action":** The text of this document can be found in a PDF at the Senate Finance Committee website: http://www.finance.senate.gov/.

79 **Ted Kennedy's HELP Committee:** I credit McDonough's *Inside National Health Reform* in the text, but, although I also relied on newspaper archives and interviews with others who were involved, I want to emphasize again how much his account provided the foundation for my reporting and description of these events in particular.

CHAPTER 7: PUNTING TO CAPITOL HILL

83 **Rahm Emanuel saw the sudden talent and leadership gap as one more reason to question whether the new president ought to push ahead:** Rahm Emanuel, Zeke Emanuel, Tom Daschle, David Cutler.

83 **"I am going to do this," he promised Orszag:** Orszag.

84 **Yet Obama took an almost instant liking to DeParle, as did Valerie Jarrett:** DeParle, Rahm Emanuel, and Zeke Emanuel.

84 **Zeke Emanuel would soon tell a friend that he thought the President was "mesmerized by her;**

maybe it's that they both lost parents early on, or something": The friend insisted on anonymity, but during one of our interviews Zeke Emanuel said almost the same thing to me.

84   **Kocher and Zeke Emanuel had been working on the spreadsheet since December**: Zeke Emanuel and Kocher. I reviewed a copy of the spreadsheet.

91   **Fowler and Baucus would arrive the next day for a lunch with Kennedy**: Fowler and Vicki Kennedy.

92   **a dinner held the night of the inaugural in a private room at Washington's Caucus Room restaurant (venue, conversation, and attendees at Frank Luntz Inauguration Night dinner)**: Luntz.

CHAPTER 8: DEAL TIME

95   **Antonios "Tony" Clapsis, a bearded, wiry twenty-eight-year-old who loved crunching numbers (background on Clapsis and his hiring)**: Clapsis, Fowler, and two other aides to members of the Senate Finance Committee.

96   **Republican senator Olympia Snowe was insisting that she would support reform only if it were paid for without any such broader tax measures**: Senator Snowe, Fowler, Senator Grassley, and DeParle.

97   **First to the table, beginning in early March, were the pharmaceutical companies, represented by several of Tauzin's deputies from PhRMA**: Tauzin, Fowler, Clapsis, Zeke Emanuel, Amgen's chief lobbyist David Beier, DeParle, and a chief executive of one of the pharmaceutical companies who was directly involved in the negotiations. I also reviewed internal memos and emails related to these negotiations.

100   **an unusual meeting took place in a conference room at the Democratic Senatorial Campaign Committee headquarters**: Extensive emails and other documents related to this meeting and to the PhRMA negotiations, including those quoted in the text, were subpoenaed by the House Energy and Commerce Committee, which made them available to reporters. In addition, members of the staff of the committee, as well as Tauzin, Fowler, DeParle, and two others who asked not to be named, were interviewed about all of the events surrounding the PhRMA negotiations and the secret campaign fund.

101   **The hospitals were next up at the Finance Committee negotiating table (hospital negotiations and deal)**: Clapsis, Fowler, DeParle, and three executives of hospitals who were kept informed of the negotiations.

102   **The latest report, for 2008, had claimed hospitals provided $36 billion in uncompensated care**: This "fact sheet" from the American Hospital Association: http://www.aha.org/search?q=charity+care&site=redesign_aha_org.

102   **That $36 billion represented only about 5 percent of all hospital revenue in 2008**: This report from CMS, showing 2008 hospital revenue of $746.5 billion: https://www.cms.gov/Research-Statistics-Data-and-Systems/Statistics-Trends-and-Reports/NationalHealth ExpendData/downloads/proj2008.pdf.

104   *National Journal* **would discover the reality, and peril, of healthcare having replaced steel as Pittsburgh's dominant industry**: *The National Journal,* January 31, 2013.

104   **Romoff soon began leading a charge to consolidate (UPMC history and acquisition strategy)**: UPMC chief executive officer Jeffrey Romoff, UPMC vice president Paul Wood, and *Beyond the Bounds,* a history of the hospital system published by UPMC in 2009.

105   **UPMC controlled 55 percent of the market for hospital and outpatient clinical services in the region**: Romoff, Wood, and a review of documents associated with the suit.

107   **Karen Ignagni, whose AHIP represented Highmark and all the other insurers, was also game to negotiate with the Baucus team (insurers' negotiations)**: Ignagni, Zirkelbach, AHIP press releases and white papers, Clapsis, Fowler, and Schwartz.

109   **the medical technology and device industry negotiations**: A senior lobbyist for the industry, Clapsis, Fowler, and DeParle.

CHAPTER 9: BEHIND CLOSED DOORS: WHITE HOUSE TURF WARS, INDUSTRY DEALS, AND SENATE WRANGLING

III **a briefing memo for the president (wrangling over the DeParle memo):** I saw one staff member's detailed entries in a journal about the wrangling over the DeParle memo, and I read the final memo. I also interviewed two White House advisers (who were on opposite sides of the dispute) about it.

117 **a large group gathered with the president in the Roosevelt Room to review a PowerPoint about healthcare reform:** I read notes of the meeting taken by an attendee and interviewed DeParle, Zeke Emanuel, Schiliro, and Kocher about it.

118 **Obama had now signed on to the mandate, though he would not go public about it until he was pressured by Baucus (Obama pressured to write letter to Baucus, which was drafted while in flight to Egypt):** DeParle, Fowler.

119 **It was about an arcane health insurance term called the medical loss ratio, or MLR (Lambrew MLR memo and debate over the issue):** I reviewed the MLR memo and the journal entries of a member of the staff who attended the meetings at which it was discussed, then interviewed three White House staff members who were involved in the issue.

121 **UnitedHealthcare's CEO had famously taken home more than a billion dollars in a severance package (UnitedHealthcare CEO settlement with SEC):** SEC press release, December 6, 2007, http://www.sec.gov/news/press/2007/2007-255.htm.

122 **President Obama had his first meeting with health industry executives:** Tauzin, DeParle, Beier, and one of those executives.

123 **They were surprised still more the next day when they were called back to the White House:** Tauzin, three of those executives, multiple subsequent newspaper articles (including the *New York Times* story cited in the text), and a member of the White House communications staff.

124 **This fiasco had been orchestrated by the economic team:** One of the members of that team and a member of the White House communications staff.

125 **DeParle upped the ante from $80 billion to $120 billion:** Tauzin, DeParle, Clapsis, and internal emails among drug industry lobbyists that I reviewed.

126 **Both DeParle's shop and the economic team were nervous about those pledges:** DeParle, Kocher, and Zeke Emanuel.

127 **Three weeks later, on July 7, 2009, the drug company CEOs met in the White House with Rahm Emanuel, DeParle, and Baucus and shook hands on the deal:** DeParle and Tauzin, as confirmed by documents subpoenaed by the House Energy and Commerce Committee that I reviewed and that committee's subsequent report: http://archives.republicans.energycommerce.house .gov/Media/file/PDFs/20120531ObamacareDeals.pdf.

131 **Harry Reid immediately turned his attention to making sure that he could keep every Democrat on board. Baucus, however, still wanted a bipartisan deal:** Although, again, McDonough's *Inside National Health Reform* provided much of the foundation for this reporting about the legislative wrangling, my sources included DeParle, Senators Snowe and Grassley, two Democratic senators who asked not to be named, Fowler and Clapsis, eleven Senate and six House staff members who asked not to be named, and a daily journal kept by a White House staff member.

131 **Dodd was constantly on the phone consulting Kennedy, who was confined to his Cape Cod home:** Vicki Kennedy.

132 **Fowler assured her that the Finance Committee bill would try to fix the age band:** Zirkelbach and Fowler.

132 **Amgen deployed the kind of muscle on Capitol Hill that had become standard:** Data on Amgen's lobbying and campaign spending was compiled for me in a special data search conducted by the Center for Responsive Politics (http://www.opensecrets.org).

133 **But Amgen had more than that. The company had David Beier:** Tauzin, Kocher, Beier, and two Senate and three House staff members who asked not to be named.

134 **With Ted Kennedy happily watching the proceedings on C-SPAN:** Vicki Kennedy.

136 **the president met with Reid, Baucus, and House Speaker Nancy Pelosi to resolve who should get subsidies:** This meeting and what was discussed were recorded in the notes of a White House staff person working on healthcare.

136 **Reid and his staff had especially little use for Baucus's romancing:** Senator Snowe, Clapsis, and Fowler.

136 **Snowe, with whom Reid had a frosty, often dismissive relationship:** Three senate staff members and Senator Snowe.

136 **Snowe was thought by some around the Senate to be difficult to work with:** Two senators and five Senate staff members.

137 **Grassley, too, persuaded Baucus to make dozens of changes:** Fowler, Clapsis, Schwartz, Senator Grassley, and two members of Grassley's staff.

138 **Baucus's efforts to accommodate Grassley and Snowe seemed to be working. Even DeParle thought so (DeParle meetings with Grassley and Snow):** DeParle and Senators Grassley and Snowe.

138 **White House "Innovation" meeting and meetings with Justice and FTC officials:** Zeke Emanuel, Kocher, and detailed journal entries of a White House staff member.

139 **Orszag and Larry Summers and their staffs had been lobbying the House and Senate staffs to include something that they argued would be a real cost cutter:** Summers, Orszag, Zeke Emanuel, and detailed journal entries of a White House staff member.

140 **approval ratings for reform were quickly dropping into negative territory, and Simas report on poll numbers and subsequent meeting where he described the "two evils":** Journal entries, including a sketch of Simas's whiteboard diagram, by a White House staff member who attended the Simas meetings, confirmed by two White House staff members.

140 **Two economics aides—Summers deputy Jason Furman and Treasury's Gene Sperling—began working on a slimmed-down, fallback reform plan:** Staff member's journal entry, confirmed by that staff member.

141 **"Why can't I explain that this is about costs and not just coverage?" Obama complained:** This, too, comes from notes entered into the staff member's journal.

142 **"Government takeover" would become the prime phrase he featured in a "words that work" memo he distributed to Republicans:** Luntz. I also reviewed his memo.

143 **Ignagni was upset although not surprised:** Ignagni and Zirkelbach.

145 **soda industry and retailers had convinced Baucus to take the soft drink tax off the table:** Staffer's journal entry and Fowler.

145 **It seemed like every day some senator or another added something new to Baucus's working draft or took something out:** In addition to journal entries from a White House staffer: DeParle, Senators Snowe and Grassley, two Democratic senators who asked not to be named, Fowler and Clapsis, and eleven Senate and six House staff members who asked not to be named.

146 **Orszag and his team infuriated Lambrew by contradicting her numbers:** Staff member's journal entry and interview with that staff member.

146 **Deliberations about grandfathering:** This was the subject of extensive, detailed entries in the staff member's journal.

CHAPTER 10: THE TEA PARTY SUMMER, "I'M FEELING LUCKY," AND "YOU LIE"

149 **During August conference calls, the drug company executives and Karen Ignagni's insurance industry bosses signaled that they had gotten the message, too:** Ignagni, Zirkelbach, and a pharmaceutical company chief executive who was involved in the PhRMA deliberations.

150 **"Of course, I'm feeling lucky," Obama answered:** Details of this meeting have been reported elsewhere, including an account by Valerie Jarrett in a *New York Times Magazine*

"oral history" compiled by Peter Baker and published on January 16, 2013; I confirmed the exact date and conversation with Schiliro.

151 **Valerie Jarrett went into high gear, too; advises Obama they can survive Tea Party Summer:** Schiliro and a member of the White House communications team.

151 **Zeke Emanuel was confident enough that he began looking ahead to when the law would be on the books (conversation with Rahm Emanuel):** Zeke Emanuel and Rahm Emanuel.

152 **One of the Catholic bishops in attendance bent his ear about abortion:** This comes from *Landmark: The Inside Story of America's New Health-Care Law,* a book by the reporting staff of *The Washington Post* (New York: Public Affairs, 2010). This anecdote can be found on page 28.

154 **they would leave the doc fix out of the bill:** Zeke Emanuel, DeParle, and Kocher; it was also recorded in journal of White House staff person.

155 **the Congressional Budget Office scoring process:** Multiple articles about the CBO; a review of congressional testimony of CBO officials; and Orszag, Gruber, Fowler, and four congressional staff people who asked not to be identified.

158 **Some healthcare experts estimated that malpractice reform could save as much as $70 billion a year (5 percent of hospital and doctor expense):** This was a consensus I gathered during my reporting for the *Time* special issue. However, because I have seen so many varying estimates, I reduced my calculation in the text to 1 percent.

158 **the best they could do was ask the president to talk to Reid and try to persuade him at least to include some kind of test programs (White House discussion regarding malpractice reform):** Zeke Emanuel and the journal entries of a White House staff person.

159 **When Ted Kennedy was told in May that he had little time left, he wrote a letter to Obama:** Vicki Kennedy.

161 **Schiliro and his congressional liaison team thought the speech had worked:** Schiliro and one member of the White House communications staff.

CHAPTER 11: SNOW JOBS, POISON PILLS, AND BOTOX

164 **The Obama staff knew Baucus's draft was coming but did not know all the details:** Zeke Emanuel, Kocher, DeParle, and Fowler.

165 **More than that, as senior political adviser David Axelrod had constantly reminded the group, Obama had spent tens of millions of dollars in campaign ads attacking John McCain for wanting to remove the tax exclusion on workers' healthcare benefits:** Zeke Emanuel and the journal of a White House staff member. Emanuel also describes this debate in a book he wrote about Obamacare: *Reinventing American Health Care: How the Affordable Care Act Will Improve Our Terribly Complex, Blatantly Unjust, Outrageously Expensive, Grossly Inefficient, Error Prone System* (New York: Public Affairs, 2014).

165 **Predictably, the economic team had a different view:** Kocher, Zeke Emanuel, Summers, Orszag, and DeParle.

165 **staff and senior Treasury Department officials began in September to go over a new list of taxes or penalties:** Journal entries kept by a person who was involved in these discussions; Orszag.

166 **the Senate Finance Committee started its debate on Baucus's draft:** Clapsis, Fowler, Schwartz, Senator Grassley, Senator Snowe, and three other Finance Committee staff members. There were also several vivid descriptions of these sessions in newspaper coverage at the time, particularly an article by David Herszenhorn of *The New York Times,* published on October 13, 2009: http://prescriptions.blogs.nytimes.com/2009/10/13/behind-the-14-9-vote-a-247-committee-staff/.

167 **The senators grilled Fowler and the staff over thousands of details, and proposed 564 amendments, of which 135 were voted on:** This tally is from McDonough, *Inside National Health Reform.*

167 **"You mean the Snowe-Schumer amendment, right, Chuck?":** Senator Snowe.

167 **The vote on a more lenient mandate panicked Gruber:** Gruber, Fowler, and Cutler.

167 **Schumer's strategy was simple:** Three Finance Committee staff members.

172 **House members' concern about, and fight over, abortion:** Most of my knowledge of the basics here comes from news clips; McDonough, *Inside National Health Reform;* and the *Washington Post* staff, *Landmark,* though I supplemented it with interviews with DeParle, Fowler, three Republican House staffers, and two Democratic House staffers. Also, a journal kept by a White House adviser tracked these developments closely.

173 **White House meeting of the healthcare reform team during the second week in November:** From notes taken by one attendee and the journal entries of another.

173 **Joe Lieberman, the Democrat from insurance-industry-friendly Connecticut, told Reid:** Three Senate staff members.

175 **She was shunned when she showed up at lunches of the Senate Republican caucus:** Fowler, Clapsis, and two other Senate staff members.

175 **Evan Bayh of Indiana still thought the tax on his medical device companies back in Indiana was too high:** Clapsis, another Senate staff member, and a lobbyist for the device industry. I also saw the industry's lobbying white paper.

176 **Blanche Lincoln of Arkansas wanted a change that would ease the penalty on employers:** This, along with the "Cornhusker Kickback," the "Louisiana Purchase," and the bargain with Lieberman, was widely reported, but I got the core of my information on all of them from interviews with Clapsis, Fowler, and three other Senate staff members, as well as from McDonough, *Inside National Health Reform,* and *The Washington Post* staff, *Landmark.*

176 **"This is essentially the collapse of health reform":** Bob Kinzel, "Dean on Health Care: 'Kill the Senate Bill,' " December 15, 2009, http://www.vpr.net/news_detail/86681/dean-on -health-care-kill-senate-bill/.

177 **Republicans hatched a plan to launch a poison pill:** Two staff members for Republican senators, McDonough, Clapsis, Fowler, and McDonough, *Inside National Health Reform.*

178 **Jay Rockefeller told the Huffington Post, "I don't think that's going to get my vote":** Ryan Grim, "Pharma Deal Shuts Down Senate Health Care Debate," March 18, 2010, http:// www.huffingtonpost.com/2009/12/11/pharma-deal-shuts-down-se_n_388895.html.

178 **Snowe sat down and quickly told the president she couldn't vote yes—yet:** Senator Snowe and DeParle.

CHAPTER 12: NEW TROUBLE, THEN MOUNT EVEREST

181 **Kocher had been talking to another potential leader working in the Obama administration:** Kocher and Park.

183 **Kocher also talked with the U.S. chief technology officer at the White House, Aneesh Chopra:** Kocher and Chopra.

183 **Nancy-Ann DeParle wrote her own implementation memo:** I did not see this memo; I was told about it by DeParle, Zeke Emanuel, and Bob Kocher.

184 **they pushed Summers and Orszag to talk to Rahm Emanuel:** Zeke Emanuel, Rahm Emanuel, Kocher, and Orszag.

185 **Negotiations between Senate and House Democrats:** Clapsis, Fowler, DeParle, Kocher, Zeke Emanuel, and Beier. Also, contemporaneous news accounts from *The Washington Post* and *The New York Times,* as well as McDonough, *Inside National Health Reform.*

185 **The Democratic negotiators spent the entirety of January 12, 2010, getting through thirty-five pages of what was going to be a more than nine-hundred-page bill. Zeke Emanuel was kicked out of the room for arguing too much:** This is from notes entered into a journal by one of the participants; I confirmed it with two participants.

186 **The policy team was sure Zeke Emanuel had instigated the article, which he indignantly denied:** Kocher, Zeke Emanuel.

186 **The groups were working on the Sunday before Election Day**: Clapsis, Fowler, Schwartz, and Baucus staff aide Sean Neary.

186 **One group adjourned to a bar**: Clapsis, Fowler, Schwartz, and Neary.

186 **Karen Ignagni called one of her contacts at the White House**: Notes taken during the call by a member of the White House staff, then confirmed by Zirkelbach (of AHIP) and DeParle.

187 **DeParle's staff was preparing a memo for the president suggesting exactly that fallback**: Journal entry by a staff member, then confirmed by DeParle and another staff member.

187 **Fowler went online to see how much it would take to open a franchise for Potbelly**: Fowler.

187 **"Leader Reid's office said we are done with health care for the year"**: White House staff member's journal entry, confirmed with three Senate staff members.

187 **The conservative Scalia kidded Emanuel**: Zeke Emanuel.

187 **At Rahm Emanuel's behest, his brother and others on the Obama team had begun playing with a drastically scaled-back proposal**: Rahm Emanuel, Zeke Emanuel, and a White House staff member's journal entry.

187 **Obama had told the staff that he had not given up yet**: Schiliro and Rahm Emanuel.

188 **Development of new strategy to turn them into one bill that could become law despite the apparent loss of the sixtieth Senate vote**: Schiliro, Zeke Emanuel, and DeParle.

190 **"I got you elected and now you won't do this? Thanks for nothing"**: DeParle.

191 **Karen Ignagni at America's Health Insurance Plans had a similar reaction**: Zirkelbach and Ignagni.

195 **"the Mount Everest" of American domestic policy challenges**: Over the course of my research I believe I read a book in which the author used this metaphor. However, when I checked my notes I couldn't find which book or author. I then solicited an email list of healthcare policy experts to ask who might have coined this phrase and got several answers indicating variations on the metaphor had been commonly used, including, for example, that writer Robert Kuttner had used it in a 2008 television interview in discussing *Obama's Challenge,* a book he had written about the coming Obama presidency. I don't think that's where I first heard it. All that I am sure of is that I did not think of it on my own. I apologize for not being able to credit who put this phrase into my head.

195 **collecting autographs from the legislators**: Zeke Emanuel.

195 **Fowler didn't collect autographs, but she was given a signing pen by Obama**: Fowler.

CHAPTER 13: IN WASHINGTON "EVERYTHING IS SLIPPING," BUT NOT IN KENTUCKY

200 **Discussions and debate at White House implementation meetings**: Unless otherwise indicated, in all cases my initial source for discussions and debate at White House implementation meetings was a detailed journal kept by one of the participants. I then confirmed what that person recorded with at least two other participants. In no case did any participant contradict anything recorded in this journal that is reported in the text.

202 **"STOP!" was the only reply he got**: Recounted in a staffer's journal and confirmed by Chopra.

202 **DeParle and Lambrew were giving biweekly memos to the president**: Zeke Emanuel, Kocher, a member of White House communications team, Orszag, and Fowler.

204 **9,625 pages of regulations covering Obamacare**: There have been varying page counts reported in the press and alleged by critics of the law, but the most careful count seems to be Glenn Kessler's in his *Washington Post* fact-checking blog. In a May 15, 2013, post he counted 9,625 pages of rules and another 7,432 pages of proposed rules. There have probably been hundreds, if not thousands, of more pages promulgated since then.

206 **he had heard a Republican staffer say something about the Commerce Clause**: Clapsis.

206 **Ignagni complained to the White House and Baucus's staff that this would cause chaos**: Ignagni and Zirkelbach, confirmed by a member of the White House healthcare policy staff.

207 **"I hate that company," she said during one staff meeting**: Recorded in the journal of someone who was at the meeting.

208   **Park had quickly and quietly put a team together to design and build HealthCare.gov (story of Park building the initial Healthcare.gov website)**: Chopra, confirmed by Park and Bryan Sivak, who replaced Park as chief technology officer of the Department of Health and Human Services.

208   **Kentucky events**: Everyone mentioned in the text spoke on the record at all times and provided or confirmed all of the information in the text. Dates and subsequent expense and enrollment figures were all checked against state records.

CHAPTER 14: AN *OFFICE* BECOMES A *CENTER*—AND IT MATTERS

210   **"Once OCIIO became CCIIO, implementing [Obamacare] became pretty much impossible"**: Everyone involved at the Department of Health and Human Services, the Centers for Medicare and Medicaid Services, and the White House was happy to talk about this, as if this kind of bureaucratic dance was as routine as talking about the weather.

214   **Number of welfare recipients in 1980 and 1997**: See this chart compiled by the Department of Health and Human Services: http://aspe.hhs.gov/hsp/indicators04/apa-tanf.htm#AFDC

216   **Non–civil servants were walled off from choosing contractors**: This explanation of the contracting process and the fact that there are 26,000 contracting officers is from an interview with Daniel Gordon, associate dean of government procurement law, George Washington University Law School.

218   **It was clear to Chopra and Park that CGI was one of those usual-suspect government contractors**: Chopra and Park.

218   **Chopra and Park tried to talk about all that to Sebelius and Tavenner and tried to go to meetings**: White House staff member's journal entries, confirmed by Sivak, Chopra, and Tavenner.

219   **Sebelius focused on drafting the rules that would govern the insurance sold on the exchanges**: DeParle, Zeke Emanuel, Ignagni, and Gary Cohen (who became head of CCIIO).

CHAPTER 15: MEANTIME, OUTSIDE THE BELTWAY . . .

220   **a patient I'll call Steven D.**: I had full access to all of Steven's medical bills, to his billing advocate Patricia Stone, and to his wife, Alice. Although it has been updated, most of this information on Steven D.'s case was first included in my *Time* special report.

225   **UPMC-Highmark suit**: I reviewed all of the documents in the UPMC-Highmark case, as well as the transcript of the legislative hearing in which Romoff and others testified about the dispute.

229   **An eighty-eight-year-old man whom I'll call Alan A.**: I had full access to Alan A. and to all of his medical bills. Most of this information about Alan A., as well as Sloan Kettering, was included in the *Time* special report.

CHAPTER 16: WAITING FOR OBAMACARE

242   **Although a poor communicator, who often left non-techies wondering how to translate what he had just said**: Three of his colleagues at CMS. Chao declined repeated interview requests made to him through the CMS press office.

242   **Chao assured his boss, CMS head Marilyn Tavenner, that he and his team would be able to get the project done on time**: Tavenner.

242   **Rebecca and Scott S.**: I had full access to all of Scott S.'s medical bills, to his billing advocate, and to his wife. Much of the information about his case was included in the *Time* special report.

245   **About $65 billion would be spent on these tests**: This is the shakiest number in the text. The actual number is probably higher. Current, reliable numbers were impossible to find, in part

because hospital lab tests are usually attributed to hospital costs in most spending surveys. But here is why I think this estimate is on the low side of the actual number: This report— https://www.futurelabmedicine.org/pdfs/2007%20status%20report%20laboratory_ medicine_-_a_national_status_report_from_the_lewin_group.pdf—prepared by the medical industry consulting firm the Lewin Group for the U.S. Centers for Disease Control and Prevention, estimated lab test spending in 2007 to be $52 billion, or "2.3% of all U.S. health-care expenditures." By 2012, total healthcare spending in the United States had reached $2.8 trillion, and 2.3 percent of $2.8 trillion is $64.4 billion. Moreover, this report from the Health Care Cost Institute found that spending for services such as lab tests have been increasing at rates exceeding 5 percent a year. A 5 percent increase per year from 2007 (when Lewin reported $52 billion) would yield a 2012 expenditure of $66 billion. So I chose $65 billion, though even that number is probably low.

245 **Cutting the over-ordering and overpricing of these tests might have easily taken $20 billion a year out of that bill:** Multiple studies and reports that I have seen, including the McKinsey reports cited above, have estimated that 30 to 50 percent of all lab testing is unnecessary and that most of it is overpriced by 20 to 50 percent. Thus, achieving $20 billion (30 percent) in savings off the national $65 billion bill would, indeed, be "easy" if moderate cuts in volume and in pricing were achieved.

246 **Hospital-affiliated in-house labs accounted for about 60 percent of all testing revenue:** This comes from a description of the laboratory testing market in the 2013 Quest Diagnostics annual financial report.

248 **Sean Recchi, a forty-two-year-old from Lancaster, Ohio:** I had full access to the Recchis and to their bills. Much of the information about Recchi's case was first included in the *Time* special report.

250 **MD Anderson probably gets a volume discount:** Three cancer specialists, including one at MD Anderson, and three hospital chief financial officers.

252 **Bruce Folken, sixty-three, went to the emergency room:** I had full access to Mr. Folken and his bills.

254 **David Cramer, a graduate divinity student at Baylor University in Texas, and the $28,000 ambulance:** As indicated in the text, David Cramer shared his story with me, as well as his correspondence with his insurance company and the ambulance company.

256 **Liz Fowler sat with Max Baucus in the front row of the spectator seats:** Fowler.

258 **the initial read at the White House was that most states, even those run by the most conservative Republicans, were likely to sign on:** DeParle, Zeke Emanuel, and a journal entry by a member of the White House staff.

260 **Cohen couldn't resist the challenge of going back to run the launch of the federal exchange:** Cohen.

260 **He was soon told by higher-ups at CMS and the White House that he should take his time:** Cohen.

261 **when it comes to hospitals, antitrust laws are complicated:** In this evaluation of antitrust laws, I was helped by talking with and reading the scholarship of several lawyers, particularly a discussion with and paper presented by William Sage, a University of Texas law professor who specializes in healthcare law and antitrust regulation.

264 **Liz Fowler was ready to leave government again (Fowler's decision to take the Johnson & Johnson job and her reaction to the Greenwald attack):** Fowler.

CHAPTER 17: A GUY IN JEANS, RED LIGHTS, AND A "TRAIN WRECK"

272 **Gunderson-Sivak meeting and their project to build the homepage:** Gunderson and Sivak.

273 **Sivak and Gunderson's cool-looking home page—which the president loved:** Park, Chopra, and Sivak.

273 **Park convinces HHS secretary Kathleen Sebelius that McKinsey & Company, the blue rib-**

bon consulting firm, should be hired: Sivak and Tavenner. (Park would not discuss this with me.)

274   **Snyder—along with Sebelius and Marilyn Tavenner, the administrator of CMS—also sat in:** The House Energy and Commerce Committee subpoenaed the list of attendees at the McKinsey briefings and made it publicly available.

274   **Snyder, who was strong-willed and turf conscious, was not surprised by the report:** A senior CMS colleague of Snyder's, Sivak, and Tavenner.

275   **Sivak and Park, who sat in on the McKinsey meetings, had hoped the report would be a wake-up call:** Sivak, Chopra.

276   **Baucus and staff had heard nothing about the McKinsey report:** Baucus staffers Schwartz, Clapsis, and Neary.

278   **Background of Enroll America:** Anne Filipic and David Simas.

278   **Going into 2013, the group had raised $5 million:** A breakdown of Enroll America's funding sources was provided by Filipic and checked partially by reference to Enroll America's IRS form 990 filings.

282   **Joshua Kushner and his partners made a set of crucial decisions:** Information on the development of "Oscar" from Joshua Kushner, Mario Schlosser, and Kevin Nazemi. In addition, I had access to all of the planning and financial projection documents they presented to potential investors.

CHAPTER 18: TWO MONTHS TO GO

290   **Everyone involved had been tied in knots trying to figure out how the names, Social Security numbers, hours worked, and details of insurance coverage for every American worker could be assembled and made to flow efficiently:** This comes from multiple journal entries from a member of the White House staff, as well as from DeParle, Zeke Emanuel, Kocher, and assistant Treasury secretary for tax policy Mark Mazur.

291   **Gary Cohen . . . did not know about the decision:** Cohen and an HHS communications official.

291   **Cohen's boss, CMS chief Tavenner, was not told until two days before:** Tavenner.

292   **a series of panicked emails:** As noted, I have seen the full text of any email that I quote. The decisions, therefore, about what portions to quote in order to ensure that the quotes are in context are mine. Most of the emails in this section can be found in a voluminous set of documents subpoenaed by the minority staffs of the Senate Finance Committee and Senate Judiciary Committee. They can be found online at http://www.hatch.senate.gov/public/_cache/files/d84dafa1-9d91-46ae-ba89-a1b38a25ef1f/HealthCare.gov%20EXHIBITS.pdf.

294   **The highest ranking official who saw that email chain was Chao:** This is based on my examination of all the addressees on the email chain and interviews with many of those listed. I am assuming but cannot be sure that someone did not send the email separately to higher-ups and that for some reason those emails were not included in the documents given to the Senate committees in response to their subpoena. Additionally, Gary Cohen told me he never saw the Grant email.

297   **Simas, who now had the title of White House deputy senior adviser for communications, made the rounds of major news outlets:** Simas and the resulting stories that I read or saw televised.

301   **Content of regular meetings Obama had about the rollout:** Simas, another member of the communications staff, and Chief of Staff Denis McDonough.

302   **"Or perhaps you could just delay everything a month? What are your contingency plans?":** Ignagni, Zirkelbach, one senior HHS official, and one senior CMS official.

303   **Generation Opportunity, which was funded largely by conservative billionaires David and Charles Koch:** See, for example, this report from the Center for Responsive Politics: http://www.opensecrets.org/news/2014/05/genopp-too-another-group-almost-wholly-funded-by-koch-network/.

CHAPTER 19: THIRTY DAYS TO GO

308   **there was "no way" the launch was going to succeed, Sivak was whispering to friends:** Two
friends of Sivak's. Sivak later confirmed this and that he talked with Sebelius and others at
HHS about his concerns.

312   **the abnormally high percentage of American workers employed in the healthcare industry—
about 16 percent versus less than 10 percent in France:** This is taken by extrapolating from
the respective percentage of gross domestic product attributable to healthcare in France,
compared to what the U.S. Bureau of Labor Statistics reports is the total percentage of the
American workforce working in healthcare-related jobs, as cited in "The Anatomy of
Healthcare in the United States," *Journal of the American Medical Association,* January 5, 2014.
As such the comparison of percentages is only an estimate.

314   **In 1936, Social Security enrollment had been delayed:** See, for example, *The New York
Times,* May 17, 1937: "25th Million Card in Security Files." The article reported that there
were one million more numbers still needed.

315   **Lyndon Johnson got Congress to delay the deadline for signing up for Medicare:** "Great
Salesmanship," *Time,* April 8, 1966.

322   **The president was not trying to underplay what he suspected would be a disaster:** Although
it is debatable which constitutes a greater failing, I cannot emphasize enough that the president and his White House staff were clueless, not deceptive, about the launch's prospects.
This is what all of my reporting before the launch and after indicates. Indeed, it defies logic
that the president or his staff would have gone forward with the October 1 launch if they
had had any idea of what was going to happen.

CHAPTER 20: THE CRASH

325   **Marilyn Tavenner was sitting by the phone:** Tavenner.

326   **The first challenge at the Department of Health and Human Services and its CMS unit:** Information on this and other events that day is from Tavenner, Julie Bataille (CMS communications director), Cohen, Cohen deputy Chiquita Brooks-LaSure, and three other
staff people at CMS.

331   **At the White House, there was also frenzied activity:** A senior White House communications staff person, plus news reports that day from multiple sources.

331   **Sebelius had assured chief of staff Denis McDonough:** Simas, and a senior HHS official.

336   **lights flickered on and off:** Tavenner, Bataille, Sivak, and a CMS communications official.

336   **Anne Filipic . . . was furious:** Filipic.

336   **Filipic's Ohio director had been a legal aid lawyer:** Enroll America Ohio director Hugh
"Trey" Daly.

CHAPTER 21: MELTDOWN IN D.C., DANCING ON EIGHT TOES
IN KENTUCKY, AND FRUSTRATION IN OHIO

349   **The White House meeting that Saturday, October 5, like those during the three days before:**
This account was provided, consistently, by four White House staff members, and later
confirmed by chief of staff McDonough.

350   **Bryan Sivak replied to an email from an executive at Amazon's Web services division:** The cor-
respondence with Amazon was first reported by Reuters. I later confirmed it with Sivak.

350   **McDonough reached out to Jeffrey Zients:** McDonough and Zients. Much of this narrative
was first reported in a story I wrote for *Time* that was published on March 10, 2014.

CHAPTER 22: THE RESCUE

356   **Dickerson agreed that weekend to join Burt in a rescue squad:** Although it should be apparent from the text, I had full access to all of the members of the rescue squad depicted

here. If the narrative depicts them doing something or thinking something, it is because they told me. Again, much of this narrative was first published in the March 10, 2014, *Time* article.

367 **McDonough and the current communications team first asked Lambrew about the cancellations:** Two senior members of the communications team and one staffer working in Lambrew's office.

374 **For Sean and Stephanie Recchi, Obamacare became good news:** Parts of this story were published in a January 16, 2014, article I wrote for *Time*.

380 **Slavitt started taking various members of the Silicon Valley surge team aside and attempted to recruit them:** Mikey Dickerson and Jini Kim.

CHAPTER 23: THE FINISH LINE

385 **Obama, wanting to make sure he was not burned by another exchange-related crisis, repeatedly asked about this:** Jeffrey Zients, Park, and a White House senior adviser.

388 **And then there was Joshua Kushner from Oscar, who told the investor crowd that Obamacare had enabled his company to exist:** Kushner. I also reviewed the deck he presented.

393 *Between Two Ferns,* **the online mock interview show hosted by comedian Zach Galifianakis:** *Politico*'s report of the effort to get Obama on *Between the Ferns* was posted on April 2, 2014.

394 **I now counted nearly $100 billion in negative changes:** Removal of CLASS Act: $70 billion; delay of employer mandate: $19 billion; miscellaneous changes in various rules and deadlines (including the cost of allowing so many people to avoid the mandate penalty because exemptions were extended to them following the "grandfathering" firestorm): $5 billion. This does not count the cost overruns associated with implementing HealthCare.gov.

395 **For example, suppose a couple we'll call the Johnsons:** I asked Ohio insurance broker Barry Cohen (who helped the Recchis enroll in Obamacare) to provide hypothetical examples of premium costs and deductibles on a spreadsheet, then selected the ones I wanted to use and rechecked them.

398 **"O-Care Premiums to Skyrocket":** *The Hill,* March 19, 2014.

400 **Obama made a surprise call into the speakerphone at the command center:** Park and White House press aide Jessica Santillo.

401 **They toasted themselves with champagne outside the Smile Center:** Park.

404 **They had hoped to get to a medical loss ratio (Oscar expenses and MLR):** Schlosser and Kushner.

406 **Mitch McConnell of Kentucky told a reporter for Louisville newspaper LEO *Weekly*:** Can be found at http://fatlip.leoweekly.com/2014/05/23/mitch-mcconnell-says-kynect -is-unconnected-to-obamacare-dodges-questions-on-nsa-spying-and-coal-making-us-sick/.

CHAPTER 24: STUCK IN THE JALOPY

411 **From 2011 to 2013, the median physicians' and surgeons' income in the United States rose 1.4 percent:** The Bureau of Labor Statistics: http://www.bls.gov/oes/current/oes291069.htm for 2013 and http://www.bls.gov/oes/2011/may/oes291069.htm for 2011.

415 **increases still seem to have averaged about 8 percent:** As footnoted, the estimate of average premium increases on the exchanges for 2015 comes from a study released by PricewaterhouseCoopers on August 12, 2014. Other studies have projected higher and lower averages; this one was in the middle. Also, the increases found in all the studies vary widely by state and even among regions within states.

423 **Medicare would have paid a total of $60,000 to $70,000 to cover this $150,000 bill:** The process by which I applied the appropriate "DRG" is described in the explanation for the material in chapter 2, regarding what Medicare would have paid for Emilia Gilbert's treatment. New York–Presbyterian Hospital later confirmed this estimate.

433   **Background of Delos "Toby" Cosgrove, the CEO of the Cleveland Clinic:** Cosgrove, and the Cleveland Clinic website: http://my.clevelandclinic.org/staff_directory/staff_display?DoctorID=237.

440   **For example, the lowest-salaried doctor:** Salaries provided by spokespeople for both UPMC and New York–Presbyterian.

453   **Before cardiothoracic surgeon Leonard Girardi operated on me I was able to check him out:** Available through the New York State Department of Health website: https://www.health.ny.gov/statistics/diseases/cardiovascular/.

453   **Louisville's Jewish Hospital and St. Mary's HealthCare:** For state and national ratings, see this State of Kentucky "Quality Indicator": https://prd.chfs.ky.gov/MONAHRQ/2012/MONAHRQ/qual/cls/pub/T_F_B.html?type=0&topic=F&tab=0&hosps=21051001. For information regarding the hospital's reputation, see the *U.S. News & World Report* rankings here: http://health.usnews.com/best-hospitals/area/ky/jewish-hospital-6510510/cardiology-and-heart-surgery. (Note that I use the *U.S. News* report as a measure of *reputation,* not actual quality.)

454   **We already spend 50 to 100 percent more as a portion of our gross domestic product:** The OECD studies cited above, which include a comprehensive chart of gross domestic product percentages, can be found here: http://www.oecd.org/els/health-systems/health-data.htm.

INDEX

ABOUT THE AUTHOR

STEVEN BRILL has been a journalist and media entrepreneur for more than thirty years. He founded and ran Court TV, *The American Lawyer* magazine, ten regional legal newspapers, and *Brill's Content* magazine. He also co-founded Press+, which has enabled hundreds of newspapers and magazines around the world to charge modest subscription fees for their digital content.

A graduate of Yale College and Yale Law School, he has written for *The New Yorker, Time, Harper's, The New York Times Magazine,* and *Esquire,* among other magazines and news sites.

Brill was the author of *Time's* March 4, 2013, Special Report "Bitter Pill: Why Medical Bills Are Killing Us," for which he won the 2014 National Magazine Award for Public Interest.

He is the author of three books: *The Teamsters; After: How America Confronted the September 12 Era;* and *Class Warfare: Inside the Fight to Fix America's Schools.*

Brill also teaches journalism at Yale, where he founded the Yale Journalism Initiative to encourage and enable talented young people to become journalists. The Initiative has trained and motivated more than one hundred Yale Journalism Scholars, who are employed at some of the world's most prestigious news organizations.

He is married, with three adult children, and lives in New York.